Death Rattlers

Schiffer Military History
Atglen, PA

DEATH RATTLERS

Marine Squadron VMF-323 Over Okinawa

William Wolf

Schiffer Military History
Atglen, PA

Dedication

I wish to dedicate this book to my wife, Nancy, and my good friend, partner, and fellow historian, Jim Lansdale. But most of all I wish to dedicate it to the brave men of VMF-323, who gave up precious years of their youth—and sometimes their lives—to defend America.

Book Design by Ian Robertson.

Library of Congress Catalog Number: 99-62987

Printed in China.
ISBN: 0-7643-0953-6

We are interested in hearing from authors with book ideas on related topics.

Published by Schiffer Publishing Ltd.
4880 Lower Valley Road
Atglen, PA 19310
Phone: (610) 593-1777
FAX: (610) 593-2002
E-mail: Schifferbk@aol.com.
Visit our web site at: www.schifferbooks.com
Please write for a free catalog.
This book may be purchased from the publisher.
Please include $3.95 postage.
Try your bookstore first.

In Europe, Schiffer books are distributed by:
Bushwood Books
6 Marksbury Road
Kew Gardens
Surrey TW9 4JF
England
Phone: 44 (0)181 392-8585
FAX: 44 (0)181 392-9876
E-mail: Bushwd@aol.com.

Try your bookstore first.

Contents

Acknowledgments

During the course of writing this book I conducted numerous telephone and personal interviews and incorporated them into the framework of the official histories. It must be remembered that more than 50 years have passed, and each man had a different vantage point in observing the course of events. Each was limited in his observations by his rank and the role he played, and therefore contributed a personal tile to the VMF-323 mosaic. It is often forgotten in the praise of pilots in air combat that their success could only happen through extensive and comprehensive training and, most of all, through the unheralded, behind-the-scenes efforts of the enlisted men on the ground. Unlike many aviation unit histories that concentrate on combat, I also tried to underscore the role of the men on the ground and Major Axtell's extensive training for the Death Rattlers' success. Throughout my research both officers and enlisted men of VMF-323 emphasized the camaraderie in the squadron. This was nurtured by the fun, boredom, discipline, and hard work of everyday squadron life during the long training period, and led to the success of the squadron over Okinawa.

Every VMF-323 member I contacted during my research was helpful and exceptionally friendly, but several members were outstanding in their assistance. Henry Brandon contributed his collection of almost daily letters to his new bride that gave me an insight into everyday life during training and combat. Brandon, James Barrett, Al Wells, George Axtell and John Ruhsam contributed extensive personal/telephone/E-mail interviews and other material. Dorothy Spangler, the daughter of pilot, Charles Spangler, lent me 22 audio tape recordings she had made in the early and mid-1990's at various reunions and via the telephone. Harley Brock did extensive work in constructing a comprehensive enlisted man's roster, and put me in contact with the enlisted men who contributed so much to the success of VMF-323. The extensive bibliography confers to the reader some idea of the assistance I was given by squadron members in writing the history and the reason for its completeness and authenticity.

By mid-1944 the restrictions on personal photography were relaxed, and consequently, members of the squadron took a large number of photos which they contributed to this history. All photo contributors are credited after the caption. Special thanks to Whitey Miller, Henry Brandon, Jody O'Keefe and Bill Drake, who each supplied a substantial number of photos. Hank Brandon, with his great memory, contributed to the identification, writing, and correction of many photo captions. As with the success of VMF-323 during the war, the success of this book came from the friendship and cooperation of all members of the squadron.

Foreword

General George Axtell. ***Courtesy George Axtell.***

This book by Bill Wolf is a tribute to the young Americans whose lives were disrupted by World War II but met the challenge it presented. They quickly utilized the initial skills they acquired in basic training at flight and technical schools when they were assigned to my squadron. Compared to the standards of today, our doctrine was limited, supervision was minimal, and the technical training of the pilots and ground support was primitive. Little did I and those other "kids" realize what could be accomplished through hard work, determination, dedication and a little luck. Needless to say, we were "gung ho" and acquired the "can do" attitude and confidence that always prevailed throughout the history of the squadron. My mission was to train the young Marines assigned to me to become a competent and cohesive fighter squadron within six months. I had to do this twice, as my first group of pilots was transferred out as replacement pilots.

My second group of pilots, which I took into combat at Okinawa, worked hard to excel. The unit quickly developed professionally, and its camaraderie was outstanding due to our recreational and social environment. We were by-passed in receiving a combat assignment and were forced into another training cycle. After the initial disappointment we went on to hone our skills and maintained our high spirits and brotherhood. In combat over Okinawa the result of our extensive training became evident, as we were the top-scoring squadron of any service. I feel it is important that Dr. Wolf brings out the fact that the squadron was a "family," and that its success was due not only to its pilots, but also to the efforts of the men on the ground.

The fondest memories of my military career and my present best and loyal friends come from this period and my association with these wonderful Marines. Each of them was professional, loyal and dedicated. The opportunity to be connected with this highly successful squadron forged my character and made me a professional, and ultimately shaped my successful military career.

Semper Fidelis,
Lt.Gen. George Axtell

CHAPTER 1
Pioneer Days
1 August 1943 to 11 January 1944

Formation

Marine Fighting Squadron 323 was commissioned on 1 August 1943, at the Marine Corps Air Station (MACS), Cherry Point, North Carolina. The squadron was assigned to Marine Air Group 32 (MAG-32) under Lt.Col. John Smith as part of the Third Marine Air Wing (3MAW) under Brig. Gen. Claude Larkin. The first commander of VMF-323 was George Axtell, a young major who would become the heart and soul of the squadron. Axtell, at 22 years, 8 months, was the youngest Squadron commander in the Marine Corps aviation branch. This, despite the fact he had only served with the Fleet Marine Force for four months and had never been in combat.

Major George Axtell assumed command of newly formed VMF-323 in July 1943. Without combat experience and three months shy of his twenty-third birthday, Axtell was the youngest squadron CO in the Marine Corps. ***Courtesy of George Axtell.***

Major George Axtell

George Clifton Axtell was born on 29 November 1920, in Ambridge, Pennsylvania. After graduating from high school, Axtell decided to escape working in industrial western Pennsylvania and enrolled in aeronautical engineering at the University of Alabama. Here he participated in the glider club and was accepted into the PFT Program, in which he earned his pilot's license. In May 1940, at the end of his second year at Alabama he applied to the Army Air Corps to become a fighter pilot, but was refused because he was underage at 19. The Navy also turned him down because of his age, so he hitchhiked to Anacostia Naval Air Station, outside Washington D.C., to try the Marine Corps Reserve Aviation unit there. A Marine Captain interviewed him and said he would be in touch in a month. With little expectation Axtell went back home and took a job as a

Major John Smith, CO of MAG-32, gave Axtell command of VMF-323. Smith scored 19 victories with VMF-223 over Guadalcanal in the fall of 1942 and was awarded the Medal of Honor. He was the only Marine ace to command an Air Group in WW-2. ***Author's collection.***

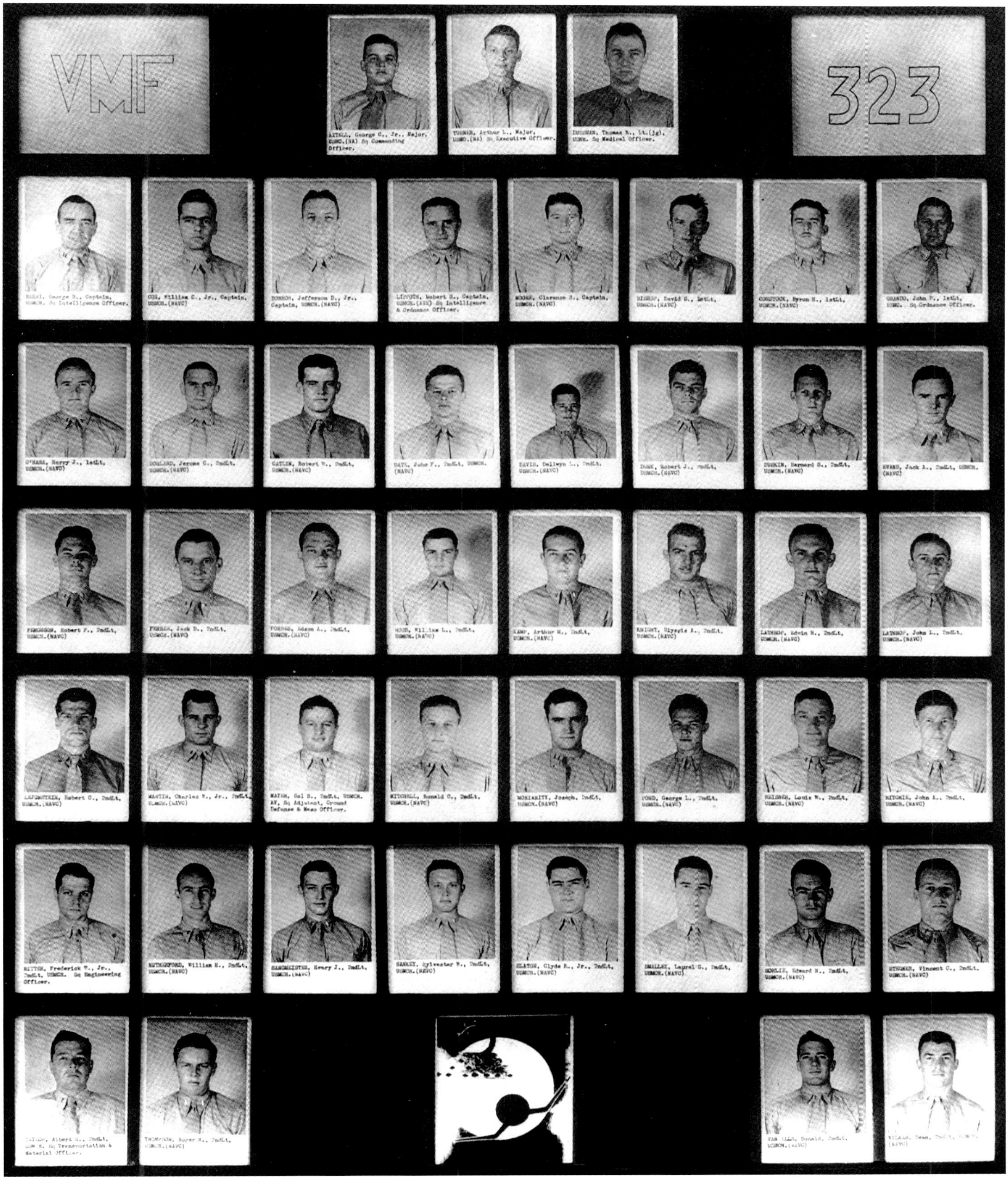

Officers at Cherry Point in September 1943. Note the rudimentary insignia at the bottom of the photo. It has the coiled snake and gullwing Corsair fighter. ***Courtesy or George Axtell/USMC.***

Major Arthur Turner was the Executive Officer. ***Courtesy of Del Davis.***

draftsman in a steel plant. At the end of June he received a call directing him to report to Anacostia on 5 July 1940, to attend flight elimination training. He successfully completed the month long program and returned to Ambridge and his job, awaiting his orders. On 4 November 1940, he reported to Pensacola as an Aviation Cadet and completed flight training in May 1941. He completed fighter training at Miami and was informed that, since he was only 20, he would not be commissioned until he reached 21 and would remain as a flight instructor in the rank of Aviation Cadet. Several weeks later a waiver was granted and Axtell was commissioned as a Second Lieutenant USMCR and ordered to Pensacola to join an instrument training squadron. In November 1941, Axtell was ordered to attend the U.S. Naval Academy Postgraduate School for meteorological engineering and completed the course in an abbreviated 15 months. While at the Naval Academy he married hometown sweetheart, Phylis Crafton, in March 1942.

He reported to Cherry Point, North Carolina, and was given command of a service squadron (maintenance squadron) for three months as a junior Major. He conducted instrument training in SNJs. Axtell recalls:

"My commanding officer at Cherry Point and MAG-32 was Lt. Col. John Smith (19 victories and the Congressional Medal of Honor at Guadalcanal, editor). We flew together and became friends. On the first of July '43, I was called in by Col. Smith and he told me to take command of VMF-323. I told him that I didn't think I was qualified because there were a lot of majors senior to me that had served in combat in the South Pacific. He gave me a cup of coffee and told me that 'I didn't know what the hell I was qualified for and that the Marine Corps knew. That my status right then was the CO of 323.' Then and there I decided that 323 was going to be the best. At first we didn't know what the hell we were doing, but it wasn't before long that we decided we could whip anybody."

"I had to form a squadron from scratch with personnel who just completed basic and advanced training courses. My assignment was to be ready to deploy to combat in six to eight months. A fighter squadron's mission is first to control the air in the tactical area of operations, then to support the infantry in its attack, and when necessary to defend the tactical position. Our squadron achieved this mission, and was deployed to California in January 1944."

Sgt. James Barrett observes: "Major Axtell was very intellectual, and his office was lit until late every night, reading and writing. He followed the book to the letter. I never saw him smile. I finally saw a photo of him after the war in Colliers magazine where he had semi-smile. We had a lot of 'hot rocks' in the squadron during combat who took unnecessary chances to become aces. He never took any chances, and he became an ace. He had to be very strict, but he was fair and was respected, and it paid off." Harley Brock adds, "Major Axtell gave each of the men enough rope to either do the job or to hang themselves."

Cherry Point

MCAS Cherry Point was established in August 1941, near New Bern, North Carolina, and began air operations in mid-March 1942, under the command of Lt.Col. Raymond Conroy.

The squadron stayed at Cherry Point only a short time, and shared the base with other newly formed units. Sgt. James Barrett remembers the state of inexperience rampant at the base: "A F6F or F4U from another squadron came in for a landing one day, and the

Capt. William Cox was the Flight Officer. ***Courtesy of Jody O'Keefe.***

inexperienced pilot folded his wings instead of letting down his landing gear, with dire consequences to himself and the plane." Young 2Lt. Del Davis describes his early days there: "In July 1943, when I joined VMF-323 at Cherry Point, the squadron was just forming and had only four or five F4U-1s. The operations officer gave me the F4U pilot's handbook and said, 'I've only flown it a couple of hops; read the book and you'll be on the flight schedule tomorrow morning.' Until then I had only flown the 250 HP SNJ, and so I decided I had better start making friends with this 2000 HP aircraft so as not to embarrass myself as the 'new guy' the next day. I started off by walking around the aircraft, not just sure how to mount the cockpit. I discovered that the Corsair was much like a horse, you got on from the left side. I read the handbook, and the next morning I walked right up to the port side and confidently got into the cockpit. The early F4U-1s were started by a shot gun shell starter, which was notorious for its multiple failures. As if I knew what I was doing, the engine fired up on the first pop. At Cherry Point the takeoffs were all out and away from a center hub, while all the landings were into the center, thus, luckily, little time was spent taxiing, and I managed to taxi out despite the huge nose sticking out in front of me. The field was very busy in those days, and all take offs and landings were controlled by aldus lights. I'll never forget the take off that day. I moved the throttle forward, not knowing what to expect. I got off the ground and wanted to raise the gear. In the early F4Us the gear handle was down below the left knee. I had tightened the shoulder harness so tight that I was unable to reach the handle. I must have flown twenty miles before I got the gear up and canopy closed."

Training was briefly interrupted by a hurricane warning. The men spent a day tying everything down from airplanes to garbage cans. The storm didn't materialize, and another day was spent untying everything.

Cherry Point Roster
August 1943

Officers

Major Axtell, George	Turner, Arthur
Captain Allen, Reid	Lippoth, Robert
Crozier, William	Moore, Clarence
1Lt. Comstock, Byron	
2Lt. Baldwin, Charles	Martin, Charles
Barnett, Dean	McDonald, Douglas
Bowen, Ralph	Mitchell, Donald
Broderick, William	O'Hara, Harry
Brown, Russell	Peterson, Conrad
Carpenter, Burson	Powers, Edward
Date, John	Rogga, Thomas
Davis, Dellwyn	Salmon, Robert
Duskin, Barnard	Sankey, Sylvester

A veteran of the Guadalcanal Campaign, Capt. Charles Moore was one of the original squadron officers at both Cherry Point and Oak Grove. Moore would later become squadron Operations Officer. *Courtesy of Henry Brandon.*

Captain Jefferson Dorroh was assigned to the squadron at Cherry Point and would and would remain with it until relieved in June 1945. *Courtesy of Henry Brandon.*

Capt. Robert Lippoth was the Intelligence and Ordnance Officer. ***Courtesy of George Axtell/USMC.***

1Lt. Fred Ritter served as Maintenance/Engineering Officer throughout the war. ***Courtesy of Bill Drake.***

Forbes, Edson
Garotto, Alfred
Good, Charles
Hendrickson, Leo
Hood, William
Horn, Robert
Hough, Donald
Jarvis, Melvin
Kamp, Arthur
Kersey, Arden
Kenney, Everett
Lejonstein, Robert
Lovelace, George
Marsh, Hugh
Sherwood, Kenneth
Skagno, Gerald
Sutherland, Allen
Taylor, Edward
Tomich, Chester
Verrant, Herce
Warren, Forest
Whitney,Gerald
Wilker, Dean
Williams, Arthur
Wilson, Norris
Wineritter, George
Wolff, James

NCO/Enlisted Men

M.T/Sgt. Bowman, Lloyd
T/Sgt. Morrison, George
S/Sgt. Brown, Robert
Culleton, John
Goodwin, Dibble
Lemmon, Archie
Salser, Floyd
Helfgott, Lawrence
Stephens, David

Sgt. Alengi, Joe
Anderson, Ernest
Barrett,James
Buckley, James
Elliott, William
Gaigal, Joseph
Garrard, Henry
Grady, Edmund
Hand, Elwood
Kaluponov, Andrew
Kelly, William
Misch, Richard
Norton, James
Stewart, Frank

Compiled by Harley Brock and Bill Wolf

Oak Grove control tower and snow-covered flight line with F4U-1s and a SNJ in the background, December, 1943. ***Courtesy of Del Davis.***

Squadron office and working area, Oak Grove, December 1943. ***Courtesy of Del Davis.***

Mechanics and plane captains take a break for a soft drink at Cherry Point on a hot August day in 1943. Paul Finney and Ernie Anderson can be identified in the foreground. ***Courtesy of Harley Brock.***

Oak Grove, Pollocksville

The squadron stayed at Cherry Point only a short time, and new personnel were added everyday. Oak Grove, Pollocksville, was one of eleven outlying auxiliary fields that were part of MCAS Cherry Point. Six of these became MCAAF (auxiliary air stations), including Pollocksville. At this time Cherry Point came under the command of Col. Christian Schilt.

Axtell: "While at Oak Grove my pilots became highly trained and qualified. The other squadrons were having a lot of landing accidents, and I opened my big mouth and said that anybody who sat down in an airplane by this time shouldn't be having any trouble. So, every new pilot coming to the group was assigned ten hours training with our squadron. Although it was a double work load, our pilots became instructor pilots. It was a blessing in disguise for our guys, as once you learn something, by teaching it you learn a lot more about it.

Photo participant, Jim Barrett (sitting right) said, "Someone with a camera recruited us to pose for some rugged action pictures to send home. The photos were actually taken by a stream which ran just a few feet from our barracks." Nick Alengi (standing) and Ed Scarcia (in water) are Barrett's macho companions. ***Courtesy of Dr. James Barrett.***

A Marine Corps PR photo of a formation of Corsairs over Cherry Point in late 1943. ***Courtesy of USMC.***

Chance Vought factory representatives held a school mechanics at Stratford CT. In October 1943. Among the -323 members attending were Fred Ritter, Lloyd Bowman, Paul Pentheny, Frank Maggliocco and Stan Woszcyna. ***Courtesy of Francis Maggliocco.***

When we first got the F4U in the service squadron I spent a lot of time studying the mechanical manuals for the aircraft. My young, green mechanics had never seen the aircraft, and they had this big maintenance book that had the schematic diagrams. They could tell me what the problem area was, and I would tell them, 'Here's what the part does, here's what it looks like on the schematics, and here's where its located on the schematics.' They knew about the part, but I was teaching them to read the schematics in order to use the maintenance book."

PC Don Hitchings: "When we first saw them (F4Us) we might as well have been looking at a jet for the first time. We had never seen engines like this and had to use the manuals to work on them. But first we found we had to sit down and figure out the manuals.

I felt sorry for the pilots. They come out of the SNJs with 550 horse power and into the F4U with 2,000 horses in a much hotter aircraft. It was single seat with instruments and controls all over the place. They had to get in and fly it with no back seat help. The low tail wheel and long nose made visibility poor for taxiing. This, along with holding the bungee-controlled stick back, made for one tired pilot before he ever got into the air."

Meeting outside the Oak Grove Command Post are 2Lts. Jack Ferree, Henry Sangmeister and Ulysses Knight. These men would be transferred out as replacement pilots in January 1944, and Major Axtell would have to start training a new group of pilots. ***Courtesy of George Axtell.***

2Lt. Joe Moriarity keeping a puppy warm from the Carolina cold. The two would go on with squadron to California but Moriarity would be transferred out while the dog stayed on and was named Gusty Fox. ***Courtesy George Axtell.***

Training was not without incident, however. Axtell: "I emphasized instrument flying because I was an instrument instructor, and if you can't fly instruments you can't get to the target. At Oak Grove, we'd be flying when everyone else would shut down. I did lose four aircraft one night. 'Lefty' Forbes led a flight that took off from Pollacksville when the weather closed in, and the inexperienced pilots became lost and disoriented. There was supposed to be GCR radars up that night, and the next morning this Colonel comes in ranting that we didn't check out the radar. But I'm not that dumb, because at midnight I had gone to the radar sites and copied their logs. I found that they had been down for parts for over 24 hours."

Edson Forbes was nicknamed 'Lefty' because he had signed as a left-handed first baseman with the Boston Braves Of the four planes: one pilot successfully landed at the closed Raleigh airport; another landed wheels up in a farmer's field; one pilot, who was low on fuel, tried to land on a highway, but hit the top of a car and somersaulted with non-fatal injuries; and the fourth pilot bailed out safely in a whiteout. Squadron members waited in the communications hut listening to this anxious pilot on the radio. When his fuel ran out he radioed a 'Good-bye' and went over the side."

Sgt. James Barrett relates: "Two Army Air Force planes, a P-47 and P-38, were mock dogfighting and collided, and crashed deep into a swamp. (2Lt.) Sol Mayer grabbed three of us and took off in a jeep. We got to the swamp, and Sol sent us in while he sat and waited for us on the road. Things didn't start off too well, as we ran into a rattle snake right away and then had to ford a river. It wasn't a big river, but it was one you didn't want to wade in if you didn't have to. We finally found the plane, but didn't recognize the pilot because he was burned to a crisp. Another rescue group came and removed the body, and we started back to the jeep and got lost. It was around noon, so we couldn't figure out the compass directions from the sun which was right overhead. We walked around for a while, and finally Sol got mad enough to fire off his pistol. Bam, Bam, Bam. We followed the sound back to an irritated Sol, who greeted us in his New Orleans accent, "I sho' was pissed off at yo'all." To emphasize his annoyance with us, he repeated it several

Boone Guyton was the Chance Vought F4U project test pilot. It is rumored that the roominess of the Corsair cockpit was due to Guyton was six foot four inches tall. Guyton visited the squadron at Oak Grove and "felt then that it was headed for greatness". ***Author's collection***

The smile on George Axtell's face would disappear as all but nine of his pilots would be soon taken as replacements for other units. ***Courtesy of George Axtell***

times. The first time I heard his accent, I thought he was from the south but making fun of people from Brooklyn." (Barrett came to the squadron as a sergeant.) "I had been at two ordnance schools, one in Memphis where I was in the top 10% of the class and was made a corporal. I was then sent to Chicago for advanced training, and on completion got my sergeant's stripes. Nick Alengi and I went through boot camp, training, and the whole VMF-323 stint together.")

Toward the end of 1943, the North Carolina phase of training was nearly completed. VMF-322, which had also been training at Oak Grove, left several days before VMF-323 and did the traditional buzz job on the field. It was something Axtell wouldn't allow -323 pilots to even think about attempting as a farewell. VMF-322 left on the train for the West Coast very early in the morning. The last thing they did before they left was to break into the laundry late the evening before and steal about half of -323's clothes. This had happened to -322 and was a farewell tradition going back to boot camp, which the -323 didn't remember until it was too late.

Captains (L. to R.) Chuck Moore, Bill Cox, and Tony Comstock confer in obviously cold North Carolina weather. ***Courtesy of Del Davis.***

2Lt. Edson "Lefty" Forbes led a division on a training mission from Pollacksville when weather closed in. Three aircraft were lost but all the pilots were safe. Forbes had signed a baseball contract with the Boston Braves before the war, earning his nickname. ***Courtesy of Dorothy Forbes.***

The squadron was preparing to leave by train for the West Coast and ready to load at Tuscarora. Sgt. James Barrett described the scene: "On Christmas Eve day, only hours before we were to ship out to California by train, an alert came in, reporting that an enemy task force was spotted in the Atlantic and was on its way to the East Coast. We had everything packed and crated. In fact, we nailed the last crate shut except for one slat. We put the hammer in and nailed the last slat with a rock.

Our aircraft were to be transferred to other east coast units, and the machine guns were removed and coated with cosmoline, which was a thick, tarry substance that was particularly difficult to remove. Gasoline was about the only thing that would take it off. The guns were uncrated, cleaned, and put in working order. We didn't have any belted ammunition for the guns, so we also had to belt our own with a belting machine. We worked all Christmas eve and through the night, and shortly after we finished at 9:30 in the morning on Christmas Day it was announced that the alert had been a false alarm. We took off a few hours and we had to remove and repack everything. We finally got to the Tuscarora station to embark. These were Jim Crow days in North Carolina. In the train station there was a poster describing the qualifications needed for being eligible to cast a vote. A certain number of bales of tobacco were required to be sold in order to vote, which would disenfranchise most blacks and many poor whites."

The train trip took a week, with a memorable stop at Phoenix where the squadron double timed through town during rare January Arizona snow flurries. The train stopped at nearly every siding to allow regularly scheduled trains to pass, but this gave the men a chance to stretch and get some fresh air from the oppressive cigarette smoke in the cars. Everyone had his own berth in the Pullman that were made up during the day and turned down at night by Black porters. Railway food in those days, when railroads were a major form of transportation, was very good, and certainly a great improvement over that served at Oak Grove. The men passed time reading, playing cards and looking out the window at countryside most of the men had never seen before."

Squadron men and officers muster at the troop train boarding site at Tuscarora, NC. The heavy woolen khaki great coats would not be needed for the remainder of the war as the squadron would train in subtropical California and tropical Hawaii and the South Pacific. ***Courtesy of Del Davis***

The troop train finally reached California, and Axtell recounts: "We got to California and stopped at El Centro in the middle of the desert, and the conductor said that we were getting out here. I told him that we were supposed to go to San Diego. The conductor said that he ran the damn train and that I could run anything else."

VMF-323 ROSTER
1 January 1944

OFFICERS

Major Axtell, George	Turner, Arthur
Captain Berry, George	Lippoth, Robert
Cox, William	Moore, Clarence
Dorroh, Jefferson	
1Lt. Bishop, David	Grando, John
Comstock, Byron	O'Hara, Harry
2Lt. Bohland, Jerome	Mitchell, Donald
Catlin, Robert	Moriarty, Joseph
Date, John	Pond, George
Davis, Dellwyn	Reiser, Louis
Dunk, Robert	Ritchie, John
Duskin, Bernard	Ritter, Frederick
Evans, Jack	Rutherford, William
Ferguson, Robert	Sangmeister, Henry
Ferree, Jack	Sankey, Slyvester
Forbes, Edson	Slayton, Clyde
Hood, William	Smalley, Laurel
Kamp, Arthur	Sorlie, Edward

T/Sgt.James "Willie" Williams, a mechanic, poses in front of the troop train after the patrolling sentry passes by. The flat cars in the background are loaded with 2 1/2 ton 6x6 trucks. ***Courtesy of Del Davis.***

VMF-323 officers watch enlisted men boarding the troop train at Tuscarora in late December 1943. The sticks the men are carrying in their left hands are brooms for the cleanup detail aboard the train. ***Courtesy of Del Davis***

Knight, Ulyssis
Lathrop, Edwin
Lathrop, John
Lejonstein, Robert
Martin, Charles
Mayer, Sol
Stegner, Vincent
Taylor, Albert
Thompson, Roger
Van Ells, Donald
Wilker, Dean

Navy Medical
Lt(jg) Dussman, Thomas

NCO/Enlisted Men

M.T/Sgt. Blake, Jerry
Bowman, Lloyd
Morrison, George

T/Sgt. Brown, Robert
Culleton. John
Grady, Edmund
McLaughlin, Thomas

S/Sgt. Alengi, Joe
Amundson, Ernest
Barrett, James
Beyerkohler, Richard
Brock, Harley
Buckley, James
Dudley, George
Elliott, William
Garrard, Henry
Goodwin, Dibble
Hand, Elwood
Kaluponov, Andrew
Kadasky, Frank
Karren, Milton
Kerndon, Louis
Micha, Charles
Parrish, Stanley
Penthenv, Harold
Stewart, Frank
Williams, James

Sgt. Borozan, Steve
Brennan, Donald
Bruno, Joseph
Bruno, John
Caron, Norman
Carver, Donald
Cresslan, Charles
Culver, Leonard
Cunningham, Harold
Daughton, John
DeMilla, Rocco
Hill, Richard
Hitchings, Donald
Holland, Vincent
Hopper, Clyde
Kroff t, Robert
Magley, Albert
Martin, James
Mascal, Edwin
Misch, Richard
Niblack, Dennis
Olson, Roger

A sentry stands guard in front of the train engine during one of the many stops on sidings to allow regularly scheduled trains to pass. These stops gave the men a chance to stretch during the long, seven day trip across the southern tier of states. *Courtesy of Del* Davis.

Edwards, John
Elson, Albert
Finney, Paul
Gates, Dan
Gawron, Edward
Gracey, Harry
Gustin, Norton
Hewlitt, Charles
Preston, George
Stovall, Eugene
Vaira, John
Walden, William
Wentz, William
Wilczek, Theodore
Wingfield, Chester

P/M 2c Yeats, Amos

P/M 3c Goff, Stanton
Sadowsky, Edward
Stagle, Robert
Rogers, William
Woodruff, Stanley

Compiled by Harley Brock and Bill Wolf

CHAPTER 2
El Centro
Desert Interlude

13 January to 20 February

El Centro Naval Auxiliary Air Station is located in extreme southern California about 10-12 miles from the Mexican border, and about 110 miles east of San Diego. It was commissioned in late July 1943, and was chosen because of its good flying weather. The squadrons that trained there flew a record number of flight hours. The base had just completed an expansion of facilities when -323 arrived. Lt. Col. Karl Voelter was the commanding officer of the base. The squadron was reassigned to Marine Base Defense Aircraft Group 43 (MABDG-43), Marine Fleet Air, West Coast, which had recently been organized (1 January 1943).

The nearby town of El Centro is the market center of the Imperial Valley, one of the richest farming areas in the world. Irrigation had transformed barren desert, much of it below sea level, into verdant pastures and lush fields of lettuce, tomatoes, melons, and sugar beets. Today the air station is home to the Blue Angels aerobatics team. The NAS is located in the middle of the southernmost and hottest desert in the United States. Although the squadron was based there from the middle of January through February, the weather remained hot—mid-80s—during the short winter daytime and, as typical of winter desert, very cold—high 30s-low 40s—at night. It was so hot that the squadron flew from early morning to about 11 am. After lunch, the afternoons were spent in ground school.

Things started out badly at El Centro for Major Axtell: "They detached over three quarters (31-editor, Axtell was allowed to chose nine to remain with -323) of my trained pilots to be sent overseas as replacements, and I had to start over again. I wasn't very happy about it, but headquarters told me that I had the best and most highly trained pilots and that they needed replacements. I couldn't argue with that. All I could do was say 'Yes, Sir' and smile. I was told not to worry, that I would catch up with the war." That left Axtell, Major Arthur Turner, the executive officer, and Captains Jefferson Dorroh, Clarence Moore, Robert Lippoth, and William Cox to form the nucleus of the new squadron, along with Lieutenants William Hood, Del Davis, Charles Martin, Gerald Bohland, Byron Comstock, Robert Lejonstein, and flight surgeon Lt.(jg) Thomas Dussman. The only good thing about El Centro was that the squadron received new aircraft after leaving theirs on the east coast.

The enlisted men who had been with -323 since North Carolina were disappointed when the old pilots were transferred to the Pacific and training the new ones had to start all over again. Ever since boot camp in 1942, they feared that they were never going to get into combat before the war would be over, and it looked even more so at that time.

Soon new pilots arrived, mainly from Southern California Marine training facilities, particularly El Toro. Pilots joining at El Centro/Pendleton were (as per paymaster list of 1 February 1944):

First Lieutenants:

Allen, Charles	Edelson, Harold	Muse, Robert
Brown, James	Keeley, Edward	Van Buskirk, William
Dillard, Joseph	Kivlin, Robert	Zehring, Frederick

Second Lieutenants:

Abner, Edward	Dolezel, Cyril	Smith, Glen
Baker, Gerald	Drake, Charles	Spangler, Charles
Ball, Vernon	Fountain, Keith	Strickland, John
Bartlett, Robert	Freshour, John	Terrill, Francis
Bierbower, James	Lejonstein, Robert	Theriault, Normand
Blaydes, Aquilla	Lynn, Richard	Tonnessen, Harold
Bourne, Raymond	Maurer, Robert	Wells, Albert
Brandon, Henry	Murray, Edward	
Broering, Warren	O'Keefe, Jeremiah	

While Axtell was away meeting with the Wing C.G. an order came in from MAG-33 for four more replacement pilots, and -323 lost Comstock and Bohland, along with Ray Bourne and Robert Maurer.

Comstock was the fourth pilot to join the new squadron at Cherry Point. Just out of high school, he had joined the RCAF in Montreal in July 1941. He won his RCAF wings, but transferred to the U.S. Navy in early 1942 and entered the Naval Flight Training Program to become a fighter pilot. Comstock was afraid the El Centro tour would mean he would be training pilots, so he volunteered for the transfer. Comstock flew with VMF-217 aboard the

Major Axtell (R) proposes a toast at an El Centro "O" club dinner. At El Centro Axtell had to acquaint himself with 34 new green pilots transferred from Southern California Marine training bases. ***Courtesy of Del Davis.***

WASP, and on 16 February 1945 damaged a Zero over Japan. He would fly the Corsair in Korea and later become a physician.

Wells: "It was only on New Year's Day 1944 that I flew the Corsair for the first time. My group at El Toro was assigned as a replacement for those pilots Axtell lost to the replacement pool."

2Lt. Charles Allen almost became a dive bomber pilot. Allen: "Joe Dillard, Razor Blaydes and I were sent to El Toro and were assigned to a dive bomber squadron there for training. They needed fighter pilots, and Dillard and Blaydes asked me to sign up with them. But I told them that the Good Lord put me to stay where I was; if he wanted me to move, I'd go. But when the fighter list came out my name was on it. One day on Okinawa, Dillard, Blaydes and I were sitting around and Dillard said, 'Do you think we ought to tell him?' I said, 'Tell me what?' Dillard said that when he and Blaydes signed up they signed me up, too. So it really wasn't Divine intervention, after all."

Larry Crawley: "While at MCAS Miramar, Bob Woods and I flipped a coin with Harry Goodyear and Bob Gilmore to see who would go where. Bob and I went to VMF-323, while they went to VMF-122."

New replacement pilot 2Lt. Henry Brandon recalls meeting Major Axtell for the first time: "We knew he was the youngest Squadron commander in the Marine Corps at that time, but everyone thought he was much older. In fact, at a get together 50 years after the war, some squadron members asked George how old he was and found he was only months older than most of us! We called him 'Uncle George,' but only behind his back."

Sgt. James Barrett: "We slept in tents at night. It was so warm during the day that the metal on the planes couldn't be touched for very long with the bare hand. But it was amazingly cold at night, and we didn't have enough blankets to keep from shivering. There was as much as 40-50 degrees difference in temperature between day and night."

Officers remaining after the mass transfers at El Centro in January 1944. (Top R to L) Lt. Bill Hood, Capt. Jeff Dorroh, Capt. Bill Cox, Lt. Byron Comstock, Major George Axtell, and Major Arthur Turner. (Bottom L to R) Lt. Jerry Bohland, Lt. Bill Martin, Lt(jg) Dr. Tom Dussman, and Lt. Del Davis. ***Courtesy of Del Davis.***

While the enlisted men were shivering in tents, the married officers lived in El Centro. The married pilots brought their wives out West for training or got married in California. Jerry O'Keefe and Hank Brandon married while they were at El Centro. The Barbara Worth Hotel was the lodging of choice, as it featured the first air conditioning units coming into use, so living was comfortable in this desert town. However, unmarried officers lived in wooden barracks on base. 2Lt. Al Wells: "We lived in wooden barracks, four to a room that were boiling during the day and freezing during the nights. El Centro was just too hot or too cold for me to remember anything else about it." El Centro was about 10-12 miles from the Mexican border. On the border was the U.S. town of Calexico, and the Mexican town of Mexicali. The men went to the bull fights and drank beer in a foreign country on Sundays.

Training began in earnest for the new arrivals, who were qualified pilots but now needed training in the basics of combat flying. The curriculum included:

(a) instrument flying
(b) overland navigation
(c) section tactics
(d) gunnery
(e) dogfighting
(f) strafing
(g) bomber escort
(h) field carrier landing practice (FCLP)

The F4U was designed as a carrier fighter for the Navy, which found it wanting and gave the fighter to the Marine Corps to sort out while it accepted the F6F Hellcat. The squadron FCLP (Field Carrier Landing Practice) was conducted on a field laid out at the Salton Sea. A few -323 pilots had previous FCLP training in Wildcats. A typical FCLP practice consisted of a four plane division. Each aircraft took off separately, and all spaced themselves at intervals to the left in a circling pattern. FCLP was important in learning the basics in landing on a carrier deck, as the procedures were the same whether landing on a carrier or practicing on the ground. However, since the field was static and a carrier would have moved into the landing aircraft's flight path, these FCLPs were faster than that of a real carrier landing. The landing procedure was to attain the correct altitude on the downward leg and then turn to the base leg. The pilot completed the requisite landing procedures: wheels down, flaps down, tail hook extended, prop full low pitch, canopy locked full open. This completed, the pilot would turn into the final approach. At this point the LSO (Landing Signals Officer) would come into view, and the pilot flew under the direction of the LSO paddle signals: too high, too low, too fast, too slow. Outstretched paddles indicated an OK to land. It was the inherent tendency for the pilot to fly his fighter into the landing, but he had to learn to trust the compulsory directions of the LSO. A correct approach was a disciplined left turn, nose high, power full on, coming in just above stall speed. If the LSO was satisfied, he would signal with the "cut" sign, one paddle whipping across his face. The pilot would then cut the throttle and flared out to catch the arresting wire. In practice most of these landings were "touch and go." If the LSO was dissatisfied with the approach, he would then "wave off" the aircraft by waggling both paddles above his head. FCPL was draining on the pilot due to the amount of concentration required. The LSO at the Salton Sea field liked to bring planes in close to him as a landing pilot would touch and go. However, one day a plane stalled out and its wing tip decapitated him.

Gunnery training was carried out over the Chocolate Mountain Gunnery Range to the north of the base and east of the southern end of the Salton Sea.

Training was usually routine, but there were times that it became more exciting, as Del Davis recounts: "In February, I was returning from a gunnery flight and got into the landing pattern at El Centro when my engine failed. I was below 500 feet, unable to bail out, and without power, so I picked out the softest looking spot I could find to put to put it down. Prior to touchdown, I pulled the shoulder harness as tightly as possible and shut off the fuel valve and battery switch. One can't believe how hard a powerless aircraft can hit an unprepared surface. The aircraft broke in two aft of the cockpit. The only injury I suffered was a cut over my eye from striking the gunsight."

The enlisted men, mechanics, and ordnance men had little to occupy them in the hot weather. Sgt. James Barrett: "Capt. John Grando joined the squadron as the head of ordnance about the time we arrived at El Centro. He was the stereotypical old Corps Leatherneck Marine; some drinking, some loving, didn't know much, wasn't very bright, and being in his early 40s was probably the oldest man in the squadron. There wasn't a lot to do for the ordnance department at El Centro, so there were always guys sitting around. Grando would drive in and see idle men and order the Master Sergeant, Ed Grady, to get them to do something, anything. Grady would have us pick up papers or something like that until Grando was satisfied and left. As soon as Grando left Grady would yell, 'OK, sign off' and we would go back to lounging around or whatever we were doing. As long as Grando didn't interfere, the ordnance men got their jobs done."

Sgt. Paul Finney: "Capt. Bill Van Buskirk was buzzing boats on the Salton Sea and hit a flock of ducks. They got stuck all over the engine, and a cylinder had to be replaced. One went through the top of the fuel cell and shattered the bulletproof windshield. It was a real mess. Then after I got finished, I damaged it again. I worked hours into the night and was so tired that when I took it out of the hanger I hit and damaged the wing tip."

Razor Blaydes carrying his parachute pack on an El Centro training flight in an SNJ, the Navy version of the AT-6 Texan Air Force trainer. ***Courtesy of Jody O'Keefe.***

CHAPTER 3
Camp Pendleton
Fun, Fun, Fun in the California Sun

February to 21 July 1944

The stay at El Centro lasted about a month before orders to transfer to Camp Joseph H. Pendleton, about 40 miles north of San Diego, were received. When the squadron transferred to Pendleton from El Centro they were supposed to fly across the mountains, but the weather closed in, delaying them. Henry Brandon's young 18 year old wife, Ann, went ahead by bus, expecting to meet him that afternoon, after which they were to find place to stay. When she arrived a base sergeant told her that the flight was delayed. He invited the worried newlywed to stay with him and his wife over night. Al Wells described the flight from El Centro: "When we flew up from El Centro the weather was not all that good, with a heavy overcast. Of course, Axtell was leading, and since we weren't instrument rated yet, he led us up the Central Valley from El Centro through the pass beyond Palm Springs, which was flanked by two mountain ranges. It was kind of crowded with 24 aircraft flying between low clouds and the ground, hemmed in by mountains. I was leading a division, which made me nervous, and I became even more nervous when another division moved in under me. Tentatively, I looked down and saw Joe Dillard flying his plane with his knees as he lit a cigarette! This was my introduction to Joe, who would become my good friend."

The ground echelon was transported from El Centro to Pendleton over the brown landscape of the coastal mountains, crossing creaking wooden bridges and trestles.

Pendleton was a huge Marine base, 55 miles deep and stretching about 22 miles along U.S. Highway 101 and the Southern California coast. Most of the base was devoted to land and amphibious training operations. For aviation training there was only one fighter strip and a tower in a river valley about 7 or 8 miles from the main gate. The camp was composed of frame and tent structures, with the mess being the only real building. The weather was mild, and the living, working, and flying conditions were very good. The advantage of Pendleton was that it was isolated, and the new pilots were there long enough to go through a good training syllabus, not once, but several times. Wells: "We all got to be good friends living with each other for the six to eight months we were there. We learned who were the good pilots and who we could depend on, which was just about everyone."

Most of the officers lived in Balboa or Laguna Beach. In Spring 1944, Laguna Beach was a small picturesque community with steep hills rising from the coast and a low key stop on coastal route U.S. 101. The town was "early California-style," as its roots as an artist's colony were being established by many colorful locals. The men who resided there found the area extraordinary: the Pacific Ocean with its coves and beautiful beaches, the town with its quaint homes and buildings surrounded by pungent eucalyptus and orange trees, all framed by the low hills inland. They would commute every morning to base, stopping at Capistrano for breakfast, where "Our Gang" movie star, Alfalfa, also ate breakfast every morning before going to Hollywood.

Unit Nicknames

In a closely knit group the members often give each other a nickname. Keith 'Lightning' Fountain says Henry Brandon was the main squadron nicknamer, "...and most of them were quite cynical. He called me 'Lightning' because he thought I was pretty slow and slept too much." Brandon gave the nickname, 'Ho-Hum,' to a laconic Southerner, Tom Blackwell.

Three Bubs: 'Big Bub'-Henry Brandon, 'Middle Bub'- Bob Woods, and 'Little Bub'- Al Wells, were called so because of their relative sizes. Bob 'Long John' Woods, 'Big Ed' Keeley, and Bill 'Moose' Martin received their nicknames from their stature.

Harold Tonnessen was known as the "Preacher," as he was the most religious officer in the squadron. He played the organ and volunteered his services to the local chaplains for musical and choral activities.

Norm 'Whitey' Miller received his name because of his hair color, but 'Red' Dillard received his for a different reason.

According to Al Wells, Joe Dillard's hair color was slightly red, but one night at Pendleton, he passed out drunk and "the young lady he was with decided to dye his bright red." Francis Terrill got his nickname because he claimed all the girls had the "Hots" for

A Death Rattler Corsair division over the Southern California mountains in the Spring of 1944. This "step down" division formation is comprised of K-91, Major Arthur Turner, K-87, Lt. Ed Abner, K-83, Lt. Charles Allen, and K-77, Lt. Bill Hood. ***Courtesy of Norman Miller.***

The operations office at Pendleton with Bob Bierbower in flight clothing on the right. Out the window a SNJ and F4U, being fueled can be seen. A Coca Cola calendar with a discrete pin up girl can be seen on the left wall. ***Courtesy of George Axtell.***

Married officers lived in Laguna Beach or Balboa on the Pacific Coast and commuted to base each morning. The Hotel Laguna (above) was a favorite Marine hangout for MACS Pendleton and El Toro. ***Courtesy of Henry Brandon.***

him, while Bob Lejonstein was called "Bird dog" because he was always chasing the girls.

Charlie Allen had the unusual childhood nickname that carried on to his adult nickname, "Seab." It was a contraction of his middle name, Seaborn. Obie "Smokey" Stover, Aquilla "Razor" Blaydes, and Bill "Duck" Drake had obvious nicknames.

Bob Muse enjoyed reading Damon Runyon novels. He was called Mindy, which was Runyan's fictional name for Lindys, the famous restaurant in New York City. Axtell had put Muse in charge of the officer's club.

Other squadron nicknames were:

The Whip-Jeff Dorroh
Hogan-Jack Broering
Zeke-Fred Zehring
Louie-James Brown
Tilly-Atilio Ferdenzi
JoJo-Joe McPhail
Bucko-Bob Wade
Eddie-Harold Edelson
Scotty-Glenn Thacker
Swampy- Albert Taylor
Wild Bill-Bill Hood
Gruesome-John Ruhsam
P.P.-Arthur Turner

Death Rattler Insignia

At Oak Grove, NC, a large rattle snake was found in the squadron area and subdued by three lieutenants. After it was killed, a photo was taken of Major Arthur Turner, -323 XO, holding it aloft. The skinned snake was later hung in the squadron's ready room.

The creator of the insignia was 1Lt. Harold Tonnessen, who was born in Norway. His father came to America alone to work, and supported the family by sending money back to Norway. He finally saved enough to bring the family over when Tonnessen was eight. Prior to the war the young Tonnessen was employed by the New York Museum of Modern Art and was a commercial artist. Tonnessen describes the design of the squadron insignia: "The original group of pilots trained in North Carolina and on their arrival on the West Coast were detached and sent out as replacements. I was part of a group of pilots from El Toro who reformed -323 under Axtell. The idea for the insignia had been roughly drawn by someone in the original group. It included a rattlesnake, and the silhouette of a F4U flying over a bull's eye. My civilian occupation was as a commercial artist, and I put these elements together in a finished form and made arrangements for their production in leather before we left the states."

Ed Abner was one of the men married in California and car-pooled from living quarters in the Balboa-Laguna Beach area to Camp Pendleton. Some of the private automobiles can be seen in the background. ***Courtesy of Henry Brandon.***

Enlisted men's tents at Pendleton (L to R) Corp. Richard Powers, Sgt. Turdio Cresentini, T/Sgt. Rocco DeMilia, and Sgt. Martin Mahady. ***Courtesy of Rocco DeMilia.***

Larry Crowley's wartime wedding at Pendleton (L to R) Gerry Baker and his wife, maid of honor, Annette O'Keefe (husband Jerry was taking the photo), bride, Mary Ellen Crowley, Groom, Larry, Crowley's mother, and Bob Woods. ***Courtesy of Jody O'Keefe.***

The rattle snake has been a constant feature of the squadron insignia over the years. The 1943 request for approval explained the design: "The circle is for the solidarity of the Squadron, a compact well-rounded unit. The rattle snake represents the vicious striking power of the airplane we fly into combat (the Vought F4U Corsair). The most distinctive feature of that aircraft (the inverted gull wing silhouette) is shown in the lower right section of the insignia."

Ray Bourne stands outside the unmarried officer's quarters. Bourne was an enlisted pilot who joined the squadron briefly at Pendleton but was shortly transferred to VMF-322. Later, on 28 May 1945, over Okinawa, he shot down a Japanese Nick and damaged another while with that squadron. ***Courtesy of Henry Brandon***

Over the more than 50 years the basic design has remained the same. However, in 1956, an unauthorized yellow stylized snake and scepter was briefly in use. Again in 1959, a new insignia utilizing the squadron's use of the Vought F8U Crusader was authorized by the Chief of Naval Operations. In 1962, this Crusader design was discontinued, and the F4U was readopted to "restore historical continuity." The squadron designation has changed over the years to reflect its mission. In June 1952, VMF (F=Fighter) was changed to VMA (A=Attack). In December 1956, back to VMF, in May 1962, VMF(AW)(AW=All Weather), July 1964, VMFA(FA=Fighter Attack). The pilots of today's VMFA-323 squadron are referred to as snakes, and a similar snake insignia remains in use.

Training

Since Major Axtell had previously been an instrument flight instructor, he insisted that all his pilots become proficient in night and all-weather flying. Squadron flight activity consisted chiefly of:

Radio navigation/D.R. navigation
Field carrier landings
Dive bombing/gunnery

Navigation training included many cross-country flights that would prove invaluable later when crossing the vast stretches of the Pacific Ocean. RON, Remain Over Night (from home base) was particularly relished by the pilots. Although these were mainly under VFRs (Visual Flight Rules), the pilots had to calculate fuel consumption and en route and arrival times on the plotting board.

Gunnery was an anticipated and invigorating phase of training. The target was a banner towed by a SBD. Before a pilot was allowed to fire on a towed target he first had to make about a dozen simulated runs. For gunnery practice a flight of two divisions would

Several of the pilots were married and lived off base. Lt. Hank Brandon and wife, Ann (L) pose in the hills over Laguna Beach with Brandon's brother, (US Army) Lt. R.J., and his wife, Betty. ***Courtesy of Henry Brandon.***

climb to 15-18,000 ft. to reach the range. The tow target was some 3,000 ft. below on a straight and level course. Each fighter would peel off individually for an overhead run. As the pilots gained proficiency they were allowed to make more vertical runs. This type of gunnery practice was not realistic in a combat sense.

Axtell: "In April 1944 while we were at Pendleton we were assigned to intercept a group of Army B-24s on a training mission. I instructed my men that when they made vertical runs on the bombers all they had to do was keep their gunsight pipper on the nose and they would then pass right by its tail and miss the bomber coming from behind. I then decided to make a run from low front quarter, coming right up close into their noses and then roll over and down. The bomber pilots must have been green, because they scattered all over after we all came so close to them."

On 3 June 1944, 16 VMF-323 F4Us joined with 16 VMF-122 F4Us out of El Centro. They flew close air support for ground troops conducting amphibious operations on the beach at Pyramid Cove on San Clemente Island. Both VMF-323 and -122 took off from Camp Pendleton for a rendezvous over the field with 28 bombers from VSMB-132 and VSMB-141. The two VMF squadrons arrived on station about five miles southeast of Pyramid Cove waiting for a call to furnish close air support. One pass was made, and the squadron returned to base.

After a training flight, Axtell had landed his plane and was taxiing in. A small belt on the cuff of his pants got caught and moved the landing gear lever. The plane was on the ground, so the main gear didn't collapse, but the tail wheel did, and he needed to be towed in. The ever-thorough, by-the-book Axtell wrote up the accident and filed a report.

On a flight led by Al Wells, the flight decided to "flathat" (ed. fly at low level) to relieve the monotony of the day's very routine training flight and to demonstrate their flying prowess to some local young ladies that needed to be impressed. After landing, as they pulled up to the flight line, Axtell came charging out to "greet" them. Axtell jumped on Well's wing and accused him of flathatting.

Lt. Hank Brandon (L) preparing a playful right cross to the jaw of buddy, Lt. Keith Fountain, on an off-duty outing to the Pacific Ocean. Brandon originated many of the unit's nicknames. He dubbed Fountain the name "Lightning" due to his very laconic nature. ***Courtesy of Henry Brandon.***

"Oh no, we never got below 1500-2000 ft," replied Wells. Axtell jumped down and looked into Well's oil cooler doors and found assorted tree matter and a length of telephone line trailing from the wing. Wells' reply to Axtell was, "I don't anything about that wire, it must have been strung between the mountains." The squadron's

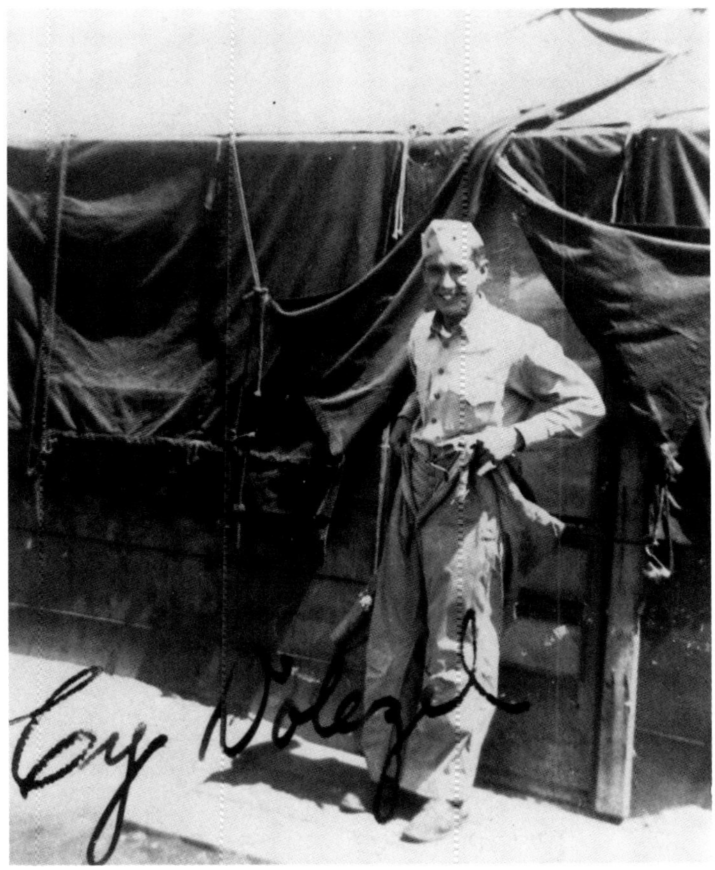

Cy Dolezel standing outside his tent. Dolezel was one of the older pilots in the squadron. ***Courtesy of Henry Brandon.***

blue Corsairs were easily identified by the large "K," plus the aircraft number on each side, just below and behind the cockpit.

2Lt. Robert M. Bartlett was scheduled for a night familiarization flight on 17 March 1944, with 2Lt. Henry Brandon on his wing. Warren Broering, "Some of the guys coming in from previous flights radioed the tower that the fog was beginning to come in and to hold all the flights. Bob went ahead and took off, but the fog rolls in pretty fast there in the summer time. He tried to stay under the fog, and on his turn back he ran into the hills near the base." On taxiing a mechanic noticed Brandon's running light out, and he returned to operations area. Brandon: "Taxiing back south I noticed the top of a small mountain about two miles to the south glow like a volcano. It took me awhile to realize that Bartlett had smacked into the mountain while making his left away from the ocean. I shut the plane down, and we got into a jeep and climbed up an old road with lots of drop offs to near where the plane hit. We couldn't get close because all those .50 caliber were cooking off in the fire. He was killed on impact and burnt. That night George (Axtell), Dr. Tom Dussman, the flight surgeon, and myself went to Laguna Beach. I got Ann (Brandon's wife) and her sister out of bed and went to tell Bartlett's wife what had happened. Going up to the door I figured George would step up to tell her the bad news, but he pushed me forward, as Bob was my friend. About this time my sister fainted, and all the commotion sort of made things easier for me to tell her the bad news." Broering, being Bartlett's best friend, escorted the body back to be interred in Kansas City.

On 25 May, 2Lt. John A. Freshour and his passenger, Lt.Cmdr. James J. Bunner, were killed when the squadron SBD crashed into a powerline near the base.

Bill Hood had a close call when he went into a screaming dive. The elevators ripped off the tail, leaving only the small 3x12 inch trim tabs to stabilize the Corsair. Hood was one of the most skilled pilots in the squadron, and was able to successfully land the fighter. 2Lt. Fred Ritter, the engineering officer: "There always was a representative available from Pratt & Whitney and Chance Vought while we were in the States. But we never had any serious problems, as it was a reliable aircraft."

At Pendleton some non-flying personnel required four hours flying time for flight pay purposes. Some of the men managed to get time in Navy blimps. It was a strange sight to see Marines hanging on mooring lines while their fellow Marines climbed into the gondola.

The Navy paid its personnel a clothing allowance, and if something wore out it was purchased new from this allowance. In the Marine Corps worn things were turned in for "survey," and these worn clothes and shoes would be exchanged for new. Someone in

Lt. Francis "Hots" Terrill (L) and Lt. Bill "Duck" Drake pose in front of the Pendleton flight line. The origin of Drake's nickname is obvious and so was Terrill's, who was known as quite the ladies man at the time. ***Courtesy of Henry Brandon***

Bob Muse, a fan of Damon Runyon novels, was nicknamed "Mindy", a corruption of famous New York City restaurant, Lindys. Muse was appointed to run the -323 Officer's club by Axtell. ***Courtesy of Norman Miller.***

the squadron found the dump where the old stuff that was turned in was discarded. The resourceful men then took these dumped clothes and had them "re-surveyed," and sent then the extra new clothes home or traded them to the Navy men.

All supplies had be obtained through San Diego. If a plane blew a tire in the morning the plane needed to be grounded for a day because the old tire had to be exchanged for the new one. The parts truck left for San Diego at 8 AM the next day and returned at 2 PM. There was a yard full of wrecked aircraft close by, and the Quarter Master (QM), Elwood Hand, would send men out on covert missions to salvage old parts. The QM would exchange these redeemed parts in San Diego for new parts that he would store in the back of the supply tent.

A mechanic revealed: "Axtell bragged about our high percentage of planes ready for flight at Pendleton. One of the secrets for this was that we had an unlisted engine that had been stolen. Because of this extra engine, one engine could always be kept ready in top condition. If an engine needed to go in for a general overhaul, this spare engine could quickly be installed and there was no need to ground the aircraft. Meanwhile, the engine that was needing overhaul would be put in shape and then become the spare."

Fun and Recreation

It was not all no work and no play at Pendleton, as Mindy Muse fondly recollects: "Pendleton was the best and funniest time of my life."

The War Diaries for June: Baseball, basketball, and volley have all been popular pastimes with all personnel both officers and enlisted during this month. On 21 June, a Squadron dance was held in the squadron area with all hands present.

Jim Barrett: "For liberty no one wanted to go into San Diego because it was filled with sailors, and it was hard to find someone without a uniform. L.A. was a much better liberty town, but was 120 miles away and required a special pass. Our normal NCO passes were 50 mile, San Diego passes. All special passes had to be picked up late in the day, but if the men wanted to leave early to get the

Onset of a legend, Squadron XO, Arthur Turner holds a very large Carolina rattle snake aloft. The hapless snake was killed on the base and later its skin adorned the squadron ready room wall. *Courtesy of Henry Brandon.*

A native of Norway, Harold Tonnessen, studied commercial art and developed the Death Rattler insignia from a rudimentary drawing done originally at Oak Grove. *Courtesy of Henry Brandon.*

The basic design of the Death Rattler insignia has remained similar throughout the years with some short-lived exceptions. In the center is an original, early 1944 leather patch. On the top left is an unauthorized, stylized late 1956 cloth patch when the VMA squadron designation reverted to VMF. On the bottom left is a cloth patch of a VMF designation. The top right cloth patch is the Vietnam VMFA insignia adopted in July 1964. The bottom right cloth patch is the Crusader F8U jet version adopted in 1959 and discontinued in 1962. ***Patches courtesy of Henry Brandon and Francis Maggliocco.***

longest liberty time possible, there was a hole in the fence. Nearly everyone used it instead of the front gate, even if they had passes. They took the coast railway from Oceanside to L.A. You had to be careful on liberty in L.A., because if a division were shipping out, the M.Ps and Shore Patrol would be out in force rounding up stragglers. You had better have a valid pass with you if they checked you. The 5th Division was shipping out, and I didn't have a valid pass and was caught and lost a stripe."

Al Wells: "While at Pendleton I met a girl who would later become my first wife. She lived up in North Hollywood, about 100 miles to the north. I went up there just about every night in a rented car and returned that same night. As there was gas rationing and mileage restrictions, I would jack up the back wheels and run off the mileage in reverse using aviation gasoline. I used to get back to base at dawn, and they had an early morning weather check flight out over the ocean to see if the weather was OK for gunnery practice. I volunteered for these flights so when I got back to base I was allowed to go to bed and get some sleep. On one of these flights I decided I would come in low and loud over the just waking base and pull up in an Immelmann (inverted loop). There were low clouds, but I thought that I would be out of the clouds at the top of the Immelmann to check my bearings while inverted to head back down through the clouds. But as I hit the top of the loop I was still in the clouds and scared the hell out of myself, as I wasn't instrument rated at the time."

SBD tires would fit on a car, but the only problem was that they would make a lot of noise, like snow tires on pavement. Also, aviation gasoline could be used in automobiles, but it needed to be cut with oil to slow it down and save the valves. After using aviation gasoline for awhile the compression got so bad that the guys who owned cars had to make sure they were going fast enough to get over the tops of some of the bigger hills.

An enlisted man, "There were nurse's quarters located some distance from the airstrip, and the recreation area was located on the hill. The nurses invited us to a party one night, but we didn't have any transportation. The only thing available was a large crane that was used to remove accidents from the runway. Even though it didn't go any faster than five mph, we requisitioned it and drove up the road with guys hanging all over it, obviously dazzling the nurses. There were also lady Marines stationed at Pendleton, and three or four of the enlisted men married them."

Getting Ready to Leave

Roger Archambault: "While at Pendleton those of us who lived on the East Coast received a 14 day leave to go home. It was the only chance most of us had for leave home during the entire time we were in the service.

On 12 June 1944, three pilots were transferred to VMF-471 at MCAS El Centro."

From 19 June onward all the squadron's 24 F4U-1s and FG-1s had been given a complete inspection and transferred to MCAS El Centro, ending all flight activity for the squadron. The squadron's only remaining aircraft, a SBD-5, conducted administrative flights to El Centro and North Island. Meanwhile, the officers and enlisted men were engaged in packing and marking equipment and belongings for overseas transfer. Ground lectures were given in these subjects: engineering, tactics, recognition, communication, and intelligence. Rotations of ten pilots were sent back to El Centro to be given additional instrument training in SNJs until all pilots completed this training. The ordnance section was being instructed on bombs and fusing, while Lts. Mayer, Ritter, and Rix instructed all enlisted personnel in combat conditioning. Since there were no aircraft available, ground school was set up and lectures were given in the following subjects: tactics, communications, engineering, intelligence, and recognition.

Jim Barrett: "We were closing down at Pendleton and ready to ship out to San Diego and were celebrating. We had a few motor scooters on base, and Bob (Capt. Robert) Lippoth decided to take a last spin around the base and fell off, breaking his collar bone. He had been with the squadron from Cherry Point and was very well

Larry Crowley (on wing) and Bob Woods show off their leather A-2 flight jackets with the new leather Death Rattler insignia. *Courtesy of Jody O'Keefe.*

"Razor" Blaydes poses with a patch on his shirt. *Courtesy of Henry Brandon.*

liked. The enlisted men particularly missed the warm-hearted, generous officer, who never returned to the squadron."

When the squadron was ready to leave Pendleton they decided they had enough confidence to try Axtell's patience and buzz the field (or more likely, he wasn't on base). Barrett: "When a F4U does a buzz job coming right at you, its flight attitude, tilted and tail up, made it look like it was going to run into the ground. It was hard to just stand there watching these little dots in the distance, getting larger and louder. When the planes were right on us, most of us ran, or at least ducked."

Bill Drake discusses the stay at Pendleton: "I believe -323 was successful because we were a unit unto ourselves at Pendleton, eating at our own mess hall, living together, drinking together, having our own mechanics and support sections. At El Toro there were many squadrons, intermixed. They could not get an identity and feeling of pride like we got."

On Okinawa the Death Rattler insignia became well known Stateside as news photographers sent home pictures of the "Where Aces Meet to Eat" scoreboard over Sol Mayer's mess hall. Here, Norman "Whitey" Miller does the "standard" mess pose. ***Courtesy of Norman Miller.***

A section of El Toro ("G" ID) passes by and gets shot at by a Death Rattler camera. ***Courtesy of Henry Brandon.***

"Gusty Fox" was the squadron mascot at Pendleton and was brought from North Carolina. The dog of undetermined breed(s) was named after the squadron's radio ID call, "Gusty Fox." ***Courtesy of Del Davis.***

The squadron's Corsairs could easily be identified by the large white "K" plus a number under the cockpit. ***Courtesy of Henry Brandon.***

Lt. Henry Brandon stands in front of his Corsair in his suit/summer/flying coveralls. The well-armed Brandon has a survival knife in a leather scabbard on his right hip and a Smith & Wesson .38 cal. revolver in a shoulder holster under hid left arm. *Courtesy of Henry Brandon.*

Lt. Keith Fountain prepares to enter the cockpit of his F4U-1D which was equipped with the raised six piece bubble canopy which afforded better vision than the earlier ten piece "birdcage" style on the F4U-1. The forward radio antenna sits on top of the cowling. Some -1D's had an additional antenna aft of the cockpit. *Courtesy of Henry Brandon.*

(L to R) Francis Terrill, Jeff Dorroh, and Bill Van Buskirk at the motor pool at Pendleton. *Courtesy of Jody O'Keefe.*

"Zeke" Zehring trying out one of his home-made props in the slip stream of a Corsair. *Courtesy of Henry Brandon.*

Hank Brandon was the assistant gunnery officer and tried to learn the rudiments of bore sighting the six .50 cal. Machine guns. Ordnance officer, John "Pappy" Grando, an old time Marine veteran, told Brandon just to "keep out of his way". *Courtesy of Henry Brandon.*

Lt. Bob Kvilin brandishing a .38 revolver, joined the squadron at El Centro but was transferred before the squadron left the States. The clap board sides and canvas-covered roof of the unmarried officer's living quarters can be seen in the background. *Courtesy of Henry Brandon.*

Atilio Luigi Ferdenzi, "Tilly", was the squadron Intelligence Officer who billed himself as the "Boston Strong Boy." *Courtesy of Henry Brandon.*

Modeling a variety of uniforms are (L to R) Bill Drake, Zeke Zehring, Keith Fountain, and Bob Maurer. *Courtesy of George Axtell.*

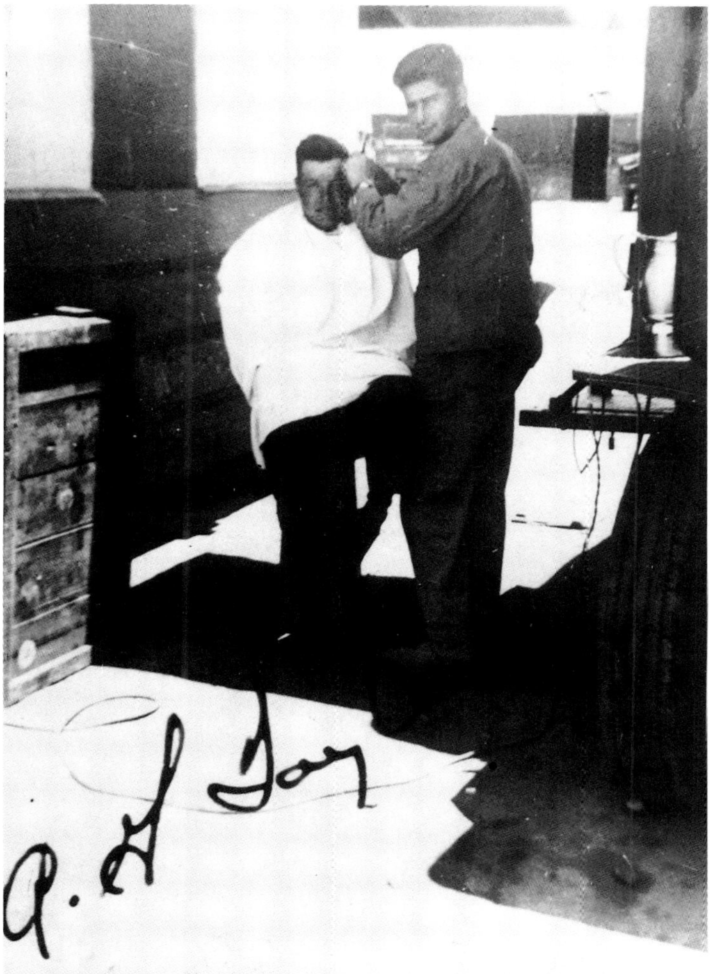

Materiels Officer, 1Lt. Albert "Swampy" Taylor receives a haircut from an unofficial squadron barber. *Courtesy of Henry Brandon.*

Harold Tonnessen was known as the "Preacher" as he was the most religious of the Death Rattlers. He played the organ and accordion and helped local chaplains with chorale services. *Courtesy of Jody O'Keefe*

Capt. Bill Cox (L) and Lt. Joe Dillard (R) argue with umpire, Lt. Bill Van Buskirk, over a call during a softball game held on the Pendleton flightline. *Courtesy of Henry Brandon.*

Fun times during liberty in Los Angeles. (L to R) Harold Edelson, Jerry O'Keefe, Ed Abner, Bob Maurer, and Francis Terrill. *Courtesy of Jody O'Keefe.*

Oregon native, Bill Hood, was one of the North Carolina trained pilots to remain on with -323. The quiet, unassuming Hood was considered an excellent pilot. He was able to safely land his Corsair after a screaming dive had ripped all the fabric off his elevators, leaving only the small 3x12 inch trim tabs to stabilize his fighter. *Courtesy of Henry Brandon.*

Hank Brandon (L) and Jerry O'Keefe (R) dressed in open collar khaki officer's shirt and garrison cap. The light-colored summer, cotton cap, previously called a field or overseas cap, was piped in gold and black braid. *Courtesy of Henry Brandon.*

Jack Broering taking part in a softball game. Athletics played a large part in the men's free time and was often very competitive. *Courtesy of Henry Brandon.*

(L to R) Jack Ball, Bob Muse, Brad Smith, Chuck Moore, and Fred Zehring celebrating at a Hollywood night club in Spring 1944. L.A. was the preferred liberty city over San Diego which was more crowded with the military. *Courtesy of Henry Brandon.*

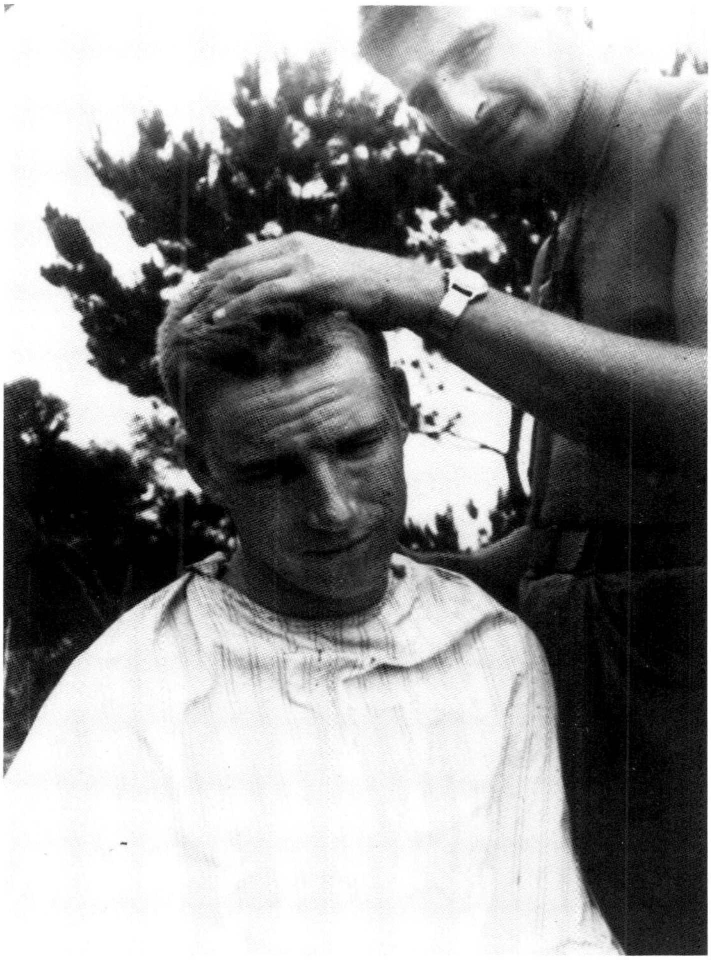

Norman "Whitey" Miller receiving a trim to his blond locks. Miller took many photos during his sojourn with -323. During post-war reunions, Miller continues to chronicle the squadron history. *Courtesy of Norman Miller.*

Quarter Master, Elwood Hand, was the Sgt. Bilko of the squadron while at Pendleton. *Courtesy of Elizabeth Hand.*

Camp Pendleton was about 40 miles north of San Diego and another 25 miles more to the Mexican border. In the standard Tijuana tourist pose on cart pulled by a zebra-painted donkey are (from the left), Jerry Baker and his wife and Hank Brandon and his wife. Baker would later be killed while his fighter was being catapulted off the USS BRETON on the way to Emirau. *Courtesy of Henry Brandon.*

Capt. Robert Lippoth on the Pendleton motor scooter. Lippoth took one last spin before the squadron shipped out to Ewa and crashed, breaking his collar bone. The popular officer was left behind and never rejoined the unit. *Courtesy of Jody O'Keefe.*

Zeke Zehring stands outside the Pendleton Command Post in full flight gear. The newly adopted Death Rattlers insignia painted on plywood is above the door. *Courtesy of George Axtell.*

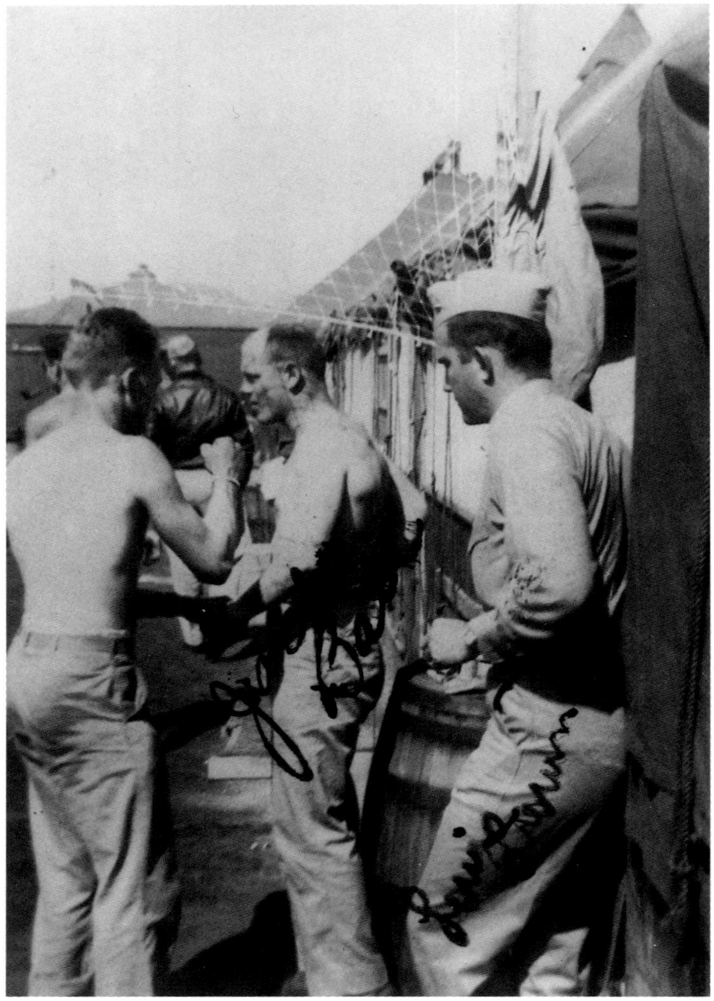

(L to R) Harold Tonnessen, Jack Ball, and Louie Brown in a bull session during a volley ball game. *Courtesy of Henry Brandon.*

A photo of a SNJ out of MAS El Toro ("G" designation) taken by a -323 pilot. The SNJ was the trainer that Naval aviators received their final training before receiving their wings. A stickler on instrument training, Axtell often had his pilots return to El Centro to receive additional instrument training in these aircraft. *Courtesy of Henry Brandon.*

CHAPTER 4
Long Island (CV-1)
21 July to 26 July 1944

Before the squadron left for Hawaii there was celebrating to do. Many of the officers and their wives had a party at the famous Coronado Hotel in San Diego to say a final farewell. Others like Al Wells and Bob Woods "borrowed" a jeep and went out on the town.

The entire squadron embarked on 21 July from NAS North Island. Henry Brandon's letter of 21-30 July: "The ship is very nice, and we are being treated very well. Fine food and nice quarters—not as bad as I imagined. I've never been out of sight of land before on a ship. Somehow or other you become very anxious for something to put your feet on except for salt water. Nothing to do but eat, sleep, shoot the bull, prowl around the ship, go to movies and attend lectures. There's plenty of time to think."

The Long Island-class carrier was laid down as a cargo ship, the MORMACMAIL in July 1939, and was commissioned as the LONG ISLAND (AVG-1). She spent her early years as a test bed for the "Baby Flattop" concept. She then trained carrier pilots and served as an aircraft ferry. The highlight of her career was her launch of the first fighters to arrive at Henderson Field on Guadalcanal, helping to save the island. Her career afterward included the mundane but necessary roles of pilot trainer and aircraft ferry. As CVE-1, she carried VMF-323 from NAS North Island, San Diego, to Ford Island, Oahu, Hawaii, arriving on 28 July 1944.

On 21 July 1944, VMF-323 embarked aboard the carrier, LONG ISLAND (CVE-1). The carrier/aircraft ferry had won fame by launching the first fighter to arrive at Henderson Field, Guadalcanal, helping to save the island. After a week at sea the squadron arrived at Ford Island, Hawaii to continue their training at Ewa. ***Photo courtesy of the US Navy.***

CHAPTER 5
Ewa
Hawaiian Holiday

28 July to 7 September

Upon their arrival at Ford Island on the island of Oahu, Hawaii, -323 Corsairs were off loaded and flown to MCAS Ewa. Several days were spent unloading and transporting the squadron's supplies and materials to Ewa.

Ewa (E-Vah), located northeast of Barbers Point on Oahu, began as a Navy dirigible base and emergency runway in the early 1930s. In late 1940, the runway was extended and a cross runway was constructed. 1941 saw extensive activity, with two runways and warm up areas being constructed. After Pearl Harbor, the construction pace accelerated, and in September 1942, Ewa was established as a Marine Corps air base. The air fields had four runways, each 300 feet wide and varying in length from 2,900 to 5,000 feet. By the time -323 arrived at the end of July 1944, Ewa was a large, elaborate established complex and inside the traffic pattern of Barbers Point. Today it is a housing subdivision.

The accommodations were very nice: new, one floor, wooden and screen barracks surrounded by lush tropical landscaping. The food was Island beef and fresh produce served in a mess hall that was modeled after a Samoan fale. The Hawaiian tour was truly a tropical holiday for the squadron.

Al Wells was the squadron's wild man: "There was a beautiful 'O' club at Ewa, and one night Mindy Muse and I stopped by for a few drinks. I didn't remember anything after the second martini. The next morning Jim Bierbower, who was officer of the day, came over to me and said, 'Little Bub, you're under arrest.' I didn't have any idea what he was talking about. He said that he didn't know any of the details, except he knew I was under arrest. I was taken to George's office, where I was told I had made an ass out of myself and had offended a one star general. George had to do something to appease the general, so he restricted me to my room for ten days except to fly and to eat, which wasn't bad at all." (Perhaps Wells should have had Bierbower intervene for him, as Bierbower later became a member of a prestigious Washington, D.C., law firm and was connected with the legal actions in the Watergate proceedings-ed.)

12 August: "I'm going to have a chart made of my teeth today for identification. We will be getting more shots soon, as you never finish taking them out here." Henry Brandon letter

18 August: "Al Wells showed us he was a real 'camper.' We went on a picnic yesterday and he put a can of pork and beans right in the fire. It exploded and covered him with pork and beans." Henry Brandon letter

As it is today, Waikiki was a favorite tourist locale. There was dancing at the Breakers near the Royal Hawaiian Hotel where 3.2 beer was served, but it was less as the men could drink it all day without anything happening. A squadron member, who shall remain nameless, describes the "good times" there:

"The red light district was very well thought out and organized. There usually was a waiting line outside the brothel door, mostly Navy. At the door there was a woman who would smell your breath, and if you had any liquor on it, you were turned away. If you passed the alcohol test you were queried on your desires, the 'usual' or 'oral.' It was a regular production line. For every two or three houses there was a military sponsored 'Pro (prophylactic) station,' where you could be given prophylactic treatment to prevent V.D. and were registered as having been so treated. If you hadn't registered and contracted V.D., there was the chance you could be court martialed. There was a major "to do" in the newspapers because the people running the brothels were making so much money they were buying property in the wealthy, high society areas of town. This was an outrage to old line Hawaiians with money."

Dibble Goodwin was a favorite first sergeant of the squadron and was the acting sergeant major of the squadron. As a sergeant

Concrete revetments on Ewa. ***Courtesy of the US Navy.***

Left: **Expanded from an emergency field and dirigible base after Pearl harbor, MACS Ewa was a large, elaborate complex with four runways when -323 arrived in July 1944. Located on the island of Oahu, today it is a housing development.** ***Courtesy of the US Navy.***

The 30 August beach hula party which got out of hand when the enlisted men threw some newly promoted officers into the ocean. Major Axtell caught the perpetrators in the act and stopped the party then and there. ***Courtesy of Jody O'Keefe.***

major he was the liaison between the enlisted men and officers. Goodwin would call the men together from time to time to explain naval law. On one occasion he told them if they got into trouble they could request a civilian lawyer and not have to take the assigned military lawyer. There was a story going around about an officer who got caught having sex in the officer's quarters and was arrested. The brass needed to find some charge against him that wouldn't jeopardize his career, so they charged him with being out of uniform because he wasn't wearing anything! He hired a civilian lawyer who got him off all together by arguing that he was wearing the uniform appropriate to the sport in which he was participating. James Barrett

30 August- "We had a beach party with hula girls. The enlisted men threw the officers, who had just received an advancement in rank, into the ocean. They threw Capt. Cox in and were about to throw Grando in when Uncle George caught them and really blew up, and ended the party right then and there. I think he is a little disgusted with that type of party." Henry Brandon letter

Harley Brock describes an incident involving plane captains who were given flight pay but had to be in the air several hours a month. "At Ewa they weren't flying much, and a lot of men needed to get into the air. Arrangements were made to get a DC-3 to carry them all at once. What a way to see the island, like a tourist bus for free. The scenery below was incredible, and I guess the pilot must have been watching it, too. We were all looking out our windows when suddenly everyone on the port side was thrown to the starboard as the pilot dodged hitting the side of a mountain. We were close to losing all our ground crew that day."

"While at Ewa squadron maintenance personnel were permitted to use armor plating material from ships sunk at Pearl Harbor for use as pilot seats and oil coolers." Del Davis

Routine training also continued. "Routine" was navigation and radio navigation, the carrying out of the month's flight syllabus, which included the following types of training flights: dummy gunnery runs and gunnery firing, division and squadron tactics, night division tactics, dive bombing (dummy and live), instrument flights, Link trainer hops, fighter direction problems, escort and interception problems, etc. Daily recognition classes were mandatory for all pilots at the synthetic training building, and lectures were given on: use of recognition signals, bombs and bomb fusing, principles and operating procedure of the use of VHF, principles of anti-aircraft, coast watchers, survival, rockets and rocket launchers, chemical warfare, company and battalion formations, and theater indoctrination, including: Palau, Philippines, Sulu Archipelago, Halmahera, Bonin, Nansei Shoto, Nanpo Shoto Islands, and Formosa. The squadron flew 1,197 hours on 740 hops during August, which was a heavy training schedule. The squadron had only flown 80 flights for 167 hours in the abbreviated July schedule at Pendleton and 954 hours in the full month of June there.

On 5 August, 1 Lt. Joe Dillard and his entire flight were restricted to their rooms for getting lost on a gunnery flight.

On 6 August, 2Lt. Glen "Brad" Smith crashed into the sea on a routine training flight at 1230 off Hilo, Hawaii. He pulled up too abruptly during an overhead gunnery run and stalled out and spun into the ocean. The body was not recovered.

Getting together after a training flight are (L to R) Lts. Larry Crawley, Dewey Durnford, Zeke Zehring, and Jerry Baker. ***Courtesy of Henry Brandon.***

2Lt. Brad Smith was killed while making a gunnery practice run off Hilo, Hawaii on 6 August 1944. ***Courtesy of Henry Brandon.***

Owen V. Gallatin, "O.V." , was left behind at Ewa with several other pilots to embark on the troopship, SEA PIKE. They would meet the squadron at Espiritu Santo after an epic 52 day voyage across the Pacific. ***Courtesy of Henry Brandon.***

8 August, two divisions led by Major George Axtell and Capt. William Van Buskirk took part in a simulated dive bombing and strafing attack on the USS MISSISSIPPI (BB-41). The two divisions flew high cover for 16 F4Us of VMF-313 and for 18 bombers of VMSB-142.

On 9 August, there was the threat of a second attack on Pearl Harbor. Ready duty strike orders were issued, which meant sitting in an aircraft in the hot sun. Many of the men were in their usual seat at the "O" Club, and several had to be escorted and dumped into their fighters by the plane captains.

11 August, 16 F4Us led by Maj. Turner intercepted six PBYs of VB-200 ten miles off Pearl Harbor.

12 August: "We had one gunnery flight today and really fouled up, as we lost the tow sleeve. I expected Uncle George to be rather angry, but he took it pretty nicely, I suppose. It was 'All the way through on it' as he says." Brandon letter

15 August, eight F4Us flew close support for 18 bombers of VMSB-142 that were carrying out a simulated attack on CAVE-81, RUDYERD BAY.

31 August, 16 F4Us led by Major Arthur Turner provided escort cover for 11 SB2Cs of VMSB-332s and simulated a strafing attack on the USS SOUTH DAKOTA (BB-57)

On 2 September, 1Lt. Ed Keeley was flying with Maj. Arthur Turner on an instrument hop and out of boredom made a run on a Navy F6F and lost Maj. Turner. Keeley was put under arrest and confined to his room for ten days, which "everyone in this outfit thinks was too severe a punishment". Henry Brandon letter

On the 6th of September, the vacation ended and the F4Us were flown back to Ford Island. The squadron was divided into two echelons to embark to their next assignment.

CHAPTER 6
USS Breton (CVE-23)
7 September to 18 September

On 7 September, 30 pilots, 3 ground officers, 90 enlisted men, 24 aircraft, and a limited amount of cargo were put aboard the USS BRETON, along with VMF-322. This echelon was transferred to the 2MAW under Maj. Gen. James Moore. The remainder of the squadron was left behind at Ewa and transferred on STAD orders with the 3MAW under Brig. Gen. Walter Farrell. At 1300 on 8 September, the carrier embarked on its ten day voyage. Meanwhile, MAG-32, under CO, Lt.Col. John Smith, and his headquarters and service squadrons were on their way to the Philippines. The Japanese propagandist, Tokyo Rose, welcomed Smith back into battle on the radio, telling him he wouldn't be so lucky this time!

The BRETON (CVE-23) was a Bogue-class carrier laid down in September 1942, and commissioned in mid-April 1943. She operated throughout her entire career with the Carrier Transport Squadron, Pacific Fleet, with which she delivered men, materiel and aircraft to the fleet. She had participated in the Saipan invasion, Battle of the Philippine Sea, and the second Bonins raid before ferrying VMF-323 from Hawaii to Emirau in September 1944. She later took part in the Okinawa invasion.

The squadron boarded the BRETON, thinking it was going to take part in the invasion of Peleliu as per the scuttlebutt of the time. They were given the maps for Peleliu, and everyone was in high spirits and looking forward to getting into the war. Their biggest fear was that the war would be over with before they could get into it. There was profound frustration when they found that they were going to Emirau.

"There was rough weather much of the time, and many people got sea sick. The food lines were very long, and extended from mid-ship along one side of the ship aft to the fantail, then back to the galley area. As one moved toward the fantail the ship would not only be moving up and down but yawing back and forth at the same time. This got to most men, and they dropped out of line. The trick was to try to hang on and get to the galley area, and when you got something to eat you were usually OK.

On the BRETON was a chief bo'suns mate who was the tyrant of all tyrants. He not only browbeat the sailors, but also the marines on board. He was roundly disliked and many detested him. He got into a confrontation with (T/Sgt. Edwin) "Tiny" Mascal, who was nicknamed for his obvious bulk. The likable Mascal had a quick temper, and he decked the CPO with quite a few approving witnesses. The incident quickly made the rounds, and the sailors took up a large collection for Mascal. CO Major Turner heard about the fight and warned Mascal that the next time he got into trouble he would face a deck court marshal." Jim Barrett

On 14 September, the BRETON crossed the Equator, and the ancient and revered crossing rites directed by King Neptune and His Royal Whore of the Royal Entourage were observed. Those who had never crossed the Equator, Pollywogs, were to be initiated by those who had, Shellbacks, which were most of the ship's crew. The Pollywogs had to eat with heavy rubber gloves. For initiation the Pollywogs had to run the gauntlet of Shellbacks wielding shillelaghs and prods shaped like three-pronged tridents. The night before the crossing, tradition has it that the Shellbacks raise the Jolly Roger on the mast. Pollywog Maj. Jack Mathis of VMF-322 decided to make a midnight run and remove the pirate flag and was caught. Accordingly, VMF-322 took the worst beating through the gauntlet, especially Mathis, who could barely stand up afterward.

Sgt. James Barrett "Gun watches at night were highlighted by the sparkling phosphorescence created by the ship's wake. I wondered if the beautiful glowing wake could be seen by enemy ships. I later found that the phosphorescence was caused by the disruption of the dinoflagellates floating near the surface." After the war Barrett went on to become a biology professor at Marquette University in Milwaukee, Wisconsin.

Warren Broering: "As the BRETON neared Emirau, the Corsairs were fitted with all three drop tanks that were empty. The men were told to sort out all the personal gear and stuff they could fit into their aircraft. There was a small space behind the seat, so that

On 7 September 1944, the first echelon of VMF-323, comprising 30 pilots, 3 ground officers, 90 enlisted men, and 24 aircraft, embarked aboard the USS BRETON (CVE-23). The Bogue-class carrier operated with the Carrier Transport Squadron throughout the war and delivered -323 to Emirau Island on 18 September. ***Courtesy of the US Navy.***

While aboard the BRETON (L to R) Cy Dolezel, Tom Blackwell, Zeke Zehring, and Jerry Baker and the rest of the squadron believed they were going into combat at Peleliu. *Courtesy of Del Davis.*

Jerry Baker (R) and Francis Terrill (L). Baker died in a catapult accident off the BRETON while Terrill died in January 1946 in a ground collision in Louisiana while ferrying aircraft. *Courtesy of Henry Brandon.*

limited the amount we could bring, and that included our carbine and steel helmet."

Probably the most discussed and controversial of any event in the squadron's history involved the catapult launch on 18 September as the BRETON neared Emirau.

Major Axtell: "Several days before the scheduled launch, my operations personnel and I held a detailed talk with the Air Department of the BRETON that was responsible for executing the catapult launch of our aircraft. We discussed the proper catapult pressure required for our aircraft. Launch pressure is calculated by the type of aircraft, configuration, total weight, carrier speed and wind over the deck. I presented my rationale that we had three empty external tanks, aircraft loaded with personal gear and mainly pilots new to this type of operation. I requested the launching pressure be increased a modest amount as a matter of common sense and safety. My recommendation was not accepted by the carrier Air Department, and ultimately the CVE captain would not overrule his officers. I launched first and had no trouble, but I maintained only marginal flying speed off the cat. I pushed my stick forward and traded what little altitude I had for speed and gained the benefit of 'ground cushion effect.' Experienced pilots can recognize this condition and recover most of the time. As I gained altitude I called the ship over my radio and informed them to increase the launch boost, as I had had only marginal flying speed on my launch. While I was talking, my wingman, Jerry Baker, was launched."

It was the first cat shot for most. Brandon describes the shot: "It didn't scare me any. You knew what to expect. You just sat back and got ready for the jolt. It was like being kicked in the butt. We were about five miles east of the coast of Emirau. I was up on the carrier bridge waiting for my turn to takeoff. I was looking down, practically into Baker's cockpit. Gerry followed all the procedures, saluted, and was launched by the hydraulic system. It looked like a pretty good cat shot. I couldn't figure out what happened. At the end of the cat, he abruptly took a stalling attitude and fell off on his left wing, hitting the water and crashing into the sea. The engine section broke off, but the aft fuselage remained afloat, and he was strapped into the cockpit fuselage section. Of course, we didn't have any choppers in those days, and it took the Escort Plane Guard boat

Bob "Long John" Woods was next on the catapult after the ill-fated Baker. "My turn went all right but it was a little scary after I saw what happened. I didn't have any time to think before I was on the cat and launched". ***Courtesy of Henry Brandon.***

15-20 minutes to get to him. It took his aircraft awhile to sink, and he drowned before they could reach him."

Harley Brock was standing on the port flight deck and described the incident from there: "We saw the plane cartwheel into the water and were making decisions in our minds as what we could do. Very soon the wreckage was just below us. The engine had been torn off, and the cockpit bubble was closed and filled with blood. There was some brief thoughts about jumping overboard, but that would have been useless with that amount of blood. We later found that the blood in the cockpit was really hydraulic fluid and that Baker had actually drowned."

Major Axtell believes: "that just after the launch Baker thought his aircraft was sinking toward the water and tried to pull his nose up and completely stalled. At the prelaunch briefing the pilots were instructed to drop the nose after the shot if airspeed appeared to be too slow and this would gain speed. This was Baker's first catapult, and he was young and excited and reacted wrongly to an unfamiliar situation. During the break in the launch operation due to the accident, the BRETON brass agreed to my, not so polite, recommendations to increase the cat pressure for the remaining aircraft. After the BRETON docked at Emirau to unload our ground crews and cargo, I went aboard and reviewed the entire operation. I informed the ship's officers on what I would include in the accident and investigative reports that are required after any occurrence of this magnitude. Needless to say, they weren't happy about my conclusions. Accidents happen in war, but there was no excuse for this one."

Henry Brandon has his own theory: "either Baker or somebody had gotten into the cockpit and let the two little clips which held the plotting board in place in the up, unlatched position. When Baker took that cat shot he took a pretty good jolt, and the unsecured plotting board hit him across the chest, causing him to lose control."

Warren Broering, who was in line to take off after Baker, has yet a different theory: "The aircraft were stacked on the deck so tightly that the pilot could not start up his engine and warm it up until the plane in front of you moved forward. Normally, the aircraft taxied to the warm up area to check the mags and let the engine get up to operating temperature. Baker started his engine and was waved forward immediately by the Signals Officer, and catapulted off with a cold engine. We were overloaded at take off, so if his engine quit for just an instant that would be all it would take to put him into the drink."

Axtell's account is more first hand and probably the explanation for this unfortunate accident of well-liked and popular Baker.

Though of poor quality, these are actual photos of the flight deck and catapult launch of VMF-323 off the BRETON. Jerry Baker was killed when his aircraft crashed into the ocean immediately after being catapulted. ***Courtesy of Jody O'Keefe.***

CHAPTER 7
Emirau
Tropical Sojourn

18 September to 25 October
The first echelon arrived at Emirau under the cloud of Lt. Baker's death during the catapult launch from the BRETON. To compound the tragedy was an incident that occurred at Baker's funeral as described by Sgt. James Barrett: "We were on large flat bed trucks which had gates on the sides and back which were loose. We were on the way back from Baker's funeral. The drivers didn't slow down for anything, and were driving on the left side of the road, Australian-style. Going around a curve one of the gates broke, and a few guys went off and broke arms and legs. Axtell was worried because most of the casualties were ordnance men, and it left him shorthanded for awhile. (S/Sgt.) Chester Wingfield broke both wrists, which were put into casts, making him totally helpless. His friend, (S/Sgt.) Glen Johnson, had to care daily for him in the sick bay. On Emirau if you broke a bone you had it set on the island and recuperated there. Later on at Okinawa you were sent out for treatment and then sent home."

Emirau was occupied by the 4th Marine Division on 20 March 1944, without Japanese opposition. The island was desired for use as a naval base and forward airfield for land-based bombers in the upcoming attacks on Jap-held islands in the Western Pacific, Truk (600 miles due north) and the Palaus (800 miles northwest), and to keep pressure on Rabaul, the by-passed Jap stronghold 250 miles to the south. Emirau of the St. Matthias Group and part of the Bismarck Archipelago, measures eight miles from east to west and is two miles wide. It has a 2 1/2 mile peninsula pointing from the center of the island's north coast. The island's climate is tropical, with high humidity and heavy rains. Hamburg Bay on the northwest coast was the principal harbor, and the flat central plateau was utilized for the two air bases. North Cape and Inshore Field were both coral surfaced heavy bomber strips with 7,000 by 150 foot runways with warm up strips at each end of the field. Inshore Field was the fighter base, with 35 double hardstands with a capacity of 210 fighters. Quarters consisted of elevated and screened prefabricated buildings and tents that housed 1,050 officers and enlisted men. When -323 arrived aboard the USS BRETON in September, Emirau was a large and extensive base.

The squadron was on standby on Emirau, awaiting further orders. Flight activity during this period was of a local nature, consisting of dummy gunnery, squadron tactics, and the inevitable Axtell-inspired instrument hops. During October the squadron flew 199 hops for 448 hours in the air.

The weather was typical of a tropical island. Henry Brandon letter: "I didn't know there was this much water in the world. It rains almost constantly, 24 hours a day, 7 days a week. There is a little stream running past our doorway. I think if it rains any harder, I could build a raft and play Robinson Crusoe for awhile." When it stopped raining it was sweltering hot, and the order of the day was to try to keep cool. Impenetrable jungle surrounded either side of the coral strip, so there weren't too many places to go. A swimming hole was dynamited by the SEABEES in the lagoon, so a lot of time was devoted to swimming and spearing lobster. There were banana plantations upstream, and the men would go on banana missions and load boats full of ripening bananas. Back at the base

Henry Brandon (L) and plane captain, Paul Finney (R) on one of the few days it didn't rain on Emirau. The squadron was waiting reassignment, hoping to go into combat in the Peleliu campaign. ***Courtesy of Henry Brandon.***

Jack Broering (R) and his plane captain on the flight line. Notice the large size of the 13 ft. 4 in. Hamilton-Standard prop. ***Courtesy of Henry Brandon.***

The Emirau coral airstrip was carved out of dense jungle which crept up to its perimeter. (L to R) Jack Ball, Louie Brown, and Razor Blaydes are standing in front of a F4U whose gun ports were protected with "100 mph duct tape" which as its name implies would come off when the aircraft reached 100 mph. *Courtesy of Henry Brandon.*

Ed Abner, dressed for the tropical jungle climate, gets ready to field the ball in taxiway softball game against VMF-322 whose white-nosed Corsairs with their wings folded in the background. *Courtesy of Henry Brandon.*

the bananas were hung in engine crates to ripen. On Sunday mornings the men could select a hand of ripe bananas and go to the mess hall, cut them up and add powdered milk and sugar for the notable meal of the week. Another highlight was the occasional beer runs up to Manus. The brass had refused to issue beer to the squadron, so Axtell decided to take matters into his own hands. Small doors were cut in the top of belly fuel tanks and were filled with canned beer. By the time the Corsairs got back from Manus the beer was ice cold from the altitude and ready to drink.

Axtell: "While we were at Emirau, Charles Lindbergh, who had been visiting Joe Foss and VMF-115 on the other side of the island, came over and flew with some of our squadron. He said we were the first squadron he'd come across that knew how to lean out engines and get the maximum performance out of their airplane. I told him, 'Mr. Lindbergh, we've been doing that since we flew the SNJs at Cherry Point.'"

The Army had left a large store of armaments in a tent that was unsecured. Al Wells "requisitioned" a brand new Browning Automatic Rifle (BAR). Wells carried it around with him for the rest of the war, having to stash it in his aircraft when the squadron moved to a new base.

On 24 October, the Commander of Task Group 59.6 ordered the forward -323 echelon to proceed to Espiritu Santo, New Hebrides Islands, to come under the control of the Commanding General, Aircraft, FMF, Pacific.

The following day the exodus began, as one pilot and 25 enlisted men left for Luganville, E.S., carried by a Curtiss R5C (C-46) Commando transport of VMR-952. During the next two days the remainder of the squadron stood by awaiting transportation. On October 28th, 24 F4U-1Ds took off for Luganville. 2Lt. Henry Brandon describes the flight: "It was a long flight from Emirau to Green Island, and then on to Bougainville and down the Slot to Guadalcanal. We stayed over night at Guadalcanal and flew the

Cy Dolezel, shirtless, holding a Thompson submachine gun, guards an unidentified Marine carrying a bag full of canned beer. One of the most strategic missions flown on Emirau was a division flight to Manus Island where specially adapted fuel tanks were loaded with canned beer and flown back. At altitude the beer would become ice-cold and ready to consume upon landing. *Courtesy of Henry Brandon.*

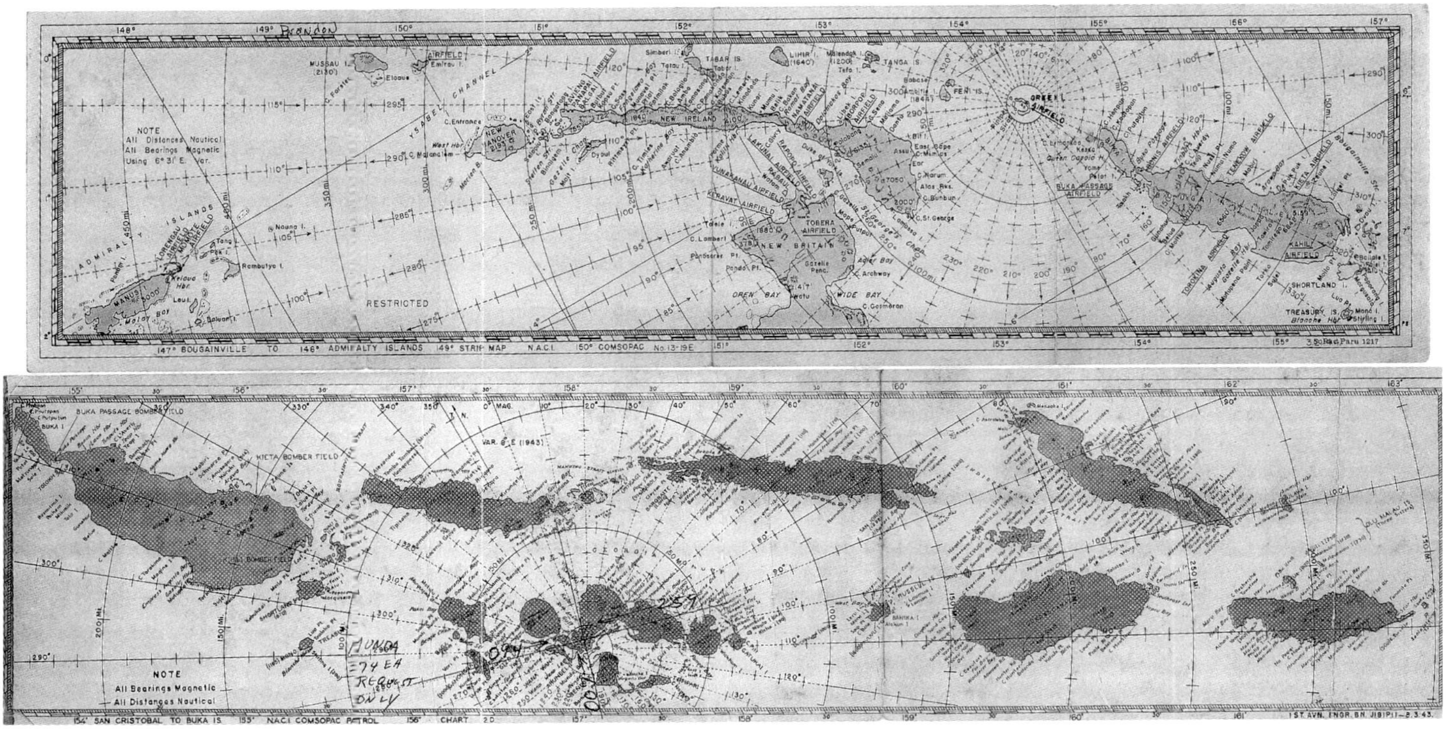

Copies of actual maps used by Henry Brandon to navigate from Emirau to Espiritu Santo via Guadalcanal. These two maps are part of a larger map and show the headings into Henderson Field on Guadalcanal and into Luganville on Espiritu. *Courtesy of Henry Brandon.*

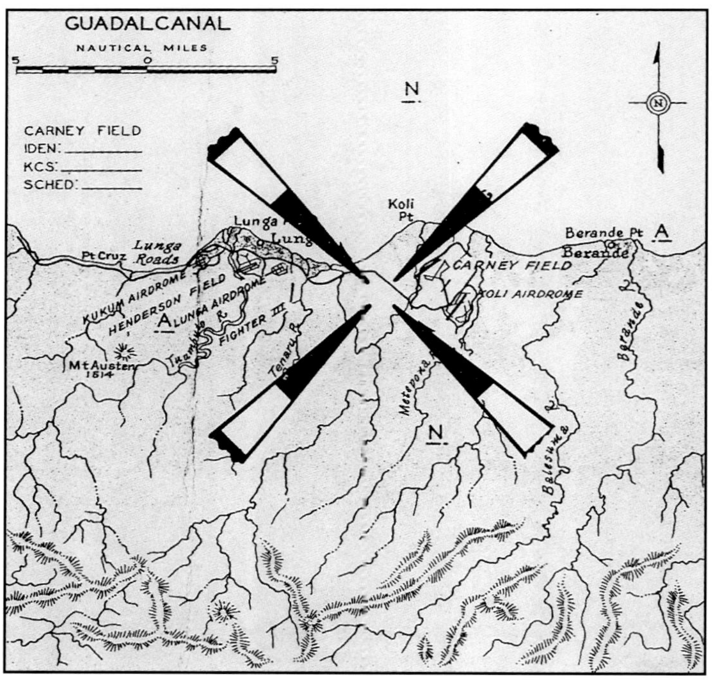

Henry Brandon's navigation map for Henderson Field. *Courtesy of Henry Brandon.*

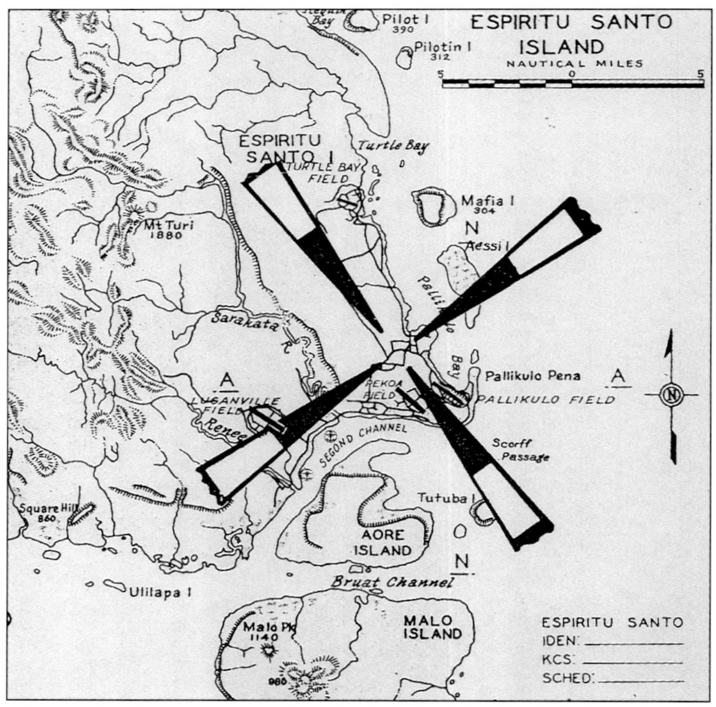

Henry Brandon's navigation map for Luganville Airfield, Espiritu Santo. *Courtesy of Henry Brandon.*

In late October 1944, the squadron landed at Henderson Field, Guadalcanal for their overnight before proceeding on to Espiritu Santo. At this time the airfield was a transition stop for units, but usually they were flying towards the Pacific battles, not away. *Courtesy of the USMC.*

When a fatigued Al Wells landed on Henderson Field after a long, tiring flight from Emirau via Green Island, he not only dropped his landing gear but also his tail hook! The -323 pilots on the ground thought he would either tear up the metal Marston matting (shown) or tear off the rear of his fighter. Nothing happened as the tail hook only bounced along the matting. *Courtesy of the USMC.*

Dr. Tom Dussman handed out "little" pills which would "kind of keep the pilots alert" on their long flight. *Courtesy of Del Davis.*

S/Sgt. Frank Maggliocco (above) and Sgt. Jim Williams stayed behind at Guadalcanal to service some -323 F4Us which had problems on the way to Espiritu. *Courtesy of Francis Maggliocco.*

next morning to Espiritu Santo. It was a long nonstop hop totally over water with a Marine (of VMR-952, which carried limited enlisted personnel and cargo) Curtiss Commando navigating for us. Since the flight was so long, the flight surgeon, Doc (Thomas) Dussman, handed out 'little pills' for the pilots to take before landing if they were feeling tired. When we asked about the pills, Dussman said that we shouldn't worry, as these would 'kind of wake you up.' Taking them, the super alert pilots watched as Al Wells went into his landing and dropped not only his landing gear, but also his tailhook. Henderson Field was covered with Marston metal matting, which had holes in it, and the pilots thought Wells would either pull up the runway or tear the rear end off his plane. The tailhook only bounced along the runway until Wells came to a stop. The next day Brandon describes the trip in a letter: "Certain parts of 'Mr. Hen's' anatomy are still numb. I did everything but stand up in the cockpit of that Corsair before landing. Took a big soft pillow to the movie last night but couldn't sit still and squirmed around for two hours."

The enlisted men were transported by R5C, Curtiss Commandos. Sgt. James Barrett: "We left Emirau for Espiritu Santo via Guadalcanal in fighter-escorted C-46s. We each had a full pack, rifle, full sea bag, and 100 pound tool box. The pilot had some doubts about whether we were overloaded for taking off from that airstrip. He decided we weren't overweight, but we just barely cleared the end of the runway before we lifted off. On the way from Emirau to Espiritu a group of ordnance men in a C-46 were to scheduled to stop at Bougainville. As the transport was about to land it was discovered that the landing gear reservoir had been depleted and the gear would not drop. The pilot asked for volunteers to urinate in the reservoir and had no problem in finding willing and able volunteers."

When -323 arrived at Espiritu Santo, New Hebrides Islands, in late October 1944, it was a declining backwater rear base. It had earlier served as a vital link for the Guadalcanal campaign. Luganville was cut out of thick jungle on the southwest end of the island. ***Courtesy of the USN.***

S/Sgt. Frank Magliocco was on the C-46 that led the 24 F4U on the 28th: "When the squadron transferred to Espiritu Santo from Emirau, a couple of our planes had problems and were stranded at Henderson Field on Guadalcanal. (M.Sgt.) James Williams and myself were left there with our tool boxes to take care of these problems. We flew into Espiritu a couple days later in a Marine B-26."

In the ferrying process, 16 F4Us arrived at Espiritu on the 29th, two on the 30th, and six on the 31st. The remainder of the personnel and gear arrived via the Commandos of VMR-952.

CHAPTER 8
The Odyssey of the Sea Pike
8 October to 29 November

On 8 October at 1400, the second echelon left Hawaii, a month after the BRETON on the SS SEA PIKE. The transport ship was a C3 type troop/cargo ship, built by Western Pipe & Steel in 1943 and operated by Moore-McCormack Lines. It measured 492 feet long, had a 70 foot beam, weighed 7,949 tons and carried 2,109 passengers and 235,000 cu.ft. of cargo. The SEA PIKE carried 20 officers and 167 enlisted men and VMF-323 supplies and materials. The SS NAVAJO VICTORY carried some of the squadron's cargo.

The intent of the voyage was for the second echelon to stand by as a reserve during the invasion of Peleliu. The ship's itinerary read like a Pacific cruise but was anything but:

8 October: left Ewa at 1400.
17 October: arrived Eniwetok, Eniwetok Atoll
21-24 October: Parry Island, Eniwetok Atoll
29 October-3 November: Babelthorp Island, Palau
3-14 November: Peleliu, Palau The echelon stood by as possible replacements in the Kossol Passage at northern end of island. A tropical storm occurred on 7-8 November. Al Bassani: "We got caught in part of a typhoon. I was lucky as I had been on boats since I was a kid. But half the ship was sick and throwing up all over the place." One squadron member broke a tibia and fibula when the ship suddenly listed and was sent to Peleliu.
14 November: left Peleliu
16-20 November: Ulithi harbor

On the 20th November, the Fleet oiler, MISSISSINEWA (AD-39), blew up with a load of aviation fuel, close by the SEA PIKE. Japanese submarines, I-36 and -47, launched five two-man kaiten suicide midget submarines into Ulithi harbor. All five kaitens were lost, but the parent submarines escaped.

22 November: crossed the Equator
23 November: Russell Islands, NW of Guadalcanal
24 November: left Russell Islands (Thanksgiving)
24 November: passed Manus through storm with a waterspout
25 November: passed Finchhaven, New Guinea
26 November: on Coral Sea
26 November: Guadalcanal
29 November: arrived at Espiritu Santo at 1200
52 days/11,236 miles

The SEA PIKE definitely was not a cruise ship, as most men lost weight on the long trip. For noted chow hound, Sgt. Thomas McLaughlin, who was very overweight, the 50+ pounds he lost were hardly noticed.

The second echelon had by-passed Emirau and disembarked at Espiritu Santo to finally join the first echelon that had been there for a month (arrived on 29 October).

The SEA PIKE was a C-3 type troop/cargo ship which carried the second echelon of 20 officers and 167 enlisted men from Hawaii to Espiritu Santo, bypassing Emirau. The voyage covered 52 days and 11,236 miles as the echelon was held in reserve for the Peleliu invasion. ***Courtesy of Western Pipe & Steel.***

CHAPTER 9
Espiritu Santo
Jungle Humdrum

Maj. Axtell on the squadron's disappointing move to Espiritu: "When we were transferred from Emirau to Espiritu Santo we sort of went backwards away from the war, and some of the men were worried that we were never going to get into the fight. We thought that we would get into the fighting at Peleliu, but we were held in reserve. I knew all these other battles in the Central Pacific were side shows and that they would have to take another big island before they could invade Japan. I knew then we would get our chance."

Espiritu Santo was chosen as the major American Army and Navy staging base when the Japanese invaded the Solomons and began construction of several airfields on Guadalcanal, 500 miles to the northwest. In late June 1942, a small recon unit explored the island. Soon the Seabees were at work, rapidly building a 6,000 foot airfield that was ready in time for the Guadalcanal pre-invasion operations in late July. It became a vital link between Henderson Field, Guadalcanal, and the airfields on Efate and Noumea.

Espiritu, known locally as Santo, is the northernmost and largest of the New Hebrides Islands. Its asymmetric shape measures roughly 75 miles long by 45 miles wide, with two north-pointing peninsulas on the north coast, a larger western and a smaller eastern peninsula. It is surrounded by numerous smaller off shore islands. It is covered by heavy jungle and contains mountains on the northwest peninsula and in the southwest as high as 6,000 feet.

When -323 arrived in late October, it was a declining backwater rear base. The squadron occupied the airfield at Luganville that was located at the southwest end of the island. The 6800 x 300 foot runway had 27,000 feet of taxiway and 75 hardstands. Nearly a quarter of the runway had to be cut out of solid coral ranging from a few feet to as deep as 35 feet. The remainder of the field utilized coral from cuts, and because of the heavy rainfall needed to be coated with emulsified asphalt. The primary quarters were Quonset huts.

Training

During the first week of November the forward echelon concentrated on setting up squadron offices and maintained their 24 aircraft in preparation for further training operations. The flight activity the next week consisted of local familiarization hops and was followed by a week and a half of dummy gunnery training, dive

Espiritu Santo VMF-323 Officers 15 February 1945. ***Courtesy of George Axtell.*** **Left to Right (FRONT ROW, MIDDLE ROW, WING): 1. Ritter, Fred 1. Drake, Bill 1. Miller, Norman 2. Durnford, Dewey 2. Dolezel, Cy 2. Thacker, Glenn 3. Lynn, Ed 3. Mershon, J.G. 3. Feliton Jim 4. Abner Ed 4. Taylor, Al 4. Reynolds, Leon 5. Martin, Charles 5. Mayor, Sol 5. Brown, Louie 6. Davis, Del 6. Ferdenzi, Tilly 6. Strickland, John 7. Dussman, Tom 7. Allen, Charles 7. Wade, Bob 8. Cecot, Felix 8. Edelson, Harold 8. Muse, Mindy 9. Graham, George 9. Bierbower, Jim 9. Wickser, Bob 10. Dorroh, Jeff 10. Woods, Bob 10. Ruhsam, John 11.Turner, Arthur 11. Terrill, Francis 11. Stover, Obie 12.Axtell, George 12. Dillard, Joe 12. Yager, Ev 13. Cox, Bill 13. Fountain, Keith 13. Ball, Vern 14. Moore, Clarence 14. Wells, Al 14. Zehring, Zeke 15. Van Buskirk, Wm. 15. Theriault, Norm 15. Nickols, Jim 16. Grando, John 16. O'Keefe, Jerry 16. Bestwick, Warren 17. McPhail, Joe 17. Crawley, Larry 18. Broering, Warren 18. Blackwell, Tom 19. Keeley, Ed 19. Spangler, Charles 20. Jefferies, ? 20. Murray, Ed 21. Brandon, Hank 21. Hood, Bill 22. Lejonstein, Bob 22. Blaydes, A.M. 23. Tonnessen, Harold 23.Rix, Paul**

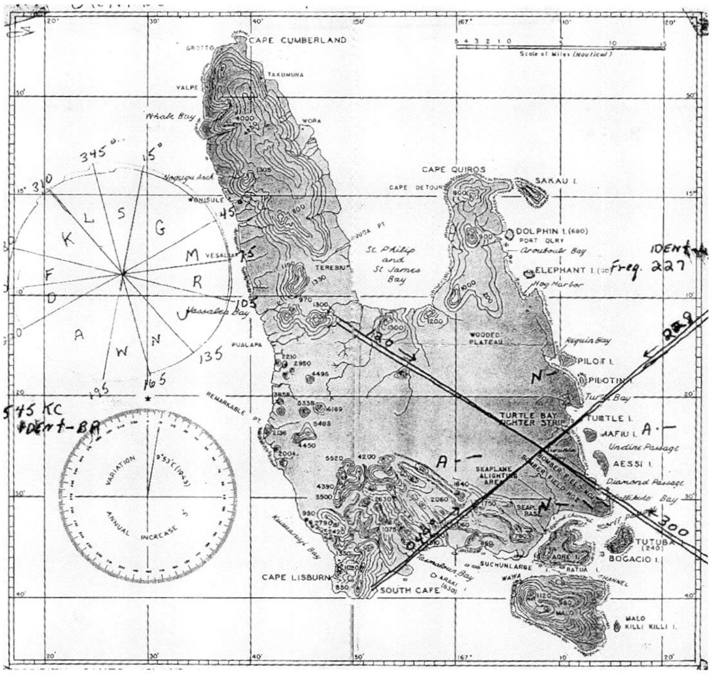

Actual map of Espiritu Santo issued to Henry Brandon on his flight there. Courtesy of Henry Brandon.

(L to R) Bob Muse, John Strickland, Harold Tonnessen, Larry Crawley, and Bill Drake demonstrate a variety of non-regulation clothing and footwear. ***Courtesy of Bill Drake.***

bombing and squadron tactics. The squadron only spent 206 hours in the air on 185 flights in November.

On 3 November, John Overton was killed in a jeep accident.

In December, Axtell stepped up the training tempo, increasing flight hours to 450 and flights to 354. Pilots flew in two groups, one in the morning and one in the afternoon. During the month the types of operational training most emphasized were: dummy rocket (135), fixed gunnery firing (62), combined tactics (40) and dive bombing (34) missions.

The use of airborne rockets, an entirely new phase of training, began during the month. Under the supervision of MAG-33, eight Mark 5 Model 1 Zero Length Launchers were installed on nine aircraft. The first group of pilots began training on 6 December, when 13 attended ground school directed by SPATU. Two full days of ground school were followed by four flights of dummy rocket runs, one flight per day. The topics stressed were tactics, estimation of glide angle, range, proper lead, effectiveness of rockets, safety, types of rockets, and movies on the training of other pilots. On 14 December, the second group of 13 pilots began the same routine of training, and 13 more on the 21st. Concurrently, 12 ordnance men participated in a three day course which emphasized types of rocket heads, safety, and the maintenance, loading arming and installation of rockets. By the end of the month no real rockets had been fired, as all runs utilized dummy heads. The pilots concentrated on

-323 Corsairs taking off from Luganville airfield located on the southwest end of the island. The base was dug out of the jungle which bordered the field. ***Courtesy of Jody O'Keefe.***

Since Luganville was a well-established base, housing was in semi-permanent Quonset Huts with corrugated steel roofs, small windows, and lack of cross ventilation that made life in them uncomfortable in the mid-day heat, humidity, and rain. (L to R) Dewey Durnford, Tilly Ferdenzi, and Bob Muse. ***Courtesy of Jody O'Keefe.***

In early December, the squadron began rocket training. Mark 5 Model 1 Zero Length Launchers were installed with 3.5 inch rockets initially being utilized and subsequently switched to the 5-inch HVAR (High Velocity Aerial Rocket). ***Courtesy of the USMC.***

Charlie Allen diving over the side in an aircraft abandonment re-enactment. The fighter belonged to Keith Fountain who cracked it up during landing on 4 December. ***Courtesy of Norman Miller.***

On 4 December, Keith Fountain bounced hard on landing, tipping his port wing, rolling up an embankment, and turning the aircraft over on its back. Fountain was uninjured but the aircraft was written off. ***Courtesy of Henry Brandon.***

20 and 40 degree dives while making dummy runs, but also experimented with 60 degree dives.

VMF-323 ordnance men built a sighting device called a harp on a water tower near the rocket range. It helped the pilots to judge dive angles and ranges for rocket delivery. Three dive angles were used in a rocket attack, with each angle using a different approach altitude. On a 20-degree dive the pilot would begin his rocket run at 3,000 ft. With the target appearing just over the port wing the pilot would make a 90-degree turn toward the target and nose over into a 20-degree dive to release his rockets. The maneuver was basically the same for the 40-degree (6,000 ft. approach altitude) and 60-degree (9,000 ft. approach altitude) dive angles. Initially, the pilots practiced with 3.5-inch rockets and then switched to 5-inch rockets.

Warren Broering: "While I attended Pasadena Junior College I took a chemistry course taught by a Professor McMorris who had

Capt. Joe McPhail joined the squadron from VMF-441 but did not see any combat with that unit. ***Courtesy of Henry Brandon.***

1Lt. Jim Feliton served as an enlisted Naval Aviation Pilot (NAP) with Joe Foss' VMF-121 flying F4F wildcats over Guadalcanal. S/Sgt. Feliton was shot down twice and rescued twice by coast watchers and natives. This photo shows Feliton with his native rescuers who are clutching their rewards for his rescue. At the end of this tour he retrained in Corsairs and was assigned to VMF-323. ***Courtesy of the USMC.***

gotten his doctorate at Cal Tech. When we were being equipped with our rocket rails at Espiritu we were shown a rocket training film and, low and behold, there was Professor McMorris in the film!"

On 4 December, 2Lt. Keith Fountain flipped his aircraft while making a landing. The Corsair bounced, its port wing fell, and the plane swerved to the left and rolled up an embankment on the left side of the runway. It turned over on its back in the soft dirt and broke in half behind the seat. Fountain walked away with just a bruise on his shoulder from the shoulder harness strap, but the aircraft had to be written off. It was later replaced by one flown in from Guadalcanal on the 12th by Del Davis.

In January, Axtell increased the training pace even further with 585 hours flown in 504 flights. Operational training consisted mainly of rocket firing runs (316), along with dive bombing (72) and gunnery (69) missions.

Capt. Felix Cecot. ***Courtesy of Norman Miller.***

1Lt. Glen Thacker describes gunnery training: "The tips of our bullets were painted different colors so that when they hit the towed sleeve our scores could be determined by counting the colored holes in the sleeve. The scores were recorded on a daily chart in the ready room."

By 13 January all 24 squadron aircraft were equipped with the Mark 5 Model 1 Zero Length Launchers. Rockets fired were of three types:

2Lt. Warren Bestwick. ***Courtesy of Norman Miller.***

2Lt. Glenn Thacker. ***Courtesy of Norman Miller.***

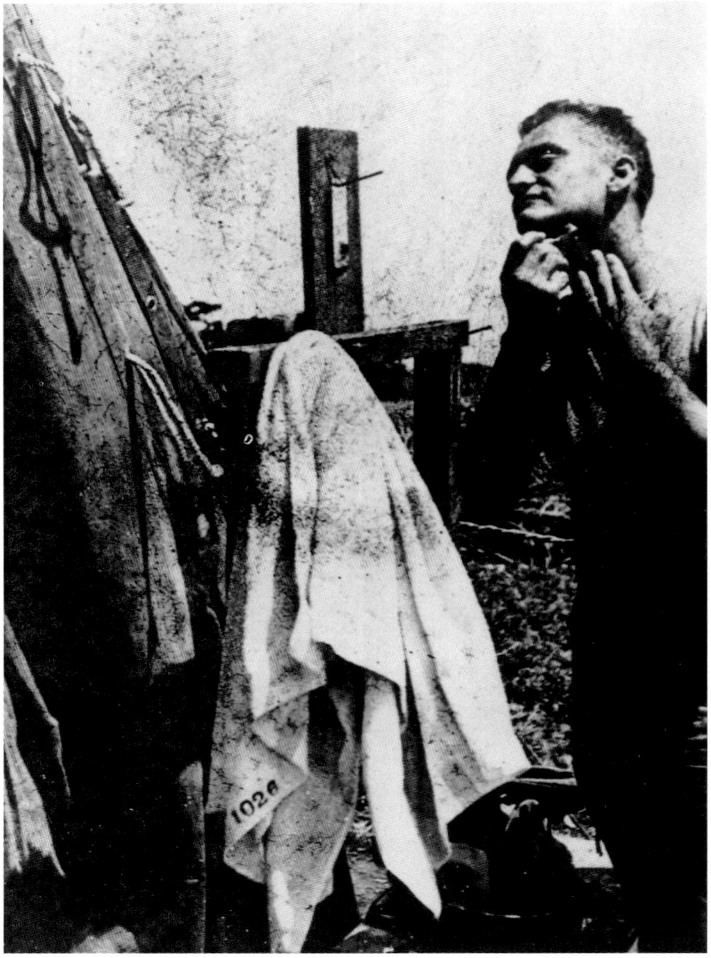

2Lt. Everett Yager. ***Courtesy of Norman Miller.***

2Lt. Bob Wade. ***Courtesy of Norman Miller.***

2.25" Mark 10 Motor with Mark 1 armor piercing head
2.25" Mark 10 Motor with Mark 2 armor piercing head
3.25" Mark 7 Motor with Mark 2 armor piercing head

Two close air support training missions were worked with the 27th Army Division. On 13 January, four flights led by Major Bill Cox worked a close air support problem with elements of the First Battalion, 165th Infantry Regiment, 27th Army Division. The mission of this flight was to make dummy strafing runs on previously designated command posts. Due to poor visibility over the target only two of the four posts could be found. On the 16th, two divisions led by Major Jefferson Dorroh worked another close air support problem with the same 27th Army unit. A simulated dive bombing and strafing attack of 12 enemy positions holding up the advance was assigned to -323 aircraft via an air support request net between the aircraft on station and the personnel manning the radio truck at the Battalion Command Post.

In January, as the squadron got closer to combat, more classes involved combat-oriented subjects: POW information, Air-Sea rescue, plane and ship recognition, close air support doctrine, and future theater indoctrination, plus the use of personal arms. Familiarization firing on the rifle range had been compulsory for all personnel, both officer and enlisted. The Ground Defense Unit practiced firing the .50 caliber AA machine gun at a towed sleeve.

On 15 January, the squadron sent out five search flights in an effort to locate a downed pilot (2Lt. John Webb) of VMF-312 who safely bailed out of his aircraft and was rescued.

2Lt. Obie Stover. ***Courtesy of Norman Miller.***

2Lt. Norman Miller. *Courtesy of Norman Miller.*

(L to R) John Strickland and Fred Zehring. ***Courtesy of Henry Brandon.***

On 31 January, Capt. Clarence Moore, the section leader, dropped a bomb at very low altitude and peppered his plane full of holes. Unfortunately for Moore, the plane he was flying was Axtell's, who wasn't very happy about the state of his favorite aircraft.

On 15 January, administrative control of the squadron was transferred to the 2MAW, Fleet Marine Force, under Maj.Gen. James Moore.

On the 16th, eight pilots were ferried to Manus on a R4D (C-47) to pick up new aircraft. Al Wells: "Bill van Buskirk and I flew up to Manus for some new planes to be ferried back to E.S. The new planes weren't ready, so we had three or four days to kill. We were hitching back to base from a movie and were picked up by a bunch of Army guys. En route we heard them complain that they had authorized leave for R&R in Australia but had no transportation. They were with a maintenance or materiel unit and had a B-25 available but no crew to fly it. They said they could get a ride to

September 1944. First Row: Hots Terrill, Seab Allen, Red Dillard, and George Graham. Second Row: Eddie Murray, O.V. Gallatin, Big Bub Brandon, Lightning Fountain, and Big Bub Woods. ***Courtesy of Henry Brandon.***

Under athletic director, Hank Brandon, sports were a large part of everyday life at Espiritu Santo. Brandon, a college basketball player, starred in the intramural games. ***Courtesy of Henry Brandon.***

Jerry O'Keefe at bat during one of the hotly contested softball games which took place between rain storms. *Courtesy of Jody O'Keefe.*

On one of their R & R outings, a motor boat was somehow commandeered and a combination water ski/surf board was improvised. *Courtesy of Henry Brandon.*

Australia from Biak, which was about five or six hours away. Van Buskirk had been a twin engine pilot and had some training with American Airlines before the war on DC-3s. We volunteered to fly them, but decided it would be prudent to fly a familiarization hop first. We got a hold of the B-25 maintenance man who knew pretty much about the aircraft, so we took off and he checked us out on the systems. With careful navigation we made it to Biak and spent the night. Late the next morning we were ready to take off when I saw the ADF, automatic direction finder, for the first time. It seemed so nice and easy, you just tuned in the destination frequency and the needle pointed in that direction. Much easier than navigating. We tuned in Manus and sat back. This worked great until we realized that the time to destination was a half hour overdue and it was getting dark. I tapped the needle to check it and realized that it was stuck. It was just dusk and the time when the clouds cast shadows on the water that look like islands. We started chasing these around

Everyone wants a picture of the squadron pet dog. Here Red Terrill puts the lens cap on his camera as Bill Drake holds the dog while someone snaps the photo with his camera. *Courtesy of Bill Drake.*

A typical native village on Espiritu Santo. The thatched roof hut in the center has "surplus" U.S. military boxes and barrels around it. *Courtesy of Don Hitchings.*

Charlie Allen (L), dog (C), and Tom Blackwell (R) try to make friends with native children, one of whom is wearing a Navy or Marine utility cap and little else. The photo was taken on the site of the rocket launching practice range. ***Courtesy of Henry Brandon.***

A group of pilots and mechanics waiting for transportation to the flight line. ***Courtesy of Henry Brandon.***

while our fuel was getting lower and the skies darker. Finally, flying around, totally lost, through dumb luck we saw some lights in the distance and landed safely with just enough light and fuel."

During January, 2Lt. Thomas "Blackie" Blackwell designed a manual lock to prevent the tail hook from descending in case hydraulic pressure was lost in flight. When the landing gear was raised, the tail wheel and tail hook had to be manually locked separately (then it wouldn't drop under any circumstances). It had to be manually unlocked on landing. It was instilled on all -323 aircraft.

Plane Captain Paul Finney had this observation of Axtell at the time: "He was one level-headed kid, I admired him. At Espiritu Santo, Axtell flew my plane and the hydraulic line burst at the accumulator in the cockpit. It covered him with red, petroleum-based

(L to R) Bill Drake, John Strickland, Louie Brown, Bob Woods, Al Wells, and Bill Martin. ***Courtesy of Henry Brandon.***

fluid. I needed an aluminum crush washer to seal the accumulator, but we didn't have any. I put it together the best I could and he took it out the next day. Of course, the same thing happened again, and he came back covered in hydraulic fluid. He had ruined two sets of flying clothing and had to manually pump down his landing gear twice. He understood I did the best I could. I never saw him riled or be unfair the whole time I was around him."

In February, there were 300 flights in 267 hours: rocket (141), dive bombing (19) and gunnery (9). There were 12 familiarization flights due to the influx of 13 new pilots on the 6th. There were 52 test flights due to the arrival of eight new aircraft on the 2nd. After operational flying was secured on the 15th, all squadron aircraft were checked and tested, and 35 test flights were flown between 15 and 28 February.

A close support training mission was flown on the 14th. Two divisions, led by 2Lt. Del Davis and Capt. Bill Van Buskirk, worked a close air support problem with elements of the 2nd Battalion, 165th Infantry Regiment, 27th Army Division. Davis' division acted as enemy aircraft and made dummy strafing runs on troops in their approach march toward their assembly area. Van Buskirk's division provided close support by simulated dive bombing and strafing of enemy positions holding up the advance of the 2nd Battalion.

New Pilots

On 2 February the squadron received eight additional F4Us from MAG-33, and four days later 13 more pilots joined the squadron from the Department of the Pacific, San Francisco, MAG-33/2nd MAW/FWF. The additional pilots were:

Capts. Joe McPhail and Felix Cecot
2Lts. Warren Beswick, James Feliton, Norman Miller
James Nichols, Leon Reynolds, John Rahsam
Obie Stover, Glenn Thacker, Robert Wade
Robert Wickser, and Everett Yager

"Espiritu Santo Claus." ***Left:*** **Christmas at Espiritu (L to R) Del Davis, Bob Woods, and Bill Drake manufacture a "tree". A main trunk had holes drilled into it and branches were inserted to take the form of a fir tree.** ***Courtesy of Bill Drake. Center:*** **(L to R) Bill Hood watch as Bill Drake, Ed Murray, Del Davis, ?? behind tree, and Bob Woods begin to add decorations to the tree.** ***Courtesy of Bill Drake. Right:*** **Old Tannenbaum, ready for Santa.** ***Courtesy of Bill Drake.***

Warren Broering: "The reason we got these new pilots and planes was that the high command expected us to sustain 50% casualties in the future."

Thacker: "I was transferred to -323 at Espiritu Santo in February 1944, with 12 other pilots. I was previously in VMF-513, which trained just behind -323 at Cherry Point/Oak Grove. I trained with Miller, Wickser, and Feliton, and we all joined -323 there. I had gotten into various scrapes with -513, so when it came time for transfers it was not surprising that the -513 staff shipped me to -323. It turned out to be a good break, because they never saw any action."

Before transferring to -323, Capt. Joe McPhail flew F4Fs in Samoa, Funa Futi, and Noumea with VMF-441 for 13 months from January 1943, seeing no combat. He returned to the States in February 1944 to become an instructor in a fighter training unit at both Jacksonville, Florida, and El Toro, California.

1Lt. James Feliton had flown F4F Wildcats earlier with Joe Foss' VMF-121 off Henderson Field, Guadalcanal, arriving on 10 October 1942 and staying until the island was secured in late January 1943. As a Naval Aviation Pilot (NAP), S/Sgt. Feliton shot down a Zero on 19 October 1942, but was shot down himself. Friendly Solomon natives brought him back to Henderson on the 22nd. Then, on 31 January 1943, VMF-121 was flying a bomber escort to Jap-held Kolombangara with Paul Fontana's VMF-112 Wolf Pack. In the ensuing air battle -112 2Lt. Jefferson DeBlanc shot down five Japanese (and was later awarded the Medal of Honor for this ac-

Sol Mayer's very informal outdoor Christmas breakfast by the river. The meal featured fresh eggs, toast, and coffee, along with hot temperatures, high humidity and numerous insects. ***Courtesy of Bill Drake.***

Al Wells is the subject of many -323 stories which usually began at the "O" club and ended in Major Axtell's dog house. ***Courtesy of Henry Brandon.***

With a cut above his right eye, Al Wells relaxes after the midnight jungle expedition up a tropical river in a "borrowed" native boat. The foray was brought about after an intense night at the "O" club. ***Courtesy of Henry Brandon.***

Owen Gallatin was an ex-enlisted pilot who later was a Korean War and Vietnam veteran. ***Courtesy of Henry Brandon.***

tion), but his fighter was badly damaged and the wounded DeBlanc bailed out. Feliton's Wildcat was also damaged, and he too bailed out, landing in a large tree on Kolombangara, and was shaken up from the fall to the ground. He was picked up by natives and taken to Coastwatcher, Henry Josselyn, on nearby Vella Lavella Island. Meanwhile, Josselyn was able to exchange DeBlanc for a sack of rice with local natives. Josselyn arranged for the evacuation of the two pilots, and a PBY finally picked them up on 12 February, returning them to Guadalcanal. At the end of his -121 tour, Feliton returned to the States, retrained in Corsairs and joined VMF-323.

Everyday routine: Monotony, some fun, waiting for combat

The four months at Espiritu grew monotonous, and the men began to wonder if they would ever see combat.

Henry Brandon's letter of 3 January to his wife stated: "Maybe something of interest will happen so I can write a more interesting letter to you." His letter of 18 January: "Today is another one of those days that nothing out of the ordinary has happened. It is just one more day I can strike off my calendar, which is one day closer to returning home. We just sit around and wait, and for what? None of us know. Our main enemy is monotony, from doing the same thing day in and day out. It is a relief to fly because of the boredom."

Brandon describes a typical day in his diaries: "Took truck down to the flight line. Hung around about an hour. Went back to barracks and put on flight clothing. Ate an early lunch. Flew at 1230 for an hour. Returned to the barracks. Read, wrote letters, bull sessions, played cards, sports. Returned to the barracks and showered. Ate dinner. Back to barracks or outside for sports. Saw movie. Returned to barracks to write, read. Went to bed."

For most men it was the first time in their lives that they had been to a foreign land, much less out of their home state. The island natives and their customs were a source of wonder to the men. The island was a feudal society. The native islanders, the Tonkinese, were under the direct supervision of the French who governed the

Tom Blackwell hanging out his laundry. ***Courtesy of Henry Brandon.***

(L to R) Pilots Tom Blackwell and Ed Keeley with plane captain, Don Hitchings. In January, Blackwell designed a manual lock to prevent the tail hook from descending in case of hydraulic pressure failure. ***Courtesy of Jody O'Keefe.***

area. The French took care of the native employment, spiritual and social needs, and were looked upon as father figures. The family unit was patriarchal, with the husband leading the way in public, followed in single file by his wife and children. Everyone, men and women, chewed betelnut, which stained their teeth, and the island was one big spittoon, with everything stained red. There was a rumor that there were headhunters on the north end of the island.

19 December: "There was an old man and his three year old son down on the beach. They traded a dozen fresh eggs, two or three pineapples, two stalks of bananas, and a couple of big cucumbers for four cigarettes and the 'privilege' of cleaning up what was left of our chow. The little boy was dressed in nothing but his birthday suit, which was the deepest shade of black. His father gave him a cigarette to smoke, think of that?" Henry Brandon letter

There were recreational activities provided for the squadron. Baseball, basketball, softball and volley teams were formed, and league competition was organized. A recreation room for enlisted personnel was equipped with reading material, writing desks, radio, phonograph and ping pong tables. There was the "O" Club for the officers with all of the above, only nicer. There was an intelligence reading room and classified library available for all officers containing a cataloged reading list, displays of recognition material, and a daily situation map. Of course, this wasn't as popular as the "O" Club.

James Barrett: "We had movies just about every night, rain or shine. We sat on benches made of metal landing strip lengths nailed to blocks of wood. One night we were sitting in the pouring rain, and at one point lightning struck about 50-100 feet behind the screen. Immediately, about half of the audience jumped to its feet. The rest of the audience looked in surprise at those standing. I was wearing wet leather field shoes and received a considerable shock, while those in rubber footgear remained seated. In another moment, lightning struck again, and the leather-shod men were once more shocked. At this point everyone decided there were safer places to be and left."

There was an ersatz French bistro on the island that was very popular. An island French family had a thatched native hut with a long screened porch with tables and chairs. Reservations had to be made two or three weeks in advance. They served seven course dinners with a small bottle of local wine. The food wasn't great, but it was fun, and a touch of civilization and a means of getting away from mess food.

Christmas was somewhat special, as Brandon's letter to his wife describes: "I opened all the packages last night and Santa was

(L to R) Seab Allen, Red Dillard, and Razor Blaydes. ***Courtesy of Bill Drake.***

nice to me. Thanks. Am writing to the tune of 'Come All Ye Faithful,' which is playing on the radio Early this AM Charles Dicken's 'A Christmas Carol' was on. I guess I have heard or read it 50 times, but it always seems right just before X-mas.

The squadron had a X-mas breakfast this AM. We got up about 8:30 and got into a truck and went out to a place on a little river where we had fresh eggs, toast and coffee, and it sure tasted good. Took some snapshots, which I will send. It sure was hot, and the flies were out in numbers, so we didn't hang around after breakfast was served. I guess today is the last day of leisure, as we start back to work tomorrow. I'll spend the rest of X-mas day reading my book, since there is nothing else to do around here. We're going to have a Christmas meal tonight, so I won't go to chow at noon. You are going to fix me X-mas dinner next year."

Then on the 26th, Brandon wrote: "We sure had a swell dinner yesterday...I'm enclosing the menu so that you can see that your husband was treated OK on X-mas day. But I would have much rather eaten a meal which you prepared for me."

Henry Brandon's letters discuss the squadron's food before it became famous at Okinawa. 8 January: "We ran out of fresh eggs today and are back to the processed eggs. They aren't too bad, in fact, I'm beginning to like them."

17 January: "I haven't been eating too much lately. Guess its because of the heat, and also because of the food, which isn't all that bad. It's just about the same day after day. Sure am going to enjoy letting you fatten me up. In fact, that's all I am looking forward to these days."

11 February: "I can say absolutely nothing in favor of the food. We had hash, potatoes, cabbage, and hominy. I ate a little of the hash and that was all. I'm sure it could be much worse, I know there are fellows who would like to have anything."

The "O" Club was the social center for the squadron's officers, and often led to the now legendary exploits that are rehashed and embellished at post war reunion bull sessions.

4 February: "There were plenty of drunks out last night. They had their usual gathering outside my window, and started throwing coconuts at all the huts." Henry Brandon letter

James Barrett: "The officers usually had permanent possession of their pistols, but when they drank too much, things would get shot at, especially lights. After a while Axtell ordered all side arms to be kept in the ordnance tent and checked out only before a flight, and brought back afterward."

Al Wells is the subject of many "O" Club stories, going back to Pendleton and his run-in with the general at Ewa.

Brandon was probably the best athlete of the unit, being a Golden Gloves boxer and college basketball player at Tennessee State University. He later coached college tennis and became an accomplished masters player. Al Wells was a little guy and was always challenging Brandon. One night they were in the "O" club and had a little too much to drink. Wells told Brandon that he was going to show him how to do a correct slow roll. They went up a hill behind the club and Wells came running down and took off into a slow roll that became a bruising roll down the hill. Brandon said, "That's nothing Al, I'm going to show you an Immelmann." Brandon came running down, did a back-flip Immelmann imitation with the same disastrous results to his body.

After an intense night in the "O" Club, Wells, Brandon, and O.V. Gallantine decided to go on a midnight jungle "expedition." They put on their jungle equipment. To start the mission off, Gallantine shot a hole in the roof of their hut. They "borrowed" the squadron 4x4 and drove to the mouth of the river and a small village. They then quietly commandeered a boat tied behind a villager's

The new meet the old, (L to R) Warren Bestwick, Norm Theriault, Dewey Durnford, Bob Wade, and Bob Muse. Bestwick and Wade joined the squadron at Espiritu. ***Courtesy of John Ruhsam.***

Unprotected, Zeke Zehring climbs a coconut tree in the Palmolive Company palm oil plantation. Orders were issued that required the wearing of helmets to ward off falling coconuts which could be and were lethal. ***Courtesy of Henry Brandon.***

house. The mission started slowly despite some concentrated paddling, but things picked up when they realized that they had neglected to untie the boat! After freeing the boat they paddled a mile and a half/two miles up the river, which was surrounded by very dense jungle and exotic nighttime noises. After negotiating a set of rapids, they slept on the bank of a coconut grove for a couple of hours and shoved off as the sun rose. Brandon thought he smelled something strange during their cruise, but it wasn't until dawn that they saw that the boat had been freshly painted. They were covered with almost indelible fresh paint that was difficult to explain back at base.

Wells: "The Navy had a PBY maintenance base at E.S., and I became friends with a pilot there. We started talking at the 'O' Club, and he told me about the beautiful girls on the island of Suva. After more than a few drinks we decided to go get his airplane and fly to this paradise. When we got to the PBY base we found his plane was torn apart. So, not to be deterred, I volunteered mine and we sneaked onto the field. Of course, the Corsair is a single seater, so I got rid of the parachute, he got in, and I sat in his lap. I unsuccessfully fired my starter cartridge and alerted the security guy, who then came over. I explained to him that I was only going to take my friend on a little flight to show him the aircraft. I fired another cartridge that caused him to raise his rifle and demand we shut down and get out, 'now!' He meant business, which was good because George would have court marshaled me if he caught us."

Wells: "One day (Robert) Muse came in bragging about his new friend, 'the Navy Captain.' In those days a Navy captain was like a god. I mean George was like a god and he was only a major. George was impressed and suggested that Muse invite the captain

A refreshment break. Unlike Emirau the squadron received an adequate beer ration on Espiritu. *Courtesy of Henry Brandon.*

Jerry O'Keefe and friends. The Tonkinese boys are outfitted in a variety of cast off Navy and Marine clothing and hats as evidenced by the rolled up pants legs and shirt sleeves. *Courtesy of Jody O'Keefe.*

to the 'O' club that night. At the club everyone deferred and kowtowed to the Captain, who in turn invited some of the squadron to his ship. It turns out that the ship was a rusty Merchant Marine tub with a crew on the verge of mutiny. Many years later I found well known author, James Michener, wrote in one of his later books the story of his wartime experiences on a merchant ship at Espirito Santo, which was on the brink of mutiny. I believe this was the ship." (Editor's note: Michener wrote his "Tales of the South Pacific" while based at Espiritu Santo.)

The USO visited the island a few days before Christmas. Bob Crosby, who was a Marine, and his Bobcats band, along with Jerry Colona and Marie "The Body" O'Driscoll appeared. They were in a rehearsal to join the Bob Hope USO show. Henry Brandon's letter home to his wife describes the event: "The show consisted of an orchestra playing pop pieces and a comedian who was pretty rough, and I wouldn't want you to see him. The women in the show drove the men to distraction." The show had to be fairly raunchy, at least for those times, because some of the officers and the chaplain lodged a complaint.

For entertainment there always was Tokyo Rose and her transparent radio propaganda that always came in loud and clear. The men thought her amusing and preferred her selection of music over that of the Armed Forces Radio. James Barrett: "She was always a source of amusement to us. We were looking forward to getting into the war, and she was trying to make us homesick for our girls, wives and mothers back home. I liked some of the good jazz she played."

A few men checked out shot guns and used them with light loads to knock down paraquets. The bird's wings were trimmed, and they were kept as pets.

Then there always was Sunday: Brandon writes: "Sunday sure is appreciated around. It feels good to have one day to do as we please."

The island, though not in the combat zone, had its own particular dangers. There were wild boars roaming the island that could be dangerous if accidentally encountered. Another danger was from falling coconuts. The Palmolive Company had a plantation on the island, and it was required to wear a helmet while walking around the island, as a man from another unit had been killed.

Fungus was prevalent because of the damp weather, and it was not uncommon to have three types growing on one's body at one time; head, crotch and feet. Albert Elson got a fungus in his ear that destroyed his ear drum. The medics would swab the fungus with Jentzen violet that turned the patient's skin purple almost permanently. Joe Dillard made metal watch bands for the men. They were an improvement over the leather and cloth bands that deteriorated in the wet climate.

Insects were a tropical nuisance, as two entries in Henry Brandon's letter attest:

8 January: "We put up our mosquito netting this afternoon. We are going to have to sleep under it, even if it makes sleeping hotter. It cuts off the breeze."

11 January: "I suppose you remember me telling you about the ants and roaches that have taken a liking to my desk. Well, if something isn't done fairly soon, I believe that I will have to make a strategic retreat, for they have me miserably outnumbered. Have knocked about ten ants off my arm since I starting writing this letter."

Brandon's letters typify the weather on Espiritu:

6 January: "It is really hot around here today as the sun is really boiling down. Our hut doesn't have any trees growing around it as most of the other huts do. About midday we go looking for a cool spot. Some of the fellows are going down to the beach this AM. If they get some transportation I may go down there myself and stay cool."

10 January: "It started raining while we were on our hop and could hardly see the runway when we returned to the field. We had to taxi back to our revetment with our hoods closed, it was raining so hard."

24 January: "We took off today in a pouring rain and prowled around for about an hour. It was really rough upstairs because of the thunderstorms. It felt just about like riding over a rough road in an automobile. We scattered back to the field and got back to the deck before it started pouring again."

Another island hazard was Major Axtell's inspections:

6 January: "This AM we had an inspection and stood out in the hot sun for nearly an hour. We stood at attention and at ease with a lot of junk on, including the tin helmet." Henry Brandon letter

27 February: "Uncle George put out an order this AM that he was going to make an inspection of our huts, but his big inspection fell through. I think he accomplished his purpose, for we had the hut looking good for a change. A pretty good trick, don't you think?" Henry Brandon letter

Mail was the item most anticipated and cherished by any serviceman. It took six days for the mail to arrive from the West Coast to Espiritu, but the return mail was faster from the island to the U.S. The mail arrived by PB2Y, and there were times when the men were especially alert for its arrival, as excerpts from Henry Brandon's letters illustrate:

22 October: "Eddie Abner received word that the stork brought him a baby girl—weighed 8lbs 10oz. The next -323 baby should be Jerry O'Keefe's. I wonder who will get the first boy? Del Davis and Maj. Dorroh are expecting."

19 December: "Maj. Dorroh found out that he became the father of an 11 lb. baby boy. He's giving out cigars, and everyone is getting plastered at his tent."

8 January: "Jerry O'Keefe informed us that he is the proud father of a baby girl, Maureen. I think that Theriault is next to become a papa, then Ed Murray and Larry Crawley."

In the backwater training at Espiritu things got a little lax and the Brass decided that discipline needed to be reinforced. Major Axtell does an inspection of his troops prior to a major review. ***Courtesy of George Axtell.***

12 January: "Norman Theriault received some bad news today. His wife gave birth to a baby around the first, and it was nearly three weeks early and died. I think I heard him say it had a bad heart."

7 February: "Guess what happened! Mrs. Larry Crawley has given birth to a baby girl, Peggy Lou Crawley, by name. Larry received word today, and he has been running around with a real smile on his face, passing out cigars."

Finally, orders to leave

The secret orders (0304-45) on 23 February, from the Commanding Officer, MAG-33, Col. Ward Dickey, divided the squadron into three echelons to be moved from Espiritu Santo to Okinawa Gunto, Ryukyu Islands:

(1) The flight echelon comprising 31 pilots (for the 31 aircraft).

(2) The assault echelon comprising 19 pilots, seven ground officers, one naval officer, 150 enlisted men, and eight naval enlisted men.

(3) The rear echelon comprising two officers and 74 men.

The packing and loading of squadron supplies and material aboard LST-744, preparatory to the squadron's movement to its next destination, continued during the last days of February and was completed by the end of the month. All three echelons were standing by awaiting further orders at the month's end.

Axtell salutes smartly as he marches his men past the Luganville base commander. *Courtesy of George Axtell.*

CHAPTER 10
Espiritu Santo to Pityilu
Flight Echelon

2 March to 25 March
On 4 March, 32 F4U-1Ds led by B-26s took off from Luganville for Pityilu, Manus Island, via Guadalcanal and Green Island The squadron landed at Henderson Field, Guadalcanal, and spent the night. In the morning it took off for Green Island. Upon landing a F4U was damaged with its pilot uninjured, but the aircraft was turned over to the RNZAF. The squadron landed on Pityilu on the 6th without incident.

Pityilu is a small island lying in the Bismarck Sea just a few miles north of Manus and Los Negros Islands of the Admiralty Island group. The base was established in May 1944, to service and repair carrier-based aircraft. Its coral-surfaced runway ran 5,500 by 300 feet, and the facility could store 350 aircraft. The receiving station could accommodate 5,000 men with 300 Quonset huts. The eastern end of the island was cleared for a fleet R&R center for 10,000 men.

During their short two and a half week stay on the Pityilu, Axtell had his pilots fly 195 local hops in 359 hours and attend recognition classes. Since the mechanics were aboard the LST, the pilots were required to work on their aircraft.

The Royal Navy carrier, HMS INDEFATIGABLE, was anchored at Pityilu, and they threw a party for the Squadron. The Brits served quality Scotch whiskey, which members of the unit hadn't seen for months. It was expected that the English would live up to their stereotype reserve, but many of the Marine pilots have commented on their rowdiness and extremely foul language. When the English visited the Death Rattlers on shore they were "treated" to Schenley's whiskey that was so bad it was nicknamed "Black Death" The whiskey had been quickly purchased by unit members before they left the States and was used to trade or barter. (Henry Brandon)

On the 26th, VMF-323 and -322 pilots and their aircraft boarded the carrier WHITE PLAINS (CVE-66) anchored in Sea Adler Harbor, Manus Island, and embarked for Ulithi anchorage three and a half days away. VMF-323 had been joined by VMF-322 and -312 at Manus after flying from Espiritu Santo, also via Guadalcanal and Green Island. VMF-312 boarded the carrier HOLLANDIA (CVE-97), which had been previously boarded by night fighter squadron VMF(N)-543 at Pearl Harbor.

Pityilu is a small island of the Admiralty Group, laying just south of Manus. When the squadron flew in on 6 March 1945, it was a large base accommodating 5,000 men and 350 aircraft. The squadron was based there until 26 March when it boarded the carrier, WHITE PLAINS. *Courtesy of the US Navy*.

CHAPTER 11
White Plains (CVE-66)
26 March to 9 April

The Casablanca-class carrier was laid down as the ELBOUR BAY (ACV-66) by Kaiser ship yards in February 1943. It was renamed WHITE PLAINS in April, redesignated CVE-66 in July, and launched on 27 September 1943. Her flight deck was too short to permit normal carrier take offs, and all launches were via her catapult. She saw action in the Marianas supporting the invasion of Saipan and Tinian, the Palau invasion, and in the Philippines. Here she distinguished herself as part of Adm. Clifton Sprague's "TAFFY 3, in the Battle of the Baby Flattops" against the Japanese fleet off Samar. She was damaged in an air attack and returned to San Diego for repairs. In her return to action she served as an aircraft ferry, taking on the F4Us of VMF-323 and -322 at Pityilu and launching them 100 miles off the Okinawa invasion beaches on 9 April 1945.

29 March: "We're aboard this ship, and its still rocking and rolling like a wild horse. 'Lightning' (Keith Fountain) is still under the weather and hopes he never sees another ship as long as he lives. He isn't the only one who is sick, there are 4 or 5 other fellows in the squadron who are sick. The food on board ship is really good. Tonight for chow we had lamb chops, carrots, and potatoes with iced tea and cherry pie for dessert. This is one thing you have to give the Navy credit for. They always have good food, and it is served on nice clean table cloths by colored messmen. There is nothing going on, and you would be able to understand what I mean if you were here. We sit around and twiddle our thumbs and wish we were home, just as we have done since we got to the Pacific." Henry Brandon letter

VMF-323 ROSTER
APRIL 1945
WHITE PLAINS

Majors
Axtell, George
Cox, William
Dorroh, Jefferson

Captain
Van Buskirk, William
Moore, Charles

1Lts.
Abner, Edward Dolezel, Cyril O'Keefe, Jeremiah Allen, Charles Edelson, Harold Strickland, John Ball, Vernon Hood, William Terrill, Francis Brandon, Henry Keeley, Edward Theriault, Normand Broering, Warren Martin, Charles Tonnessen, Harold Brown, James Murray, Edward Wells, Albert Dillard, Joseph Muse, Robert Zehring, Frederick

2Lts.
Bierbower, James Drake, William Fountain, Keith Crawley, Lawrence Durnford, Dewey

Compiled by Harley Brock and Bill Wolf

The WHITE PLAINS (CVE-66), after taking part in the invasion of Saipan and Tinian, distinguished herself and was damaged in the "Battle of the Baby Flattops" off Samar, the Philippines. After repairs in San Diego she served as an aircraft ferry for VMF-323 and -322, launching them 100 miles off Okinawa. ***Courtesy of the US Navy.***

CHAPTER 12
Ulithi
Pacific Spring Board

By mid-1944, Eniwetok was too far east to serve as the advanced base for the fleet, and Ulithi Atoll was occupied unopposed on 20 September 1944, as part of the Palau invasion. The atoll's location was ideal for the future tactical plans for the invasion of the Western Pacific, particularly the Philippines/Leyte and Okinawa that were 900 miles and 1,200 miles, respectively, to the northwest. After September 1944, Ulithi was the supply axis for the Western Pacific.

Ulithi was the typical Pacific atoll, a large open-enden lagoon formed by low islands and exposed coral reefs. In late March the members of -323 entered the lagoon aboard the USS WHITE PLAINS. They were awed by the sight of hundreds of U.S. Navy warships, their support and supply ships, Merchant Marine vessels, along with about 50 Royal Navy ships. Six Fleet fast carriers, the WASP, YORKTOWN, HORNET, HANCOCK, TICONDEROGA and LEXINGTON, painted in their gray and blue camouflage formed a "Murder's Row" in the large harbor.

Al Wells: "This was probably the most impressive thing in terms of force I have ever seen in my life. I remember seeing the movie, 'The CAINE Mutiny,' after the war. The guys from the CAINE were in awe when they went to testify aboard a true aircraft carrier. Well, that's how I felt. Looking into the Ulithi Harbor there were half a dozen or more of these carriers and over a hundred warships. I knew then there was no way we could lose the war."

While the WHITE PLAINS was at Ulithi, the carrier FRANKLIN (CV-13) had limped into the harbor after sustaining two 550lb. bomb hits, which started huge fires and explosions on the 19 March fighter sweeps off southern Japan. Rumors were rampant about the damage to the carrier that had lost 724 killed and 260 wounded and was the most extensively damaged carrier to survive the war.

When the WHITE PLAINS sailed into Ulithi, the pilots were awed by the sight of six ESSEX Class carriers which were dubbed "Murderer's Row." Pictured from the front: WASP, YORKTOWN, HORNET, HANCOCK, and TICONDEROGA. Back left is the LEXINGTON. ***Courtesy of the US Navy.***

CHAPTER 13
Okinawa
Finally into Battle

9 April

The WHITE PLAINS left Ulithi on 28 March, and was enroute and cruised off Okinawa Shima by 8 April. The flight echelon was intended for minimal self-sufficient until the LST arrived soon after.

VMF-322 and -323 on the escort carrier, USS WHITE PLAINS, had to stand off Okinawa for several days after the invasion, waiting for Kadena to become operational due to damage from artillery and aerial bombardment. The Captain and crew of the carrier were very anxious to get the Marines launched and then retire from the Kamikaze threat, back to CONUS. On 8 April, the task force and invasion fleet were under threat of Japanese air attack when the two squadrons were scheduled to be launched. A VMF-322 Corsair piloted by 1Lt. Forrest Warren was spotted number 1 on the catapult. However, the WHITE PLAINS was advised that the Seabees were completing work on the field at Kadena and that launch was to be delayed. Since Warren's fighter was already on the catapult he was volunteered for lone CAP for the carrier during the delayed launch. The carrier's flight deck was crowded with aircraft, and Warren asked what would happen if Kadena were not ready before he ran out of fuel and he could not land back on the crowded carrier deck? The reply was that the carrier would do several directional changes to calm the water and that he was to make a landing in the calmed water next to the carrier! That's what he was told. Luckily, the launch commenced shortly, and Warren was able to land safely on Kadena.

Axtell, with Brandon on his wing, landed on Kadena after being catapulted off the WHITE PLAINS. The pilots hid some Schenley's "Black Death" whiskey bottles in their aircraft to be used later for barter. (Brandon later bartered whiskey for a blood-stained Japanese battle flag from Sol Mayer, who had traded for it.) After 21 months from its formation the squadron was finally in combat.

This cake was presented to VMF-323 and -322 on 8 April, by the Captain and crew of the WHITE PLAINS prior to their being catapulted from her decks to Kadena airfield on Okinawa. The WHITE PLAINS was eager to leave the combat area due to the kamikaze threat. *Courtesy of the US Navy.*

A reconnaissance photo taken from the north in October 1944, during the first US raid on Okinawa. Kadena airfield lies in the foreground surrounded by the mosaic of farmlands while Yonton airfield is being bombed in the distance. *Courtesy of the USAAF.*

CHAPTER 14
LST-744
We'll Meet You There

1 March to 8 April

The ground assault echelon consisted of 20 pilots, eight ground officers, one Naval officer, 150 Marine enlisted men and eight Navy enlisted men. During the last days of February the cargo was loaded, and the men boarded on 1 March.

The LST was 327 feet long and had a beam of 50 feet. It had range of 6,000 miles at a speed of nine knots.

Sgt. Robert Carleton diary: "The LST is brand new. It has hot and cold fresh water showers. The living quarters are good, and so is the chow. We are the only outfit on board, so there is plenty of room. Each room has a radio."

Corp. Roger Archambault: "We called it the USS SEMAPHORE. The crew was great, the living quarters clean and neat, and the food excellent. The LST carried all the necessary personnel to start our combat operations."

VMF-323 ROSTER
APRIL 1945
LST-744

Major
Turner, Arthur

Captains

Grando, John	Cecot, Felix
Graham, George	McPhail, Joe

The lack of Japanese opposition on the beaches allowed the early capture of the Yonton and Kadena airfields. The two airfields, only miles apart, lie on the horizon of this photo. ***Courtesy of the US Navy.***

1Lts.

Broering, Warren	Lynn, Richard
Davis, Dellwyn	Mayer, Sol
Dussman, Thomas	Ritter, Frederick
Ferndenzi, Atilio	Spangler, Charles
Feliton, James	Thacker, Glen

2Lts.

Bestwick, Warren	Stover, Obie
Miller, Norman	Wade, Robert
Reynolds, Leon	Wickser, Robert
Rix, Paul	Woods, Robert
Ruhsam, John	Yager, Everett

W.O.
Jeffers, Larry

M/T.Sgts.

Becker, Raymond	Grady, Edmund
Blake, Jerry	Hand, Elwood
Bowman, Lloyd	Herndon, Lonnie
Brown, Robert	McLaughlin, Thomas
Culleton, John	Misch, Richard
Dudley, George	Morrison, George
Elliott, William	Parrish, Stanley
Garrard, Henry	Yongeberg, Eugene

T/Sgts.

Amundson, Ernest	Elson, Albert	Nilblack, Dennis
Barrett, James	Frankanicz, Sam	Penthany, Harold
Buckley, James	Finney, Paul	Preston, George
Brower, ??	Himmelberger, Arthur	Sloan, Albert
Caron, Norman	Hitchings, Donald	Vaira, John
Cochrane, Jack	Lee, Melvin	Warren, Milton
Daughton, John	Martin, James	Williams, James
DeMilia, Rocco	Mascal, Edwin	Woszcyna, Stanley

S/Sgts.

Alengi, Joe	Dennis, Thomas	Hurlburt, Elmer
Bennett, Jerome	DiPaola, Arthur	Johnson, Glenn
Boyce, Joseph	Downs, Francis	Krofft, Robert
Brennen, Donald	Flegel, Wayne	Magley, Albert
Bruno, John	Gracey, Harry	Magliocco, Francis
Carver, Donald	Gustin, Norton	Melson, Kenneth
Chessman, Charles	Hewitt, Charles	Schress, ??
Coogan, Edward	Hill, Clyde	Stovall, Eugene
Clevenger, Clarence	Hill, Richard	Walden, William

Supplies and equipment being unloaded from LSTs, LSMs, and LCTs beached at high tide at Hagushi Beach soon after L-Day. Note the large number of fuel barrels in the foreground which were drained into fuel trucks which transported the gasoline to Kadena. ***Courtesy of*** **the** ***US Navy.***

Culver, Leonard	Hill, Thomas	Wingfield, Chester
Holland, Vincent		

Sgts.

Ansel, Eugene	DeRock Lawrence	Quill, Ralph
Barr, Earl	DiBenecitto, Michael	Russell, Gilbert
Boenzi, Neal	Drolet, Maurice	Saari, Lynn
Boss, Ralph	Folcarelli, Anthony	Sherwood, Leslie
Bouchard, Roland	Gates, Dan	Shipton, Bart
Bouchillon, Howard	Griffin, Marley	Sieber, Clyde
Butcher, William	Hopper, Clyde	Silechia, Vito
Beye, William	Kaelber, Charles	Stafford, Dennis
Carleton, Robert	Kenyon, Robert	Stevens, James
Comerford, John	Londraville, Arthur	Tomsett, Richard
Cox, John	Neeb, Norman	Versaci, Benedict
Crescenti, Turidio	Olson, Roger	Weirich, Robert
Cunningham, Harold	Powers, Richard	Yanuss, Quenton

Corporals

Archambault, Roger	Doktor, Robert	Orlandella, Frank
Baldwin, H.	Dwyer, John	Ostendorf, Otto
Beaulieu, Charles	Gilbert, Richard	Ostroski, Thaddius
Burgess, John	Hinton, Thomas	Scarola, Edward
Burns, Karl	Hudspeth, Charles	
Caldwell, Wilbur	Jackson, Eugene	Jenner or Kenner,
Cassel, Roy	James, Joseph Edwin	
Cook, Ernest	Kennedy, John	
Corotta, Arthur	Knopf, George	
Desibia, Edward	McGregor, Harry	

PFCs

Clark, Thomas	Lach, Walter	Steinle, James
Fenton, James	Singletary, Robert	Tomlinson, Fred

Corpsmen

Eggleston, ??	Rogers, William	Whitten, Payson
Goff, Stanton	Sadowski, Edward	Woodruff, Stanley
Mynatt, James	Slagle, Robert	

Temporary Duty

SSgt.Baker	Sgt. Bokros	Corp. Anderson	MT Frye
Sgt.Herbert	Sgt. Cupciella	Corp. Cerluse	MT Kuck
Sgt. Michael	Sgt. Kadja	Corp. Williams	

Field Cooks

Coluccio, Daniel	Kozlowski, Edward	Vaguoni, Nicholas

Assistant Cooks

Gregorczyk, Anthony   Gregory, William

Compiled by Harley Brock and Bill Wolf

The itinerary of LST-744:

1 March left Luganville at 1230 to board the LST

1 March left Espiritu Santo at 1700

4 March anchored at Guadalcanal at 1300 left at 1500 and anchored at Tulagi at 1800 Purvis Bay, Florida Is

Beachhead shipping under attack on 6-7 April during the first kamikaze attack. Fallout from the intense AA fire could be almost as dangerous as the Japanese. It wasn't long before troopships and LSTs were prohibited from firing. ***Courtesy of the US Navy.***

5 March took on fuel
10 March. Received first mail since 27 Feb.
11 March took on provisions
12 March took on water
15 March left Tulagi at 0800 with 12 other LSTs and 6 destroyers in convoy. Rough weather.
24 March Ulithi at 1330 rainy and cloudy
25 March loaded limited cargo for VMTB-223
26 March left Ulithi in rough weather
28 March issued invasion money 10 yen/$1 100 sen=1 yen
31 March in China Sea
1 April arrived at Kerama Retto Easter Sunday, April Fool's Day and L-Day
2 April First airs attack early afternoon Tony? Hit LST-599
4 April landed at 1000 worked day and night
two air raid alerts that night but no planes attacked.

The long layover at Guadalcanal/Tulagi allowed the ground and service elements of MAG-33 to join the Northern Attack Force and proceed toward Ulithi.

As soon as the LST left Tulagi it ran into rough weather. James Barrett: "The LST ran into a heavy storm, and I had gun watch at the time. I was standing in the open pulpit turret, and when I looked at the LST along side, I could see that the first third of its bottom was out of the water. The LST was so long and shallow drafted, as it cut from one wave trough to another, it would hang over the top of the wave. At the bottom of the trough I had to actually look up to see the top of the next wave."

PC Donald Hitchings, "The thing (LST) rode like a bathtub, up, down and around. On the way to Okinawa we were part of a tremendous convoy. You couldn't see either end."

Pilot Del Davis: "The flotilla consisted of more than 50 vessels, mostly of the LST family. We were loaded with all our necessary supplies, including many 55 gallon gasoline drums strapped on the main deck. In order to reach the outside upper deck, one had to squeeze through the bulkhead hatch and climb over the barrels of fuel. All this fuel did not convey a very comfortable feeling, considering the threat of enemy action occurring just over the horizon."

Full-time pilot and part-time heavy machinery operator, Del Davis. Davis had worked in the oil fields before the war and helped offload the bulldozers and build landing ramps. ***Courtesy of Bill Drake.***

The LST, Landing Ship Tank, was 327 feet long with a beam of 50 feet. The ground echelon embarked on the new LST-744 from Espiritu Santo on 1 March and arrived off Okinawa on 1 April. It was beached on the Hagushi beaches on the 4th. A bulldozer can be seen on the right after it had smoothed off the landing ramp area. ***Courtesy of the US Navy.***

Joe McPhail: "The decks were loaded with 55 gallon drums of 100 octane fuel. Our intelligence officer, Tilly Ferndenzi, was scared to death the whole time he was on the LST. He wore his Mae West the whole time he was aboard, even when he slept."

The men aboard the LST were just as impressed with Ulithi as were those on the WHITE PLAINS.

James Barrett: "As soon as we dropped anchor at Ulithi, among the many hundreds of ships, a LCVP came along side and delivered mail which was sent from the U.S. West Coast two days earlier. It was impressive to think about the organization that went into knowing precisely when and where LST-744 would be on that day. There were hundreds of ships of all kinds to the horizon."

On 2 April, the assault squadron arrived off the shores of Kerama Retto aboard LST-744 and laid anchor. Kerama Retto is a series of eight steep, rocky hilly islands that lay 20-25 miles to the southwest of the invasion beaches and possesses a large natural anchorage. Their strategic location caused them to be invaded on 26 March and secured by 29 March.

"We had individual bunks which were also our general quarters area. During a general quarters alert, a NCO got excited trying to get to his area, which on the LST was his bunk. During an alert everything is one way, so even if you are only ten feet away from your area you have to run all the way around the ship to get there. In his excitement, he ran the wrong way, knocking over sailors who were running the right way, and ended up not living down this episode." James Barrett

Mel Lee with his bulldozer. Lee was ordered to plow shut the entrances of caves and bunkers suspected of harboring Japanese soldiers and infiltrators but sometimes contained Okinawan civilians. ***Courtesy of Mel Lee.***

On 4 April LST-744 left the Kerama Retto anchorage at 0630 and embarked in heavy seas toward the east coast of Okinawa Shima. At 0900 the LST anchored among the transports laying off the Hagushi invasion beaches. The deteriorating weather spared the fleet from Japanese air attack that day. During the 5th, the LST continued to lie at anchor, and the rain and overcast again kept the Kamikazes away. From the LST the men watched the shelling from our battleships at night. Each battleship had its own colored shell for identification in ranging on a target.

James Barrett: "When we were anchored off Okinawa waiting to land on shore there was a large AKA ammunition ship along side us. If it were hit by kamikazes it would demolish everything around it. The ship was so worried about being hit that it would often have its LCVPs out making a smoke screen. You could always hear when the planes were coming because the guns in the distance would open up first, and the firing would come closer and closer, and soon the guns on your ship would be opening up. We shot down some of our own planes. I saw two old F4Fs being launched by a carrier, and as soon as they gained altitude they were shot down by our own AA fire." An old Navy anti-aircraft policy was, "Shoot them all down and sort them out later."

At 0715, the next day a kamikaze got through CAP. Pilot Glen Thacker: "We were watching this air show. It all seemed far away, but suddenly a Jap plane came in low over the water so that the ships couldn't fire at it without hitting each other. Then before we knew it the LST to the left of us was hit about deck level by the kamikaze, and the pilots from another squadron (VMF-312) came streaming out onto the shore." AA fire had knocked off a wing, but the plane crashed and penetrated the main deck of the LST-599, exploding and starting fires. LST-599, which was carrying 30 officers and 169 enlisted men of VMF-322, suffered a loss of 7 wounded and all 424 tons of gear, including some VMF-323 gear. When all the loss claims were made, it was found that 848 tons of gear were lost! The men of 323 watched the LST fire control put out the fires, but most of the gear was lost and 21 men were wounded, but none killed. The men of -323 spent the remainder of the day at anchor scanning the skies for kamikazes.

On the 6th, the LST weighed anchor, hit the beach at 0900, and began unloading. By this time the pre-invasion fears of a repeat of the blood bath on the beaches of Iwo Jima had subsided as U.S. forces had driven far inland and the beach head was free from the threat of Japanese infantry attack and long range artillery. The 6th was also the day the Japanese began the first of their ten massed suicide attacks they code named kikusui, "floating chrysanthemums." That day the Japanese sent 699 aircraft (355 kamikazes) toward Okinawa. The sky continued to be overcast with strong winds, and the kamikazes held off until 1700 when four or five got through the CAP. The entire anchorage area blazed away with AA fire. The transport and LST anti-aircraft fire were undisciplined and unrestrained, firing on bearings that caused the spent flak to fall on surrounding ships and the beach head. Pieces hurtled from the sky, and a helmet was a necessity. There was no injury to -323 personnel or damage to the cargo.

Once the invasion force reached the beachhead the AA fire got out of control. Every gun on hundreds of ships would start shooting at a plane and follow it down to the sea, so at the end they would be shooting at other ships and personnel on shore. Orders were finally given to LST gunners to no longer allow them to fire their guns.

Del Davis: "The LST beached during a tropical storm, and unloading was canceled for a while due to heavy seas. There were air raid alerts, and enemy aircraft could be seen strafing the beach and ships in the anchorage. The pontoons of the LST adjacent to ours had broken away and broached in a 180 degree position that put the 'drive off' end to seaward and its deep end on shore. I observed the opportunity to move the squadron's equipment ashore. The executive officer of the LST was a Navy Lt.(jg), and he permitted us to utilize the anchor wench to try to position the pontoon adjacent to our LST's opened ramp doors. Aided by low tides we were able to get the pontoon around the numerous coral formations in the immediate area and into the proper position. But we were confronted with an eight-foot drop off on the beach shoreline.

At approximately 0200, we were checking the feasibility of staging the squadron's equipment ashore. It was a clear night, and the Fleet had not generated smoke to cover the landing operations. Enemy aircraft strafed the beach area from north to south, and it seemed like every bullet was fired directly at me with my name inscribed on it. I wanted to get off that LST ASAP! The LST had been loaded, first off, last loaded and there was a small bulldozer adjacent to the ramp doors. I had worked on the oil fields and pipeline business prior to my entry to the military and decided to launch the dozer off the high end of the ramp. I had watched experienced tractor drivers jump tractors from railway cars at the oil fields, and I was confident that I could take the 'giant step' onto the sands of Okinawa. We placed driftwood under the ramp for a softer landing, and I launched that little dozer onto the beach without a hitch. We began to build an off-loading ramp to fill in the eight foot drop.

Just as we were directing the rolling stock to move down the newly built ramp, a jeep drove up and a large, burly 06 jumped out and shouted, 'Who's responsible for this?' I proudly said, 'I am, Sir.' He proceeded to inform me that I had interfered with the unloading scheme and that I would forever regret what I had done. He asked me how long it would take to clear the ramp, and I told him within 30 minutes. To my great relief and surprise, he said, 'Well done, lieutenant.'"

At daylight, I shut down the dozer and was checking the pontoon when an enemy aircraft made two attacks along the beach. During one of these attacks, I was hotfooting down the pontoon towards the LST, and midway down the pontoon the attacking aircraft made hits on the pontoon. I managed to lodge my leg into the separation between the pontoons. I received cuts on my leg and a subsequent coral infection which resulted in my being grounded for the first day of flight operations on 10 April."

Tech.Sgt. Mel Lee, an equipment operator attached to the Transportation Department of VMF-323, was one of the first off his LST on 6 April. He and his bulldozer were assigned to build and maintain sand-coral ramps from the drop run of the LSTs to shore so that the rolling equipment would not get bogged down. It was of utmost importance that the refueling trucks were moved ashore and to Kadena before the aircraft arrived. Lee describes the scene at the landing beaches: "Things were hectic, we worked all day and night on the 6th getting our equipment ashore. I remember watching a kamikaze come over through the heavy AA and hit our sister LST. Fortunately, there were only a few casualties, but the equipment in the hold suffered damage. The worse thing for me was watching all the gun crews shooting at enemy aircraft and sometimes our own. I remember one officer shouting at them to stop shooting at our own planes. It seemed like they shot at anything flying."

Lee continues, "We were in position and had the fuel trucks ready by the 8th ready to refuel the Corsairs when they arrived the next day at Kadena. During the first week I spent a lot of time working a bulldozer in and around our squadron area, digging shelters in the sides of hills or underground and bulldozed new roads. Our Marine bulldozers were small compared to Army Engineers' and Seabees' heavy D7 and D8 Caterpillars. The Seabees were building roads in the area and would leave their equipment unoccupied and unguarded. I decided to borrow one of the D8s and moved it to our area and complete my work in half the time and returned it. At night I worked a shovel dozer with the Seabees and loaded trucks with coral to be used for the enlargement of the airstrips and taxiways. Several times the Japs came over at night while I was working. I jumped off the shovel dozer and hid in the steel bucket. Most of the time I worked alone in a large coral digging pit. This was no

An artist portrayed Mel Lee covering Japanese strong points in this sketch entitled "The Okinawa Obliterator." ***Courtesy of Mel Lee.***

fun, and I was very scared. During the first week one of our guards had shot a Jap infiltrater outside our tents. If anyone approached me I couldn't hear them over the noise of the diesel engine. I was always worried about Jap snipers or infiltraters, so I kept a loaded .45 Thompson submachine gun on my lap."

Lee: "Another one of my duties with a bulldozer was knocking down villages suspected of having Jap infiltraters hiding in them. I did not enjoy this one bit, as I would never know if I were crushing some poor frightened Okinawan or a Jap. For this duty I acquired the nickname 'Okinawan Obliterator,' and had a cartoon drawn of me on my bulldozer."

S/Sgt. Frank Magliocco: "I got off the ramp of the LST and walked towards shore. All of a sudden I stepped into some kind of hole and went in over my head. I don't know if it was from a bomb crater or what. I had my pack and rifle—thank God I didn't have my tool box, or I would never have come up. (T/Sgt.) Don Hitchings pulled me out, I was like a drowned fish. I remember walking onto the beach to the trucks and looking up and seeing a poor Navy Hellcat being peppered by our own AA fire."

T/Sgt. James Barrett was unloading a LST and was handling crated drop tanks. The man above him lost his grip on a crate, and Barrett turned to escape by jumping off the ramp onto the rain-slicked deck. He twisted his ankle, and it swelled so much that it appeared to be broken and he was air evacuated to Guam. It was diagnosed as a sprain, and after three days he was sent back to duty at Kadena and arrived about a week later. Barrett was 323's first Okinawa casualty, and not its last.

T/Sgt. Jim Barrett was the squadron's first Okinawan casualty when he slipped while unloading an LST. He was evacuated to the Marianas Islands with a suspected broken ankle which was later diagnosed as a severe sprain. Barrett (R) is seen here with T/Sgts. Ed Grady (L) and John Vaira (C). ***Courtesy of Rocco DeMilia.***

7-8 April

These days were spent unloading and transferring cargo to Kadena. Since Axtell was the junior squadron commander of the three squadrons to be stationed at Kadena, -323 was assigned the undeveloped portion of the field. They needed to redo everything to prepare for the flight echelon arrival. Shops, messing facilities, latrines and bivouac areas had to be immediately set up. The men worked day and night on the 7th and 8th, and by the 9th when -323 pilots and Corsairs landed on Kadena, all was in readiness to service the aircraft and accommodate the men.

CHAPTER 15
Sea Bass
Another Epic Sea Odyssey

22 March to 2 May
The one officer, 1Lt. Albert Taylcr, (War Diaries state two officers) and 74 enlisted men loaded the SEA BASS in early March at Espiritu Santo to begin a 52 day odyssey across the Pacific. The SEA BASS was an identical C3 type troop/cargo ship to the SEA PIKE that the ground echelon had previously sailed for 54 days from Ford Island, Hawaii, to Luganville, Espiritu Santo, in September to November. Both were built by Western Pipe & Steel in 1943. It measured 492 feet long, 70 foot beam and weighed 7,949 tons. The SEA BASS carried 2,838 passengers and 184,900 cu.ft. of cargo and was operated by the Matson Lines.

Sea Bass Itinerary
1-21 March wait and load at Espiritu Santo
22 March leave E.S.
25 March arrive Noumea, New Caledonia
28 March leave Noumea
31 March arrive Banskin, Marshall Is.
02 April leave Banika
02 April arrive Guadalcanal, Solomon Is.
04 April depart Guadalcanal
07 April arrive Eniwetok, Marshall Is.
23 April depart Eniwetok
25 April arrive Saipan, Marianas Is.
27 April depart Saipan
02 May arrive Okinawa

Harley Brock recounts the journey: "Conditions aboard the ship were like the other one (SEA PIKE). Salt water showers, two meals a day which you couldn't eat, and wall-to-wall men. We had some stretches of rough weather, and it usually took a day to recover from the sea sickness and clean up the mess. The ship was delivering cargo, and so we were all over the South Pacific. We went to Noumea, the Russell Islands, Guadalcanal, and then we went up to Eniwetok, which was a large forward base. We anchored off shore and half of us got ashore, eager to take advantage of the PX and recreation areas. But the news of the day (13 April) was that President Roosevelt had died, and everything was closed. We pulled up anchor and got underway and arrived at Saipan (Marianas Islands) at night and anchored. Just about sunrise we were nearly rolled out of our bunks by the roar of aircraft engines passing overhead every minute. We all rushed topside to see what was happening. What a sight! It was the biggest airplane I had ever seen in my life. A B-29. They just seemed to run off the runway and dip down a bit and fly right over our ship. They were so close we could read the numbers off the planes. We steamed quickly to Okinawa where the big battle was going on. We arrived on May 1st at night and anchored. Most of the men went down the cargo nets and onto landing craft to the island. I stayed aboard and helped unload the cargo the next day."

Joe Bassani: "Between the 54 days on the SEA PIKE getting from Hawaii to Espiritu Santo and another 50 or more days on the SEA BASS getting from there to Okinawa, we were beginning to feel more like sailors than Marines."

The SEA BASS sailed an epic 54 days from Espiritu Santo, over the South Pacific before reaching Okinawa carrying 74 enlisted men of the third echelon. This echelon finally arrived at Kadena three weeks after the flight echelon took from the WHITE PLAINS. ***Courtesy of the Matson Lines.***

VMF-323 Roster APRIL 1945
Troopship SEA BASS

1Lt.
Taylor, Albert

M.T/Sgt.
Stewart, Frank

T/Sgts.
Borozan, Steve
Cross, Robert
Micha, Charles

S/Sgts.
Brock, Harley
Chapman, Odie
Gawron, Edward
Regan, John
Uphouse, Earl

Sargeants
Clark, Joe
Cohen, Samuel
Fitzgerald, Gerald
Griffoni, Joseph
Kennedy, James
Kyne, Gerald
Langston, Don
St. Clair, Robert
Shegogue, Donald
Tipler, Frank

Corporals
Bassani, Joseph
Bickford, John
Cerniello, Alfred
Downes, Francis
Dubin, Isadore
Fox, Lester
Harrison, Chester
Heynolds, Robert
Masclarete, Joseph
Maslakowski, Edward
McDonald, Raymond
Morris, John
Mutter, Howard
Naylor, George
Nespola, Frank
Siegel, Clyde
Stransky, Paul
Toomey, Howard

PFCs
Cooke, Thomas
Courtney, Howard
Dell, Harold
Dube, Raymond
Freeman, Christian
Zabra, John
Hopkins, Harry
Larsen, Arnold
McGartland, John
Miksic, Markus
Navarro, Robert
Palumbizio, Alfred
Quesenberry, Genious
Sabtino, Leonardo
Tocci, Frank
Withrow, Richard

1Lt. Albert "Swampy" Taylor was the officer in command of the third echelon aboard the SEA BASS. ***Courtesy of Henry Brandon.***

Asst. Cook
Belanger, Gerard

Privates
DeStefano, Bart
Lewison, David

Compiled by Harley Brock and Bill Wolf

CHAPTER 16
Okinawa
The Final Battle, A Background

Reasons for the Okinawa Invasion
When the Marianas campaign was successfully concluded in the summer of 1944, Staff planners looked to the northeast. MacArthur desired an earlier return to the Philippines, and his wish was granted. Formosa was considered, and the 10th Army was formed to invade the island now known as Taiwan. However, it was found that the Formosan coast offered no suitable landing beaches, and a new target had to be chosen. Okinawa in the Ryukuyus Islands group, only 350 miles from the Japanese homeland, was selected. The reasons for this choice were that from Okinawan bases:

(1) Naval and air forces could attack the Japanese home islands and their sea approaches, industry, and demoralize its people with constant military pressure.

(2) Support could be given to future operations in the South China Sea and on China.

(3) Cut Japanese air and naval communications from the home islands to its occupied territories on the Asian mainland, Formosa, Malaya, and the Netherlands East Indies. Conversely, cut the source of raw materials from these areas.

(4) Provide airfields and anchorages for the invasion of Japan. The island had enough space for new airfields in addition to those the Japanese had already built, along with the protected bays and harbors on the island's coasts. It was estimated that there were over two dozen potential airfield sites which could accommodate five Very Long Range (VLR) bomber wings, two fighter wings, numerous medium and light bomber fields, and a depot field.

Okinawa
Okinawa Shima is the central island of a chain of islands named the Ryukyu Islands (Nansei Shoto), which separates the East China

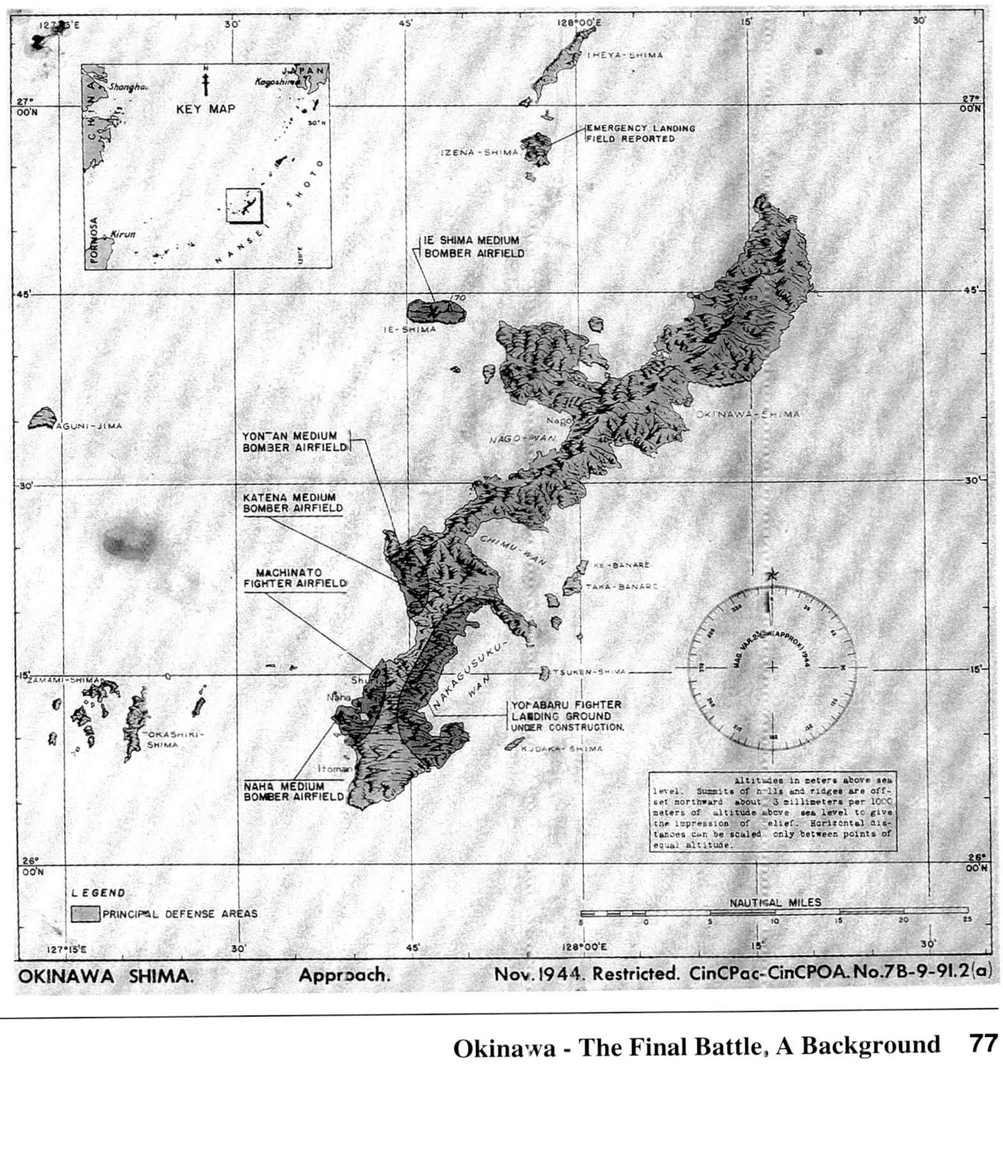

CinCPac-CinPOA pre-invasion cloth survival chart of Okinawa Shima printed in November 1944, showing the disposition of Japanese airfields and principal defense areas. Note the Kadena is spelled Katena. *Courtesy of Henry Brandon.*

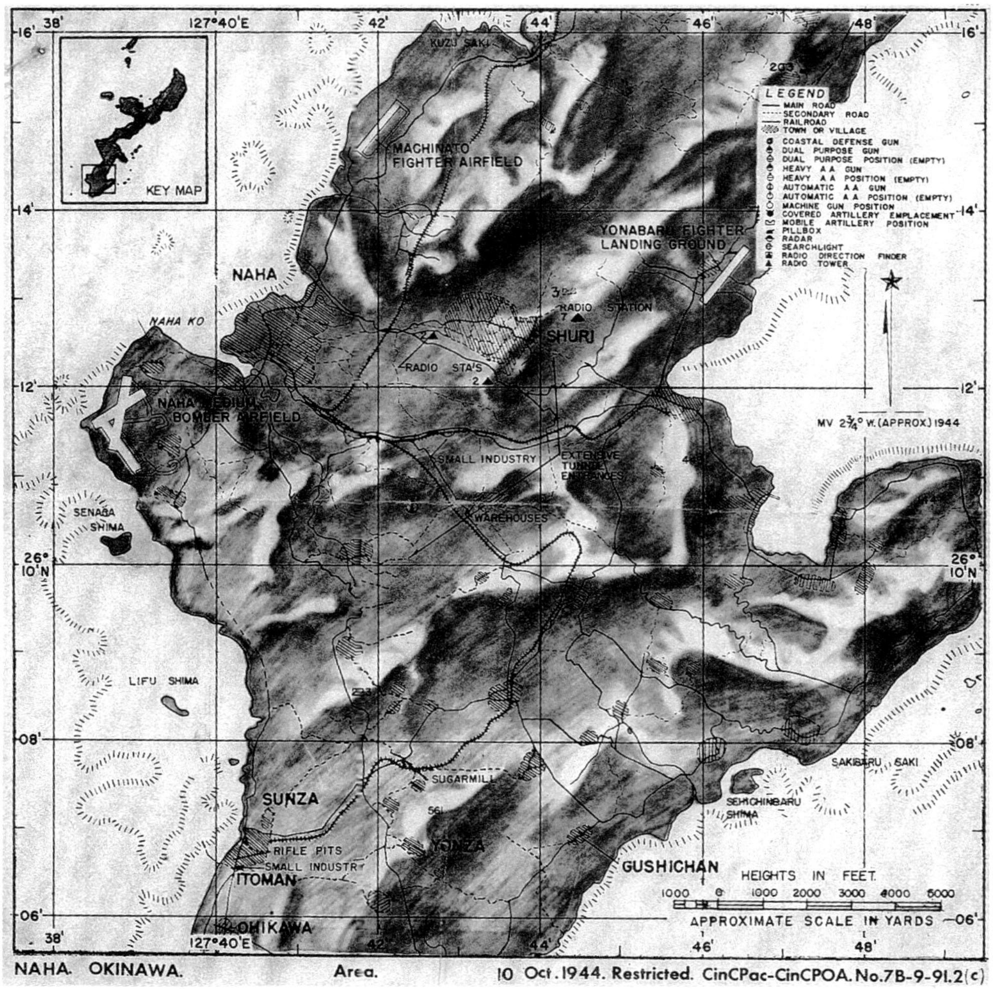

October 1944, pre-invasion map of the Naha area were the heavy ground fighting would take place in May and June. *Courtesy of Henry Brandon*.

Sea and the Pacific Ocean. It is the largest at 67 miles long, north to south, and varying in width from two to 15 miles. It has a jagged coastline, with deeply carved bays and inlets, and a perimeter of coral reef that confines seaward approaches. One third of the way from the southern end of the island a narrow isthmus divides the island. North of the isthmus is rugged hill country, with elevations reaching over 1,500 feet and covered with heavy, jungle-like vegetation. The southern third of the island is low hill (under 700 feet) terrain interrupted by steep limestone scarps and terraces covered by small stands of pine and grasses. This southern sector also has large tracts of gently sloping land used for agriculture. The climate is subtropical, with moderate winters and hot summers, with high humidity throughout the year. May through September are marked by frequent, often torrential, rains with the typhoon season running from July to November. During the rest of the year, except for short rains, the climate is usually good.

The Japanese geographical terms; gunto, retto and shoto translate to chain of islands while jima or shima translate to island. Wan means bay and misaki means point.

OPERATION ICEBERG

The Okinawa invasion began on 1 April 1945. (NOTE: L-Day, "LOVE DAY," of OPERATION ICEBERG, the invasion of Okinawa on the Hagushi beaches took place on 1 April after seven

Kadena after its capture on 9 April. The cloud at the end of the runway is dust from construction. *Courtesy of John Ruhsam*.

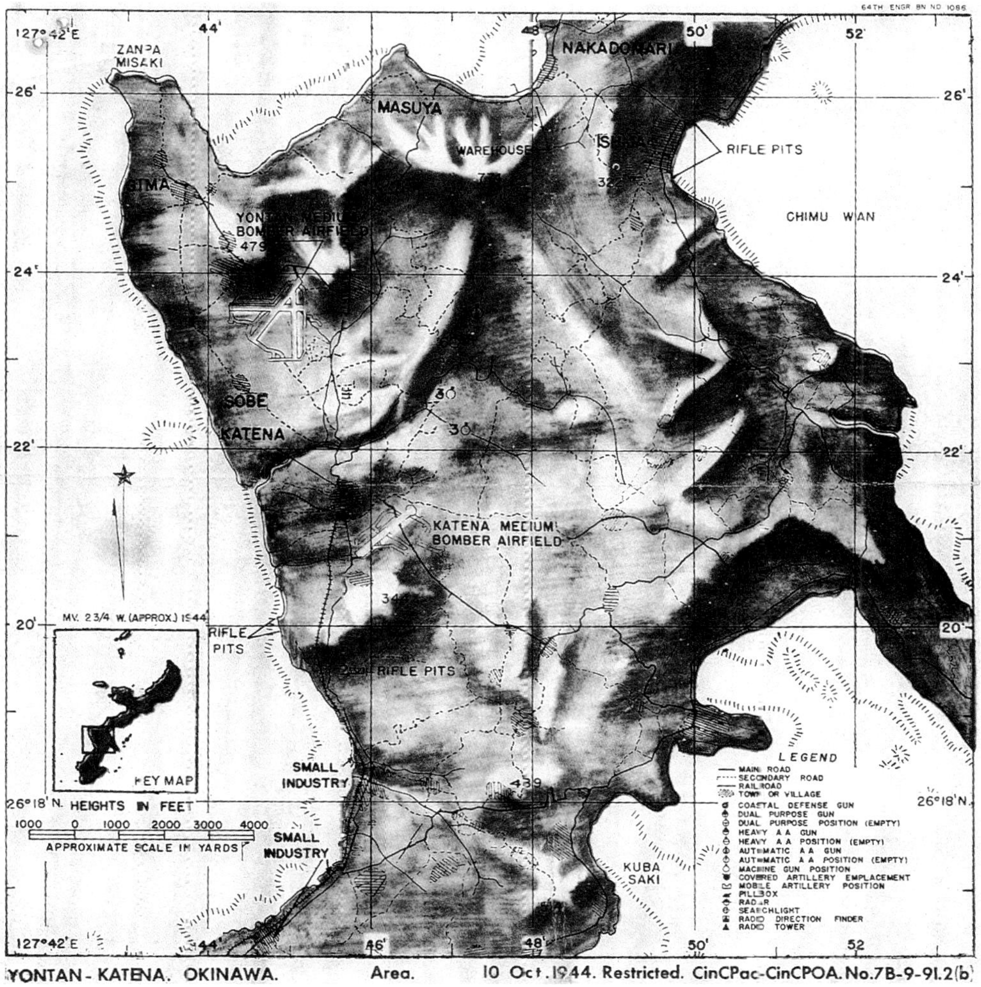

October 1944, map of Kadena and Yonton airfields which were used as medium bomber fields by the Japanese. Kadena was built on a plain on the south center of the island, just off the west coast. ***Courtesy of Henry Brandon.***

days of softening up by ten battleships and eleven cruisers and by carrier-based aircraft, which dropped tons of explosives on Japanese defenses.) Simultaneous landings by the 3rd Marines and 24th Army Corps took place on the west coast, south and north of Bisha Gawa, and 20 miles north of Okinawa's major city and port, Naha. Surprisingly, only light resistance was met, and the rapid advance captured Yontan and Kadena airfields. Kadena was captured by the 17th Regimental Combat team of the 7th Division shortly before noon. The reason for the quick advance here was because Japanese commander, Hiromichi Yahara, decided to reinforce more defensible areas than the airfield's flat open areas. He did move artillery-equipped units into the rugged hills above the airfield to harass the field.

AIRFIELD CONSTRUCTION

Shortly after the invasion construction troops landed. The 1901st Aviation Engineer Battalion and CBMU 624 began work on Kadena on 4 April, under occasional enemy shelling and sniper fire. Their initial undertaking was to concentrate on getting the airfields operational as soon as possible, initially clearing runways and filling bomb craters. Both Yontan and Kadena were damaged by the pre-invasion aerial and naval bombardment, and Jap-laid mines and a

A huge highway traffic circle outside Kadena built by the 130th SeeBee Battalion to aid the flow of supplies, not only to Kadena, but also to the infantry fighting in the north. Kadena airfield can be seen in the distance. ***Courtesy of John Ruhsam.***

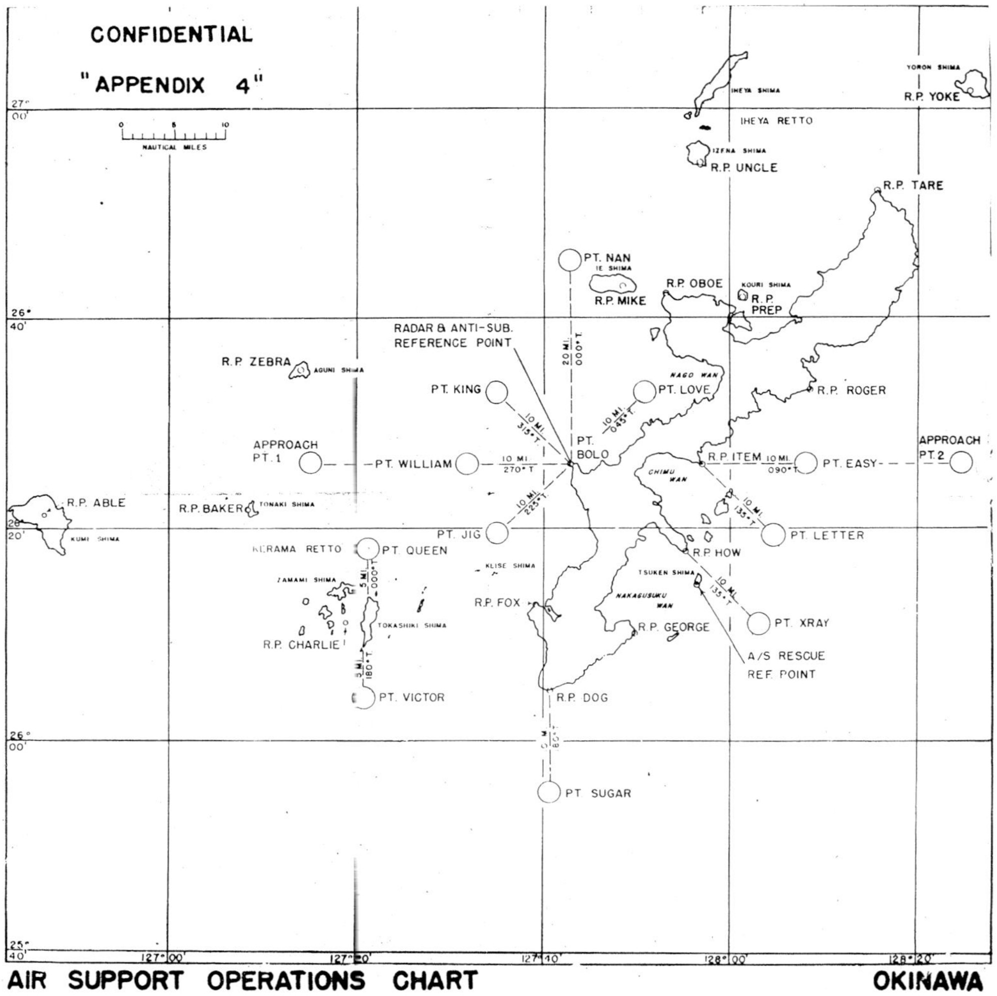

An Air Support Operations chart showing the navigation reference points. Point BOLO was the center station of the Okinawa operation. *Courtesy of the US Navy.*

Work on the landing field continued during daily flight operations. Here a -323 Corsair comes in for a landing while a grader waits to begin work again. *Courtesy of the USMC via Steve Stuczynski.*

few booby traps further impeded the work. Kadena was ready for operations on the morning of 9 April, when Axtell and the Death Rattlers catapulted off the WHITE PLAINS and landed on Kadena.

Marine engineers and Seabees began repairing the runways at Yontan and Kadena. The runways were lightly surfaced and heavily damaged by naval gunfire, aerial bombing and Japanese demolition. Yontan was put into use on 7 April, but Kadena presented more far-reaching problems. It suffered more damage, and the source of coral for resurfacing was some distance from the field. Nonetheless, Kadena was proclaimed ready for dry weather use on 9 April, and by 1 May both fields were officially declared all-weather operational. Both fields were, in fact, all-weather from their first days of operation. Ultimately, it was found that the Japanese airfields were too short and their construction too light for our heavier aircraft. The hardstands were too small and the taxiways too narrow. In the latter part of the month, construction troops resurfaced and extended the existing runways, built and widened taxiways, and built hardstands, warm-up aprons, and fuel storage facilities. The original Japanese runway was rebuilt one quarter at a time, half the length and half the width, so that the base could remain operational. Damage-control parties occasionally were filling bomb craters while the field was under attack, and at no time were operations shut down for any period of time due to enemy damage.

Major Axtell comments on the Kadena runway: "The weather and condition of the runway has received considerable discussion. Until the Army engineers and Seabees got well into expanding and widening the runway, we found on our arrival, the primitive Japanese main runway had an excellent drainage system, so we were able to operate in days of heavy rain without hindrance. We were assigned the northern side of the field, which was undeveloped. We found that all the newly constructed taxiways and roads on our side of the field would become nothing but mud during rains and were unable to support the weight of aircraft or vehicles. The lack of adequate drainage had made the newly constructed taxiways almost impassable and dangerous. The situation of having Kadena fighters unable to takeoff became one of great concern. Admiral Halsey came ashore to determine why we were not operating. He inspected the runway with senior commanders, and he and I drifted to the rear of the inspection team. As we walked I told him why we couldn't operate and he said I was the only person who had the guts to stand up and lay the facts on the line. He told me he would get the engineers off their asses and correct the drainage problem. Several days later things were better, but still treacherous, but we could get to the main runway."

CHAPTER 17
Okinawa Air War
The Enemy

KAMIKAZES OVER OKINAWA

After the failure of the *Sho-Go* plan in the Philippines, the Japanese Imperial GHQ issued a new directive for the future defense of the homeland. The directive determined that the conclusive battle of the war would be conducted on Japan, but that a concentrated effort would be made to defend the Ryukyus. Japanese air power was to be conserved until the enemy had actually landed, and then their invasion fleet would be destroyed by a coordinated sea and air special attack elements. Also, the previous Japanese canon of defense that emphasized unyielding resistance no matter the cost and the need to halt the enemy invasion on the beaches had proven costly. Therefore, the Japanese embraced a new defensive strategy to protract every land battle as long as possible in order to exact the maximal casualties and expose the Americans to Japanese naval and air forces. The intent was to dissipate the enemy invasion into a costly, demoralizing stalemate.

The Japanese High Command had recognized that their pilots were no longer well trained enough to attack enemy shipping by conventional methods. American pilots decimated them in air-to-air combat before they were able to reach their targets. With no prospects of victory in the air, unorthodox methods needed to be adopted. So, it was decided that *tokko tai,* special attack pilots, were to be utilized to crash into enemy warships, "one plane, one ship." The Navy would ultimately lose 2,525 kamikaze pilots, mainly drawn from over 1,700 preparatory trainees. The remainder were volunteers ranging from lieutenant to ensign, including over 100 valuable Naval Academy volunteers. The Army would lose 1,388 suicide pilots mainly drawn from apprentice pilot officers and young airmen.

During the battle for the Philippines, the Japanese had sent out 650 kamikaze aircraft that sank 16 ships and damaged 150 others. At Iwo Jima only one major attack was mounted. In it 25 suicide planes of 40 total attackers sank an escort carrier, damaged a large carrier and two other ships. It was at Okinawa that the kamikaze fury would be vented on the invading American warships.

Operation TEN-GO (named after Tennozan, the site of a great sixteenth century battle) was formulated as a massed air attack on the American Okinawan invasion fleet by both kamikaze and conventional aircraft. However, between 19-23 March, the Japanese Fifth Air Fleet had sent 193 aircraft out to attack the fast carriers of TF-58 that were attacking airfields on Kyushu on the southern tip of the Japanese homelands. In the battle, only 32 returned. In conjunction with B-29s of the XXI Bomber Command, forays of fighter sweeps destroyed another estimated 350 Japanese Army and Navy Air Force aircraft on the ground on Kyushu. At the outset of the Okinawa invasion, the principal Japanese air counterattack forces had been severely diminished, and replacements had to be hurriedly recruited from other already depleted JNAF air fleets and JAAF air armies.

In preparation for battle, ancient Samurai warriors had tied their hair with a folded white cloth. Here, to symbolize courage, the ceremonial hachimaki head band is tied prior to a kamikaze mission. *Author's collection.*

Young school girls wave cherry blossoms to kamikaze pilots departing from Chiran Air Base on Kyushu in April 1945. ***Author's collection.***

For the Okinawa campaign the Japanese Navy kamikaze pilots and aircraft were drawn almost without exception from the operational training establishment. The Army, however, made increasing use of pilots from combat units, along with those from training units. Both Navy and Army tactical units continued to fly conventional missions. Both services established kamikaze operating procedures with the emphasis being put on dive bombing. Only rudimentary navigation training was necessary, as pilots could follow the nearly continuous chain of islands leading from Kyushu to Okinawa. At times the poorest trained pilots had to be led visually to the target by experienced bomber pilots. It was for this reason that few kamikaze missions occurred at night, and those that did were on moonlit nights. There was a definite deterioration of pilot quality as the campaign proceeded.

Kamikaze tactics were ever changing, as the Japanese searched for ways of avoiding Allied fighter, AA and radar. Generally, during the massed kikusui attacks of the TEN-GO operation, reconnaissance and "snooper" aircraft would appear in increased numbers about two hours before sunrise. Japanese reconnaissance flights designated targets for the day's mission. Just before the major attack, single aircraft or small formations of aircraft would fly in at all heights to draw off and dissipate the CAP. The major force of suicide and conventional aircraft and their escorts would then swarm a pre-designated area, expecting to overwhelm the CAP there and hit the unprotected shipping. Ideally, diving from astern reduced the effectiveness of the target's evasive action and exposed the pilot to less AA fire. Both the Japanese Naval Air Force (JNAF) and the Japanese Army Air Force (JAAF) targeted carriers as the most prized objective. The parked aircraft and large elevators were the most vulnerable part of the carrier. However, ordering a pilot to attack a specific target and his being able to fly to its general area, identify it, and then penetrate its defensive screen was another thing. Many times the CAP or AA was so daunting around the target that the pilot was willing to settle on a hit on any target. Consequently, relatively unprotected destroyer radar pickets and landing craft were often the target not of choice. Logistical problems also surfaced. Since many of the aircraft used were older or obsolescent, there were parts and maintenance difficulties, especially concerning engines. These older aircraft were smaller and lighter and were unable to carry the heavier bombs needed to cause significant damage to the larger and more heavily armored capital ships. This accounts for the fact that no major Allied warship (battleship, fleet or light carrier, or cruiser) was sunk by a kamikaze. Three escort carriers were the most important ships sunk. However, stories of destroyers and other small ships surviving multiple suicide hits are legend. Japanese gasoline supply and quality also declined. The serviceability rate for the special attack units was generally 20% on Kyushu. The fighter sweeps and bomber raids over Kyushu interrupted the entire flow of the Japanese attack plan.

The initial phase of the invasion took the Japanese by surprise. On 23 March, TF-58 began its pre-invasion softening up of Okinawa, and the adjacent Kerama Retto Islands were invaded. It wasn't until two days later that the procrastinating Japanese High Command issued an alert for TEN-GO to prepare for an attack on anticipated enemy invasion fleet and amphibious forces. By the 29th, the Ameri-

Extensive kamikaze damage being surveyed in the Kerama anchorage where the Navy brought its damaged ships for repair. ***Courtesy of the US Navy.***

A dead, burned kamikaze pilot lays next to the wreckage of his aircraft. ***Courtesy of Don Hitchings.***

cans had established an intricate offshore defensive network. Commander of Japanese East China Sea Air Forces, Admiral Soemu Toyoda, had intended on amassing 4,500 aircraft for the initial attacks on the invasion forces, but the March homeland aircraft losses curtailed his plans. It wasn't until the 6th of April that he managed to marshal 700 aircraft on Kyushu and Formosa. There were to be ten planned concentrated kamikaze attacks which were code named *Kikusui,* "floating chrysanthemums." The attacks were to be launched from Formosa and the Sakishima Gunto Islands to the southwest, from Kyushu on the southern tip of the Japanese homeland, and from the Amami Gunto Islands midway between Japan and Okinawa. The ten TEN-GO attacks occurred between 6 April and 22 June, comprising 1,900 (1,050 JAAF and 850 JNAF) kamikaze sorties.

The determined *Kikusui* attacks were difficult to suppress, because a resolute suicide pilot could hit a ship if he weren't shot down first. Many kamikaze aircraft, heavily damaged by AA fire, crashed their targets with devastating results. The attacks were most effective against smaller warships. The larger ships were more heavily armored and armed, and because they were more valuable, they were afforded better covering protection. It was for this reason that the majority of ships lost to kamikazes were destroyers and destroyer escorts, especially the picket destroyers. These lonely, lightly armed ships were placed 15 to 80 miles offshore to patrol in small circles in order to pick up approaching enemy aircraft with their radar and vector awaiting CAP to them. Since they were the proverbial sitting ducks they were often attacked.

To counter the Japanese air threat a comprehensive defensive perimeter was established. Carrier Task Force CTF-58, under V.Adm. Mark Mitscher, the Royal Navy carriers of Task Force 57 and USN Escort Carrier Group provided CAP for the fleet and the invasion troops. In addition, they carried out attacks on the Japanese strike bases, especially on Kyushu, where the Fast Carrier Task Force made two large scale fighter sweeps of the island. The kamikaze threat became so grave that on 20 April, Admiral Spruance requested the B-29s of the XXI Bomber Command in the Marianas to strike airfields on Kyushu, even though airfields were not viable B-29 bombing targets.

The primary problem with the air defense was its inability to provide both direct support missions for the ground forces and CAP for Kerama Retto and all the elements of the fleet: the invasion force, the bombardment force, the carrier force and the radar pickets. The initial air defense plan required one division (four fighters) to cover the southwest approach (Formosa and Sakishimas), six divisions to cover invasion shipping and the island's airfields and troops, and five divisions to cover the northern approaches (Kyushu and Agami Shima). This defensive dispersal of 12 divisions (48 aircraft) was not always possible to accomplish after L-Day (1 April), because the demand for close support aircraft took away from CAP. After L+5 up to six divisions (24 aircraft), augmented by aircraft flown off the fast carrier and Support Carrier Group, were available for CAP. However, by L+8 (9 April) these carrier CAP forces were relieved by the Marine Corsair equipped VMFs operating from the captured Kadena and Yontan airfields, which had taken some time to become operational. The Marine flyers soon assumed a large portion of the responsibility for island CAP, picket ship CAP and close support for the troops. With these additional aircraft it was possible to fly daily picket ship CAP, and on days of forecasted normal activity, fly five divisions on CAP and stand two divisions on alert. When large Japanese raids were forecast it was possible to put up seven divisions and stand another three divisions on alert.

The total number of Japanese air raids on Okinawa for the entire Okinawa operation was 896, including 3,700 JNAF and 1,100 JAAF sorties. During the ten *Kikusui* attacks beginning 6-7 April and ending 21-22 June, a total of 1,465 kamikazes (860 JNAF/5th Air Fleet and 605 JAAF/6th Air Army) took part. There were a total of 1,900 sorties, as additional sporadic independent suicide attacks were carried out by 140 JNAF and 45 JAAF kamikazes, and 250 more from Formosa (50 JNAF and 200 JAAF) between the *Kikusui* attacks. The kamikazes sunk 26 of 28 of the total ships sunk (the other two were sunk by conventional air attacks) and damaged 164 of the 225 total during the *Kikusui* interval. During the entire campaign, mostly due to air attacks, 36 ships were sunk and 368 damaged. Of these, 31 were later determined to be damaged beyond economical repair, and 150 required dockyard repair and were thus put out of action. A total of 4,907 Navy personnel were killed from all causes and 4,824 wounded, many due to kamikaze attacks. For the entire campaign approximately 7,800 Japanese aircraft were lost to all causes. Many of these were destroyed on the ground during Allied air attacks on their bases. Of an estimated 3,000+ Japanese aircraft lost in combat, 1,900 (1,050 JNAF and 850 JAAF) were kamikazes, for a total of 63% of all combat losses, as compared to 14% in the Philippines. American air losses from all causes were 763 aircraft. (Figures from USSBS: Campaigns of the Pacific War and USSBS #62 Japanese Air Power.)

The aerial combat success of the Death Rattlers was tied to the ten kikusui raids. Almost three quarters (74.5%) of their victories (92 3/4 of 124 1/2) were scored during these attacks. Also, their record 24 3/4 victories on 22 April were against a massed suicide attack that was not part of a planned kikusui program.

The irony of the success of VMF-323 over the kamikazes lies in this observation by Axtell: "Intelligence reports about the kamikazes were very closely held before we got to Okinawa. We had heard about them in the Philippines, but no details were released. The funny thing was that intelligence spent a lot of time telling us about all the dangerous snakes that infested Okinawa, and we never saw one snake!"

Ruhsam: "When we got into the battle over Okinawa the war was essentially over. Although when we saw the determination of the kamikazes, and then when we came ashore and saw the captured Baka rocket bombs, we wondered how many of these the Japs were going to throw at us. But we were confident and were eager to get into aerial combat. We had superior aircraft and air superiority. We soon found that the kamikazes were no threat, that they had used up their best pilots and aircraft."

JAPANESE KIKUSUI ATTACKS

Attack #	**Date**	**Number of Planes Navy**	**Army**	**Total**	**VMF-323 Victories**
1	6-7 April	230	125	355	N/A
2	12-13 April	125	60	185	6
3	15-16 April	120	45	165	10 1/2
4	27-28 April	65	50	115	14 1/2
5	3-4 May	75	50	125	25 3/4
6	10-11 May	70	80	150	10
7	23-25 May	65	100	165	8
8	27-29 May	60	50	110	2
9	3-7 June	20	30	50	16
10	21-22 June	30	15	45	0.
	Total	860	605	1465	92 3/4

CHAPTER 18
Picket Ship CAP

In order to contend with the kamikazes an early warning system of 16 radar picket ships were stationed around Okinawa to monitor the most probable air approaches to the island. Established on 26 March, the stations were located from 15 to 80 miles from Point "BOLO," which was located on the Hugushi Beachhead. Destroyers or destroyer escorts were stationed on one of 16 radar picket stations with a fighter director team on board. The picket ships were to steam 24 hours a day at 15 knots within a radius of 5,000 yards of the center of their station. These stations were dispersed so that contacts could be relayed from picket to picket without losing contact. The picket ship was to pick up incoming Japanese aircraft via continual radar and visual searches. The fighter director was to vector nearby CAP, usually consisting of two divisions, to the intercept. Many enemy aircraft were thus destroyed before they reached the island, and the island was given timely air raid warning. The majority of the destroyers were of the Fletcher class, lightly armed with five Bofors and seven single 20 mm, and that was not enough fire power. By 14 April, the picket ships became the specific targets of the kamikazes, and Gen. Wallace ordered that continuous two-plane CAP be maintained over the most vulnerable stations (those to the northwest of Okinawa-editor). Each flight leader was to report directly to the picket captain he was protecting. The picket would control the flight in order to keep it out of the ship's AA range. After the landing beaches were secured, one or two AA armed LCIs (Landing Craft Infantry), LSMs (Landing Ship Medium), and minesweepers were released to give additional AA support to each picket destroyer. Standing orders were that any aircraft approaching within 12,000 yards was to be fired on. CAP pilots had to take care in their patrol perimeter and in their pursuit of Japanese aircraft attacking a picket. By 10 April, the more exposed stations were reinforced with an additional destroyer and four LCIs. On 16 May, the land-based radar stations on Ie Shima and Hedo Saki became operational, and the number of picket stations was reduced to five. By July the kamikaze threat subsided to nil, and only two pickets remained on station covering the approaches to Kerama Retto. The last destroyer to be sunk was the CALLAGHAN, which went down with 47 crew. Ironically, this last gasp suicide attack was carried out by an ancient fabric and wooden floatplane. In all, thirteen destroyers were sunk and 88 damaged by kamikazes.

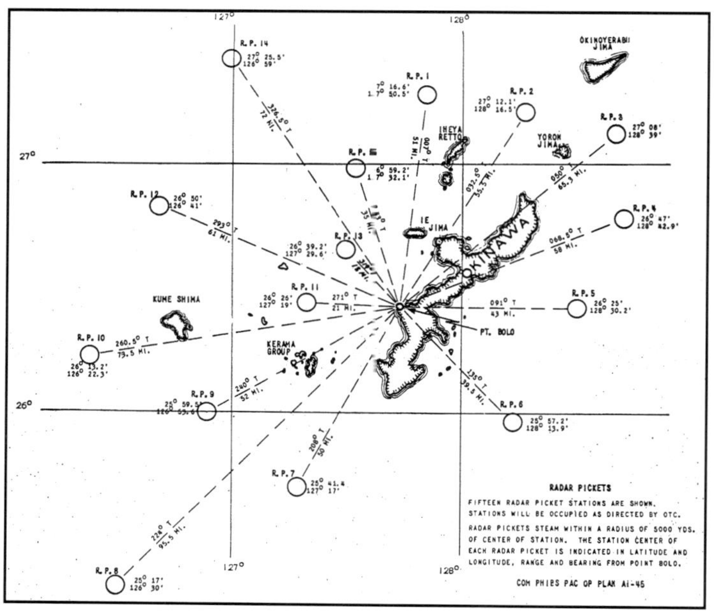

Secret wartime COM PHIBS PAC OP radar picket station location map. The 15 stations were located from Point Bolo in range in miles and bearing. ***Courtesy of the US Navy.***

The Fletcher-class destroyers which served as radar pickets off Okinawa suffered heavily from the onslaught of the kamikazes as they patrolled the defense perimeter. Pictured is the HAZELWOOD whose bridge was crashed on 28 April, with the loss of her captain and 45 men. The destroyer standing by is the CALHOUN. ***Courtesy of the US Navy.***

CHAPTER 19
Close Air Support
TAF Background

Because Yontan and Kadena were undefended and captured early, the Tenth Army TAF initiated land-based operations earlier than planned. On 2 April, Gen. Mulcahy and his staff set up their CP midway between the two airfields. Mulcahy was the land-based agent for CASCU (Commander, Air Support Control Unit), which operated on Adm. Kelly Turner's flagship offshore. The headquarters of Gen. Fred C. Wallace, the ADC (Air Defense Commander), was set up close by. Land-based aircraft, radar air warning and control units and anti-aircraft artillery units were under ADC control. It was the ADC responsibility to coordinate these three individual elements with the overall air defense network of the invasion. ICEBERG plans proscribed that TAF would undertake air defense of Okinawa once the amphibious landing phase was concluded. Because the kamikaze campaign was being successfully directed against the naval units, the Navy continued to control air operations over the Ryukyus until the island was declared secured. Gen. Wallace held that ADC efforts were to be conducted against the kamikazes. From day-1, Mag-31 (under Col. John Munn) and-33 (under Col. Ward Dickey) directed CAPs from Yontan and Kadena to that end.

MARINE CLOSE AIR SUPPORT ON OKINAWA

Since their pioneering dive bombing feats in "protection of American property" action in the Nicaraguan civil war of 1927, Marine Corps aviation prided itself on its close ground support abilities. For two decades Marine air doctrine and training had stressed close air support, and the success of their air operations in the Solomons and Philippines confirmed this proficiency. Col. Vernon McGee, commander of the Landing Force Air Support Units, stated, "Okinawa was the culmination of the development of air support doctrine in the Pacific."

Because Japanese airpower was considered the primary threat to the invasion, the maintenance of air superiority was the objective of the Marine flyers once they took over at the newly captured Yontan and Kadena airfields. This air superiority responsibility would remain their obligation for much of the campaign. The need to protect the fleet and invasion beaches from air attack caused ground commanders to worry that air support would languish. However, Navy (joined by some Marine) squadrons from the carriers were assigned to air support, eventually performing 60% of those missions that became more necessary as Japanese resistance stiffened. It seemed odd for Navy aircraft, returning to their carriers after a close support mission, to pass outbound Marine flyers, the experts in close support, on their way to CAP duties.

Because of the large number of aircraft involved and the scale and complexity of the land battle, the chain of command controlling tactical air was more elaborate and centralized than previously seen in the Pacific theater. Initially, all air operations were controlled by a naval support control element on board the HQ ship, ELDORADO. It delegated the direction of aircraft in support of the two corps of ground troops fighting on the island to two auxiliary control units aboard other ships. Carrier fighters, mostly Navy and some Marine, had flown all the support missions (which were relatively few, as initial Japanese resistance was much less than anticipated) for the first eight days after L-Day until the Marine's Corsairs were able to occupy Yontan and Kadena airfields. With the arrival of the Marines, all troop support control on Okinawa became a Marine-directed function as the Tactical Air Force (TAF), TF 99.2. It was commanded by Major General Francis P. Mulcahy,

USMC Major General Francis P. Mulcahy was the commander of the 10th Army's Tactical Air Force and the land-based agent for CASCU (Commander Air Support Control Units). ***Courtesy of the USMC.***

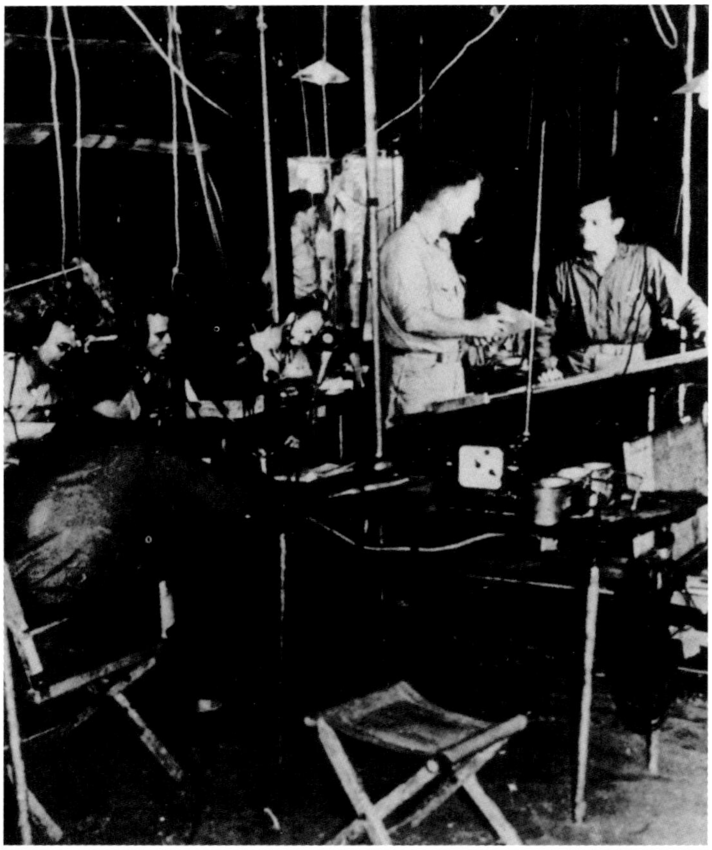

The command center of LFASCU-3 (Landing Force Air Support Control Units). The unit was commanded by Co. Vernon Magee at 10th Army HQ and coordinated he recommendations for close air support by LFASCU-1 and -2. ***Courtesy of the USMC.***

CASCU (Commander Air Support Control Units) who, because of poor health, was later relieved on 11 June by Major General Louis E. Woods.

Two shore-based landing force air support control units, LFASCU, were assigned to 3rd Corps (LFASCU-1 under Col. Kenneth H. Weir) and 24th Corps (LFASCU-2 under Col. Kenneth D. Darby). The requests for air support from these two control units were screened by LFASCU-3 under Col. Vernon E. Magee at 10th Army HQ and were in liaison with tactical air components. A LFASCU was situated near Corps headquarters and was connected directly by land wire to front-line troops and to the Corps information center, which kept it in constant communication with artillery and naval gunfire. An examination of TAF and carrier unit commitments and support priorities were analyzed, and the mission was approved or not. If Marine aircraft were involved, LFASCU-3 ordered the mission directly to TAF operations center. In any case, the artillery officer at Corps or 10th Army HQ had the final word on questions concerning air, ground and artillery/Naval gun coordination.

On a more first hand basis Air Liaison Parties (ALPs) under the Joint Assault Signal Companies of each ground unit provided front-line control of ground support missions. The requests from ground units for air support were reviewed for need (e.g. could other supporting arms, such as artillery, fulfill the request?). The request was then passed on to the LFASCU at Corps HQ. If the request were approved there, the LFASCU would order the number and type of aircraft and the type of armament required for the mission. An air coordinator or airborne traffic controller in a "Grasshopper" light observation plane would site the target for mission aircraft. He directed them to the target, then observed the results and directed other runs on the target if they were needed. ALP would direct (not control, as the front line was too narrow, e.g. the Japanese and American troops were too close to each other) the missions if this airborne director's visibility were impaired or not in the air. These frail VMO (observation) planes flew 1,388 sorties of this type. They would fly past cave openings at the same level so they could look directly at and see if a Jap gun was located inside.

This ground support control system was a necessarily complicated procedure to prevent repetition of fire and general confusion. If individual ground units had been allowed to make requests for support it would have been difficult to effectively coordinate the simultaneous air strikes of a large number of aircraft of the three different services along the very compressed front. The major fault of this system was the delay between the request for and the execution of the mission, but as the days went by the delay time decreased and the efficiency increased. LFASCUs handled a total of 10,506 close support sorties, 3,287 by LFASCU-1 and 7,219 for LFASCU-2. Magee's shipboard ASCUs controlled another 6,809 sorties.

In the opening stages of the operation there was little need for troops to call for close support, as they met surprisingly little resistance. As the 6th Marine Division moved north toward the Motobu Peninsula, Japanese opposition became more determined. Japanese troop concentrations, artillery emplacements and observation posts were dealt with by air strikes. To the south, Okinawa's defenses—caves, ridges, and ravines—all fortified by ingeniously camouflaged blockhouses and pillboxes connected by underground tunnels provided abundant close support targets. The XXIV Corps offensive

An ALP (Air Liaison Party) briefs a TBF squadron. The ALP units provided direct front line control of direct air support after consultation with a LFASCU. ***Courtesy of the USMC.***

Union Air Terminal, A captured Japanese bunker, used by combined officers of TAG, ACT, NATS, and TC. This was the Okinawa center for the greatest air transport system in the world at the time. ***Courtesy of USMC via Steve Stuczynski.***

to the south met a solid wall of Japanese fortifications. Artillery and naval shelling were often ineffectual in penetrating these defenses, and air support was called to deal with them. A total of 817 sorties (for an average of twelve per day of combat) were flown in the XXIV Corps support. As many as 43 missions were flown in one day, with 139 aircraft dropping 1,000 and 2,000 lb. bombs on the Shuri Line on 19 April. Much of the fighting in the south by Marine units was at such close quarters that air strikes were not practicable without the danger of hitting friendly troops.

The ground support aircraft met several problems during the campaign. Rain and low ceilings, especially between 19 May and 5 June, reduced operations. Often flights that were able to take off found the target area so socked in that the pilots had to attack secondary targets or drop their bombs at random on Jap territory. There were problems with mediocre maps that made pinpointing targets difficult and dangerous to friendly troops that were often pinned down close to the attack. There were ten drops on friendly troops causing 16 deaths and approximately 50 wounded, which considering the total 17,404 sorties flown is not unreasonable. Japanese antiaircraft, though often skillfully mustered, was not numerous and caused little damage. Only 91 American aircraft were shot down by AA, as opposed to 602 Japanese by American gunners.

By the end of June, at which time Japanese resistance on Okinawa had ceased, the TAF commanded by Maj. Gen. Louis E. Woods had over 750 aircraft. Included were one Marine Air Wing, an AAF fighter wing, and an AAF bomber wing with one light, one medium and two heavy bomber groups. On 14 July, the TAF was disbanded, as by that time Okinawa-based air operations were bomber missions.

The results of the close support missions on the enemy can not be accurately assessed. During the battle, 562 Marine tactical missions were flown (of 1,904 total), some with as many as 75 aircraft. They dropped a total of 1,805 tons of bombs (of 7,144 total tons) and 683 napalm tanks (of 1,573 total), and fired 15,865 rockets (of 49,641 total). [from Evaluation of USMC Operations in WW-2 (revised 31 Dec. 1945)]

George Axtell: "Too much emphasis was placed on air-to-air combat and its role. It was necessary for us initially to gain air superiority to protect the fleet. The greatest satisfaction that I received was from the delivering of close air support day in and day out to our infantry. I got a hell of a lot of personal satisfaction to hear from a ground controller what an accurate and effective job we had done after a mission." Axtell would make his wingmen nervous with his habit of personally surveying from low level the damage inflicted by a close air support mission. At 800-1,000ft, they were particularly vulnerable to gunfire.

The Marine meteorological station on Okinawa. In this posed photograph one of the weathermen is seen climbing the anemometer mast while the other has just released a weather balloon. Okinawa's subtropical foliage can be seen in the foreground. ***Courtesy of the USMC via Steve Stuczynski.***

A beautiful photo of Death Rattler Corsairs returning from a close air support mission. Note that a rocket on aircraft #43 is hung up on the launching rail, not am uncommon occurrence. Since -323 was assigned to CAP and picket patrol, close support was a secondary role. ***Courtesy of USMC via Steve Stuczynski.***

Axtell continues: "I flew hundreds of hours, many on instrument conditions, on CAP or over Radar Picket Ships holding at altitude awaiting an assignment to intercept. The opportunity to engage the enemy in combat was a crap roll—it happened to me I only three times."

Al Wells: "About a quarter of our sorties were ground support. I actually enjoyed them because on CAP or over the picket ships nothing happened. You would fly around for three, four, five hours and go home bored to death."

Troop confidence in air support can be measured in that only about half of the close support missions they requested could be provided. The Marine Corsairs earned the nickname, "Sweethearts of Okinawa."

Spectacular, if staged, PR photo of F4Us in a close air-ground support demonstration. ***Courtesy of USMC via Steve Stuczynski.***

TACTICAL AIR FORCE (TAF)
TG 99.2
M.Gen. F.F. Mulcahy USMC
AIR DEFENSE COMMAND
TU 99.2.1
B.Gen. W.W. Wallace USMC

MAG-31
Col.J.C. Munn
7 April
VMF-224 Maj.J.M. Poindexter
VMF-311 Maj.P.L. Shuman
VMF-441 Maj.R.O. White
VMF(N)-542 Maj.W.C. Kellum
Hedron 31
Servron 31

MAG-22
Col.D.W. Torrey
21 May
VMF-113 Maj.H. Williams
VMF-314 Maj.R.E. Cameron
VMF(N)-533 Maj.M.M. McGruder
Hedron 22
Servron 22

MAG-33.
Col.W.E. Dickey.
9 April.
VMF-312 Maj.R.M. Day*
VMF-322 Maj.F.M. Rauschenbach
VMF-323 Maj.G.C. Axtell
VMF(N)-543 Maj.C.C.Chamberlain
Hedron 33
Servron 33

MAG-14.
Col.E.A. Montgomery.
8 June.
VMF-212 Maj. J.P. McMahon
VMF-222 Maj.H.A. Harwood

Hedron 14
Servron 14

301st FIGHTER WING
(USAAF)
Col. T.S. Olds

318 FIGHTER GROUP
Col. L.M. Sanders
13 May
19 FS
73 FS
333 FS
548 FS (N)
364 ASG

413 FIGHTER GROUP
Col. H.R. Thyng
20 June
1 FS
21 FS
34 FS

507 FIGHTER GROUP
Col. L.F. Stetson
30 June.
463 FS
464 FS
465 FS

Dates are time of arrival on Okinawa
Names are CO at time of arrival on Okinawa

*KIA

CHAPTER 20

The Weapon

F4U-1D/FG-1D Described

During WWII a total of 11,425 Corsairs were manufactured by three companies, Vought F4U-(6674 aircraft), Goodyear FG-(4017), and Brewster F3A-(735). All Corsair variants were characterized by their gull or bent wing, which when viewed from the front inclines from the circular fuselage to meet the landing gear on each side. The other predominate feature was the long radial engine cowling capped on one end by a large propeller, and a cockpit located well aft on the fuselage. The cockpit location had the pilot sitting behind the trailing edge of the wing.

The empty weight was 8,971 lbs., with the pure fighter version weighing 11,962 lbs. and the fighter-bomber version weighing in excess of 14,000 lbs.

During World War II, Corsair pilots achieved an 11 to 1 kill ratio, 2,140 enemy to 189 Corsairs lost. In the ground support role it excelled to such an extent that by mid-1944, the Navy recommended that F6F combat squadrons leaving combat to re-equip exchange their Hellcats for Corsairs.

Plane Captain Donald Hitchings was with -323 from its formation. "The Corsair we had on Okinawa was an entirely different airplane from the one we had in North Carolina. There were well over 100 major changes. They made factory changes in the landing gear, the tail wheel, and the oil cooler. The early F4Us had the 'Bird Cage' canopy, which gave way to the bubble. We made changes in the field once we got overseas."

Engine

The engine was a R-2800-8W Pratt & Whitney Double Wasp two row radial boasting 2,130 hp and 2,700 rpm.

The starter was originally the cartridge system in which cartridge gases drove a piston in the cylinder that turned the gear train that drove the engine. In later -1D models an electric inertial starter was used.

The huge propeller was a hydraulic three blade 13 ft. 4 in. aluminum Hamilton Standard Hydromatic. It was the world's largest at that time, and to provide the ground clearance and to have a normal sized landing gear the gull wing configuration was developed. The propeller control in the cockpit was part of the engine control on the left side.

The engine was air cooled, with the air entering the cowl annulus. The air passed over cylinder ribs, was directed around baffles and exited the rear of the cowling through a sequence of encircling cowl flap partitions. Some of the early Corsairs at Pollacksville had hydraulic cowl flaps that leaked oil badly. When the pilot finally was in level flight after the blind Corsair takeoff and he could finally see something out to the front windshield, he found it was spattered with oil.

The engine water injection system, patented by Pratt & Whitney before the war, gave WAR EMERGENCY or COMBAT power for a maximum of five minutes, which was a lifetime in combat. A

The classic Corsair long "Hog" nose, huge 13 foot 4 inch Hamilton-Standard propeller, and gull wing configuration are evident on this F4U-1D on exhibit at the National Museum of Naval Aviation at Pensacola. The aircraft is painted in the markings of Greg "Pappy" Boyington of VMF-214, the "Black Sheep". ***Author's collection.***

A view of the components of the famous F4U gull wing assembly. ***Author's collection.***

The frameless, raised bubble canopy replaced the early "bird cage" version which had heavily framed window sections and was cramped in height. The bubble, along with an adjustable seat and raised tail wheel, increased the Corsair's field of vision from atrocious to poor! *Author's collection.*

The early birdcage canopy consisted of ten pieces, separated by partitions which gave the canopy its name. *Author's collection.*

tank and pump system cooled the cylinders with a water-alcohol mixture that was injected into the engine cylinders. It mixed with the fuel-air mixture in the main stage supercharger area and resulted in 20% higher power and increased speed for a short period of time. Also, when the pilot pushed the throttle past a certain gate, the fuel mixture would be leaned out and permitted the engine to operate at a higher manifold pressure. The water injection button was protected with safety wire and needed to be pushed to engage.

The internal fuselage fuel tank was set in tandem with the cockpit, which kept the Corsair fuselage rather slender when compared to other P&W Double Wasp fighters, the P-47 Thunderbolt and F6F Hellcat. It carried 237 gal. and was placed just behind the firewall directly over the wing. The fuel tank and its fuel lines were self-sealing. There were two underwing center section pylons for drop tank attachment. The U.S. Navy 154 gal. or the Lockheed 165 gal. drop tanks could be hung on these attachments.

PC Don Hitchings, "The Pratt & Whitney was tight to work on because of its close fitting cowling. We used all kinds of methods to get at some of the bolts. This was before magnetic tools, so we would put chewing gum on the end of a socket wrench so we wouldn't drop the nut. I often wished I had another joint in my arm. I insisted that my crew be sure everything was 100% right before it went into the air, no ifs, ands or buts whatsoever. Some of the replacement parts we got didn't fit too well. I remember at

The tail wheel was hydraulically retracted into the fuselage while the arresting gear fit onto an external fastener. The arresting gear was raised and lowered by a separate hydraulic actuator in the cockpit. Late model Corsairs had raised tail wheels for better visibility. *Author's collection.*

On Okinawa engine overhaul was done at Yonton. The large Pratt & Whitney R-2800 Double Wasp was supported by a makeshift sand bag and wooden workstand. It had as 18 cylinder two row, air-cooled radial engine producing 2000 HP. *Courtesy of Steve Stuczynski via USMC.*

The plane crews serviced their Corsairs in the open, come rain or shine. *Courtesy of the USMC.*

A 55 gallon drum serves as a sophisticated workstand for this -323 plane crew. *Courtesy of John Ruhsam.*

Pollacksville I had to put three different wings on a Corsair before I found one that fit. Cowlings were another problem."

COCKPIT

The cockpit was entered from the starboard side via steps, hand grips and a walkway. The canopy was operated externally by a push button on the upper forward end of the sliding section. Internally the canopy was operated by a pull handle. It has been said, because Vought F4U project test pilot, Boone Guyton, was six foot four inches, the Corsair cockpit was spacious.

Al Wells describes the cockpit: "The Corsair cockpit was large, but in the vertical dimension rather than in width. Someone suggested that a pilot could take evasive action from enemy fire by releasing his seat belts and dodging around the large cockpit. While being comfortable for the large pilot, smaller pilots like me were at a disadvantage. The bucket seat could be adjusted vertically nine

Air for the oil cooler entered through the inter cooler airscoop that was located in the leading edge of the wing, passed through the coolers and exited through the underwing flaps. *Author's collection.*

Plane Captain, T/Sgt. Don Hitchings, found the "Pratt & Whitney difficult to work on due to its tight fitting cowling. I wish I had another joint in my elbow." *Courtesy of Don Hitchings.*

Main Instrument Panel: The forward panel had the Corsair flight instruments arranged on the left and the engine instruments on the right. ***Author's collection.***

inches, one inch at a time. But if the seat were raised or seat cushions added so the shorter pilot could see then his feet would barely touch the rudder pedals. This left him in a near standing position, which was uncomfortable for long periods of time. Usually in a fighter you sat and the pedals were in front of you. In the Corsair your feet actually hung down, which was awkward because your shins instead of being horizontal were vertical, and to get the brake you had to raise your toe. You could get some adjustment (six inches-ed.) on the rudder pedal and some tilt on the brake. Also, it was a reach to employ full forward stick." The Corsair had no actual cockpit floor, only seat rails and the pedal troughs. Looking down the pilot could see into the interior of the fuselage. This open space allowed the pilot to dangle his feet and stretch his legs. However, it was a catch-all, and doing negative G's could cause a cloud of dust, and in a roll one would find out what a mechanic had left behind. A seat belt and shoulder harness were provided, as was a relief tube.

Wells: "At El Toro, I had become good buddies with Charlie Spangler, and he encouraged me to go into fighters. He introduced me to Col. 'Sad Sam' Moore, who had made a name for himself at Guadalcanal. Moore said that I wasn't tall enough to be a fighter pilot. He got up from his desk and came along beside me. I pulled myself up as tall as possible, and he saw I was as tall as he and Spangler, and that's how I got into fighters."

INSTRUMENT AND CONTROL SYSTEMS

The instrument layout consisted of flight instruments and engine instruments.

The flight instruments included:
airspeed indicator directional gyro clock
altimeter gyro horizon compass
climb indicator turn & bank indicator
The engine indicators included:
cylinder temperature indicator fuel pressure gauge tachometer fuel quantity gauge
oil pressure gauge manifold pressure indicator
oil temperature indicator RPM indicator

The principal surface controls consisted of runs to the ailerons, elevators and rudders that were all moved manually by the pilot. Elevator and aileron control runs from the pilot's stick were of the push rod type, while the rudder control run was a continuous cable running over pulleys from the cockpit pedals to the rudder horn.

A heavy bungee spring was connected to the elevator controls and tail wheel door mechanism. This lessened stick forces during landing and came into action when the landing gear was dropped.

The trim tabs were provided on the port wing aileron, on the elevators, and rudder, and were controlled by hand wheels on the port side of the cockpit. Balance tabs on the ailerons and elevators were connected directly to the control surfaces and required no control by the pilot.

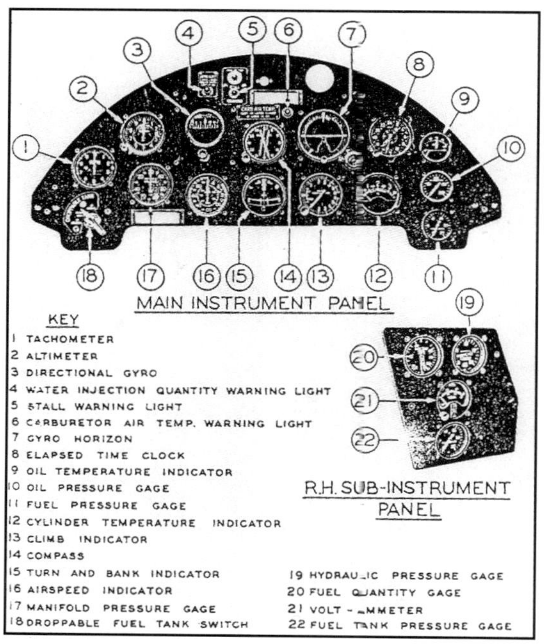

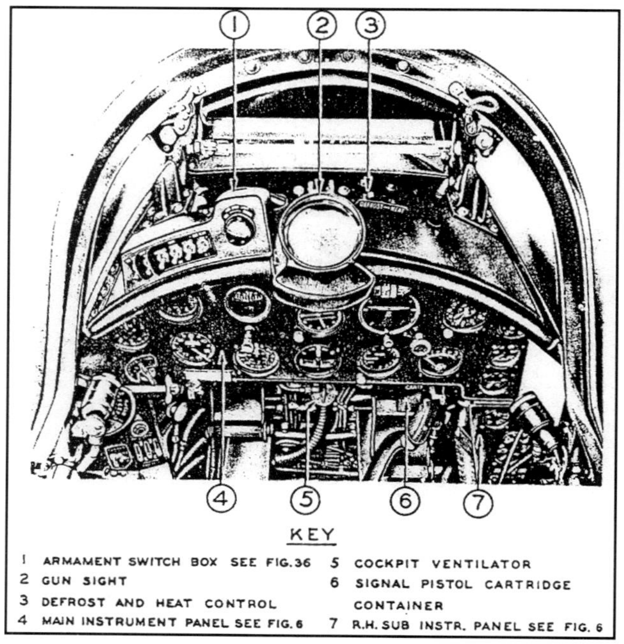

Diagram of the Main Instrument Panel. Author's collection/ ***F4U Pilot's Handbook.***

LEFT COCKPIT. Note the engine throttle above, the curved stick, and pedestal-mounted rudders. The floor of the Corsair was open to the fuselage and could collect a variety of flotsam which would become evident in a roll and in negative G maneuvers. *Author's collection/F4U Pilot's Handbook.*

RIGHT COCKPIT. The Corsair was large and comfortable and had an adjustable seat. The right cockpit contained circuit breakers and electrical switches. *Author's collection/F4U Pilot's Handbook.*

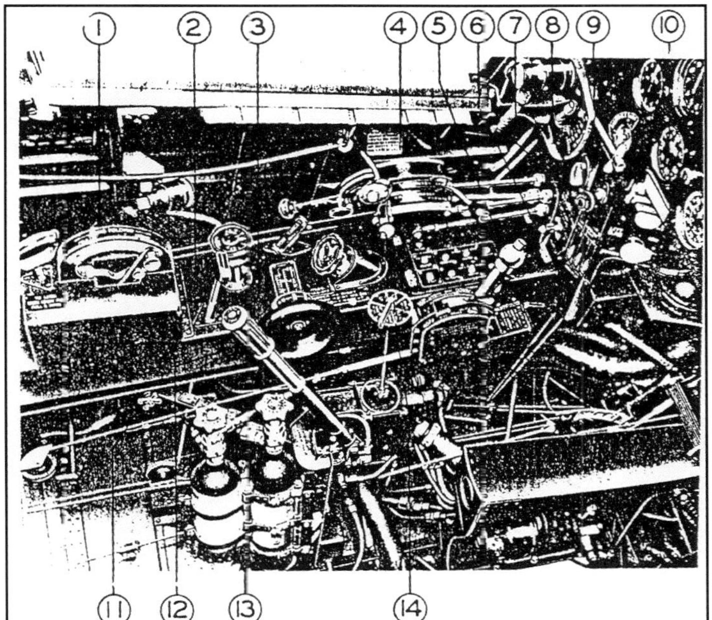

Radio and Identification Systems

The radio equipment included AN/ARR-2 and AN/ARC-5 sets and were mounted on a shelf in the fuselage behind the cockpit. Recognition equipment included AN/APX-1 or ABA sets. The controls were located on the starboard side of the cockpit. Al Wells: "The sets were HF, not the VHF like today, but for the time it wasn't too bad. Compared to today it was awful. It wasn't unusual for someone in a division not to be receiving."

Armor Protection

A large piece of armor weighing 53 lbs. was placed directly behind the pilot for posterior protection. A curved 25 lb. hardened aluminum plate placed forward of the cockpit above the fuel tank acted as a deflection plate. Of course, the huge P&W engine afforded the pilot ample protection from head-on attacks. A removable quarter inch steel plate could be placed under the pilot's seat. A piece of optical bullet-resistant glass was placed behind the curved outer windshield glass.

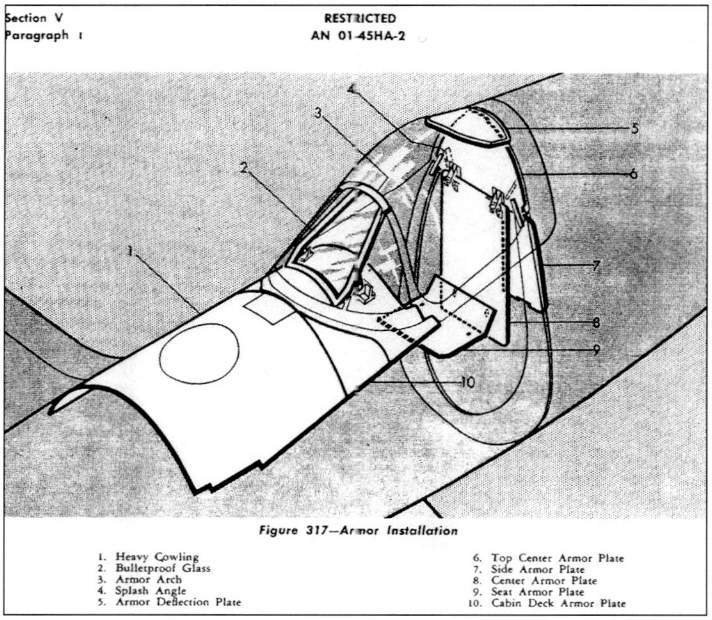

ARMOR PROTECTION ***F4U Pilot's Handbook.***

Heating and Cooling

A cockpit combustion heater provided heat for the cockpit and for defrosting the windshield. A butterfly vent located just below the bulletproof glass controlled the flow onto the windshield and cockpit.

Fresh air entered through a foot operated butterfly vent located forward and between the foot troughs.

Oxygen System

The oxygen system was of the diluter demand type. The oxygen bottle was located at the right side of the pilot's seat. This positioning was considered by pilots to be dangerous in case of a hit. The diluter demand regulator was located just forward of the bottle and connected to the mask.

Machine Guns

Standard armament consisted of six Colt Browning M-2 .50 caliber machine guns firing 2,350 rounds in about 30 seconds. Two guns could be turned off. The guns were charged hydraulically by pushing two gun charging knobs located to the left just below the instrument panel. The upper knob controlled the three starboard guns, and the bottom knob the three port guns. The hydraulic chargers allowed the pilot to quickly and readily charge the guns and focus on flying the fighter. The trigger controls were electric and located on the stick.

The guns were boresighted to converge and impact a six foot target at 1,000 feet, "the harmonization point of the guns."

Gunsight

An illuminated MK 8 two ring reflector gunsight was located on a padded mount above the instrument panel. It was a simple arrangement of a single electric light bulb inside a small housing, a reticle, a lens and reflector plate. The sight was used by looking at the target through a glass plate. On the plate a light bulb projected a center dot called a "pipper," and two surrounding rings that showed the pilot where to aim. The pipper showed exactly where the guns were pointed, and the outer rings determined the deflection. The gunsight required the calculation of an accurate deflection angle that was difficult in the swirl of combat. With repetition and experience the pilot was able to compute automatically the position of the pipper under that particular combat circumstance. There was a spare bulb fastened to the sight that could be changed in flight.

Gun Camera

Type N-6 or AN-N6 gun cameras were electrically operated 16 mm motion picture cameras activated by the trigger control switch. They were mounted inside the leading edge of the starboard outer wing panel behind a curved laminated glass faired into the wing. The camera was focused on the convergence point by a boresight adapter. A small, self-contained heater warmed the camera bay.

MAINTENANCE

Unlike the fighter squadrons of today, VMF-323 was manned and outfitted to operate independently. Organic to the squadron was a motor transport section, medical section with a flight surgeon and corpsmen, and a mess hall unit with cooks and bakers. There was a large aircraft maintenance section that was able to perform all aspects of mechanical undertaking, along with an ordnance unit.

Pilots of VMF-323 were assigned an aircraft, but it often was flown by others, especially since the squadron often had more pilots than aircraft. Assigned to each aircraft was a Chief Plane Captain, two ordnance personnel, and two assistant plane captains. Del Davis: "This may seem to be overkill in numbers, but it really paid off under combat conditions. These people were highly trained and available, so we used them to our advantage."

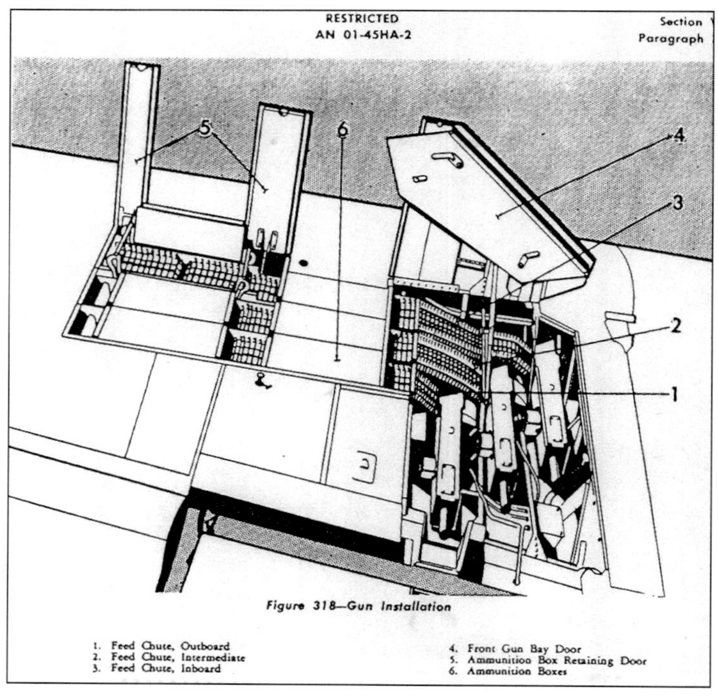

GUN INSTALLATION ***F4U Pilot's Handbook.***

The F4U-1D packed six M-2 .50 caliber machine guns firing 2375 rounds. Here armorers service the guns and ammo boxes. ***Courtesy of the USMC.***

Del Davis: "For some reason good metal wax was not available to us in the forward area. We called upon our wives and friends in the States to send us automobile wax. We waxed the aircraft from top to bottom. We believed it gave us a few extra knots, and the aircraft were certainly beautiful to behold."

Some crews even provided their aircraft's pilot a pair of in-cockpit shoes. The pilot would sit up on the wing before entering the cockpit and the crew would remove his always muddy boots and put on the cockpit pair. The cockpit needed to be as clean as possible so that during negative "G" forces nothing was floating around the cockpit.

The camaraderie between the plane captains and pilots is illustrated by this story related by Glen Thacker:

"I was scheduled to fly a strike mission, and my Corsair was loaded down with bombs and rockets. As I was moving down the runway, nearly reaching takeoff speed, my engine started to misfire. I aborted the takeoff and taxied back to the end of the runway to try again. I went over the complete cockpit check list and thought everything was all right I attempted another takeoff, but two-thirds of the way down the runway the engine misfired again. This time I

Armorer, S/Sgt. Ed Coogan, servicing the port wing .50s. ***Courtesy of Mel Lee.***

T/Sgt.Paul Pentheny working on the compact P & W engine which had many inaccessible areas. Plane captains possessed chronically skinned knuckles. ***Courtesy of Harley Brock.***

A F4U double ace. Plane Captain, S/Sgt. Charles Chessman, servicing a Corsair with ten victory flags. The three top -323 aces had seven victories each but different pilots flew the same fighter and scored victories. *Courtesy of Harley Brock.*

took the plane back to the flight line and parked it. I didn't know what was wrong.

The next day when I went to the flight line the plane captain of that aircraft took me to one side, away from the others, and told me that there was nothing wrong with the plane. He told me that I was trying to take off with the wrong fuel setting. It was supposed to be set on reserve, and I had set it for main tank. He didn't tell anyone about my mistake, and stuck his neck out by letting it go as a 'mechanical.'"

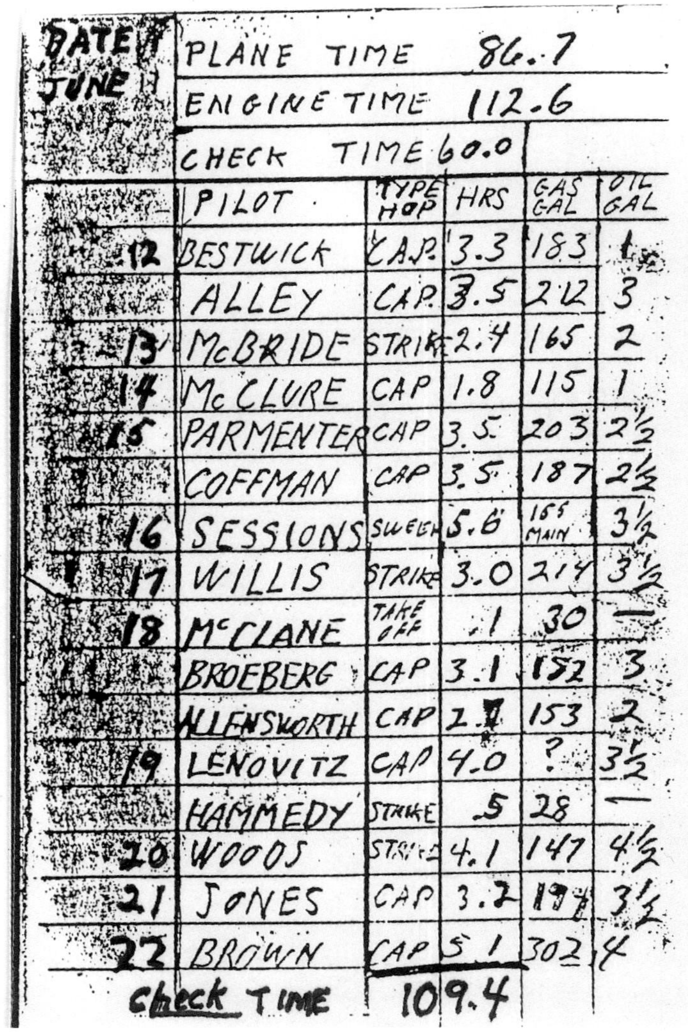

DATE JUNE 11	PLANE TIME 86.7				
	ENGINE TIME 112.6				
	CHECK TIME 60.0				
	PILOT	TYPE HOP	HRS	GAS GAL	OIL GAL
12	BESTWICK	CAP	3.3	183	1
	ALLEY	CAP	3.5	212	3
13	McBRIDE	STRIKE	2.4	165	2
14	McCLURE	CAP	1.8	115	1
15	PARMENTER	CAP	3.5	203	2½
	COFFMAN	CAP	3.5	187	2½
16	SESSIONS	SWEEP	5.6	155 MAIN	3½
17	WILLIS	STRIKE	3.0	214	3½
18	McCLANE	TAKE OFF	.1	30	—
	BROEBERG	CAP	3.1	152	3
	ALLENSWORTH	CAP	[illegible]	153	2
19	LENOVITZ	CAP	4.0	?	3½
	HAMMEDY	STRIKE	.5	28	—
20	WOODS	STRIKE	4.1	147	4½
21	JONES	CAP	3.2	[illegible]	3½
22	BROWN	CAP	5.1	302	4
	CHECK TIME		109.4		

Plane Captain, Paul Caron's log book for F4U #37 for the 12th-24th, June 1945. It logs pilot name, type of hop, flight time, gallons of gasoline and oil used. The log shows that 16 different pilots flew the fighter. *Courtesy of Paul Caron via Frank Maggliocco.*

Maintenance was done outside in any weather. In the early days at Kadena the mechs had to contend with the everyday rains, Japanese artillery, and the threat of Jap infiltrators and snipers. They often had to do double duty, helping to fuel the returning aircraft in the day and then servicing at night. *Courtesy of Henry Brandon.*

Charlie Spangler (L) and Keith Fountain wax a Corsair to add a few extra knots of speed. Metal wax was unavailable so the pilots wrote home for car wax. *Courtesy of Keith Fountain.*

CHAPTER 21
Flying the F4U-1D Corsair

Flight Clothing
Mae West, oxygen mask, side arm, dye marker, shark repellent, fishing kit, hand flares, signaling mirror, life raft, maps and current charts and parachute.

Starting the Engine
Early cartridge starters were nothing but trouble, and every start was an adventure. When the pilot was ready the PC inserted the shell into the breech of the starter, grabbed the CO_2 fire extinguisher, and stood by the right wing with thumbs up. The PC always knew if the CO_2 bottle were full by its weight. Sometimes the engine started and sometimes it didn't. If it didn't, there would be a flood of gasoline from the engine onto the tarmac. If there was a backfire the fuel would ignite in a whoosh of flames 20 feet high. The pilot would evacuate while the PC rushed in to put out the flames.

A well dressed Del Davis enters the cockpit of his F4U. Davis is outfitted in a Mae West, parachute, oxygen mask, side arm, survival kit, maps, and current charts. ***Courtesy of Del Davis.***

Al Wells continues, "Actually, the starting procedure was somewhat complicated. The large prop had to be turned over by hand four or five times, the fuel booster pump switched on, the priming switch clicked several times, the ignition switch activated, and the cartridge fired. We could shoot as many as three or four of them before we were able to start the engine. Tilly Ferndenzi, our Intelligence Officer, came over to give us a hard time, 'You guys are supposed to be the best pilots in the world and can't even start your engines.' We told him he didn't realize how complicated the starting procedure really was. He got into the cockpit and fired the cartridge, and damn if all the Pratt & Whitney's 2,000 horses didn't turn over and roar to a start. He never let us forget about this. Later, electric starters made things easier."

Warren Bestwick: "The Pratt & Whitney was a powerful engine. Very few aircraft could have flown the loads out of the Okinawan mud like we did."

Takeoff Checklist

F4U CORSAIR CHECKLIST
TAKEOFF

Wings Spread and locked
Fuel Tank Selector RESERVE
Mixture AUTOMATIC RICH
Supercharger Control NEUTRAL
Propeller Control Maximum RPM (down)
Cowl Flaps 2/3 open
Intercooler Flap Closed
Oil Cooler Flap Open as required
Rudder Tab 6 degrees RIGHT
Aileron Tab 6 degrees RIGHT Wing DOWN
Elevator Tab 1 Degree nose UP
Alternate Air Control Direct (in)
Wing Flaps Set as required
Tail Wheel LOCKED
Manifold pressure Limit 53.5" Hg.

Ground Handling
The long 16 foot noses over the P&W engine, the aft cockpit location, and its tail down attitude were the source of the legendary tales of the Corsair's poor visibility. Charles Lindbergh, who was a Vought factory representative during the war, once commented that the Corsair's forward visibility was no less than that of the *SPIRIT OF ST. LOUIS*, which had none! The forward visibility was improved from the early "birdcage" canopy -1 models by design changes to the bubble canopy, the adjustable seat, and a new raised

It is apparent why pilots had difficulties in taxiing the Corsair with its cockpit situated aft of the wing, exposing a 16 foot nose which pointed skyward. Note that the cowl flaps are in the open position and the wing flaps in the down position, making it easy for the pilot to use the flap step to climb onto the wing. ***Author's collection.***

Photo of a -323 F4U taking off from Kadena, The pivoting of the oleo strut can be seen as the wheel rotates to fit into the wing. ***Courtesy of Norman Miller.***

tail wheel in the -1D versions in late 1943. Nonetheless, on the ground the only forward view was upward at about 30 degrees into the sky!

Henry Brandon describes taxiing: "The easiest method of taxiing was to have a groundman wing walk you out. He would lead along under the tip of the wing where the pilot could follow his hand signals. Otherwise, it was S-turns with the tail wheel disengaged to allow it to swivel. But the disengaged tail wheel made the aircraft directionally unstable, so you had to be careful. Fortunately, the hydraulic wheel brakes were very good and could be used with low power to steer. But you had to avoid braking too hard because the aircraft could nose over. Also, you couldn't ride the brakes, which would overheat. It took a lot of practice to get it right."

Al Wells adds, "Between not being able to see and holding the bungee controlled stick back and working the brakes, you were one tired pilot before you ever got into the air."

Takeoff

Before takeoff the tail wheel was locked. The rudder tab was set to offset the torque of the large propeller, or the rudder force needed for a straight takeoff would be excessive. The aileron tab was set to prevent the left wing from pulling down as the fighter became airborne. The takeoff run for the fighter version at 12,500 lbs. was 1,250 feet, while the fighter-bomber version at 14,000 lbs. was about 1,450 feet. A slow initial throttle opening kept the F4U on a straight, fixed course down the runway until the tail came up and the rudder and ailerons became effective. This counteracted propeller torque and any cross wind.

In-Flight Characteristics

The Corsair trimmed easily for a climb, with minimal changes for gear and flap retraction and for speed and power changes. The large Hamilton Standard propeller pulled the Corsair into an impressive climb rate. In level flight the aircraft could be trimmed for hands off flying, and demonstrated positive stability in cruise and high speed modes. Aileron control allowed light stick force, allowing the Corsair to reach maximum roll even at high speed dives. The Jap Zero had poor aileron control at high speeds and thus it rolled heavily. Marine pilots used this high speed dive capability to evade, diving the aircraft and then rolling it to left or right before recovery to lose the pursuing Jap. The Corsair dove well due to its weight, high power and relative aerodynamic cleanliness. Lowering the landing gear could act as a dive brake, but plenty of altitude was needed to pull out due to trim changes and heavy elevator control. The Corsair was initially judged to have poor stall characteristics, espe-

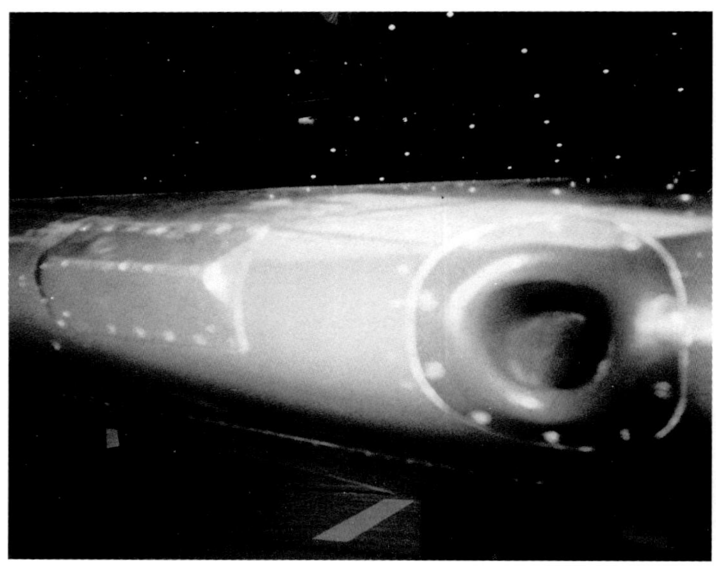

Outboard from the faired machine gun port is a leading edge spoiler. Early tests found that during power-on landings a serious left wing drop occurred which could flip the aircraft over on its back. To remedy the problem this spoiler was installed on the starboard wing (only) near the crank. ***Author's collection***

cially dropping its port wing, which could be a problem upon landing. (This was later rectified by adding a spoiler on the right wing to make the stall symmetrical-ed.)

Landing Checklist

F4U CHECK LIST
LANDING

Stall Warning Switch ON
Tail Wheel LOCKED for field landing
Fuel Tank Selector RESERVE
Mixture AUTOMATIC RICH
Supercharger Control NEUTRAL
Propeller Control 2300 RPM
Cowl Flaps CLOSED
Alternate Air Control Direct (in)
LANDING GEAR EXTENDED
Wing Flaps Set 30 degrees or as required

Early production versions suffered numerous landing difficulties, which were corrected in successive models. By 1944, most of the problems were solved. The oleo strut had been particularly troublesome, producing some wild bounces, but they were reworked and gave a remarkably smooth landing even with a high sink rate.

Al Wells describes the landing: "The landing approach was made with a close in base leg and tight turn, keeping the runway in sight and gear level until the fighter was over the end of the runway. Then plant it. The Corsair was not a ground looping aircraft, it had a soft gear because the oleo had been redesigned for carrier landings. After touchdown the pilot checked out each window and past the long nose to stay on the straight and narrow."

The pilot's notes recommended: "On landing, roll in 20 degrees right rudder trim, holding the resulting pressure with left rudder as a precaution in event of a go-around. The sudden application of power in a go-around caused immense and immediate left torque, which if not countered by the trim could flip the aircraft. Also, in case of a go-around and because the F4U dropped like a rock, the fuel mixture on final approach was set at rich and the prop pitch at flat."

Glen Thacker on the F4U: "I was just so happy to be flying that I never noticed anything bad, even the birdcage canopy model.

Glen Thacker: "The longer you flew the F4U the more it became second nature and part of you. By the time I got to Okinawa everything about the aircraft was perfect for me". ***Courtesy of Henry Brandon.***

The longer I flew the F4U, the more it became second nature and part of you. By the time I got to Okinawa everything about the aircraft was perfect for me. The plane had become very simple and so easy to fly. The controls were hydraulically assisted. The stick was like a feather. I really flew it, as fast as it could go, and pushed it to the limit and never had any trouble. The most exciting thing for me was getting in the cockpit for takeoff. Taking that smooth powerful Pratt & Whitney to flying speed and then jerking those wheels up and you were off. Some young pilots complained about all the gauges and instruments, but it was just like the gauges on an automobile dashboard. They're really just some basic ones, maybe eight or ten, but after awhile all you needed was a quick glance to tell you if everything checked out. I got so that I felt nothing was ever going to happen to it. It would always get you into the air, and then you would go and do whatever you were supposed to do and it would get you back."

CHAPTER 22
F4U Armaments and Tactics

Machine Guns

The F4U-1D packed six Browning-designed Colt M2 forward firing 50 caliber aircraft machine guns; three mounted in the inboard portion of each outer wing panel. The three guns in each wing were installed in echelon to permit the feed chutes to reach the breeches. Access for the guns and ammunition boxes were located on the upper wing surfaces. The ammo storage capacity was 400 rounds for each inboard and middle gun (two 200-round boxes each). Each outboard gun had 375 rounds (the smaller capacity 175 round box was the aft outboard box, which was shallower to fit the contour of the wing). The total of 2,375 rounds was carried in disintegrating belts in various combinations depending on squadron preference and mission requirements to utilize the effect of tracers, armor piercing, and incendiary bullets. Some Corsairs were equipped with four 20 mm cannon, two in each wing, carrying 200 rounds per gun for a total of 800 rounds. Most pilots preferred the six .50s, as they fired three times the rounds in a denser pattern in a faster rate of fire. Strafing was most effective against motor transport, troops and materiel in the open or in shallow trenches, and temporarily neutralized open mortar, artillery and AA positions. Its primary effect on enemy troops was to hold them away from their firing positions as friendly troops advanced.

Electric heating pads attached to each gun prevented low temperature jams and were activated by a cockpit switch.

On a mission, the gun ports were protected from debris by so-called "100 mph" duct tape.

There were two types of strafing attacks:

(1) Flat or small angle run (area strafing): It could be initiated at any altitude depending on the selected speed of the firing run. It derived its name from the point of opening fire that was reached at a low altitude and at a small angle to horizontal. The pilot could not keep an individual target under sustained fire for any length of time. However, a long target area, such as uncovered personnel and dispersed materiel, could be keep under fire, and resultant ricochets could cause further damage.

(2) Steep or high angle run: This firing run was made at a steep angle to the horizontal and allowed the pilot to direct extended fire at a selected target until he was forced to pull when he closed on the ground. Often, if targets were available, the steep angle run would continue as a low angle attack.

Rockets

Four Zero Length launchers were mounted on the outer wing panels. Two types of rockets were available: 3.5 and 5 inch warheads mounted on standard or high velocity bodies. HVARs, high velocity aerial rockets, were preferred because of their longer range, flatter trajectory and greater penetrating power.

Rocket attacks were standardized into three classes: class A 20 degree, class B 30 degree and class C 50 degree.

Napalm

Napalm is a powder that thickens gasoline to a gel. It was named so because it is made from the aluminum salts of **nap**hennic and **palm-**

The starboard wing of this FG-1D displays three recently fired .50 cal. Machine guns. Inboard the guns is the rectangular Plexiglas window that protected the An or An-N6 16mm gun camera. ***Author's collection.***

Each wing housed three Colt-Browning M-2 .50 caliber machine guns. Access panels for the guns and ammunition containers were situated on the upper wing surfaces. Ammunition storage capacity was 400 rounds for each inboard and middle gun and 375 rounds for each outboard gun. ***Author's collection.***

2nd MAW rocket assembly area on Okinawa. During the campaign rockets were first used extensively in the Pacific. A total of 15,691 rockets were launched by TAF in its close support role. *Courtesy of USMC via Steve Stuczynski.*

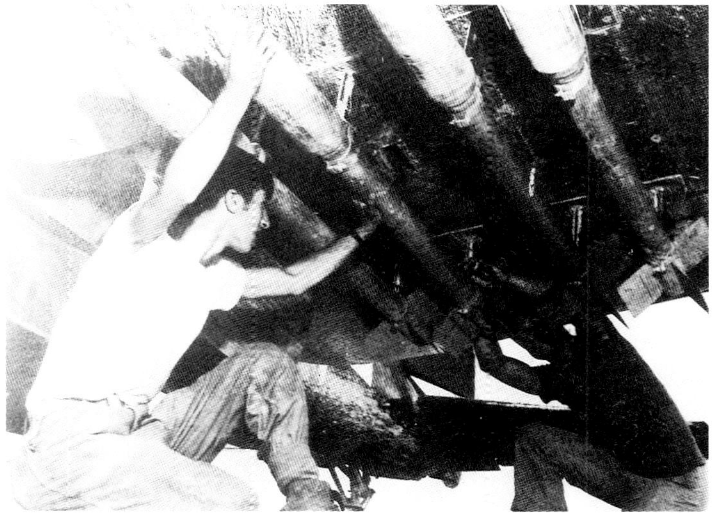

Five inch HVAR (High Velocity Aerial Rocket) being loaded on underwing zero-length launch rails. Just before takeoff, the safety pins were removed and the rockets were charged. *Courtesy USMC via Steve Stuczynski.*

itic acids. Napalm fires were difficult to extinguish, and a 150 gal. tank could burn out a 90 x 150 foot area and was difficult to extinguish. Napalm was first considered most effective in the incineration of enemy troops entrenched in pill boxes and caves. Before long it was found that this method was not particularly effective, and napalm was most useful in destroying skillfully placed Japanese camouflage prior to rocket attacks in order to expose Japanese positions. The F4U-1D was able to carry three napalm tanks: 160 gal. on the center line pylon and two 150 gal. on each wing pylon. The napalm was ignited by a white phosphorus igniter. The cowl was used as a sighting device.

Another spectacular Hollywood-type PR still of a Marine platoon equipped with a flame thrower, bazooka, and riflemen being assisted by the close support of a division of Corsairs. *Courtesy of USMC via Steve Stuczynski.*

It was estimated that a salvo of all eight rockets could equal the destructive power of a broadside from a naval destroyer. *Courtesy of the USMC.*

Usually only one napalm tank was loaded as a mixed load of bombs or rockets were carried. Napalm was useful in destroying skillfully placed Japanese camouflage prior to rocket or bombing attacks in order to expose enemy positions. ***Courtesy of Norman Miller.***

An ordnance man operates a bomb crane to hoist a 1000 lb. bomb onto a dolly which transported the bomb to the fighters. The F4U-1D could carry three bombs, including the 2000 lb. with a maximum load of 4000lbs. ***Courtesy of the USMC via Steve Stuczynski.***

Bombs

Early F4Us were capable of carrying only one bomb of any size, including the 2,000 lb. The -1D and -4 were designed to carry three bombs, including the 2,000 lb., with a maximum of load of 4,000 lb. Twin pylons were installed under the wings to carry bombs to a maximum of 1,000 lbs., two jettisonable fuel tanks or napalm tanks. The three bomb load was varied in weight type, with the limiting factor being sufficient takeoff space (e.g. the 4,000 lb. load included one 2,000 lb. on the center line and two 1,000 lb. bombs on each wing pylon). In addition, a third tank could be carried on a center line attachment point.

Switches located above the instrument panel armed and selected the bomb to be dropped. Both bombs and rockets were fired by a thumb switch on top of the stick. Selection depended on the position of the bomb-rocket switch.

There were three types of bombing runs:

(1) Dive bombing: a high angle diving attack of 60 to 70 degrees braked by the main gear, whose fairing acted as a dive brake. Dive bombing was best accomplished by designated dive bombers.

(2) Glide bombing: high speed, accelerating attack delivered at 30 to 55 degrees without the use of dive brakes. The initial ele-

A 150 gallon napalm tank could burn out a 90 x 150 foot area. Here a -323 F4U dives on a ridge in south Okinawa where Japanese had to be blasted out foot-by-foot by advancing infantry.

ment of surprise and built up speed make the attacker a difficult target going in and out.

(3) Low-level run: an attack at 20 degrees and at a very low altitude and short range.

Whenever possible bombing runs were to be made parallel to the line of supporting troops, as generally bombing is more accurate in deflection than in range.

During the Okinawa close air support operations the use of 1,000 and 2,000 lb. bombs was most effective against heavily fortified positions, as the reduction of Shuri Castle demonstrated.

The Corsair in air combat vs. the ZERO

In November 1942, an Intelligence Summary report comparing a captured Zero to the F4U-1 stated: "The Zero was far inferior to the Corsair in level speeds and diving speeds at all altitudes. It fell short in climbs starting at sea level, and above 20,000 feet the Zero could not stay with the Corsair in high-speed climbs. The superiority of the F4U-1 was very evident and would persist even when carrying heavier loads. In combat with the Zero, the Corsair could take full advantage of its speed, along with its ability to pushover and roll at high speeds if surprised. Due to its much higher wing loading, the F4U-1 had to avoid any attempt to turn with the Zero except at high speeds, and could expect the latter to out climb the Corsair at moderate altitudes and low speeds. In this case, the Corsair should be climbed at high speeds and on a heading which should open the distance and prevent the Zero from reaching a favorable position to attack. After reaching 19,000 or 20,000 feet, the Corsair had superior performance in climb and could choose its own position for attack."

The main landing gear was hydraulically retracted by rotating 90 degrees aft via large hinges. It consisted of 32"x8" tires with multiple disc brakes, oleo strut, and dive brake fairing. This fairing was used as a dive brake to slow the fighter by dropping the landing gear when beginning the dive. ***Author's collection.***

Left: **The F4U-1D was able to carry three napalm tanks, a 160 gallon on the center-line pylon and two 150 gallon tanks on each wing pylon.** ***Courtesy of the USMC via Steve Stuczynski.***

CHAPTER 23

Death Rattlers Board of Directors

Squadron CO, Major George Axtell, was well-respected by his pilots and enlisted men despite his young age. His Plane Captain, Paul Finney described the young Major as "One level headed kid. I never saw him riled or unfair the whole time I was around him." Even today most of the squadron members refer to him as Major or General Axtell. *Courtesy of Norman Miller.*

Capt. Jeff Dorroh was the Operations Officer. *Courtesy of Norman Miller.*

Major Arthur Turner was the squadron Executive Officer (XO). *Courtesy of Dr. James Barrett.*

Capt. Bill Cox was the Flight Officer. *Courtesy of Henry Brandon.*

Axtell's right hand men: (L to R) Jeff Dorroh, Ops; Dr. Tom Dussman, Flight Surgeon; Tilly Ferdenzi, Intelligence; and Paul Rix, Communications. *Courtesy of Norman Miller.*

Capt. Chuck Moore was the Flight and Safety Officer. *Courtesy of Del Davis.*

1Lt. Atilio Ferdenzi was the squadron Intelligence Officer and Historian. *Courtesy of Henry Brandon.*

Dr. Tom Dussman was the squadron Flight Surgeon and Malaria Officer. He was a Lt.(jg) detached from the Navy. *Courtesy of Henry Brandon.*

Ordnance and Chemical Officer, Capt. John Grando, was probably the oldest man in the unit. He was described as the stereotypical old Corps Leatherneck Marine by his men. *Courtesy of Norman Miller.*

1Lt. Albert Taylor was the Materiel Officer and is pictured riding to the Kadena Flight line. *Courtesy of Jody O'Keefe.*

1Lt. Fred Ritter was the Maintenance/Engineering Officer. ***Courtesy of Henry Brandon.***

1Lt. Sol Mayer was the legendary Mess Officer. ***Courtesy of Norman Miller.***

The officers and men of VMF-323 in May 1945, at Kadena, Okinawa. ***Courtesy of Harold Cunningham via Roger Archambault.***

CHAPTER 24
April
The Death Rattlers Go Into Combat

Introductory Dangers

The War Diary for early April states: "During the period covered in this report, constant air alerts and frequent bombing raids have been experienced. On several occasions the general squadron area has been subjected to heavy Japanese artillery fire. Many times the pilots and ground crews have been forced to operate from this field under these adverse conditions."

However, initially there was less danger from the Japanese attacks than from the fallout from the concentrated AA fire from our off-shore shipping. On 6 April alone, four Americans were killed and 34 wounded, including Col. Raymond Scollin, the prospective commander of Kadena. L-day, 1 April, the first day of the invasion, in contrast, only yielded 28 killed, 104 wounded and 27 missing out of the 50,000 landing troops.

"Our AA fire was more dangerous to us than the Japs. The stuff was falling from the sky, and I got a small wound on my left hand. The Corpsman sprinkled a little sulfa powder on it. It wasn't enough for a Purple Heart or even any sympathy." Frank Magliocco

"The most dangerous thing on the ground was the fall out from all the AA guns shooting at the Japs. These pieces of shells and bullets came down like rain and could kill someone without a helmet. Sol Mayer had a Thompson submachine gun which he would use on Jap planes flying at 15,000 feet! One day I came up behind him with my BAR while he was wasting ammo. I squeezed off about ten rounds, and old Sol jumped about ten feet in the air. He got the point and never played AA again." Al Wells

Shelling, bombing and strafing of Kadena:

09 April-morning strafed and bombed

15 April-strafed and bombed

16 April-shelled

21 April-bombed and strafed

27 April-air raid in fox holes all night

28 April-air raid and some shelling: 3 or 4 shells hit nearby tents had shrapnel holes. No sleep

29 April-air raid

03 May-air raid and shelled

04 May-shelling, Corp. Karl Burns hit by shrapnel and evacuated

12 May-air raid

14 May-air raid with some bombs dropped nearby

16 May-bombed in morning

24-25 May-air raid 2000 to 0500 Could see fire on Yontan AA claims 4 Japs at Yontan

28 May-air raid phosphorous bombs dropped near tower, 3 crash trucks burned and several men killed

03 June-air raid warnings but Japs don't get through

05 June-air raid and paratroops attack drill

09 June-air raid bombs dropped in distance

16 June-0430 air raid some bombs dropped nearby

During April, either Yontan or Kadena was bombed or shelled almost every night. During that period, three Marines were killed and 26 injured, while three aircraft were destroyed and five dam-

Corsairs at standby alert in early June. When was occupied on L-Day, 1 April, the first day of the invasion, pre-invasion bombardment damage needs to be quickly repaired so the F4Us of VMF-323 and-322 could be launched from the WHITE PLAINS and begin operations. ***Courtesy of Norman Miller.***

Kadena on 20 April. The Japanese airstrip was found to be too short, to have inadequate taxiways, and were unable to withstand the weight of the heavier American Corsair fighter. Development and improvement proceeded rapidly as seen in this photo. ***Courtesy of the USMC.***

The Kadena control tower. The original Japanese tower is on the left while the newly constructed Marine tower is on the right. *Courtesy of Bob Woods.*

Officer's quarters consisted of tents which were improved by their inhabitants as the weeks went by. Cots were brought in and wooden floors added. *Courtesy of Bob Woods.*

aged. Most of the attacks were nuisance flights of lone aircraft disturbing the Marine's sleep. The most effective attack took place on the 28th when the Japanese dropped 18 bombs on Yontan that night and strafed both fields off and on between midnight and 0400. The next night Japanese artillery fired 28 shells on Kadena just after midnight. The two attacks caused one casualty, three slightly damaged aircraft, and lots of lost sleep.

On many nights the Japanese sent a bomber over the area on a nuisance bombing raid. This Jap raider was nicknamed "Washing Machine Charlie" or "Louie the Louse," after the same named intruder which had flown over Guadalcanal in 1942. At 2-3-4 o'clock the air raid sirens would start up. The sleep-incoherent men would ignore the siren until the thundering of the thousands of land and ship-born anti-aircraft batteries prompted them into the often water-filled foxholes next to their tents. They mostly slept in the raw or in a pair of shorts, so that after huddling in the mud until the raid was over, they could go over to the ever filled rain barrel and rinse off. The shower of dissipated AA debris perforated the tents with holes that would leak profusely in the heavy rain. A total of 64 nuisance raids were recorded over the island during the 46 days from 9 April until V-J Day.

"We had a foxhole just outside our tent at Kadena, and when a raid came over we jumped in. You could actually hear the 'psfft,' 'psfft' sound of the shrapnel coming down. It was definitely very dangerous, as it had a dozen or so sharp edges on it. One night after a raid I went back to my tent and found a piece of shrapnel on my pillow which had tore through our tent canvas." James Barrett

M/Sgt. Thomas McLaughlin, after a night of raids and alerts during the day, heard another siren go off, dropped everything he was doing, and jumped into a ditch and broke his ankle.

"Joseph 'Jesse' James and his buddy, Wilbur Caldwell, were two young naive kids who were sort of enlisted squadron mascots.

BEFORE. Another view of officer's row in dry times. A low, sandbagged foxhole can be seen in the center of the photo, between the circle of tents. *Courtesy of Del Davis.*

AFTER. "Canal Street." Another view of the officer area, which was pitched in a grassy area and which quickly became a mire after a rainy period. *Courtesy of Jody O'Keefe.*

An improved tent with a covered vestibule and a large sand bagged fox hole very nearby (foreground). The men made good use of them in the early days of the campaign. ***Courtesy of Jody O'Keefe.***

Hots Terrill (L) and Jerry O'Keefe outside quarters under construction in mid-April at Kadena. Wooden framework and planking was collected and utilized to improve the tents. The ubiquitous five gallon Jerry can used for water can be seen behind O'Keefe's left hip. ***Courtesy of Jody O'Keefe.***

James had promised his mother that he was going to shoot down a Jap airplane for her. During one raid, they fired on an attacking Japanese plane with their rifles, and somehow the plane was hit, probably not by them, but they claimed a shared victory." James Barrett

During the early weeks on Kadena the squadron was harassed by a hidden Japanese artillery piece. "Pistol Pete" or "Kadena Pete" was named after the artillery piece which had bombarded Henderson Field on Guadalcanal. Pistol Pete turned out to be six 150 mm pieces cleverly hidden from aerial observation. Before the initial invasion on 1 April, Japanese commander Col. Hiromishi Yahara decided not to defend the flat, open Yontan and Kadena airfields. Instead, he positioned an artillery-equipped combat unit in the rugged hills to the north of the airfield. They were hidden in caves above the plain, which had been zeroed in before the invasion. The artillery pieces were moved out of the caves, usually in darkness, and shells were fired at Marine positions. They were neutralized by pounding them by day with massed 155 mm fire to immobilize them by causing casualties and damage to the cave entrances so they couldn't be moved at night. At night heavy interdiction fire was laid down to prevent their use. This routine continued until each gun was silenced or overrun by Marine infantry. Lt.Col. Frederick P. Henderson, IIIAC Artillery Operations Officer in charge of eliminating Pistol Pete, stated: "the next morning at first light (if) we found them still there (we) went to work polishing them off. Kadena Pete didn't bother us anymore, and the flyers and brass were all happy."

Pistol Pete made a firm impression in the minds of the Squadron, as numerous stories are told about the gun(s).

The shower was the product of the engineering of Red Dillard and Hank Brandon. Brandon says: "We received many criticisms and suggestions for improvement but everyone made use of it." ***Courtesy of Henry Brandon.***

It's finished, don't forget to bring your soap. ***Courtesy of Henry Brandon.***

Bill Hood (L) and Glenn Thacker in boots walking along a perpetually muddy "Main Street" on their way to the shower. ***Courtesy of Harley Brock.***

"Pistol Pete," one of six Japanese 150mm artillery pieces which were concealed in the hills north of Kadena. The pieces were named after a similar harassing artillery piece on Guadalcanal. ***Courtesy of the US Army.***

Del Davis stands outside his tent. There is a large shell hole, behind and right. ***Courtesy of Del Davis.***

Jerry O'Keefe poses in the entrance of a sandbagged bunker. Not only did "Pistol Pete" intrude on the squadron but Japs often sent a single aircraft over nightly to disturb the men's sleep and force them into foxholes or shelters. ***Courtesy of Bob Woods.***

Zeke Zehring and a piece of heavy equipment used to construct and reconstruct the runway after "Pistol Pete" finished his dirty work. ***Courtesy of Henry Brandon.***

Avid reader, Mindy Muse (L), walking with Jerry O'Keefe who could be ribbing him about the Japanese "gas attack." ***Courtesy of Norman Miller.***

Pilots had to taxi a long distance to the runway. Normally, the pilot had to S-turn to see over the long nose of the Corsair, but the Kadena taxiway was too narrow to do this. Two enlisted ground crewmen were assigned to "wing walk" at the wing tips to guide the pilot on Kadena's unfamiliar, muddy taxiways. During the first days of operations, in the pre-dawn morning, the first two Corsairs, Chuck Moore and his wingman, Henry Brandon, were being walked down the taxiway, when Pistol Pete opened up fire on the field. The barrage was stepping rounds towards the taxing Corsairs. The ground crew naturally ran to take cover, leaving the Corsairs helpless to maneuver through the mud and darkness. The pilots rose up out of their cockpits, yelling at the walkers to get back on the wing tips. Henry Brandon

The men had listened to the gas attack lecture and hung up the masks in their tents and forgot about them. One day a shell came in, and the strong smell of the cordite caused Bob Muse to think it was a gas attack and he yelled "Gas, Gas." Everyone in the tent scrambled to find and don their masks, but Muse couldn't find his. The unprotected Muse began to turn purple, and everyone thought the attack was for real. Muse locked at everyone expecting to be given their mask, but with no mask being volunteered he finally had to escape. With his face purple and contorted he took off for the safety of the "high ground" and became the butt of several days of ribbing.

After Pistol Pete was eliminated, the constant rolling thunder of the artillery barrages to the south disrupted the men's sleep, especially during the reduction of the Shuri Line. This went on until 4 May, when the Japanese staged a final Banzai charge preceded by a 12,000 round artillery barrage.

The nightly shelling and bombing put nerves on edge, and the threat of Japanese infiltraters was ever present. Flight Surgeon Dr. Thomas Dussman heard noises near his sick bay that was located on a knoll away from the rest of the camp. T.Sgts. Stanley Woszcyna and Paul Finney, followed by Don Hitchings were walking back in the dark from working on their aircraft on the flight line that was some distance from camp. The nightly password was usually given at dinner, but the sergeants were working and missed it. The armed

A well-known photo of Yonton airfield under attack. The intensity of the AA return fire lit up the sky showing the Corsairs of VMF-311, "Hell's Bells," stationed at the base. The fallout from this AA fire could be very dangerous and accounted for several fatalities. ***Courtesy of the USMC.***

Dussman challenged them for the password, but before they could explain he fired. Woszcyna was shot through the hip, and the bullet then hit Finney in the stomach. Finney, "I've never held this against him too much. I think being alone over there all the time wasn't a good situation because it made him a little more uptight than the rest of us. I guess he was sleeping or something and could have thought we were Japs. He hit two out of three of us, but it took him three shots. But if we had been Japs we would have gotten him! We were put on a hospital ship, and I was sent to a hospital on Saipan while Woszcyna ended up on Guam. They took my shoes away on the beach at Okinawa, and I didn't get a pair back until I was ready to go back to Okinawa a month later. We came back to Okinawa on a LST."

Keith Fountain, "On one of the first nights on the island we heard this running sound, and then a 'bang, bang,' and then somebody hollered, 'Did you get him?' The answer was, 'No, I think the son-of-a-bitch got away.' It turned out that a Jap had gotten hungry and was rummaging through our camp. There were a lot of domesticated goats running loose on the island, and just about every night one got shot."

"The only thing close to being a Japanese booby trap were the vegetables available from their abandoned gardens. Intelligence advised us against eating them, as the Japanese used human manure to fertilize them." -Henry Brandon

The War Diaries state: "The pilots themselves have operated from this field under the most hazardous operating conditions. With very few exceptions pilots have had but 2,400-2,500' of useable runway, due to the constant construction being carried out to improve the field. This shortness of runway coupled with strike loads carried by our aircraft, including 8 rockets, 2-500 lb. Bombs, or two pylon tanks filled with napalm, plus full ammo loads, have made takeoffs no mean feat." However, the pilots weren't alone in facing danger.

PC Donald Hitchings, "We serviced the planes around the clock. One of the problems as Plane Captains was that we didn't get much sleep. The personnel on the oil and fuel trucks worked hard all day without stopping, as the first missions would take off at dawn and continue on all day until the last patrol before dusk. So at night not only did we have to service the planes, but also oil and fuel them. If a patrol came in around dark we had to go out and put out roadside kerosene lamps to mark the runway. Then we had to worry about the Japs who follow our planes in because they were low on fuel and easy targets. We tried to grab naps while the patrols were in the air."

Melvin Lee: "We had to keep our fuel trucks running back and forth between their refueling station on the shore and Kadena. The airstrip was narrow and short, and we stationed our trucks along side. We had to move often, as the Seabees were very busy enlarging the field. Once a Corsair landed we rushed out as it taxied to a stop to refuel it, so it was ready to take off immediately if the Japs

Left: **The Japanese shelling, infiltrators, and nightly air raids put nerves on edge. T/Sgts. Stan Woszcyna and Paul Finney had missed the pass word for the evening because they were working late. As they passed the isolated infirmary tent of a sleepy, Dr. Tom Dussman (pictured), the physician issued a challenge and with no pass word replied, shot and wounded the two sergeants.** ***Courtesy of Jody O'Keefe.***

Stan Woszcyna was hit in the hip by Dussman. ***Courtesy of Harley Brock.***

Ground crew, like Mel Lee, here manning a starter cart, were in danger from Japanese shelling and air raids as they often worked through the night getting the aircraft ready for the next day's missions. ***Courtesy of Rocco DeMilia.***

came. It was scary work for the drivers in those trucks carrying 500 gallons of aviation gasoline, never knowing when Pistol Pete was going to start shelling or a Jap bomber would come over.

Paul Finney was wounded in the stomach by Dussman. Both he and Woszcyna were air-evacuated to hospitals in the Marianas and returned to duty a month later via LST. ***Courtesy of Harley Brock.***

10 April Mission/Death of James Brown

Al Wells: "We landed at Kadena on April 9th and were greeted by some Light Colonel who gave a big speech on how they were really going to take care of the pilots. He told us that operations were going to be conservative, and there would be no flights in bad weather. The next morning they got us up at 0400, and Sol (Mayer) made us a good breakfast. It was a memorable day, as it was my birthday and also that of my buddy, Louie Brown. To find out who was senior we even wrote home to find our birth hour. The weather closed down to practically 200 feet, and it was raining like hell. We all got into our cockpits and just sat there waiting on the rain. Louie and I had saved a bottle of whiskey and couldn't wait to celebrate when group ops canceled the mission. But we were ordered to take the flight off, and I knew there would be no way in hell we were going to join up in this mess." Henry Brandon continues: "I was concentrating on finding my section leader below the overcast. I saw a flash out of the corner of my eye and thought it was naval gunfire, but when Louie Brown didn't come back I knew what I saw. He probably just lost it in the weather and went in. We should never have taken off in that, nothing was accomplished."

Kadena was defended by Army Anti-Aircraft units. ***Courtesy of John Ruhsam.***

Jack Broering sitting on the wing tip of a Japanese Ida or Sonia which was destroyed in the pre-invasion bombardment. The rectangular holes in the fuselage were cut by souvenir hunters. ***Courtesy of Bill Drake.***

12 APRIL COMBAT

Combat 1

Since they had landed on the 9th, the weather had been bad. On the 10th and 11th only one mission had taken off, and the death of 1Lt. James Brown was blamed on the weather. 1Lt. Al Wells describes the mission:

"On the 12th the weather was getting better, and we were in our cockpits waiting for someone to make up their minds on doing something. I was shooting the bull with the plane captain who was standing on the wing when tracer bullets tattooed the runway. We all started our engines, but it had rained so hard that almost everyone was stuck in the mud. At least a couple guys nosed up on their props trying to get their aircraft moving. I was on fairly solid ground, so I got to the runway before anyone else, even though I was scheduled about sixth to go as I was in the second division. No one else was around, so I didn't know what the hell to do. So, I'm a sitting target on the runway which ran east and west. It was just getting gray out, and I saw an aircraft headed south making a glide bomb run on a little building they had put up as a control tower. It made a direct hit, which made me mad because they had killed some of our people in the tower. I took off and was able to get the Jap in my sights as he crossed the runway, pulled up, and made a gradual 180

Sgt. Rocky DeMilia sitting on top a covered AA gun guarding Kadena. ***Courtesy of Rocco DeMilia.***

This Japanese Army Tony Ki-61 fighter of 19 Hikko Sentai was captured when its pilot mistakenly landed on Yonton thinking it was still in Japanese hands. The fighter was to be test flown by Marine pilots but its engine caught fire and grounded the aircraft. ***Courtesy of Hank Brandon.***

Jack Broening inspects an abandoned Japanese bunker near the base. ***Courtesy of Bill Drake.***

During the early days at Kadena rain and mud were a major problem. This bulldozer is hopelessly stuck in the deep mud. ***Courtesy of Norman Miller.***

On the squadron's first mission of the war, on 10 April, 1Lt. James "Louie" Brown became its first fatality when he crashed shortly after take off in bad weather. ***Courtesy of Henry Brandon.***

degree turn headed back toward Japan. He never knew I was there because he continued his gradual turn without evasion. Every AA gun on the island was shooting at me and him. I was very careful to remember the gun check list: turning on the electric gun switches and charging them hydraulically. I tried the gunsight, but I couldn't get it dim enough as it was too dark outside, so I turned it off. I was right behind him (a KI-61 Army Tony) and fired. The only thing I did wrong to that point was that I couldn't stop shooting, I was so excited. It was so dark you really couldn't see the water, and I almost followed him in. I pulled up and started climbing, thinking: 'Boy, there must be more of them.' The aircraft was performing poorly, and I couldn't figure out why until I looked down and saw I hadn't put the gear up I had remembered everything except this little point."

Well's after action report states that he sighted the Tony a mile ahead and above, got on his tail and closed from 6 o'clock below. The Tony made no evasive turn until he opened fire at 200 feet. Wells kept firing as the Tony made a sharp diving turn to the left and burst into flames and crashed into Nakagasuki Wan.

The action report also stated, "The remainder of the flight was uneventful." For pilots in their first combat this was an understatement. 2Lt. Henry Brandon was waiting on the runway just behind Wells, taxied around the new bomb crater, and took off in the dark in search of a possible partner of the Jap. As he turned his head to begin his search, Brandon looked over and saw, instead of a Jap, a large blue Navy F6F, which came out of nowhere, flying right next to him. Brandon remarks, "I think we scared the heck out of each other." On their return to land at Kadena the pilots found that they had to land on a runway cut in half by the Jap bomb. They had to make a carrier approach, chop throttles, hit the brakes and hope there was enough runway left to stop.

Combat 2

After the first massed kikusui kamikaze attack on 6-7 April, in which 355 (230 JNAF and 125 JAAF) Japanese aircraft attacked Okinawa, the next kikusui was scheduled for 12 April. The Japanese mus-

A GMC 2 1/2 ton 6x6 truck plowing a clearing through a muddy road for a truck supply convoy to the front. ***Courtesy of the US Army.***

1Lt. Al Wells scored the first Death Rattler air victory just after take of on 12 April when he shot down a Tony in the early dawn over Nakagasuku Bay. After the combat Wells wondered why his fighter was acting so sluggishly when he found, in his excitement, he had forgotten to retract his landing gear on take off! ***Courtesy of Al Wells.***

A -323 Corsair sitting on a wet taxiway. The original Japanese taxiways were very narrow and couldn't support the weight of the heavier American fighters. There were numerous stuck-in-the-mud incidents once an aircraft strayed off the taxiway. ***Courtesy of Rocco DeMilia.***

tered 185 kamikaze aircraft (125 JNAF and 60 JAAF), 45 conventional torpedo bombers, nine Betty/Ohka combinations and 150 escort fighters. As in the first kikusui, the raid was carried out in the early afternoon. Much of the brunt of the attack was absorbed by picket station #1, which was located 35 miles northwest of the Motobu Peninsula.

Sixteen Death Rattlers took off from Kadena at 1330 for a CAP, but two returned to base for mechanical reasons shortly after joining up. All pilots were looking forward to finally meeting the Japs, especially after Al Wells' victory that morning. During the flight Japanese aircraft approached from the north and the squadron, split by air control, chased after them.

Six of the fighters were vectored north to the Motobu Peninsula, Point "O." The flight was led by Capt. Felix Cecot with 2Lt. Leon Reynolds on his wing. Capt. Joe McPhail led the second section with 2Lt. Warren Bestwick on his wing, while the third section was led by 2Lt. Glen Thacker with 2Lt. E. Yager on his wing. 2Lts. Bob Wade and John Ruhsam had returned to base earlier. Joe

First Death Rattler victim. The Kawasaki KI-61 was a front-line Japanese Army fighter introduced in April 1943. First thought to be of Italian design the new fighter was dubbed "Tony" by Allied Intelligence. ***Courtesy of James Lansdale.***

Capt. Joe McPhail hadn't been in the cockpit since leaving Espiritu on Valentine's Day. While on CAP his flight was vectored toward some bogies. When he saw "some blue planes chasing some brown planes" he knew he was in the right place and shot down a Zeke. *Courtesy of Norman Miller.*

2Lt. Warren Bestwick (L) shows Bill Drake the victory markings for the two Zekes he shot down on the 12 June afternoon mission over the Motobu Peninsula. Bestwick would add a Tojo to his total on 15 April. *Courtesy of Jody O'Keefe.*

McPhail was excited to be back in the cockpit of his Corsair, as he hadn't been in the air since Valentine's Day over Espiritu Santo.

McPhail describes the battle: "We contacted the fighter director, who vectored us over the Motobu Peninsula towards some bogies (Bogies were unidentified aircraft, friend or foe, while identified enemy aircraft were called in as bandits-ed.) coming down from the north at 18,000 feet. He had us climb to 23,000 feet and circle there. The director said the bogies were just ahead of us, but no one could see them. There were lots of clouds which cut down the visibility. As I was looking down on the deck, I saw some blue airplanes chasing some brown airplanes. I thought, that's were I wanted to be. I called out their position, and Warren and I made a descending left turn. We had made a 180 degree turn and lost about 2,000 feet when four Zekes appeared right under us at 19,000 feet, heading south. They were in a tight formation, flying almost abreast in two-two plane sections like we flew. I picked up the rear plane on the right and fired at about 400 yards, above and behind, but I was too far away. The Zeke saw the tracers and made a series of small evasive turns. I waited a little bit and fired, getting hits which tore off pieces around the cockpit. He then blew up. I was going so fast that I blew by the other Zekes, who scattered. I then rolled over and split-essed to get out of there. As the speed picked up, the ailerons started fluttering and the stick slammed left and right, and I couldn't stop it. Finally, I used the trim tab to pull out at about 9,000 feet. I looked for my wingman (Bestwick) and was unable to find him and went home."

Bestwick continues: "Captain McPhail shot at the rear plane on the right. His Zeke crossed under the rest of their formation and exploded in flames. I picked up the second plane of the first Jap section and fired a long burst and saw it catch fire. The Zeke, however, pulled up and made it impossible for me to stay on his tail. By that time the first plane of the second section had broken off to the right and down, so I continued my run and fired a 20 degree deflection shot from behind. This plane also exploded. While looking

2Lt. Felix Cecot claimed a Jack probable over Ie Shima on the way back to Kadena for his only claim of the war. *Courtesy of Norman Miller*.

1Lt. Del Davis (*Above,* A) , 1Lt. Charlie Spangler (*Below,* B), and 2Lt. Dewey Durnford (*Opposite, Top left,* C) conspired to tear a hapless twin-engined Betty apart to share one-third victory apiece and end a successful first day's combat for the squadron: six victories and two probables. *Courtesy of (A) Del Davis, (B) Dorothy Spangler, and (C) Author.*

John Ruhsam (above) dropped back to escort his wingman, Bob Wade, back to Kadena because of a mechanical with Wade's fighter. On the way Ruhsam shot down a Zeke over the Motobu Peninsula. When he landed Kadena was being shelled and he had to hurriedly escape his aircraft on the taxiway and jump into the nearest foxhole. *Courtesy of John Ruhsam*.

down I saw my first Zeke spiraling down in smoke, but didn't see my second Zeke after firing on him. Unable to find Capt. McPhail, I started to get my bearings when I saw three Zekes above and ahead of me, doing slow rolls in column. I started to climb and follow them, but they spotted me and turned and started to bracket me. I made a diving 180 degree turn to the left and saw no more of those Zekes. They didn't follow me very far, because I turned to look for them after flying away for about a minute. While returning home I saw four planes 3,000 feet above and to the right of me flying in the opposite direction. I turned toward them to investigate and saw they were Zekes. They made a slight turn toward me but continued north. They were still 2,000 feet above and several miles past. Being low on gas, I returned to base." (Note: these Zekes were old model 21 versions and were probably from the Genzsen Kokutai training division that was in that area that day.)

Thacker had followed Bestwick on his original pass and went after the fourth Zeke in the formation. He made a beam run from 3 o'clock, on the same level, and his six machine guns tore pieces off the fuselage. The smoking Zeke rolled, pulled through tightly, and got away, giving Thacker a probable kill. He and Yager returned to base.

The fighter director vectored six other fighters northwest from Ie Shima. This group consisted of flight leader Major Arthur Turner and his wingman, 2Lt. Obie Stover, while 1Lt. Del Davis led the second section with 2Lt. Robert Woods on his wing and 1Lt. Charles Spangler led the third section with 2Lt. Dewey Durnford on his wing. Flying at 25,000 feet, 71 miles northwest of Ie Shima, the flight sighted a bogie at 10 o'clock, 8 miles away and 4,000 feet below. Del Davis, "The weather was clear with very good visibility, and we had no trouble picking up the target. It was apparent that the target had also observed us, as he turned away to the northwest and started a rapid descent to the sea and leveled off at 13,000 feet." Spangler and Durnford peeled off, closely followed by Davis and Woods. Spangler closed from 5 o'clock and opened fire at 800 feet. He hit the Jap, now ID'd as a Mitsubishi G4M Betty, tearing off the top of its rudder. His bullets continued up to the port engine, setting it on fire. At the same time Durnford opened fire at 200 feet and hit the cockpit. Davis continues: "I opened fire at about 200 feet from the 5 o'clock position, aiming at the tail turret gunner who was banging away at me. At this moment I was shocked as the Betty executed a hard right level flipper turn into me and exposed the starboard waist gun and top turret, which all began to fire at me. I finished my firing pass and observed pieces falling from the starboard engine. I executed a hard right turn and pulled up to about the 45 degree angle and rolled back to the left in order to keep him in sight, and quickly pulled back through and rolled back to the left and fired into the starboard cockpit and right wing root area inside the right engine. The wing separated and the aircraft dove into the sea." The three pilots shared the victory, regrouped and spent the remainder of the mission working with the fighter director without result.

Cecot and Reynolds continued north at 22,000 feet after the Japs that were reported at 20,000 feet. Cecot spotted the battle below and dove to 5,000 feet to fire at a Navy J2M Jack fighter. As the Jack rolled, Cecot hit it in the belly and saw it smoking, but was prevented from seeing the results of his hits as he sped past and got credit for a probable. Reynolds' hydraulic system was out and he was unable to retract one wheel. Nonetheless, he and Cecot chased the Japs for another 20 minutes before returning to base.

After takeoff Bob Wade was unable to retract his gear. He kept working on it, trying to keep in formation, but he kept falling behind and returned to base. It was standard procedure for mechanicals returning to base to be escorted. Ruhsam describes the action: "Wade dropped from formation and returned to base as he could not hold more than 145 kts. with rated power. It was my responsibility to see he was not left alone, and I throttled back so he could close on my wing. All around us we could see action, it was a picture I shall never forget. There, in the beautiful blue sky among the puffy cumulus clouds, were planes everywhere, some in flames, some in attack, and we were unable to join in the melee. I turned back toward Kadena with Wade on my wing, and as I looked down there below me I saw a Jap Zero at 3,500 feet making a turn toward three Navy Corsairs. All I could see were meat balls, those large red circles on the wings of the Zero. Big red meat balls! All I needed to do was to roll over into a left high side run, something I had been doing in gunnery practice for all these years. Everything was in slow motion, it took forever for him to come into my sights, time just stood still. At 300 yards and nearly full deflection I squeezed the trigger and all six guns started firing, and it seemed like I shot off all my ammunition. I was sure that my tracers had hit him in the cockpit and engine, but training taught me to break away and maintain my speed. As I broke up and away I looked down and saw the Zero begin to shed parts and break out into flames, and it hit just offshore at Nago Wan. Wade was directly behind him, and I thought that he had shot him down. He later told me that he hadn't fired and that I had destroyed him. We returned to base and landed. On the roll out there were no instructions from the tower, which I thought was odd, but after a couple of unanswered radio calls I taxied in. There were no linemen to greet me, and I disgustedly shut the engine down and sat there for a second when the ground a 100 feet in front of the plane erupted. It didn't take me long to realize that the airfield was being shelled and that the cockpit of my plane was not the place to be. I got out and jumped into the nearest foxhole."

The luster of this first successful large scale encounter was marred when Pistol Pete decided to shell the field. Warren Bestwick: "As I landed the tower warned me that the field was being shelled. We had Seabees and Army Engineers working on the field at the time, and they left their equipment out as they took refuge in foxholes. As I was taxiing S-turns these runway workers motioned me, 'Go, Go, Go.' So I thought they were motioning that everything was clear and I stopped S-turning and went ahead. Actually, they were motioning me to get away from them as they thought the gun was aimed at my aircraft. One of them had left his grader right in the middle of the runway, and I ran into it. My prop hit one of those large balloon tires and it exploded, and I thought surely a shell had hit me."

A note in the Material data section of the action report commented: "Pilots experienced considerable hydraulic trouble because mechanics were unable to work on the planes. Lack of time, poor operating conditions, and the fact that the squadron had just reached the field were also reasons for mechanical trouble."

12 April: Brandon: "I am writing this letter by candle light on a rickety cardboard box. We are living in tents right on the ground. I must admit we don't have many of the comforts of home, but I must admit I don't mind too much. I was lucky enough to locate an old cot. 'Lightning' (Keith Fountain) and Charley Allen are sleeping in sleeping bags on the ground, and I know they haven't been sleeping too well."

In his 12 April letter to his wife Henry Brandon wrote: "We are living in tents right on the ground. I must admit that I don't have many of the comforts of home but I admit that I don't mind too much". Here the pilots move their cots outdoors to catch some sun between missions and the rain. *Courtesy of Henry Brandon.*

Bob Muse chose his tent mates masterfully. They were Mess Officer Sol Mayer, Intelligence Officer Tilly Ferndenzi, and Supply Officer Swampy Taylor. Muse liked to brag that his tent mates kept him well-fed, well-informed and well dressed!

13 April Mission

On 13 April, VMF-323 F4Us were scheduled for a dawn CAP mission from Kadena. Corsairs of VMF-322 were lined up close to the edge of the runway (perhaps due to the muddy conditions). They had moved to this position that night from the same position on the opposite side of the field. One of -322's Corsairs had gotten stuck in the mud on the right side of the runway with its long nose sticking out on the runway. Two Death Rattler Corsairs, piloted by Capt. Charles Moore and Henry Brandon, successfully made the predawn takeoff. Brandon was #2, and as he made his right hand turn he noticed a huge explosion over his right shoulder. The #3 man, Larry Crawley, in the flight had struck the implanted -322 Corsair with his right wing tip, but was able to complete his takeoff successfully. The #4 man, Keith Fountain: " I was hugging the right side of the runway because the night before -322 airplanes had all been parked on the other side, and I wanted to stay away from them. The visibility was poor and it was raining. I had my aircraft under control, but my wing tip hit the nose of that Corsair and I careened and hit the aircraft on the other side of the runway. The collision resulted in a large explosion that blew off the entire nose section of my aircraft. I was sitting in the open and undid my seat belt and ran away. It was a miracle that I survived at all. The aircraft had a full load of gas." The -323 pilot survived with first and second degree burns to the exposed areas of the face, wrists and ankles. Fountain was air evacuated to Fleet Hospital, Guam, and returned to the unit three weeks later. In the following fire, .50 caliber machine gun rounds exploded, making the rescue very hazardous. Two pilots from VMF-322 were killed. Corpsman/1/c James Maynatt of -323 was killed by the exploding ammunition and was buried in the 1st Marine Division Cemetery on Okinawa. Eight planes were damaged, five beyond repair.

George Axtell on flying in poor weather conditions: "I had been an instrument instructor previous to Cherry Point and had emphasized instrument flying throughout our training. On Okinawa we were one of the few squadrons which would launch under severe weather conditions because we had the confidence to do so due to our training. We would stay out in weather where we couldn't see anything for long periods, and then the weather would suddenly clear or we would find holes. Because of our ability and willingness to stay out in poor weather and conserve fuel, we got the opportunity to be vectored to and intercept large formations of Japanese."

13 April

The squadron kept aircraft ready to scramble. Del Davis: "We were ready to scramble from the alert pad and kept our aircraft engines warm for immediate takeoff. The oil pressure was a major factor and required frequent engine run ups (depending on outside temperatures) to prevent engine failure when high power was applied. We warmed up every half hour or so and were able to apply maximum power in a matter of seconds, which was -323 policy. Other squadrons really didn't want to be scrambled from the alert pad and purposely did not keep their engines warm for immediate launch."

John Ruhsam describes his feelings and the conditions early at Kadena in a letter to his parents. "I'm trying to write this on my knees while waiting for a 'scramble.' We are on alert all afternoon, just waiting for action. I don't want to say more than I'm allowed, but they tell us that we may tell of personal experiences and heaven knows there have been plenty of these. The old war has been red hot in this portion of the hemisphere. Bombed, strafed and shelled. We lay in a fox hole every night. Have shot at infiltrating Japs, in fact one was killed about 100 feet behind our tent. Wade had another shot at five yards with his .38 but the results were questionable. I can't deny that at times I have been scared as heck and at times I get really jumpy. This is real war, but I can say that I am damn proud to be a Marine. The reputation we have is well earned, and those who know will agree 100%. We are a fighting outfit par excellence. Now that I have arrived here I'm glad I made the choice and am a Marine. I'll never feel second best.

I'm working with the best flight! Capt. McPhail is our division leader, Warren Bestwick (a peachy fellow from Montana), Wade and myself. Wade and I alternate as section leader and wingman. It is a real nice feeling to know you have someone on your wing you can trust.

The weather has been miserable, raining and cold. The mud is horrible. You take two steps and your boots weigh ten pounds more. The first couple of nights we sat in our tents as cold as I have ever been, the rain pouring outside. The candle would jump and flicker from the concussion of the artillery barrage. When things finally became quiet we were able to get a comfortable night's sleep in our sleeping bag. But then 'Washing Machine Charlie' would come over and we would have to run for our wet fox holes. There is hardly ever a morning that some snooper wouldn't wake us up. Usually he would fly over about 0330 in the morning, and then we couldn't get back to sleep."

14 April Close Air Support #1

Mission: 0812-1050 Provide close air support by bombing and rocket firing on enemy artillery positions holding up front line troops in south Okinawa. These close support missions were part of the softening up process for the assault on the Japanese Shuri Line. This defensive complex was a series of underground strong points and killing zones set in the ridges, escarpments, and draws of the highlands that stretched across the narrow, five mile wide, southern neck of the island. In addition, the Japanese took advantage of the thousands of concrete lyre-shaped tombs that dotted the terrain and were utilized as defensive positions. The assault on this very compact battlefield, which began on 19 April, was to provide the most savage fighting of the campaign.

The mission started out badly, as two rockets were accidentally launched on deck before takeoff. Al Wells describes the incident: "-323 was on the north side of the strip and -322 on the south side, and several rockets were launched into their living area. -322 was ready to kill Grando, -323 ordnance officer. Fortunately, there were no casualties or damage to installations."

Major George Axtell led 15 Corsairs from Kadena at 0812. The Air Support Control Unit (ASCU) gave the target location via the Air Support Net. The Air Coordinator flying in a TBF further identified the target by flying over it and giving terrain features. Upon nearing the target, Axtell went down to further verify the targets that were near Machinato A/D. Each aircraft carried two 500 lb. G.P. bombs and eight MK.7 3.25 inch rocket motors with 5 inch MK I armor piercing heads.

Six Corsairs initiated dive bombing runs between 7-8,000 feet with dive brakes deployed, attaining a speed of 280 knots and releasing 500 lb. bombs between 1-2,000 feet at an angle of 50-60 degrees and recovering near the deck. Six bombs were dropped on a grid coordinate as the actual targets were not seen, since the Japanese camouflage was excellent.

All 15 Corsairs hit the second target that was a grass hut area that intelligence had reported to harbor concealed artillery. Rocket attacks were made after a run of 6,000 feet along a slant range of 1,500-2,000 feet at an angle of 40-50 degrees with four rockets launched per run. The second target was only seen after one of the pilots reported spotting gunfire flashes from a few native huts. A total of 66 rockets and 13 bombs were directed at the huts, and four artillery pieces were observed to explode.

Four F4Us suffered shrapnel holes from the exploding target and were repairable on base. The accidental discharge of the two rockets prior to take off was traced. It was found that all switches were on off position and all safety precautions were taken. It was thought that the cause was a current being supplied by a flashlight battery used in connection with the zero voltage kit. A current ran into the launcher, and since corresponding launchers on both wings were on the same wiring circuit, the rocket on the opposite launcher would fire. The rocket expert from TAF recommended that different zero voltage kits be used.

Capt. Joe McPhail stands outside the "Biltmore." By the end of April the tent accommodations were much improved. Wooden flooring was installed and attempts at drainage were made. The tent side flaps rolled up to help dry out the inside of the tent. ***Courtesy of John Ruhsam.***

14 April Close Air Support #2

Mission: 1550-1820 Area bombing, rocket firing and strafing of underground positions in the northern end of Shuri town.

Major Axtell led the second close support mission of the day, but after a half hour on station, due to poor communications between ASCU and Axtell, Maj. Turner took the lead. Each fighter carried two 500 lb. G.P. bombs and eight rockets. The mission was on station at 1630, at which time Turner contacted the ASCU and received the coordinates to gridded target charts. The approach to the target was designated north-south. The target area consisted of buildings and underground installations in the northern section of Shuri Town.

Dive bombing runs were begun at 8,000 feet north of the target using dive brakes, as 45-50 degree dives were made releasing at 2,500 feet with pullout at 1,000 feet. The pilots dropped both bombs on the first run.

The rocket runs followed the dive bombing. These runs were initiated at 6,000 feet north of the target and fired at 1,500 feet in 40 degree dives on automatic fire. Since there was no enemy AA fire a normal climbing turn to the left was used to join up.

Because of the underground nature of the target, along with the smoke and haze over the target, assessment of damage was difficult. An estimated 60% of the bombs and rockets hit the target area, and damage was done to grass huts during scattered strafing runs.

15 APRIL COMBAT

On Friday the 13th, it was announced that President Franklin D. Roosevelt, only three months into his third term, had died. At the same time, the existence of the kamikazes was finally made public in the American press and was naturally buried by news of F.D.R.'s death and funeral. Their effectiveness was not made known, and the kamikaze pilots were depicted as reluctant volunteers, or banzai fanatics as the Ohka suicide rocket plane nickname, "Baka" (fool) insinuated. During the second kikusui on the 12th, the Kamikazes had hit eleven ships, killed 267 and wounded 427.

1Lt. Bob Wade destroyed two Tonys over Kawata Wan as the squadron scored six more victories on the 15th. ***Courtesy of the USMC.***

Axtell: "A lot of time on CAP and picket ship patrol you just sat and looked at blue ocean. The Navy took the first pick on the patrols. Certain CAP stations were useless, but we grabbed every mission we could in the north because the kamikazes came down north from Kyushu."

Combat 1

At 1705, four F4U-1Ds took off on a scramble CAP, flying cover for a picket ship and were vectored out 65 miles southeast of the northern tip of Okinawa. After about an hour and a half of patrolling, two Japanese Navy D3A Val bombers were spotted incoming at 6,500 feet. Three Marine pilots, 1Lt. Joe Dillard, 1Lt. Harold Tonnessen, and 1Lt. Francis Terrill all went after the Jap from 8,000 feet and made high beam runs into the bullets of the Jap rear gunner. The Val flew straight and level as the trio attacked from 3 o'clock. The Val then tried to turn and flee, but the trio opened fire

Posing before their successful mission 15 April are (L to R) Charley Allen, Zeke Zehring, Tom Blackwell, and John Strickland. Allen and Strickland shared a Zeke while Zehring scored a Tony. ***Courtesy of Jody O'Keefe.***

1Lt. Fred Zehring chased a Tony inland, so intent on pumping bullets into the already doomed Jap that he was unable to pull out of his attack and crashed into a mountainside. ***Courtesy of Henry Brandon.***

at 600 feet. The rear gunner was silenced, the Val snap rolled, caught fire and split-essed into the sea.

Tonnessen describes the return home, "After this long action was over Joe led us home only to find Kadena was under a nuisance bombing attack by a single Japanese aircraft. It was almost dark by then and, as we circled off the island waiting for an all clear, Joe polled the flight as to fuel supply. Everyone reported EMPTY. Joe decided to go in and take our chances. I had been flying tail-end Charlie, and as we circled the field for break off, my engine quit. We had only half the width and half the length of the runway available for landing due to construction workers improving the field. I radioed that I was coming in. I pulled up my landing gear and headed for the part of the runway under construction. The aircraft skidded nicely until it hit a truck and had to be written off."

The Action Report states: "Our offensive tactics were aggressive, and the teamwork was excellent."

Combat 2

At 1730, three divisions led by Major Arthur Turner took off on a dusk CAP and proceeded to their assigned areas. After an hour the division, consisting of 1Lt. Charles Allen and his wingman, 2Lt. Thomas Blackwell, and second section leader 1Lt. Joe Strickland and his wingman, 1Lt. Frederick Zehring, spotted bogies.

At 1830, the division, orbiting at 6,000 feet, sighted four Zekes and two Tonys off the north coast. The Japanese were cruising at 1,000 feet in a southerly direction. Strickland and Zehring dove on the Japs, who scattered and pulled away. The Marines separated, and Zehring went after a Tony and managed to close from above at 6 o'clock. With the Corsair on his tail, the Tony pushed over in a power dive, and was hit by all six 50s that started the engine and fuselage burning. Even though the Tony was seemingly out of control and headed for the mountainous shore of northwestern Okinawa, Zehring pressed home his attack. He followed the Tony down, pouring bursts into him, until the Jap crashed into the side of a mountain, five miles inland. The aggressive Zehring, perhaps too intent on his attack, was unable to pull out of his dive, and crashed into the mountain near his victim, and a half minute later his fighter burst into flames.

Combat 3

After spotting the four Zekes and two Tonys, the division split up. Strickland and Allen sectioned up and sighted a lone Zeke cruising below them at 190 knots in a southeasterly direction. The lieutenants commenced a high side run from 4,000 feet, above and at 6 o'clock. The Zeke made a sharp diving turn to the left at the same time that Allen and Strickland opened fire at 500 feet. The Zeke began smoking, and the pilot tried to get out of the cockpit. Another short burst put an end to that, and the pilot slumped back into his seat and was seen to crash into a mountain for a shared victory. The official After Combat Action report stated that in the battle a Corsair was hit in the wheel doors by light AA fire. It damaged the hydraulic system and caused the wheels to buckle on landing, totaling the fighter. 1Lt. Charles Allen relates the true story:

"After we made contact with the Jap planes, as usual when the hassle started the whole division went to shit and everyone went their way to win the war right at that moment. After we shot down the Zeke we all stayed in the same vicinity, and the next thing I heard was that Zeke (Zehring) had gone in. I spotted a column of smoke and went down to circle and spot what I could. Shortly thereafter all hell broke loose in my plane, and I knew my plane had been hit by gunfire. With smoke in my cockpit and the engine running a little rough my first thought was to get the hell out of this thing. I took a little time to look around for enemy planes, but all I saw was this lone Corsair way up above and to the left. I opened the canopy, unbuckled my seat belt and shoved the stick forward to assist going out. Well, the Man Upstairs no doubt had other plans for me, for when I tried to leave my knees got caught under the wind screen and I was stuck. My luck hadn't run out yet, because the plane made a nose up movement and the next thing I knew was that I was sitting back in my seat minus my helmet and goggles. The engine was still running, and I was still flying, so I decided what the hell, I might as well stay as long as the engine keeps going because I can always go over the side. I headed toward base, and as I got near I started broadcasting in the blind to the tower to let them know my predicament. Not knowing if they would hear me, I told them I was heading straight east into the east-west runway. When I got near the end of the runway, I put the gear handle down, but was I surprised when I bellied in and slid down the runway. As I hurried to get out of the plane, I found that the field was strafed by two Jap planes, and I had to run to the nearest foxhole.

After the all clear, I went over to my Corsair to inspect the damage. The top cylinder had been shot out, the hydraulic system was out, and there were bullet holes in the left flap too close to the cockpit.

Later on in the day, after debrief, 'Ho Hum' (Thomas Blackwell) came up to me and said, 'Seab,' (Allen's nickname), I don't know just exactly how to tell you this. After a long pause I said, 'Well, I was the one who shot at you.' Since it turned out the way it did, I told him to forget about it, but if it had turned out differently I would have been as mad as hell! The squadron was so close that in the heat of battle I knew these things happened, and it was hard to be angry and hold a grudge."

Combat 4

This division of four Corsairs, on dusk CAP off Point *Roger,* was led by Capt. Joe McPhail with 1Lt. Warren Bestwick on his wing, and had 2Lt. John Ruhsam as second division leader with 2Lt. Robert Wade on his wing. At 1900, the flight was vectored toward bogies approaching from the north and sighted four Army Ki-61 Tonys in column 1,000 feet below at 7,000 feet, near Kawata Wan. This air controller's vector provided inaccurate altitude information, and the flight entered the fray with insufficient altitude advantage. McPhail dove after the rear Tony, but hadn't seen three Army Ki-44 Tojos flying 1,000 feet above, behind and on the opposite side. McPhail missed his 20 degree deflection shot and overran, allowing all four Tonys to turn into him. To make matters worse, the Tojos also headed for McPhail.

Bestwick spotted the Tojos, pulled up into them and staggered the lead plane with 1,200 rounds on a head-on run and had to pull up violently to avoid a mid-air collision. Bestwick didn't see the

Tojo crash, but Wade saw a plane hit the water and believed it to be the same Tojo. Bestwick was awarded with a probable.

Meanwhile, Ruhsam hit the tail-end Tony with a long burst from 6 o'clock at 300 yards. Ruhsam, "We tangled with 7 Japs, 3 Tojos and 4 Tonys—faster than Hell and headed for no good. They were fast and had speed and it took forever to catch up. This was a case of 'he who has the fastest plane gets the first shot.' I managed to get behind one of the Tonys and gave him a long burst, but he didn't burn. He just started a long slow turn, spiraled down, hit the ground and blew up. While I was watching I lost track of my division and began to pay attention to any other Japs who may have still been around. I looked up and saw a lone Tony who was in perfect position to make a run on me. I guess he didn't see me as he did nothing, but I immediately went into water injection and hauled back on the stick to get more altitude. I tried to stay under him where he couldn't see me. But he did see me, and the next thing I knew, he just ran away from me, using his altitude for speed. I returned to base alone. It was dark, and I could look around and see our formations with their recognition lights on. As I approached Kadena I was told to circle as the field was under attack. Finally, the attack was over and I was cleared to land."

Wade chased a Tony, but the Jap chopped the throttle and Wade overran. The Tony pilot fired three bursts at Wade, and one 20 mm shell hit in the area of his right wing lock. Fortunately, it didn't explode, as it could have torn the wing off. Wade dove away after another Tony and devastated him on the third burst from 400 yards. The Tony trailed smoke and burned as it hit the ground. Wade headed north at 5,000 feet trying to find his flight. He detected a Tony five miles ahead, decided to drop his centerline tank and fire-walled his fighter. It took him ten minutes to catch the Jap off the northern tip of Okinawa, and he exploded him with a short burst from over 300 yards. This Tony dove into the water and burned. John Ruhsam revealed that Wade had been wounded in the combat and had swore Doc Dussman to secrecy because he didn't want to leave combat.

1Lt. John Ruhsam had claimed a Zeke on the 12th and then got a Tony while flying with Bob Wade on the 15th. Upon returning to base, Ruhsam found Japanese aircraft in the landing pattern and the field under Japanese air attack and had to circle the field until the Japs were finished. ***Courtesy of John Ruhsam.***

"I wondered why he started to wear a bath robe around the tent, and he told me, 'To hell with the Purple Heart, I want to stay in combat.' He could have gone home, and most guys would have jumped at the chance."

The other three pilots chased a Tojo away, but were unable to close on it with drop tanks. Wade rejoined the flight and the division headed towards Kadena. Their return was hairy. It was dark, they were low on fuel, and to top everything the field was under a bombing and strafing attack, and "friendly" AA fire was shooting at anything in the sky. Ruhsam, "The Japs got into the traffic circle with us when we returned. They had their lights on, and we couldn't distinguish them until they strafed and dropped three bombs on the field." The division landed safely, but perhaps not too soundly.

Del Davis relates an unusual experience on this day: "My division was on combat patrol at 18,000 feet over the northwest section of the island. The sun was going down but fairly good light remained. We were vectored to an enemy target and all hell broke loose. We were 'squirrel-caged,' as we had literally flown into a large formation of enemy aircraft. There were lots of tracers in the air, and each side was getting off snap shots at each other. The enemy scattered, I lost my wingman, and it had become quite dark by then. We were trained to join on a friendly aircraft ASAP to provide mutual support. I suddenly observed an aircraft off my right wing, and we moved closer together, wing tip-to-wing tip. I turned on my wing lights, and I think we both realized that we were 'unfriendly' at that same instant. I hacked the throttle and rolled into him, hoping to get a shot at him from the 6 o'clock position. But he rolled right with me and we were canopy-to-canopy, head-to-head, this pilot was here to stay. To this day, I'll never know just how we separated, but I had the forethought to turn off my running lights, and luckily this talented pilot just disappeared in the darkness. He had escaped, but had a 350 mile flight back home to Japan."

An anonymous pilot on the mission adds, "Maj. Turner led us to our position up the Okinawa coast, and I spotted four Tonys coming down the coast toward us. I guess he didn't see them, and I called the clock position on them. We had the altitude advantage and could have picked them off nicely, but Turner refused to turn the lead over to me as I was first lieutenant and he was a major. So the Tonys went on by us, but they were picked up by a division behind us."

16 APRIL COMBAT

During the afternoon of the 15th, Task Force 58 launched a fighter sweep over Kyushu and destroyed 29 JNAF Fifth Air Fleet planes in the air, and a further 51 on the ground. This sweep put a crimp on the force available for the third kikusui. The Japanese decided on an early morning launch of 165 (120 JNAF and 45 JAAF) kamikazes and a like number of conventional bombers and decoys.

Combat 1

After a 0730 scramble, 1Lt. Jim Feliton and his wingman, 2Lt. Dewey Durnford, were vectored northward to picket station No. 14, some 30 miles north of Ie Shima, to intercept bogies incoming from Kyushu. The visibility was perfect, no clouds or haze, and Durnford identified a single Kawasaki Ki-48 Lily twin-engined light

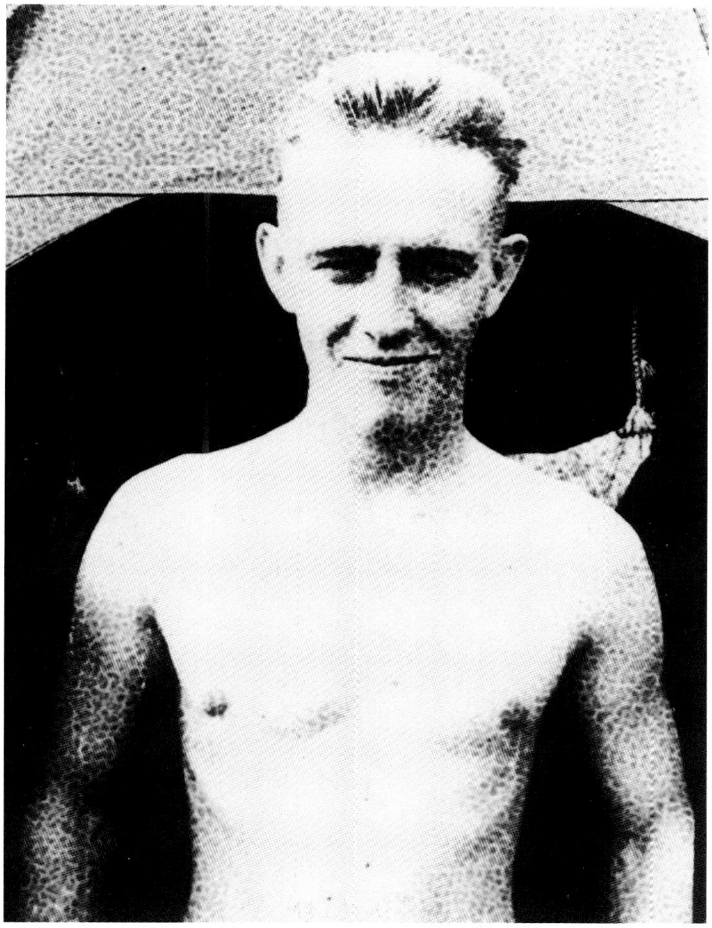

2Lt. Dewey Durnford shot down a Lilly bomber which had been attacking destroyer picket ships. On his return to base he intercepted and destroyed a Japanese bomber he identified as a Helen,. During the attack the enemy bomber dropped a winged aircraft from its belly which Durnford described over his radio as a "papoose." *Courtesy of Norman Miller.*

The bomber Durnford identified as a Helen was actually a G4M Betty as seen in this photo of Japanese pilots relaxing before take off. Under the belly of this Betty the "papoose" can be seen. It was a piloted, jet-propelled kamikaze flying bomb. *Author's collection.*

The Ohka, "Cherry Blossom," kamikaze was dubbed Baka, or "Fool," by the Americans. The Japanese claimed 300 were launched, but the Bakas were only credited with one destroyer sunk and two damaged. The Baka shown here was one of six captured in underground bunkers at Kadena. *Author's collection.*

bomber off in the distance, south of a damaged destroyer. Durnford saw the Lily turning back to the north for another run on the destroyer that had a badly damaged superstructure and was on fire. (This destroyer appears to be the PRINGLE DD-477, operating with DesDiv 90. She was hit by a kamikaze which struck her bridge and plowed through her superstructure deck. She broke in two and quickly sank with 43 dead, 62 missing and 258 survivors.) Durnford called the Lily's position to Feliton who couldn't find it, and told Durnford to go after it. He shoved the Corsair into a dive from 8-10,000 feet, and as he approached the target at about 1,000 feet above the water, he cut his throttle back to keep from overrunning. Durnford started his firing run from the 8 o'clock position, which exposed him to the bomber's turret gunners, but gave him better accuracy and more effective firepower. He closed to about 300 feet and began to fire, but noticed white wisps floating past the Corsair and Lily. It didn't take him long to realize that this was "friendly" anti-aircraft fire from below. Both planes were closing on the destroyer, each firing at the other. Durnford led the Lily in his gunsight, fired a short test burst and saw that his tracers were on target. He then followed with a long salvo that hit the Lily, which nosed over and fell into the sea short of its target. Durnford quickly pulled up to the left to escape the furious AA fire and rejoin his division.

The second division of the flight was forced to return to Kadena because of oil covering the division leader's windscreen. The remaining two Marine flyers were then quickly vectored south to intercept a bogie which had penetrated the air screen. Climbing to 12,000 feet, the Corsairs accelerated for 15-20 minutes toward the accurate bogie vector, which they picked up heading toward Kerama Retto at 2 o'clock and high on a converging path. The target was ID'd as a twin-engined Nakajima Ki-49 Helen bomber (see note). Feliton began his starboard attack as Durnford took a high portside position, the SOP for attacking bombers. Feliton rolled into his firing run and made his reversal as he neared the Helen. Nothing happened, as his guns had jammed, and he continued on, breaking off toward Durnford, who had begun his run.

On the afternoon CAP, a division led by 1Lt. Charles Martin (above) followed by wingman, 2Lt. Everett Yager and a second section of 1Lt. Ed Keeley and his wingman, 2Lt. Larry Crawley, pounced on a hapless single-engined Jap Kate bomber. All four pilots shared in the victory with a quarter share each. ***Courtesy of Del Davis.***

Textbook bomber attack procedure was to position the two attacking fighters on either side of their target at the 1 and 11 o'clock positions. The attacks were to alternate, port then starboard, each fighter changing sides and reattacking from the 4 and 8 o'clock positions, then breaking off at 6 o'clock or until the target was destroyed. Durnford had learned from his previous shared 1/3 victory over a Betty four days before that the Jap bombers were lightly armed. A concentrated firing pass from a slightly high 4 or 8 o'clock position running through (not to) the 6 o'clock position would increase target area and accuracy. He rolled in from his starboard and leveled out during his reversal. He fired a short burst from 8 o'clock leading the Jap's nose, another moving through 7 o'clock, and a final burst so close to the Jap that he was only 50 yards from its stern. He pulled up away from the attack with Jap tracers spewing around him and his cockpit filling with smoke. Durnford, convinced he had been hit, loosened his seat belt, opened the canopy, got a leg overboard and was ready to bail, when he recognized that the smoke had cleared. He got back into the aircraft and checked the gauges. Everything was functioning, and he rebuckled his seat belt and looked around and saw the Jap's engine on fire. The smoke from it had entered the Corsair's cockpit and had panicked its pilot.

Durnford made his second run, rolling to the left, and as soon as he was high out of his reversal, he fired a long downward burst from 4 o'clock on the Jap's starboard, hitting the engine and causing part of the wing to tear off. The strickened aircraft rolled on its starboard and fell into the ocean. As he fired, Durnford had noticed a small, winged craft drop from under the bomber. Durnford radioed that the bomber had been carrying "a papoose." Later, the papoose was identified by intelligence as a Baka bomb. (See note) The CAP was over, and Durnford returned to Kadena with two victories.

NOTE: The Baka bomb was not a bomb but a small piloted, suicide aircraft. The Japanese named the aircraft "OHKA," that translates from the Japanese as "Cherry Blossom," but was called "Baka" by the Allies which translates to the far less poetic "Fool." The model 11 was the only operational version, and a total of 755 were produced. It was a twin-ruddered, mid-winged cantilevered monoplane measuring 19 ft. 11 in. long, 3 ft. 10 in. high, with a 16 ft. 9 in. wingspan. It was powered by three rockets mounted in the rear fuselage and providing 8-10 seconds thrust of power, all at once or in succession. The warhead weighed 2,650 lbs. and contained five fuses. The cockpit contained the conventional pilot's stick and rudder arrangement, giving the pilot very good control of the aircraft. Contrary to Allied propaganda, the cockpits were not locked. The Ohka was carried to the target by specially modified Mitsubishi Betty G4M2 bombers. The aircraft carrying the "papoose" was identified by Durnford as a Helen, which looks very much like a Betty, especially to a pilot concentrating on his gunsight while maneuvering his fighter through the enemy's tracers! The Baka was carried by formations of heavily protected Betty bombers to a point within 30 miles of the target at 16-18,000 feet where it was released and the Bettys returned home. After release the Baka pilot could either glide towards the target or fire his rockets simultaneously to increase speed or singly to increase range. However, in combat, ideal tactics could not be implemented. Allied fighter air patrols ranging from 50 to 100 miles from the fleet would cause the Baka-encumbered and extremely vulnerable Betty to jettison its ward prematurely. It is for this reason that many Baka targets were the outlying destroyer pickets. The Baka that Durnford saw was one of six launched (unsuccessfully) that day, along with 126 kamikazes (42 returned) during Kikusui 3, the code name for one of the ten planned suicide operations on Okinawa. Six Bakas, hidden in underground bunkers, had been captured at Kadena during the first day of the invasion. Their Betty mother aircraft had been destroyed on the ground during the pre-invasion bombardment, or had escaped to Japan. Japanese propaganda boasted that over 300 Ohkas had been launched, but the exact number is difficult to determine. One destroyer (MANNERT L. ABELE) was definitely

2Lt. Ev Yager's quarter share in the downed Kate was his only claim of the war. ***Courtesy of Norman Miller.***

sunk, two others damaged, and two more possibly damaged by Bakas. So giving the Baka the benefit of the doubt, it had less than a 2% success rate. So, for the results achieved, perhaps the name "Baka" was appropriate. Adm. J.J. Clark, with tongue in cheek assessed the Baka: "The Baka failed because it was a one-shot mission; the pilots never got any practice."

Combat 2
Major George Axtell and his wingman, 1Lt. Ed Abner, had taken off on a scramble CAP at 0730 and reached patrolling altitude of 23,000 feet, 20 miles northwest of Ie Shima.

Axtell: "My wingman Ed Abner and I were assigned to a combat patrol point under the radar control of a picket ship at 23,000 feet. During the first hour of the mission we were repeatedly intercepted by Navy carrier-based F6Fs. We turned into them, made identification (the F4U's gull wings) and they would break off. We land-based fighters and the carrier fighters were under different combat flight controllers, and overall coordination of operations was very loose. Our patrols overlapped, and each flight had to identify any apparent bogey (aircraft whose identity was in doubt).

In response to the Fighter Director aboard the destroyer we were vectored on a course and altitude to identify the bogies. As full power was added, we turned to the assigned heading. I made my usual visual check in all quadrants, and as I was turning, I glimpsed at what I thought were F6Fs. They were high above us, coming out of the sun, making an apparent pass in our direction. I called the F6Fs to Abner and told him, 'Let's press on.' Soon I noticed red flashes going all around and into my aircraft. I looked into my mirror and saw two large red setting suns and made an immediate violent snap roll. I ended up behind the Franks (or Jacks-ACA report), while Abner took evasive action by diving to the deck. I was mad, embarrassed and determined to close on the Japs. At full power I was barely able to keep them in range, firing bursts at higher and higher angles of deflection in an attempt to score some hits. Oil was streaming over my canopy, and I had to abort my flight. Under very low power I made it back to Kadena with holes in my engine, main tank and flaps. Abner had landed an hour before and reported the incident, and everyone thought I had been shot down."

The Hamps and Jacks made high side stern runs out of the sun from 27,000 feet. Abner saw red flashes flicker over his wings and realized that there were two Hamps on his tail. The standard procedure to evade tailing aircraft is to turn into them, but this maneuver put Abner's Corsair into three high speed stalls. One of the two Hamps dove past the stalling Corsair, and as Abner brought it out of the stall he was able to dive on the Hamp's tail. He put the Pratt & Whitney into water injection and closed rapidly from above, and at 6 o'clock opened fire at 300 yards with his guns jamming momentarily. He continued to close getting hits on the top of its fuselage, causing it to smoke and drop its left wheel. Abner dropped his flaps to slow down and closed to 50 yards from astern. He got off three bursts, and the Hamp went over on its back and dove straight into the sea and exploded. Abner pulled up his flaps, and the second Hamp passed him in a dive followed by a Navy F6F that was firing at the Hamp. Abner pursued the two and moved in from above at 6 o'clock. He fired three bursts, and the Hellcat joined him. The Hamp started to smoke and fell to 100 feet, where it exploded for a shared victory.

Combat 3
The second round of morning CAPs left Kadena at 0930, led by 1Lt. Charles Martin with 1Lt. Larry Crawley on his wing, and 1Lt. Ed Keeley leading the second division with 2Lt. Everett Yager on his wing. The flight was vectored away from Okinawa and then back. The four Corsairs at 3,000 feet spotted a Navy B5N Kate attack bomber about four miles off Zampa Misaki (Point *Bolo*), a peninsula jutting from the Huguishi Beachhead at 1,500 feet. Martin led the attack from 6 o'clock high and began firing at 300 yards, getting hits on the engine. The Kate made shallow turns as the other F4Us closed in. Crawley followed Martin in and scored hits on the Jap's wing roots from 300 yards. Keeley closed at point blank range and took his cut, followed by Yager. After being on the receiving end of 24-.50 caliber machine guns the Kate started burning, its wing blew off, and it crashed into the water. One F4U was hit by the rear seat gunner's 7.7 machine gun. Five holes were found in the cowling and wing root and were repairable on site.

16 April Death of Maj. Jack Mathis

Also on the 16th, both VMF-323 and -322 flew cover for destroyer pickets which were reluctant to release them until after dusk because of the kamikaze threat. At 1945, VMF-323 division leader, Capt. Chuck Moore, had led his Corsairs back to Kadena. With IFF (Identification Friend or Foe) operating on proper code, Kadena tower advised Moore that he would flash field landing lights only momentarily because of impending Japanese attack. With Moore navigating, his division landed safely. The field had been under constant repair, and there was heavy equipment parked along the right side of the runway. Mathis, VMF-322 division leader, was also approaching the field and was given the same brief flash of runway lights. However, he lined up on the wrong side of the lights

1Lt. Ed Abner, shown here reclining on the wing of his Corsair, shot down a Hamp and shared another Hamp with a Navy F6F Hellcat. In the early days CAP control was very loose and Navy and Marine flights chronically intercepted one another. ***Courtesy of Norman Miller.***

On 16 April, 1Lt. Bob Lejonstien's aircraft lost oil pressure and he was forced to ditch. He was picked up by a DD and transferred to a LST which dropped him off on the beachhead. Despite having a bandaged head he was unable to hitch a ride back to base and had to walk. Axtell greeted him by telling him since he wasn't hurt too badly, he was on the next day's flying schedule! ***Courtesy of George Axtell.***

and plowed into the heavy equipment. Axtell and other -323 personnel rushed over and pulled Mathis' dead body from the wreckage.

16 April Bob Lejonstein MIA

On 16 April, an eight plane CAP led by Capt. Bill van Buskirk took off from Kadena at 0800 for picket duty. After flying for about 3 hours the unit was returning when 2Lt. Bob Lejonstein's engine started to become erratic and the oil pressure was gradually falling off. Since he was only at 1,500 feet Lejonstein decided he had better make a decision pretty quick, either to get more altitude to bail out or try to make it back to base. His decision was made for him, as the prop slowed and then just stopped, a big blade appearing just in front of his windscreen. Too low to bail, Lejonstein peered down and saw the ocean was calm, but as he dropped lower the swells got bigger and bigger. He decided he couldn't go into the swells head on, as he would be demolished if he crashed into one. He turned and set down the Corsair gently into a trough behind the crest of a swell for an ideal ocean landing. He forgot to tighten his harness straps, and when he hit the water he lurched forward, hitting his head on the gunsight and opening up a gash on his forehead with his raised goggles. He got out of the slowly sinking fighter. When he was in the water he noticed blood and scrambled to inflate his life raft and get out of the water and away from any sharks. He inflated the raft but found it to be a floppy piece of rubber. The raft's inflation valve had been left open, and all the CO2 escaped, leaving Wickser to depend on his Mae West. Fortunately, a minesweeper was nearby and picked him up. His head wound was bandaged, and he stayed over night being listed as MIA back at Kadena. The next morning he was transferred to a LST, which dropped him off on a beach and pointed him in the general direction of Kadena! Despite the bandage on his head he was unable to hitch a ride and had to walk back to base. After reporting his story to Axtell, the CO told Lejonstein that he was glad the pilot was not badly injured and that he should report to make another hop the next day. There is a discrepancy in the official records which list Bob Wickser as the MIA. A reunion video made in 1982 has Lejonstein relate the above story. In my interviews, Al Wells, Jerry O'Keefe and George Axtell insist it was Lejonstein who was the MIA.

17 April Close Air Support #1

Mission: 0600-0930 Destroy enemy machine gun and mortar emplacements in the northern portion of the Motobu Peninsula in support of friendly troops. The Sixth Marine Division had moved from the invasion beaches to capture Nago, the largest town on the north end of the island, without encountering significant resistance until L+12. However, when it drove into the Motobu Peninsula, jutting out into the East China Sea, things were to change. The troops of Col. Takesiko Udo occupied prepared defensive positions on 1,200 foot Mount Yae Take. Yae Take's dense vegetation and steep ravines were strewn with mines and guarded by machine guns and mortars. The defenders, determined to fight to the death, had to be blasted out of the intricate cave network at high cost to the attackers.

Major Axtell led seven F4Us at 0600, carrying two 500 lb. G.P. bombs and eight rockets to station. ASCU, via the Air Support Net, radioed Axtell the target location. He went low over the target to further verify and to aid him in establishing an accurate aiming point for the aircraft on station above.

A view of Ie Shima airfield taken by a -323 pilot. Ie Shima, an island off the Motobu Peninsula was invaded on 16 April. On the 17th and 21st VMF-323 flew close air support missions in the area. ***Courtesy of Norman Miller.***

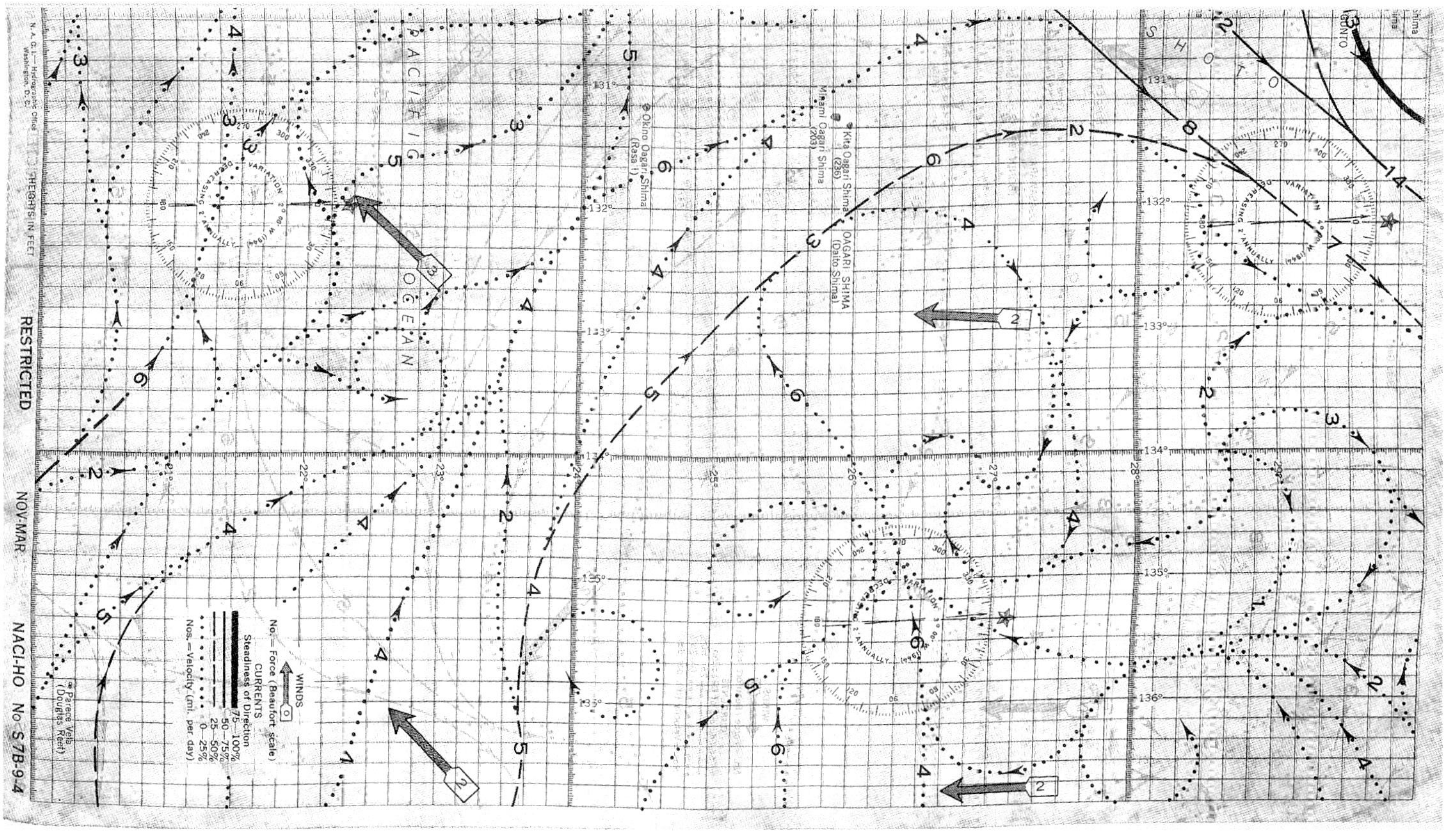

Two actual cloth emergency drift charts for the navigation of rubber rafts in case of ditching at sea. *Courtesy of Henry Brandon.*

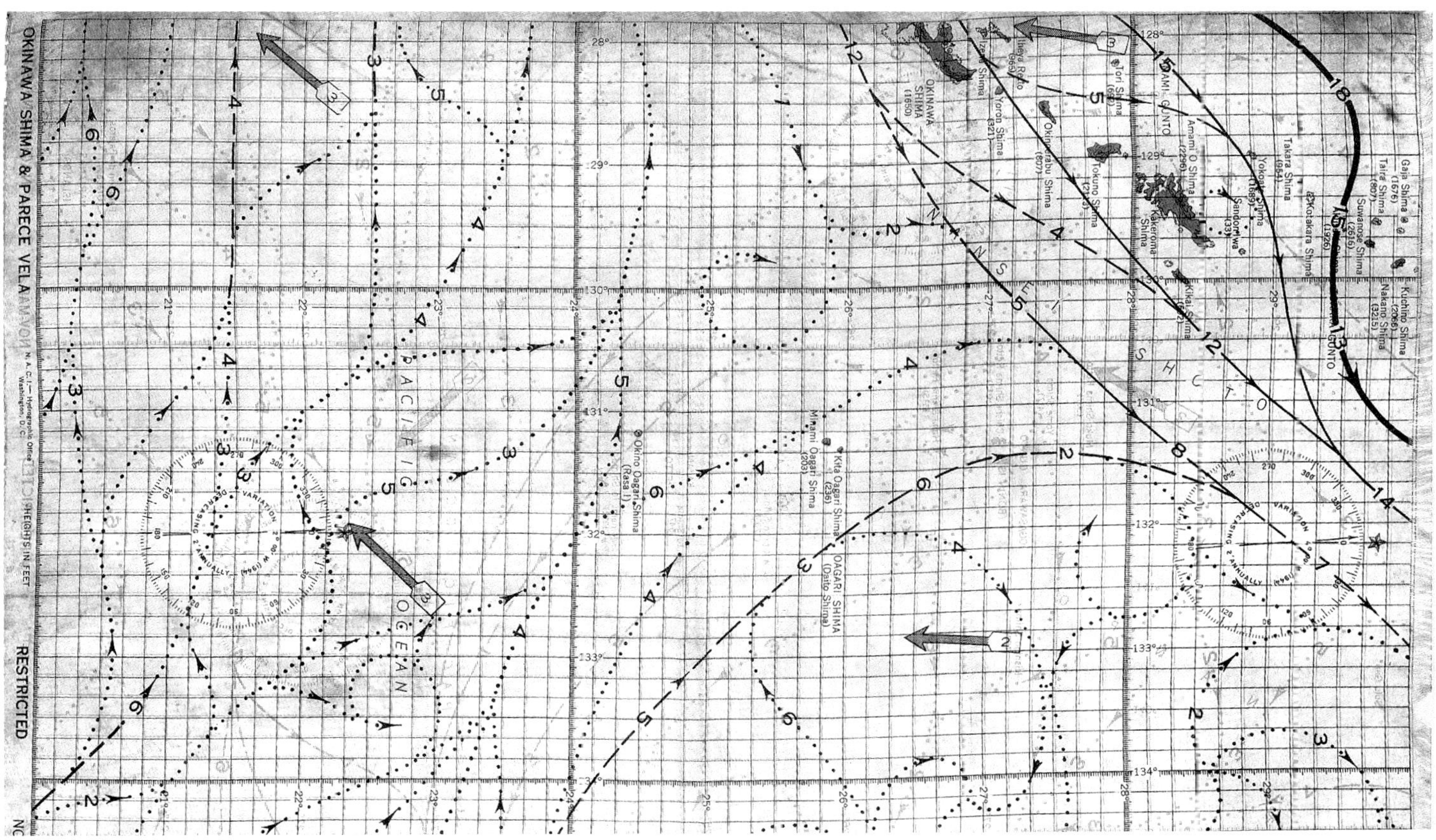

Ordnance Officer, Capt. John Grando, was driving the jeep during the runway accident on 17 April. A taxiing Corsair, unable to see the jeep over its long nose, hit it with its prop, killing T/Sgt. Al Elson and injuring T/Sgt. George Morrison and S/Sgt. Glen Johnson. ***Courtesy of Jody O'Keefe***

After observing the target area, Axtell climbed back to 2,500 feet and went into his rocket run at an angle of 25 degrees, releasing two rockets at 1,000 feet to further pinpoint the target. The aircraft waiting on station then made one glide bomb run with their dive brakes down, from 6,000 feet at a speed of 240 kts., releasing one bomb at 1,500 feet. They pulled out at 800-1,000 feet after clearing the target and retirement was made low on deck. The flight was then ordered back to Kadena. Although all bombs and rockets were in the marked target area, no emplacements were observed, as the target was well camouflaged. On landing a F4U suffered wing damage when a rocket fell off.

Post mission analysis stated: "Having the flight leader, on getting target designation, go down low on target to pinpoint it prior to his actually pinpointing it for the rest of his flight by way of rockets or bombs seems to be the most effective way to ensure accurate close air support."

Shuri Castle was left a mass of rubble by naval, infantry, and air attack. After its capture, the walls, moats, and thick surrounding forest looked like a World War One no-man's land. Shuri City in the distance was also totally destroyed. The Death Rattlers flew several support missions there in late April. ***Courtesy of the USMC***

17 April Close Air Support #2

Mission: 1030-1305 Attack enemy troop concentrations, mortar and artillery emplacements two miles east of Hamamoto in the northern part of the Motobu Peninsula.

After rearming in an hour from the earlier morning mission Axtell led two divisions off Kadena at 1030, each fighter armed with two 500 lb. G.P. bombs and eight rockets. After the general target area had been established by use of gridded target charts, Axtell dove low over the target for better observation. He noted buildings in and about the area, but failed to detect emplacements of any kind as they were either underground or extremely well camouflaged. He climbed back to 6,000 feet and started his rocket run to pinpoint what he thought was the target area for the rest of the flight on station. After he retired, the flight made their runs, firing all their rockets in salvoes of four, making their approach at 15 degrees at 240 kts. and releasing at 800-1,000 feet with a pullout of 200 feet.

At the termination of the rocket run, a glide bomb run on the target was made at 15 degrees from a pushover altitude of 2,500 feet, 235 KTS. speed, a bomb release at 1,000 feet and a pullout at 500 feet.

An estimated 75% of the ordnance hit the marked target area, but its effect was not known due to the camouflage. On this day major Japanese resistance on the Motobu subsided, and all resistance ended on 20 April.

17 April Death of Albert Elson

On the morning of 17 April, Capt. John Grando and T/Sgt. George Morrison were riding in the front seat and T/Sgt. Albert Elson and S/Sgt. Glen Johnson were in the back seat of a jeep which was traveling along a taxiway. These ordnance men were out to investigate the accidental firing of rockets being loaded earlier that morning. In the noise, confusion, and dust of a mission forming for takeoff, the vehicle turned to cross the taxiway, and was overtaken by 1Lt. Harold Tonnessen's taxiing aircraft. The F4U was notorious for its poor forward visibility over its 16 foot nose while taxiing. On this narrow taxiway the pilot could only see slightly forward left or right while turning by tapping the brake pedals to turn. The F4U's propeller hit the rear of the jeep, killing Elson and injuring Morrison and Johnson, who were evacuated to Guam. Morrison suffered a broken hip and Johnson a broken leg.

A small tomb located near Kadena. *Courtesy of Bob Woods.*

18 April Close Air Support #1

Mission: 1030-1305 Destroy by bombs, napalm, rockets and strafing the barracks, compound area and castle in the southeast part of Shuri. The Tenth Army continued to attack the Shuri Line with costly, unimaginative frontal assaults. Lt.Gen. Simon Buckner's troops used what he described as the "blowtorch and corkscrew" approach in fighting the entrenched Japanese. The blow torch was the flame thrower, and the corkscrew was the demolition charge; both delivered at close range by tanks and infantry. To relieve the bloodshed, naval and air support was called in to knock out strong points. The Shuri Castle, built in 1544, had coral walls 20 feet thick and 40 feet high. Lying on a high knob of ground at the southern edge of Shuri Town, it was the constant object of naval and air bombardment. The three Death Rattler support missions of the 18th were part of the softening up process for the 19 April American advance by three divisions against the Japanese 62nd Division's Machinato Line.

At 1030, Major Jeff Dorroh led four F4Us armed with one 500 lb. bomb, eight rockets, and one 165 gal. pylon napalm tank. The target area was easily identified in 4/10 clouds and haze from an altitude of 1,500 feet, from which the napalm attack was initiated. The F4Us went into a low level glide angle of 15 degrees at a speed of 235 Kts. and leveled off close to the target to an altitude of 100 feet. Using the cowl as a sighting device to release the napalm, large fires were set off with two of four hits in the target area.

After retiring low on deck, the flight climbed to 2,500 feet and made a rocket run, at 15-20 degrees, slant range of 3,000 feet. All eight rockets were salvoed at once, and large holes were noticed in the barracks and compound area after the run, but there were no explosions.

A glide bombing run was made next. The run began at 3,000 feet, at a 40 degree angle and released at 1,000 feet. The bombing damage seemed to be slight, and was followed by 6,000 50 cal. rounds of strafing on the target.

Burial tombs built into hillsides were scattered over Okinawa. This aerial view shows the architectural types and layouts. The Japanese used these tombs as ready-made gun emplacements and pill boxes in their defensive campaign. ***Courtesy of Henry Brandon.***

18 April Close Air Support #2

Mission: 1330-1600 Orders were to attack the radio towers and block house east of Shuri and the trucks and houses around Inasomi and Tamagusuku-Mura.

Major Axtell led two divisions armed with one 1,000 lb. G.P. bomb and eight rockets. ASCU designated the two target locations and Axtell dove to verified them, and then returned and fired rockets at the first target and a bomb at the second.

The two radio towers east of Shuri were the object of the first attack, a west to east rocket run with pushover from 2,700 feet, 10 degree dive, and a slant range release at 2,400 feet and pullout at 600 feet. Damage was seen to be slight, and it was determined that radio towers were poor targets for rockets.

The second target, the objective of the dive bombing attack, was seven radio towers and one blockhouse. The pushover was made at 3,000 feet through cloud cover and smoke at 10 degrees, and release at 150 feet with pullout at 100 feet. The aircraft were protected on their low pullout by the use of eight second delay bombs. Eight bombs hit the area, but three were duds. Damage on this target was also judged to be slight, with some huts and other dwellings on the periphery of the area damaged and on fire.

The Inasomi and Tamagusuku-Mura areas were "well strafed." A total of 13,630 rounds being used on 15 to 20 trucks, eight of which burned (the others seemed to be out of gas and did not burn). A large explosion followed one of the strafing runs on Inasomi, and it was believed that an ammunition dump had been hit. The post mission analysis concluded that the strafing attack did more visible damage than either the rocket or bombing attacks.

Close up of a tomb near Kadena which had been vandalized by American soldiers as an ancestral skull has been placed in the entranceway. ***Courtesy of Henry Brandon.***

Al Wells continued his strafing attack: "After all the excitement I forgot to turn off all the switches. The sky was clear but bumpy, and somehow my fingers on the stick activated the trigger. I fired off a few rounds on my approach to the field and it scared the hell out me. I didn't hit anything, or I would have heard about it."

18 April Close Air Support #3
Mission: 1630-1830 Destroy Japanese AA positions northwest of Shuri Town.

Major Arthur Turner led a division on the last support mission of the day carrying a 500 lb. G.P. bomb, eight rockets and a 165 gal. napalm tank. Turner was given grid coordinates and had to approximate the well-camouflaged target with a bomb. He then led the division in east-west dive bombing runs, followed by rocket runs, napalm drops (two duds), and finishing the mission with a strafing attack. Results of the mission were considered superficial.

20 April Close Support
Mission: 1330-1605 After having flights canceled on the 20th due to bad weather, -323 was assigned to lend support to the Shuri offensive.

Major Axtell led eight Corsairs armed with two 500 lb. G.P. bombs and eight rockets to station at 1345. Two targets were assigned via ASCU without the Air Coordinator, but were soon canceled. The divisions orbited until 1540, waiting for a target to be assigned. At this time Axtell informed the ASCU that he was running low on fuel and requested a target upon which to unload on before returning to base. Permission was granted to strike targets of opportunity in Itoman Town, south Okinawa.

A sequence of west to east attacks followed. Glide bomb runs and rocket runs were made, encountering scant AA fire. Results were ineffective due to the lack of specific target designation by an Air Coordinator.

20 April Accident
A division led by Captain Bill Van Buskirk took off at 0525 for a CAP. On takeoff 1Lt. Harold Edelson's landing gear folded. Edelson was uninjured, but his aircraft was written off.

21 April Close Support #1 and #2
Missions: Sesoko Shima is a small island lying off the west coast of the Motobu Peninsula. After the conquest of the Peninsula several strong points remained on the island to harass the mainland, and air support was requested to neutralize them.

Two -323 missions were sent out. The first, four aircraft led by Major Dorroh, left at 1105 to hit gun emplacements and an observation post. The second, another division led by Capt. Moore, left at 1430 to strike pillboxes, caves, and radio towers on the northwest section of the island.

Dorroh's division was assigned three targets. The first target was a complex of camouflaged burial vaults used as gun emplacements and was hit by 20 rockets, knocking out two with direct hits and leaving the other two gun vaults flaming. Their second target was an observation post and was left burning by eight 500 lb. Bombs, followed by strafing attacks. The third target, gun emplacements, was knocked out by seven rockets and strafing. On their return, two aircraft were found to have suffered minor damage from their own bomb blasts.

Moore's division attacked their first target, a fortified concrete tower, causing slight damage with seven bombs, four rockets and strafing. Their second targets were pillboxes and fortified caves covering an area of 50 square yards. Twenty rockets were fired, 17 hitting the target area, and this attack was followed by strafing, which also caused slight damage.

21 April Close Support #3
Mission: 1530-1730 Japanese artillery positions northwest of Shuri Town were attacked to prevent their continued harassment of the American attack on the Shuri Line.

Major Arthur Turner led a four plane division on gun positions identified by their flashes 200 yards apart. The first set of four guns were hit by 21 rockets which scored hits or near misses destroying three or four. Five bombs were dropped from low level on the second target. Both guns were silenced and believed to be destroyed.

22 April Combat "The Big Turkey Shoot"
The Japanese had lost over 700 kamikazes and as many conventional bombers and escorts since the start of their TEN-GO operation, and only a few scattered Japanese aircraft appeared. Shortly before sunset the Japs sent a large joint JNAF formation from Kyushu and a JAAF formation from Formosa. This was not a kikusui attack, but did more damage than the next—the fourth kikusui—on the 27-28th.

After five days of boring CAP without aerial combat and six uneventful flights that day the Death Rattlers were looking for action. Major George Axtell, followed by his wingman, 1Lt. Ed Abner, and his second section led by 1Lt. Jerry O'Keefe and his wingman,

1Lt. Bill Hood, led eight Corsairs. This group was followed by Major Jefferson Dorroh leading 1Lt. Charles Allen and 2Lt. Normand Theriault (one F4U aborted) for CAP at 1500. The first three hours of the CAP were uneventful.

After three hours of patrolling, Axtell's four plane division was vectored to 25,000 feet to intercept a high flying Jap bogie. Before they could reach their assigned altitude they were revectored to dive on a large formation of 35 low-flying Japs to the northwest.

At 5,000 feet they detected a large formation of Val dive bombers flying directly towards them and heading towards two destroyers about 40 miles north of Aguni Shima. Axtell's Corsairs rolled over, dove through cloud cover, and intercepted the Japs, identified Val dive bombers. The Val formation split up and took evasive action, some heading for cloud cover at 2,000 feet. Axtell attacked the Vals with beam runs from slightly above and all 10-45 degree deflection shots. Fifteen minutes later, Axtell had shot down five and damaged three to become an ace in one mission. Axtell's wingman, Al Abner, shot down two Vals and damaged another, all on a single high stern run. The first Val smoked and crashed. He hit the second Val and its bomb exploded, forcing Abner to fly through the debris. Abner's fighter suffered a shattered wing tip and damage to both wing roots, along with a few bullet holes in his fuselage. Despite the damage, Abner hit the tail of another Val before he returned to base. 1Lt. Charles Allen downed a Val and claimed another as a probable.

It was Jerry O'Keefe's turn. Dropping full flaps to remain in firing position, O'Keefe flamed four Vals from a point blank 6 o'clock position. He was scissoring with a fifth Val and made a head-on run. The Val kept on coming, looking like he was going to ram the Marine. O'Keefe pressed the trigger until the Val winged over, and O'Keefe had to pull up violently to avoid collision. He left combat with ammo in only two machine guns. "It was one of the most exhilarating, brief moments of my life." O'Keefe had become an instant ace.

1Lt. Bill Hood followed section leader, O'Keefe, into the Jap formation and shot at three planes on his first pass. A Val was hit in the tail from 400 yards with a 40 degree deflection shot and was credited as damaged. His next target was an ancient Nate Ki-27 fighter that burst into flames and crashed after a stern shot. His last target on this run was another Val that was flamed by a stern shot,

1Lt. Jerry O'Keefe became an instant ace shooting down five Vals. O'Keefe described the combat: "It was one of the most exhilarating brief moments of my life." ***Courtesy of Jody O'Keefe.***

Major George Axtell shot down five Vals and damaged three others to become an ace. ***Courtesy of Norman Miller.***

1Lt. Charles Allen got a Val and a Val probable. *Courtesy of Norman Miller.*

Major Jeff Dorroh shot down six Val sand damaged two others. Dorroh's total was one less than the Marine record one day total of seven set by Capt. James Swett of VMF-221 on 7 April 1943, when he shot down seven Vals over Bougainville. *Courtesy of Jody O'Keefe.*

1Lt. Ed Abner, shown here with an elephant design on his landing gear fairing, shot down two Vals and damaged another on a single run. *Courtesy of Henry Brandon.*

but was not seen hitting the water and listed as damaged. Hood pulled up in a wing over and was joined by other carrier-borne Corsairs in pursuing the Vals. His next victims were hit by point blank stern shots; the first rolled and crashed, while his second victim snap-rolled and crashed for shared victories. Hood's next shared victory came when he and another Corsair made a simultaneous head-on run on a hapless Val. These three shared victories were probably made with pilots off the carrier RANDOLPH (CV-15). Hood's last victory came on a point blank stern run at a Nate. The nimble Nate tried a sharp turn, but Hood was at 100 feet and couldn't miss.

Before the engagement, Major Jefferson Dorroh's three plane section was orbiting at 5,500 feet. They were vectored to dive through the clouds and located the same formation that Axtell had bounced just seconds before. Upon seeing the large formation of Japs, Major Dorroh had deactivated two of his machine guns to conserve ammo. He went after two fleeing Vals in a high beam run. He hit the first Val around the cockpit and fuselage, and it went into a steep turn towards the water. Dorroh could not hang around to see it crash and was credited with a probable. He recovered low on the water and approached another Val from slightly above at 9 o'clock. The Val went into such a quick, violent turn that Dorroh had to drop his gear and lower his flaps to continue the pursuit and not overrun. Using four guns, he got hits in the cockpit and fuselage, killing the pilot before the Val crashed into the sea for his first victory. He quickly got victory #2 with an attack from above at 5 o'clock. Another vector gave Dorroh another Val victory. Pulling up his nose, he gave it a one second, full deflection shot at 1,000 feet. He then sighted another Val just below the clouds at 2,000 feet. He fired from 9 o'clock, and the Val started to burn, made a steep diving turn, and crashed for victory #4. Another run was made on a Val,

The Aichi D3A, Val, was a two man, fixed gear carrier bomber which had bombed Pearl Harbor. It was obsolete at that time and by Spring 1945, was relegated to land-based Kamikaze units on Kyushu. It was the most numerous of -323's 124 1/2 kills, accounting for 51 3/4 of its victories, Zekes and Nicks were next, falling 16 times each. On 22 April 22 3/4 Vals fell to Death Rattler guns. *Courtesy of Jim Lansdale.*

and wing and cockpit fragments were seen flying off, but Dorroh only claimed a probable as he lost it in the clouds. Dorroh missed his next Val on the first pass but set it on fire with a 9 o'clock pass. It exploded when it hit the water for victory #5, another ace-in-a-day. Dorroh was not done for the day. On the way back to Kadena, he joined Lt. Charles Allen of Axtell's element. They spotted a lone fleeing Val, and Dorroh urged Allen to get it, but he was out of ammo. Dorroh set it on fire with another deflection run for his sixth victory of the day.

1Lt. Charles Allen had followed Dorroh on the original interception and made a high stern run on his first victim. The Val flamed around the cowling, nosed over and crashed. He made another high stern run and flamed a second Val, but Allen overran and did not see it crash and claimed it as a probable.

1Lt. Normand Theriault also followed Dorroh in and closed on the tail of a Val, hitting it with a three second burst. It flamed and split-essed into the water. He hit his next Val with high stern 30 degree deflection shot, knocking off pieces of its wing and causing its engine to smoke. Three carrier-borne Corsairs showed up to fire on the strickened Val, and Theriault was forced to claim a 1/4 victory. He quickly went into a right flipper turn and got on the tail of another Val. His 50s hit the cockpit, starting a fire that caused the Val to crash into the sea. All Theriault's attacks were made at point blank range.

1Lt. Bill Hood shot down two Nates and then claimed three shared victories with the Corsairs of other Marine units for 3 1/2 victories for the day. *Courtesy of Henry Brandon.*

Axtell, O'Keefe and Dorroh began the day without previously destroying an enemy aircraft, but by its end were "instant aces." Seven -323 pilots returned to base with 24 3/4 total victories (the fraction due to shared victories with VMF-224 and 441 pilots who claimed an additional 8 1/2 victories in the battle), three probables and six other Japs which got away with obvious damage. This was the highest daily total for any air squadron in the Okinawa campaign. The total bag of Japanese planes shot down for the day was 54. The Marine aviators were credited with 33 1/4 and the Navy the remainder. Dorroh's six victories were the most in one day since 7 April 1943, when Capt. James Swett of VMF-221 shot down seven Vals over Bougainville. Axtell, Dorroh and O'Keefe received the Navy Cross for this action.

Debriefing after the battle noted that that there were no rear gunners in the Jap aircraft, and that they exploded upon impact, as their bombs were fused instantaneously, both observations verifying their kamikaze status. VMF-323 pilots noted that they wasted too much ammo and would have had problems if they had run into more Japs. Five pilots had released their drop tanks too soon and returned to base low on gas.

It is interesting to note the large number of Navy Aichi Vals claimed shot down, when in fact the low wing, spatted fixed-gear, dive bomber was largely an obsolete aircraft replaced by the Kugisho Judy. The Army's Mitsubishi Ki-51 Sonia and Nakajima Ki-27 Nate were both low wing, spatted fixed-gear fighters which could be mistaken for the Val in the duress of air combat. The JAAF expended them in their kikusui attacks.

Del Davis notes: "We also launched as late as 1730, a time when the enemy was most active. One disadvantage to this was that the fleet was justifiably anxious and would open fire on just about anything flying by. Our aircraft had three lights on the bottom; amber, white and red. We were instructed to use the assigned color code of the day. But no one could see the colors from more than a half mile off, and so this was an ineffective IFF (identification, friend or foe) device. You definitely didn't want to get within a half mile of the fleet's guns! Our navigational aids were very poor. The ZB/YE nav-aid at Kadena was a simple fade and build tone, which told you when you were over the field. On one of my missions I was returning late over a 6,000 foot overcast top. I started my let down into the overcast, did a reverse turn at 3,000 feet, and tracked the nav-aid inbound to the airfield, breaking through the clouds at 1,500 feet. But we found we were crossing the beach easterly toward Kadena, and every AA gun in the fleet had opened fire on us. I dove the formation steeply to the deck and broke sharply to the north. The only good thing about the AA was that any enemy fighter that had trailed our formation home would be driven back into the clouds."

The brass congratulates the victors in the 22 April air battle which netted a record 24 3/4 Japs and three "aces-in-a-day" (5 victories in a day). Front Row: (L to R) Ed Abner (2 victories), Jerry O'Keefe (5), Charles Allen (1), Bill Hood (3 1/2). Back Row: (L to R) Jeff Dorroh (6), George Axtell (5), Gen. Francis Mulcahy, Col. Ward Dickey, and Norm Theriault (2 1/4). Mulcahy was the commanding general of the 10th Army TAF and 2nd MAW while Dickey was CO of MAG-33. ***Courtesy of Jody O'Keefe.***

22 April

Norman "Whitey" Miller describes a non-contact mission. "Our flight was led by 1Lt. Jim Feliton and consisted of his wingman, 1Lt. Harold Tonnessen, my section leader, 1Lt. Glen Thacker, and myself. We were headed out for picket ship patrol, flying through scattered cloud. Soon we ran into some heavy black cloud, and I

1Lt. Norm Theriault made point blank attacks and shot down two Vals and then was forced to share a 1/4th victory with three carrier-borne F4Us which finished off the Val Theriaut first set on fire. ***Courtesy of Norm Theriault.***

A PR photo of Jerry O'Keefe at Yonton. Note that the same Corsair, #897, was also used in the Norm Theriault photo. ***Courtesy of Jody O'Keefe.***

thought it was too dangerous to fly too close to Scotty (Thacker), so I broke away from the formation. As I did so I was not looking at my gyro horizon instrument, which would have shown me the attitude of my plane. As the clouds got thicker and soupier, suddenly I just panicked. There's the myth of the old mail pilots flying by the seat of their pants, but I didn't know if I was right side up or upside down. All I could see in my panicked state was my altimeter racing clockwise one time and counter clockwise another as I made worried adjustments to the stick. I was afraid of stalling and spinning in. Finally, I came out of the clouds only 200 feet above the water, totally disoriented. I headed for a clear area to gain my composure and bearings and headed back toward Kadena. This was the scariest of any of my days of flying. The irony was, despite all my instrument training, that in my panic I had not thought to use the one instrument that could have helped me make a gradual descent through the clouds."

Combat chef extrordinaire, Sol Mayer, prepares to reward new instant aces, (L to R) Jeff Dorroh, George Axtell, and Jerry O'Keefe with a steak dinner with all the trimmings. ***Courtesy of the USMC via Jody O'Keefe.***

24 April CAP Mission

Four F4Us led by Major Arthur Turner flew a morning CAP. Warren Broering: "We were flying CAP off the little island of Ie Shima, and the weather kept getting lower and lower. We tried to keep on station and used Ie Shima to keep ourselves oriented as to Okinawa. Finally, we got down to 150 to 200 feet and suddenly there was another division of Corsairs doing the same thing we were, and we could have lost all eight of us in nothing flat. We asked the command ship for permission to return to base, and they said, 'No, you stay out there.' Turner told them if we were going to have to stay, we were going to climb through this stuff, because it was too dangerous to stay down here. We tucked ourselves close to Turner, who did a great job on instruments as we climbed to 24,000 feet before breaking out of this soup. We stayed up there for an hour and a half and spent the whole time worrying how we were going to get back down to find the base. But we were lucky—when we came down there was an opening right over the field."

New Pilots

Harold Hohl: "At the end of our training we had checked out in the F6F Hellcat night fighter for several days. We then did some FCLP with the Corsair in preparation to join a carrier squadron, but finally they decided what they wanted to do with us. I joined -323 on Okinawa with the first replacement pilots, along with Jerry Conners and Jim Carey, towards the end of April. We had left San Diego around April 1, went through Hawaii and on to Guam, where we picked up replacement aircraft to fly into Okinawa."

A.M. Blaydes: "I came to Okinawa after the squadron flew off the WHITE PLAINS to Kadena. On Pityliu, we were staging to put the aircraft aboard the carrier, and we had just got the planes fueled

Commandant, Gen. Alexander Vandegrift (2nd left) visits Major General Francis Mulcahy and the three Death Rattlers who became aces-in-a-day: (L to R) Axtell (5), Vandegrift, Mulcahy, Dorroh (6), and O'Keefe (5). Courtesy of the USMC.

Jerry O'Keefe receives the Navy Cross for his five victories. ***Courtesy of Jody O'Keefe.***

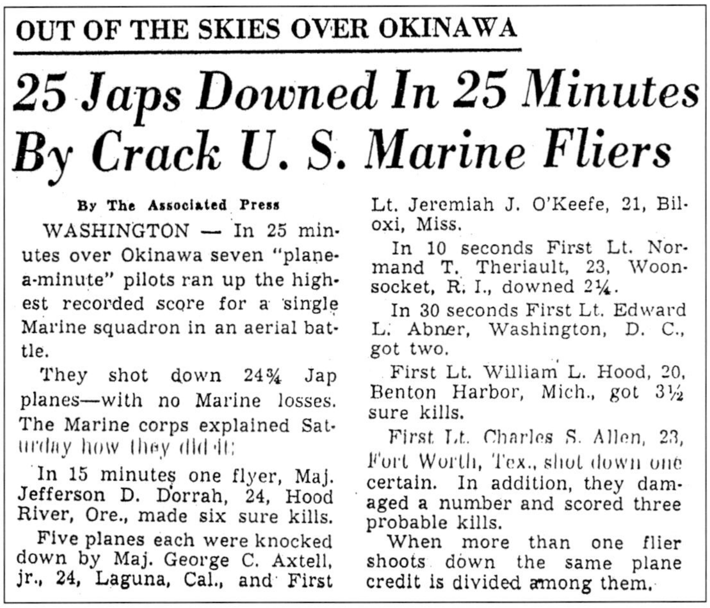

OUT OF THE SKIES OVER OKINAWA

25 Japs Downed In 25 Minutes By Crack U. S. Marine Fliers

By The Associated Press

WASHINGTON — In 25 minutes over Okinawa seven "plane-a-minute" pilots ran up the highest recorded score for a single Marine squadron in an aerial battle.

They shot down 24¾ Jap planes—with no Marine losses. The Marine corps explained Saturday how they did it:

In 15 minutes one flyer, Maj. Jefferson D. Dorrah, 24, Hood River, Ore., made six sure kills.

Five planes each were knocked down by Maj. George C. Axtell, jr., 24, Laguna, Cal., and First Lt. Jeremiah J. O'Keefe, 21, Biloxi, Miss.

In 10 seconds First Lt. Normand T. Theriault, 23, Woonsocket, R. I., downed 2¼.

In 30 seconds First Lt. Edward L. Abner, Washington, D. C., got two.

First Lt. William L. Hood, 20, Benton Harbor, Mich., got 3½ sure kills.

First Lt. Charles S. Allen, 23, Fort Worth, Tex., shot down one certain. In addition, they damaged a number and scored three probable kills.

When more than one flier shoots down the same plane credit is divided among them.

L.A. TIMES/Associated Press dispatch on the record combat. ***Courtesy of Jody O'Keefe.***

and oiled. Keith Fountain motioned me over to hold up his wing until the pressure built up so he could fold them. I stepped off the wing of my aircraft onto the runway, which was covered with Marsden Mat over coral, and my foot slipped and I hurt it. I went to have it looked at and found that I had broken a metatarsel bone and needed a cast. The doctor was going to send me back down to Espiritu Santo, but I talked him into waiting. While I was recuperating I was flying a Navy Captain around. He had a civilian license but couldn't sign out this Piper Cub. So, I signed it out and he flew it. We got to be good friends, and I told him my story about being left behind. There was a SBD on the base. and I asked him since I was qualified in it, if I could fly it up to Manus. There I could catch a MATS plane to Okinawa. I did get one to the Philippines where I tried to get to Okinawa. I was detained by a Navy commander who asked for my orders, and I told him that I lost my flight bag with my orders in it. He told me to wait a minute. As soon as he left I took off and ended up at another airfield and spoke to a Marine squadron CO who I had known before. He thought it was funny that I was going AWOL to get into combat instead of the other way around. I led a flight of 2nd lieutenants to Iwo Jima and hurt my foot again. I had it x-rayed again and found I had rebroken it, this time right behind the previous fracture. The Navy flight surgeon said he would let me fly with my foot taped if I could use the Corsair's brakes. I got in the cockpit and mashed my heels against the pedal with a great deal of pain. All flight surgeons have soloed at some time in their career, and he knew that you were supposed to use your toes to brake. He asked me if I always braked that way, and I told him I didn't know there was any other way! The next morning I landed at Yontan and then flew the three miles over to Kadena, about a couple weeks late."

28 APRIL COMBAT

Four days went by with very sparse Japanese air activity and without a shipping loss before the Japanese launched their fourth kikusui. Of the 165 aircraft (120 JNAF and 45 JAAF), 25 began their attack between 2,000 on the 27th and 0400 on the 28th. At dawn the picket stations began to be harassed, but it was not until after seven CAP missions without seeing a Jap that the Death Rattlers were vectored to large formations of incoming bogies.

Combat 1

First Lieutenants Vernon Ball, Francis Terrill, Bill Hood and Ed Murray were scrambled on CAP at 1615, and were vectored to 15,000 feet over Izena Shima by the Fighter Director. The flight was then moved north to 25,000 feet, 50 miles north of Izena Shima. At this time at 22,000 feet, Lt. Murray sighted four Vals cruising along at 180 knots in a southerly directing at 15,000 feet toward shipping in the area. The entire division nosed over, each choosing a Val to engage.

Hood dove 7,000 feet and closed on a Val from above at 5 o'clock at 350 knots. He opened fire at 1,500 feet on the Val, which took evasive action with gentle climbing and diving turns. He closed to 200 feet and saw his tracers hit the entire length of the fuselage and into the cockpit. The Jap flamed and split-essed into the ocean.

Terrill sighted his Val below and dove to initiate a run from 6 o'clock above. He opened short bursts of fire at 300 feet and saw tracers hitting the entire length of the fuselage. The Val began to smoke badly and spun into the water.

Murray sighted his Val and dove to make a pass from above, closing at 8 o'clock, and opening fire at 900 feet. His adversary smoked, but soon burned violently and immediately crashed into the sea.

Ball nosed over, made his pass from above at 7 o'clock, and opened fire at 1,500 feet, and after a short burst flamed the Val, which typically split-essed onto the ocean.

All four Vals had taken evasive action by effecting steep, diving turns to starboard and port, but to no avail, as all were shot down on the Corsair's first firing pass. The kamikaze Vals carried

(L to R) Harold Hohl, Jim Carey, and Jerry Conners joined the squadron after it had landed at Okinawa. ***Courtesy of Norman Miller.***

A GMC 6x6 delivering the pilots to the flight line for another mission. Seab Allen is waving at the camera. ***Courtesy of Norman Miller.***

1Lt. Vern Ball shot down two Vals for his only victories of the war. Because the Vals were kamikazes they had no rear gunners and were easily approached from the rear. ***Courtesy of Norman Miller.***

Downing two Nates to go with his five Vals on the 22nd, Jerry O'Keefe's #26 shows seven victories which made him the highest scoring Marine ace over Okinawa at the time. ***Courtesy of Jody O'Keefe.***

no rear gunners, so the Marines were able to close to point blank range.

After dispatching these Vals, the four Death Rattlers joined up and were vectored west. Almost immediately four more Vals accompanied by an Ida were sighted in the area headed toward shipping to the south. The Ki-55 Ida was an obsolete Army advanced trainer whose pilot, unable to navigate, was probably along for the kamikaze ride.

Ball and Terrill dove 5,000 feet and made a simultaneous run on one Val at 15,000 feet. Ball opened a short burst of fire at 1,500 feet from above at 6 o'clock and closed fast due to the speed of the dive. Ball fired a few more bursts and noticed the burning as he pulled by. Terrill, on his wing, saw the Val splash.

On retirement the Ball and Hood sections paired up. Hood had spotted two Vals at 12 o'clock, five miles ahead, and 5,000 feet below. Hood and Murray began to bracket the Japs on the port side,

1Lt. Joe Dillard (L) shot down a Kate for the last of the squadron's 14 1/2 victories for the day while 1Lt. Bill Hood (driver) became an ace when he claimed two Vals. ***Courtesy of Norman Miller.***

Three double victories. 1Lt Vern Ball (2 Vals), passenger seat, 1Lt. Charles Spangler (0), driver, 1Lt. Francis Terrill (2 Vals), standing, and 1Lt. Jerry O'Keefe (2 Nates). ***Courtesy of Norman Miller.***

The Nakajima Ki-27 Nate played a major part in the early war Japanese success but was superseded by the Oscar as the Japanese Army's front-line fighter. It became a home defense fighter and trainer before being phased out in 1943. It was used by the Army as a kamikaze over Okinawa. ***Courtesy of James Lansdale.***

while Ball and Terrill did so on the starboard. As the division dove in their run the Vals split, one going left and the other right in diving turns. Ball dropped 50 degree flaps, cut his throttle and made a 4 o'clock run on the right-turning Val. A few well-aimed bursts from 1,500 feet set the Jap on fire and into the ocean. Meanwhile, Terrill closed on the second Val from above at 6 o'clock, also opening fire from 1,500 feet, and the Val caught fire and split-essed into the ocean.

That left the remaining Vals and the Ida. Murray and Hood started their runs at approximately 1,200-1,600 feet, with the Vals and Ida 800-1,000 feet below. Murray made two passes. On his first pass he shot down the hapless Ida. During his next run on the Val he was joined by an unidentified F4U out of Yontan, which opened fire at the same time and got credit for a shared victory.

Hood finished the battle by splashing his Val with two runs. On the first he dropped 800 feet from 1,600 feet and his bullets ripped pieces off the fuselage and engine cowling. But he had trouble finishing off the Val because of his high speed and the Val's low speed. On his second run he slowed and fired from 4 o'clock from above at 1,500 feet and was able to concentrate his fire to set the Jap on fire and to crash into the ocean. The victory made him an ace.

Henry Brandon: "I flew the first mission of the day, and when I returned to Kadena Jack Ball told me that I was scheduled for runway standby in his place as his aircraft had been damaged. I told him that he could take mine, as I was tired from my dull CAP. I guess I lost my only chance at combat, as Jack shot down two Vals that day."

Great PR photo of Jerry O'Keefe after getting his seventh victory. ***Courtesy of Jody O'Keefe.***

An abandoned Japanese building was used as a latrine at Kadena. ***Courtesy of Norman Miller.***

Combat 2

At 1730, on the eleventh and last mission of the day, two divisions left Kadena. One division was led by Major George Axtell and comprised of 2Lt. John Ruhsam (wingman), 1Lt. Jerry O'Keefe (section leader), and 2Lt. Dewey Durnford (wingman). The second division was led by Capt. Joe McPhail and comprised of 1Lt. Ed Keeley (wingman), 1Lt. Del Davis (section leader), and 1Lt. Robert Muse (wingman).

Once airborne the Fighter Director vectored the flight to a point approximately 70 miles northwest of Zampa Misaki, which lies on the west south central coast. The flight orbited this point, and as the Fighter Director was unable to give any information on the altitudes of approaching bogies, Axtell deployed his flight. Two F4Us at 8,000 feet, two at 10,000, two at 12,000, and two at 15,000.

O'Keefe, in Axtell's division, headed east at 15,000 feet and recalls the encounter: "I called the rest of the flight that I saw five bogies, as they were too far distant for me to be certain of their identity. I suspected they were Japanese because their group included five planes rather than the four, eight, or twelve planes we usually had. It surprised me that when I called out the bogies at 3 o'clock down and headed south that no one else in the flight saw them. I requested Axtell to let my section investigate, and we began a slow turn to the south and began bearing down on the bogies from behind and above. As I got closer I became more certain that the bogies were bandits and radioed the confirmation. Major Axtell then descended with the remainder of the flight, following us. I armed my machine guns and hand signaled Durnford on my right wing to move out further right so he could attack from the rear at about the 5 o'clock position. Then I could attack from the left rear position at about 7 o'clock. My excitement was running high—as we chased these aircraft I could see now they were Nates flying in a V-formation and headed towards our shipping in Okinawa Harbor. I lost sight of Durnford, but we were so much in tune with each other that I thought he would be in range to fire with me on the

A hokey "official" Marine Corps PR photo with the caption: "As fighting continued on Okinawa Marine Corps fighter pilots find time for a little relaxation between missions. A native cart is one means of transportation between their tents and the mess hall." Riding the cart are Del Davis (front), and Leon Reynolds (rear), and pushing are Bob Wickser and Bill Martin (in shorts). *Courtesy the USMC.*

"Red" Dillard (L) and Bob Muse check out the intelligence board. Posted on the board was "recognition dope" and the notice that Intelligence was relocated to the ready room. *Courtesy of Bill Drake*

Nates. The Japanese pilots were unaware of our approach and did not make any move to evade our attack. I opened fire on the leader, aiming at his plane about amidships, shooting from probably 300 yards. He took a hit just in front of his cockpit and exploded. I attempted to fix aim on the next closest plane, but couldn't do so in time and missed him with a short burst as I dove past in a shallow dive. I pulled up and around to the left as quickly as I could, and only detected a single plane in a dive for the ocean below. I went after him, flying straight down on his tail and didn't miss him again. I fired into his plane from directly behind and he exploded. Durnford and I teamed up again and rejoined Major Axtell's flight." (Durnford had followed O'Keefe and exploded two Nates on his first run.) The two Nate victories gave O'Keefe seven victories, making him the leading Marine ace over Okinawa at the time.

Meanwhile, Axtell spotted a Nate trying to escape and was going too fast, trying to catch up and overshot on his first pass. He recovered, pulled up, and made another less hasty run, opening fire at 900 feet at 8 o'clock above. A short burst splashed the Nate.

John Ruhsam describes his part in the combat: "I was on the wing of our CO, Maj. Axtell, and it was the first time I had flown with him. I was a bit apprehensive, as are most lieutenants flying with majors for the first time. Wade and I joined the squadron late as replacements, and we were never quite sure that we had been accepted by those who had been flying together for so long. We were vectored toward the north, as radar had picked up Jap planes headed toward the island. As we did not know their altitude, Axtell split us up into sections. Two were to remain at 8,000 feet, two at 10,000, two at 15,000, and he and I climbed toward 20,000. On our way I spotted a formation of five Japanese planes below. No one else saw them, and Axtell turned the lead over to me. I assumed then that the flight would join with us and we would make a coordinated attack. However, that was not the idea of those below us. They had identified the Japs as obsolete Nates, and before I knew it there were several of the enemy burning below me. I thought, 'John, you spotted those planes and now you're not even going to get a shot at them unless you do something mighty fast!' I rolled over at 15,000 feet and split-essed on an overhead run at the remaining Nate. I was in a steep dive, so I jettisoned my belly tank, charged my guns and lined up on the Jap. I fired one short burst and saw the little flickering of my bullets when they hit. But then I was in the only cloud in the entire Pacific that day. I knew if I continued on course I was going to run right into the Nate. I did the only thing that I knew and stood on the right rudder. I broke out of the cloud just as I just missed the Nate, with my wing going between his wing and elevator. But now the ocean was right in front of me and I was going hell-bent for it. With both hands on the stick I hauled back as hard as I could, knowing that I was going to pull right up in front of the Jap. It was the only time that I came close to blacking out in combat. I couldn't see a thing with the G's I was pulling, but I also knew that there wasn't much room between me and the ocean, either. As I came out of the dive and regained my focus, I heard Axtell, who had come up behind me, tell the rest of the pilots to stay away from the Nate as he had him burning. I was chagrined. Not only had I missed a chance to get another victory, but in the process had nearly bought the farm. To make matters worse, I was the only pilot who had dropped his belly tank, and I was flying on the CO's wing. I was so embarrassed that I vowed not to complain or to say a word on the way back. I was worried about my fuel, and leaned out the fuel mixture so much that I was burning more air than gasoline. I was mighty happy when we got near Kadena and the skipper said, 'John, you go on and land first.'"

Combat 3

At 1500, 1Lt. Joe Dillard and his wingman, 2Lt. James Bierbower, took off, and three and a half hours later were vectored to a Navy B5N Kate torpedo bomber by a formation of picket ships. In the twilight haze, the Jap was headed towards the ships at 1,000 feet, but saw the Marines and turned to flee. Dillard closed from 5 o'clock level and Bierbower from 7 o'clock level. The Kate tried to make a turn in each direction, but found he was bracketed and flew straight on course. Since there was no rear gunner in this kamikaze, Dillard closed in from 300 feet and fired. The Kate was hit in the wing roots and set on fire on the first burst, and went into a diving port turn and crashed about 50 miles northwest of Ie Shima at 1845. On the way back to base, Dillard lit up his customary cigarette. It was the last victory of a successful day, the Death Rattlers depriving the Japanese of 14 1/2 aircraft.

30 April Close Support

Mission: 0915-1145 Strikes on artillery positions and supply dumps in the built up area south of Machinato Airfield that was being attacked by American troops.

After being assigned to fruitful CAPs and Picket CAPS, scoring a record 24 3/4 victories on the 22nd and another 14 1/2 victories on the 28th, -323 was assigned a close support mission. Major Axtell led two divisions of -323 Corsairs and was joined by six more VMF-312 F4Us.

Only 2,500 feet of runway was available at takeoff. Pilots used 20 to 30 degrees of flaps to take off with a full load of gas, ammunition, two 165 gal. Napalm tanks, and eight rockets. Since friendly troops were within 400 yards of the target, the pilots were thoroughly briefed. The target was easily found despite the 2,500 foot ceiling, and were further pinpointed by white phosphorous shells.

Napalm tanks were released first, causing fires in the entire target area. Of the 28 napalm bombs loaded, 23 hit the area, two could not be released because of shackle trouble, two just fell off for unknown causes near the target, and one had fallen off during taxiing to the take off position.

Rockets were fired next and 96 hit the target, though two would not fire because of electrical problems and 30 were not fired because some pilots were not on target and did not wish to fire due to the proximity of friendly troops. After the rocket attack, each plane made two strafing runs, firing 17,000 rounds, to finish the attack that was judged to have caused serious damage.

Al Wells describes the attack: "Intelligence had reported that there was Jap artillery hidden along this road and that we were to strafe the area and flush it out. We had to strafe some buildings, which were only native huts. It was cruel, because we had to de-

"Take Your Atabrin Tablets" sign encourages the use of the anti-malarial medication which was rumored to cause impotency. The administering Corpsmen had to check under the men's tongues to be sure the tablet had been swallowed. ***Courtesy of Jody O'Keefe.***

stroy the homes of the Okinawans. In most cases they had moved out, but the natives had an awful time during the battle. I was on a low approach on a row of huts, shooting with my machine guns. A flash appeared at the top of the roof in front of me, so I launched my rockets. Because of my low altitude they arrived at the same time I did. The building blew up right in my face, and a log which was part of the structure stuck in my oil cooler on the right wing, and I was losing oil pressure fast. Luckily, I was close to the field and was able to land before the engine seized."

Kadena night partner. Death Rattler, Bob Wade (3rd left) visits members of VMF-543(N) whose F6F-5Ns shared Kadena. This squadron shot down 15 Japanese aircraft. *Courtesy of John Ruhsam.*

30 April

John Ruhsam describes life and times at Kadena in a letter to his parents. "You should know where I am if only from the newspapers. Time continues to roll along at a terrific clip. We are busy all the time, and don't notice how fast the days go by. Here it is May already.

All is well, I really enjoy life here, we are outdoors all the time and I do a lot of flying. The food is excellent due to a real mess officer. Every once in a while we really have some excitement. The full moon hasn't helped the situation, and the last three nights have been a little bit of hell. The nights have been one continuous air raid, and on top of that we have been shelled each of those nights. This makes sleeping rather difficult, and with the early morning alerts and long flights, I get really tired. All part of the game, I guess.

Tomorrow is the first day I have had off since we landed a month ago. I don't know what I will do. Hope I can sleep late in the morning, but one gets so used to getting up early, you wake up regardless. I will probably go down to the harbor and see if I can go out to the ships and take a warm shower. I made some friends on the boat coming over, so I may look them up. The cook promised me a pie or cake if I came around.

Here it is 9 o'clock already and no air raid yet tonight. I'm going to hit the sack because I'm so tired."

Take your medicine

There were atabrin notices posted around the base, with a prominent one at the mess hall door. Also prominent around the mess hall door were orange spots on the wet ground where the men stood in line and spit out their atabrin. They were supposed to take atabrin tablets for malaria, but there was a rumor that it made you impotent. After the rumor started the corpsmen had to make sure that the men swallowed the tablet by looking into their mouth.

Sharing Kadena: VMF-312, VMF-322, and VMF-543(N)

(See Photos this page.)

The Legend of Sol Mayer

Sol Mayer began his military career as a Army Aviation cadet, but washed out two weeks before he would earn his wings because he lowered his flaps instead of his landing gear, which in some cases is fine but not during landing. A month later, he enlisted in the Marine Corps, went through the trauma of boot camp, and did well enough to be sent to Quantico to become an aviation ground officer. He began this career as an adjutant, but the paper work got to him. "It took them years to unravel some of my work." He then moved on to become a defense officer that stateside was no challenge. "Who was going to attack us, anyway?" Finally he was made a mess of-

VMF-322 accompanied -323 throughput its Pacific training stints at Ewa, Emirau, and Espiritu Santo. The squadron was commanded by Major Frederick Rauschenbach and scored 29 victories. The unit's Corsair's were distinguished by their white noses. *Courtesy of the USMC.*

VMF-312 was also stationed at Kadena under Major Richard Day. The Corsair's of "Day's Knights" were identified by the checkerboard marking on the noses and vertical stabilizers. The squadron scored 59 1/2 victories over Okinawa. *Courtesy of the USMC.*

Sol Mayer billed himself as the "Fighting Man's Mess Officer" and made it his business to make sure his "boys were the best fed outfit on Okinawa." Lt. Col. Mayer later was the head messman in Korea when he fed the First Marine Air Wing. ***Courtesy of Henry Brandon.***

G.I. Sol with his trusty Thompson machine gun and a souvenir Japanese samurai sword he collected on one of his souvenirs-for-food forays. He would go to the front and collect Jap souvenirs and trade them to the Navy off shore for food. ***Courtesy of Norman Miller.***

ficer. "As a mess officer I found my true calling. I came from a long line of Louisiana plantation owners with a partiality for good food."

When he got to Okinawa, Mayer found that the supply situation had changed, and his reputation was in jeopardy. "At Espiritu Santo, it was easy because we were in a rear area and food procurement was no problem. But when we hit Okinawa I only had what the Table of Allowances called for.

Thirty days of D- and K-rations, and the 10-in-1, which isn't a bad ration, except it is canned and my boys weren't used to eating that. To keep my reputation I came up with a plan. I needed to find people with food who needed something I could give them. The Army would never get any liquor. Our pilots were given these small bottles of brandy by the medical department when they finished their flights, and they gave them to me to trade."

Harold Tonnessen: "We pilots were allowed these little jiggers of brandy after every flight, which had to be signed out from Doc Dussman. I was a tea-toter and always have been, but one day I happened to be at the dispensary and looked at the log book. You should have seen how different ways my name was spelled and signed."

Mayor traded with the Army supply dump on the beach, which was loaded with B-rations which were good canned foods, but Mayor still didn't have fresh meat or eggs. "The Navy guys off-

The mess hall was known as "Mayer's Mess, Where the Aces Meet to Eat." A score board was posted above the door to tabulate the squadron's victory total. There are 81 Japanese flags displayed here, which dates the photo at the end of April. ***Courtesy of Henry Brandon.***

Glenn Thacker (L) and George Graham. *Courtesy of Norman Miller.*

Not only aces ate at Mayer's Mess. Here armorer, Joe Bassani, strikes the standard "mess pose." *Courtesy of Joe Bassani.*

shore never set foot on Okinawa and wanted some momento of their duty there for back home. I took a few of my boys out toward the front lines to pick up some native pots and household stuff from the destroyed and abandoned villages. I took these out to the ships a little at a time and began to build up my reputation and our food supply. After awhile the Navy guys asked me for battle souvenirs—Jap rifles and bayonets. I went to the front-line troops to try to trade, but their price was too high, a couple of bottles of bourbon for a bayonet or flag. I didn't have enough liquor to keep this up, so I had to devise another plan."

Major Axtell continues: "Sol was a frustrated grunt, and he requested temporary duty with the infantry on the front lines. I made my jeep available to him, plus several cases of bourbon for his use in potential bargaining. He actually participated in attacks on the front-lines, and by all reports did it very professionally. He picked up Japanese souvenirs with the intention of trading them for food with the Navy laying offshore. His salesmanship was outstanding. The squadron mess after the first two weeks was furnished with white table cloths, silverware, fresh eggs, steak, potatoes, you name it. It was open 24 hours a day and fed anyone who stopped by."

Warren Broering, "The Sunday evening meal was special, and you had to be showered, shaved and have on a clean uniform or else you couldn't get served. That sounds like an insignificant thing, but it did feel good to be clean, to sit down to a linen table cloth with napkins held by napkin rings. Sol made you feel pretty elegant. Generals and Admirals would often come and join us for these Sunday meals,"

Harold Tonnessen: "Sol had great cooks working for him. They could make Spam taste like a Virginia ham. Thanks to Sol we were eating in a covered mess hall, while the other squadrons were still eating out of cans in their tents."

Mayer studied maps and picked up intelligence scuttlebutt in his mess to find out where the next attack would begin. With his ever present flat-billed aviator's cap, armed with his Thompson submachine gun, .45 pistol, and a large trench knife, he would take his truck out to join an infantry unit ready to jump off into battle. Legend has it on one foray Mayer went into combat with a unit. When all their line officers fell, he took charge and led the attack up a ridge, routing 500 Japs entrenched in their caves. After the battle he went into the still smoldering caves and collected weapons, helmets, battle flags, and the coveted Samurai swords. He later sent several cases of beer up to the infantry to thank them. Soon, he would again take his truck out, play soldier for an afternoon and, after the battle, fill his truck with souvenirs and head for the beach."

Mayor continues: "I found a Navy Duck to take me out to the ships with my souvenirs. I had to bribe the Officer of the Deck to let me on board, and then bribe the Supply Officer to finally get down to serious trading. Souvenirs for boxes of fresh and frozen meat; beef, chicken, pork, turkey, bacon and other food for the mess. Later, I got ice cream, eggs, fresh bread, real butter, and even apple pie. Some of our boys ate better than they ever did at home. Eventually, I had so much food that I could trade it with ground commanders for more souvenirs, so I started doing business by the truck load. The front line guys would get their first steaks since they left the States. The Marine Generals would come down to eat my food—the other squadrons didn't have anybody like me. When all these guys went home the general put me in charge of the whole show.

After the war I left the Marine Corps to make my fortune. When Korea came along, they called me up again. Would you believe they sent me to Fort Lee to learn how to run a mess hall! When I got to Korea I worked my way up from a first lieutenant to a light colonel. I ran the mess for the whole First Air Wing and traveled throughout Korea and Japan to take care of my boys."

MONTHLY SUMMARY

APRIL

Personnel: 292

Officers:	Marine: 61	Enlisted: Marine: 223
	Navy: 1	Navy: 7
Personnel lost: 4		
	1Lt. James Brown	T/Sgt. Albert Elson
	1Lt. Frederick Zehring	HA/1/c James Mynatt
Aircraft on hand:	27 F4U-1Ds	4 FG-1Ds
Aircraft lost:	8 F4U-1Ds	1 FG-1D

Missions: 122/20 flying days
Combat Air Patrol: 65
Picket Ship Patrol: 43
Close Air Support: 14
1655 hrs./659 indiv. flights/656 combat missions
Encounters: AA: 4 Enemy A/C 13
Enemy A/C destroyed: 54 3/4
probable: 6
damaged: 6

Al Wells (L) and Francis Terrill. ***Courtesy of Norman Miller.***

CHAPTER 25
May
A Magnificent Month

1 May: "I can make my daily report. Tonight for chow we had beef hash, potatoes, cabbage, hot rolls, and coffee. I know that I am losing weight now, but its not because of the chow, for it has been very good. I guess its because we are busy for a change. This place looks about like the country around Nashville. Except for more rain the climate seems the same as there for the time of the year, for it has been really pleasant. There are rolling hills and valleys with pine trees growing on the hillsides. It sure seems funny not to see the coconut trees and tropical plants which we have been accustomed." Henry Brandon letter

3 MAY COMBAT

The first days of May had seen little activity due to bad weather, and no ships were lost. The rain and low cloud cleared by early afternoon, and the Japanese launched their fifth kikusui attack, with 125 aircraft (75 JNAF and 50 JAAF) taking part. The first raids were directed towards radar picket stations #9 and #10, which lie 60 miles to the southwest and thus indicated that these were Army attacks organized from Formosa or the Sakishima Islands The Death Rattlers were patrolling to the east of the real action on this day.

A four plane dusk combat air patrol took off at 1715 and was led by 1Lt Charles Allen, followed by his wingman, 1Lt. John Strickland, and second section leader, 1Lt. James Feliton and his wingman, 2Lt. Thomas Blackwell.

Picket ships vectored the flight to a bogie flying in about 15 miles southwest of Aguni Shima headed toward friendly shipping ten miles to the south. Blackwell tallyhoed the bogie, now identified as a Judy dive bomber, which in this case was carrying a torpedo. The Judy was 500 feet below and 3,500 feet out. It made a momentary turn toward the F4Us but quickly decided that discretion was the better part of valor and quickly dove away. Feliton pulled up to the left to bracket, while the second section pulled up to the right. The Judy continued to dive, turn, and climb to evade, but to no avail followed by the bracketing Corsairs. Soon Blackwell was in firing position on a high stern run. He opened fire at 900 feet and kept firing as the Judy pulled up. He scored hits in the wing roots, cockpit, and fuselage, causing the Judy to explode.

4 MAY COMBAT

The Japanese had initiated their fifth kikusui at dusk the day before, with the Navy losing four ships. This phase of the kikusui involved JNAF kamikazes of the Fifth Air Fleet from Kyushu. There was a thick haze that made the camouflaged kamikazes difficult to detect by shipboard AA and CAP. Also, the wakes left by the frantically maneuvering destroyers made them highly obvious from above. VMF-323, patrolling north of Aguni Shima, was to be in the thick of the action. When the 16 Death Rattler Corsairs took off for Kadena at 0730, they were warned of bogies approaching their patrol area and anticipated action. Little did they realize that in the next hour they would participate in one of the greatest days in squadron history. By 0750 there were bogies flooding the picket radar screens, and the Fighter Director vectored each four plane -323 division to a different position.

Combat 1

Capt. Bill Van Buskirk led his division 20 miles north of Aguni Shima, followed by his wingman, 2Lt. Harold Hohl, and second section leader, 1Lt. Cy Dolezel and his wingman, 2Lt. Bill Drake.

Tom Blackwell (L) and Ed Keeley. Blackwell exploded a Judy on 3 May. Both pilots survived the war but both died just after returning to the States. Blackwell died in an aircraft accident while Keeley died in auto wreck in California. ***Courtesy of Henry Brandon.***

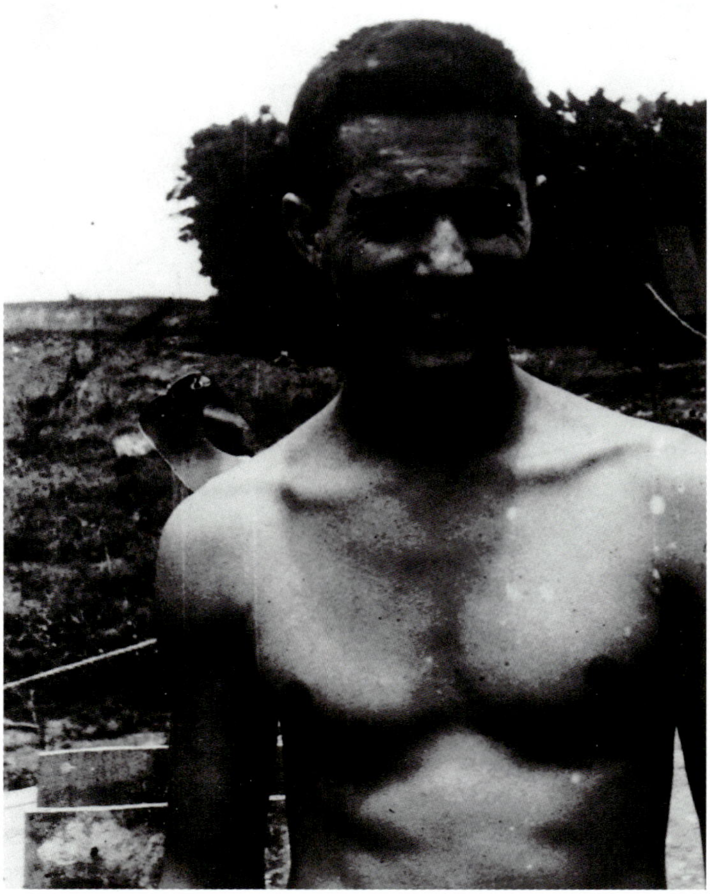

2Lt. Jim Bierbower was a junior pilot and relegated to the fourth, 'tail-end Charlie' position of his division and therefore had little chance to score. When his division leader had radio problems Bierbower took the lead and shot down a Tojo for his only victory of the war. ***Courtesy of Norman Miller.***

1Lt. A.M. Blaydes shared a Val and then a Dinah with Joe Dillard for his only claims of the war. ***Courtesy of Norman Miller.***

Several aircraft were milling around the area, and Van Buskirk and Dolezel investigated and teamed up to shoot down a twin-engined Army Ki-46 Dinah fighter that was heading towards a destroyer, low in the water. Van Buskirk pulled up and went after a Val diving on a LCM that was providing AA support for the picket destroyers. He exploded the Val 200 feet off the water, and parts of the plane started a fire on the LCM's fantail. Hohl went after a Val and was joined by an unidentified Corsair to share its destruction. Harold Hohl: "May 4th was my first hop, and I really didn't understand what combat was all about, being a young, green second lieutenant. I was really surprised when we saw bogies. All air discipline and tactics went out the window, and it was everyone for himself. You didn't wait for the section leader, or your wingman, you just went. There were bogies in the area, and I activated my guns, but when I hit the plungers I only activated one side. I didn't know it until I landed and saw that the tape over the gun ports on one side wasn't broken."

Bill Drake also shot down a Val. The division joined up and headed toward the northern tip of Okinawa, where Dolezel splashed a Val flying at wave top for the division's final kill.

Combat 2

A division led by 1Lt. Joe Dillard was also in the area of the Van Buskirk division. Dillard downed two Dinahs and one Val, and then coupled with his wingman, 1Lt. Aquilla Blydes, who shared the destruction of another Dinah and Val.

1Lt. Francis Terrill, leader of the second division, was credited with a Val and 1 1/4 Dinahs, the 1/4 with unknown pilots of another unit. He also damaged two Dinahs and two Vals. All his hits were scored on high stern runs.

Glen Thacker describes his combat: "I had flown 15 missions by this time. We were vectored by Central Control to a picket ship. We reported to the picket that we were on our way at 5-6,000 feet, climbing gradually. I'm already starting to get bored because nothing ever happened on these patrols. The picket ship told us that they had picked up so many bogies on radar that they weren't going to vector us. We were just supposed to keep our eyes open. I checked the gun switches and adjusted the gunsight luminescence in anticipation. And it wasn't two minutes later that I looked at about 2 o'clock 1,000 yards down when I spotted a Betty right on the water, flying in the opposite direction. At that time, whenever anybody saw a Jap they just yelled 'tallyho' and went after it without waiting for anyone else in the squadron. I picked out an interception point and dove straight down in a steep angle. After a short time I'm about 500 yards out from the Betty at 1 o'clock and heading for it. The Betty didn't take any evasive action as I closed to 150-200 yards and started firing at 3 o'clock. I was closing fast from the dive and pulling a lot of G's and firing until 5 o'clock when I went past him. I had hit him good and saw flames. I leveled out, but when I looked around to find him there was nothing, no flames or explosion, no debris at all. I knew I got him.

I had no time to look around, as there were a large number of planes, Japanese and American, milling in front of me in a large spiral. They were just flying in a tight circle, so I entered this melee that was so tight you had to worry about a collision with every turn. It was 15 minutes of the most intensive flying I had ever done. You had a Corsair fly into your sights as often as a Jap. But I did manage to get off three or four bursts. I got a good hit on a Val, which I couldn't follow up because of confusion of planes. I got to the edge of the circle and saw a lone Dinah which was flying straight and level out of the circle. I was 200 feet above and 150 feet behind him, and I fired and he went straight into the water. I came back and I'm milling around with Corsairs of other squadrons which are trying to reform. I'm looking for Blydes, Terrill, or Dillard, but I'm in no hurry, as the fight's over. So I looked down and counted seven ships below and also saw three Corsairs leaving the area, so I took off after them assuming it was my division. I'm at 500 feet, and I looked up and here comes another Japanese plane in. He was above me to my right at 200 feet and descending at 20 degrees. He was going so slowly he looked like he was stopped, and I couldn't get the nose up to get a shot at him. He was coming down toward the ships in an easy glide, so I swung around to the right, and as I did the Jap released his bombs towards a ship. I held my breath as the bombs just missed, and I closed behind him at 600 feet level. I was about to fire when I saw tracers whizzing past me from another Corsair above and behind me. The Corsair was so close that he looked like he was going to settle down on me, and I had to get out of the way. I swung out to the left. The Corsair had its flaps down and kept pumping lead into the Jap bomber. The Corsair broke off, and I followed the flaming Jap. It looked as though it would go in at any time, but somehow it kept flying, a ball of flame. It leveled off in a lazy turn about ten feet just off the water towards our ships. We are both circling to the right, but he was in a much tighter turn and at about 70 mph with my Corsair's stall speed at 105 mph. I don't know how he stayed in the air. He was creeping along, engulfed in

1Lt. Joe Dillard got four total victories: two shared (with A.M. Blaydes), then two Dinahs and a Val. The shooting was so good that Dillard ran out of ammo. ***Courtesy of Norman Miller.***

1Lt. Cy Dolezel got a Val and shared a Dinah. ***Courtesy of Bill Drake.***

Division leader, Capt. Joe McPhail, shot down a Nick while on CAP over Ie Shima but missed further action when he had to escort Warren Bestwick and his ailing P & W back to base. ***Courtesy of Del Davis.***

1Lt. Bob Muse was credited with a Jill which was attacking the destroyer, HENRY A. WILEY. At an after the war reunion Muse was made a honorary WILEY crew member for helping to save the warship. ***Courtesy of Jody O'Keefe.***

2Lt. Harold Hohl (L) shared a Val but found when he returned to Kadena that in the excitement of his first combat he had charged only half his guns. Hohl is shown here with 2Lts. Jim Carey (C), and Jerry Conners (R). All three joined the squadron on Okinawa. ***Courtesy of Jody O'Keefe.***

flames that trailed out 20 feet behind. I could tell he was about to stall, as his nose was up and tail down, but he kept going. I couldn't take my eyes off of him, waiting for him to hit the water. Suddenly, out of the corner of my eye I saw a ship, and the bomber was so close I couldn't do anything but watch in shock. Two seconds later he hit the ship on the port side, amidships, and it broke in two. (LSM(R)-190 on Picket Station #12 was hit about the time Thacker was in the area and sank rapidly. The rocket-launching landing ship (medium) suffered thirteen killed and 18 wounded.)

I met up with the division. Blaydes and I still had some ammunition left, but Terrill and Dillard were out and returned to Kadena. We stayed out on patrol, making long runs in one direction and then back. We did that a few times in a wide formation. I'm about 500 yards from Blaydes at 8-10,000 feet. We're scanning the sky, and I see a Jap bomber (Helen) right near Blayde's plane. I don't know where he came from, all of a sudden it's there, flying in the same direction as if we were flying in loose formation. He's a little above and in front of Blaydes, and Blaydes never saw him I don't

Capt. Bill Van Buskirk shot down a Val and shared a Dinah for his only victories of the war. ***Courtesy of Henry Brandon.***

1Lt. Francis Terrill had a busy day in becoming an ace by shooting down a Dinah, then shared another Dinah with three other pilots, shot down a Val, followed by damaging two more Dinahs and two Vals. ***Courtesy of Henry Brandon.***

think the bomber pilot saw me at first, either. I turned in towards him at a 45 degree heading, and he turned over in a slight dive and released his bomb. He then went into a steep dive directly away from me. Since his dive angle was steeper than mine he was faster, and it took me awhile to catch him. I'm approaching him, and I was worried about a fixed tail gun and lowered my flight path so he would shoot over me. I knew I didn't have much ammo left, as I closed right behind him at 200 feet. He made a little turn to the right just above the water, but we were too close to the water, so I just leveled out as he made a sharp right. I looked around and saw him spiral straight down and explode into the water. Blaydes congratulated me on my shooting, but I had gotten a victory without firing a shot!

When I landed two ground crew members showed me two bullet holes only three feet behind the cockpit. It must have been from the Corsair which hit the Jap that rammed the LSM."

Combat 3

The four plane division was led by Capt. Joe McPhail and his wingman, 2Lt. Warren Bestwick, while the second section was led by 1Lt. John Ruhsam, followed by his wingman, 1Lt. Bob Wade. The Corsairs were ordered by the radar controller to proceed north to Ie Shima, which was an island about 25 miles north of Kadena and just off the Motobu Peninsula to the east They were to orbit at the usual CAP altitude of 30,000 feet. The sky was hazy with some puffy clouds at about 5,000 feet, but mostly clear with generally good visibility. John Ruhsam: "Most of the CAP missions were dull, and we would sit up there, circling for four or five hours at 25,000 feet with the sun coming in the cockpit. We didn't get much sleep, and the oxygen systems weren't what they are today, and we would doze off in the cockpit. Any time I would get sleepy and my head would drop, my wingman, Bob Wade, would come right up next to me and let loose with six .50s, and wow! That would wake me up in a hurry!"

1Lt. John Ruhsam became an ace and ran his score to six victories, as seen in this PR photo, as he knocked down four Vals and damaged three more. He could have scored more victories but he ran out of ammo. ***Courtesy of John Ruhsam.***

Just off Ie Shima a lone Army Ki-27 Nate fighter was approaching from the north about 10,000 feet below. The fighter was identified by its fixed gear, which was covered with spats. The fighter had been obsolete for several years, and at the time was used as a home defense fighter and trainer. All four pilots, eager for the easy kill, made hard starboard turns to get on the tail of the approaching victim. Ruhsam got there first and fired a burst, but was going too fast and overran. He broke below and to the left to make another run. McPhail was right behind and hit the Nate, which rolled over on his back, and a fire started between his gear. The Nate never pulled out and dove straight into the water.

Soon Bestwick's Pratt & Whitney started to belch black smoke, indicating an oil problem. Operating in two plane divisions, McPhail escorted Bestwick back to Kadena and radioed that he would rejoin when Bestwick landed safely. Meanwhile, Ruhsam and Wade climbed back to CAP duty in widening circles and saw a picket destroyer on fire about 25 miles northwest of Ie Shima. The Marine's land-based radar controllers had not reported enemy contacts, and there was nothing on the radio. So the pair descended in a widening circle, searching the area in the vicinity of the smoking picket for Jap attackers. (The picket was probably the destroyer, MORRISON DD-560, stationed at picket station No. 1 that was struck and severely damaged by a kamikaze about 0825, and had reported Corsairs pursuing a Val.) Abruptly, ahead and to the right a two seat, Navy Val dive-bomber appeared. There were also several other green and brown camouflaged Vals lingering around. Ruhsam perhaps too quickly fired off a volley and hit the Val in the starboard wing with his tracers, tearing off pieces. The Val carried a rear gunner (so it probably was not a kamikaze), and Ruhsam saw the streaks of its tracers coming at him. Tactics dictated that the duo would sandwich the Val and one of the Corsairs would turn in and make a firing run. The Jap would then be committed to turn into his attacker, and then the other Corsair would get low (to avoid the tail gunner) on his tail to finish off the attack. Wade was occupied with another Val as Ruhsam pulled away from his damaged Val. He made a hard starboard turn and moved low and across to port to again get on the fleeing Val's tail. Ruhsam cut his throttle fully, but was too close to get the Jap in his sights and had to let his fighter fade back to 100 feet and then fire. This time the Val fell away and exploded into flames. As Ruhsam turned away another Val flew across his nose. He fired, and the Jap flew into his bullets and fell in flame into the ocean for an easy victory. Wade had dispatched his Val and rejoined Ruhsam near the deck, as their combats had eaten a lot of altitude. At about 500 feet, the section encountered another Nate directly ahead. Ruhsam moved in, but as he did the nimble Nate rolled into a split-ess toward the sea and took off in the opposite direction. It was impossible for Ruhsam's large F4U to follow this maneuver, but as the Jap pulled out of this lifesaving strategy, Wade was waiting for him with a short, fatal burst into the cockpit.

By this time, McPhail had returned and was fervently calling on the radio for a position so he could get in on the action. McPhail:

1Lt. Bob Wade also became an ace when he claimed two Vals and two Nates (he damaged three other Nates) for six total victories. Like Ruhsam, he used too much ammo and was only firing with three guns on his last victim. ***Author's collection.***

1Lt. Glenn Thacker downed a Helen and damaged a Val. Thacker was credited with the Helen without firing a shot but suffered bullet holes from a "friendly" Corsair. ***Courtesy of Norman Miller.***

Seven new aces in three weeks of combat over Okinawa. (L to R) Front Row: Bob Wade and Jerry O'Keefe. Back Row: Bill Hood, Joe Dillard, George Axtell, and Jeff Dorroh. This photo was taken after the 24 3/4 victory day on 4 May. Author's collection.

"They told me they were over by some clouds but there were clouds everywhere." Wade and Ruhsam were busy chasing more Japs, throwing the tactics they learned to the wind: keep the altitude advantage, as altitude could always be swapped for speed, and never dogfight a Jap. These Japs were kamikazes with minimal training and were flying outdated aircraft. The two Marine pilots had to slow down to get on the victim's tail and fire. If the Jap didn't go down on the first run, they pulled around in a tight circle and made another firing run. Ruhsam set another Val on fire and flew nearby, waiting to see the results of his attack, when Wade came from astern to attack. The Val blew up in front of him, and his Corsair flew right through the fireball, but through pure luck escaped hitting any pieces. The stressed Wade separated from Ruhsam, who was off chasing more Japs. Ruhsam got behind another Val and fired, killing the rear gunner, when he ran out of ammunition. He followed the wounded Val just off the wave tops, debating what to do next. Ruhsam: "The Jap was right down on the water, and I was thinking about cutting his tail off with my prop. I'm flying right on top of him, no more than 8-10 feet away, when several tracer bullets streaked past my left wing toward the Val from behind. It was Wade, with only one gun shooting, but he abruptly ran out of ammo. Here were the two of us, out of ammo, looking right down at the panicked Jap pilot. He could have pulled up and got us both, but he did

The Mitsubishi Ki-46 Dinah was a high performance twin engine Army air defense fighter. On 4 May, -323 encountered a number of Dinahs, probably escorting kamikazes of the fifth kikusui and shot down 5 1/4. ***Courtesy of Jim Lansdale.***

(L to R) Joe Dillard, 1Lt. Ted Brown (three victories) of VMF-311, and John Ruhsam receiving congratulations from Major General Francis Mulcahy. ***Courtesy of John Ruhsam.***

Major Arthur Turner was leading an attack on Japanese regimental HQ at Shuri Castle. Lowering his landing gear to slow for his napalm drop, he was hit by AA fire and crashed behind enemy lines. Scuttle-butt was rampant about his fate before he died. ***Courtesy of Jody O'Keefe.***

1Lt. Francis Terrill scored the day's only victory, a Hamp, while on a picket ship patrol.

what any pilot would do and made a port turn to escape. But he was so low, his wing tip hit the water and, zap, he just disintegrated and was gone. After 30 minutes of intense dogfighting the two exhausted Marines turned back toward Kadena for the short trip home, each with four victories, which made them aces. In debrief both pilots believed they could have scored more victories if they had conserved ammunition on the easily destroyed Vals.

Combat 4

The fourth division, led by 1Lt. Vernon Ball, with 2Lt. James Bierbower on his wing, and his second section leader was 1Lt. Robert Muse, with his wingman, 2Lt. Obie Stover.

2Lt. Bierbower was one of the younger pilots in the squadron, and so had little chance to score, being relegated to the chronic assignment of fourth pilot in the division—the tail-end Charlie—a position which required him to protect the others. First Ball's radio went out and Muse took over, but soon Muse's radio malfunctioned also and Bierbower took the lead. He saw an Army Ki-44 Tojo fighter making a high and above run on a formation of four unsuspecting Navy F6F Hellcats, flying at 2,000 feet 25 miles north of Ie Shima. Every other pilot in the division also saw the Tojo, but Bierbower, seeing an opportunity, fire-walled the Corsair and kicked in the water injection. With three other Corsairs screaming down behind him, Bierbower got to the Jap first and hit it with a short salvo, and it burst into flames. The Tojo almost joined the Hellcat formation when Bierbower hit it. On fire, it skidded under the still unaware Hellcats, shot upwards and disintegrated in a flash of fire directly in front of the startled Navy pilots, who took off in every direction.

Later in this flight, Muse observed some AA bursts 20 miles west of Ie Shima, and he and Stover were vectored to 8-9,000 feet. There were AA puffs exploding around the two, either becuase they were being mistaken for the enemy, or there was an enemy aircraft in the vicinity. Muse radioed the control officer to report the friendly fire and turned to get out of there. As he turned, he saw a Jill bomber coming in toward the destroyer 100 feet off the water. Muse dove through a wall of AA fire and caught the Jill with a quick full deflection shot as it passed low over the destroyer, followed by Muse. Miraculously, there were no holes in his Corsair. Muse found that the destroyer was the HENRY A. WILEY (DD-749) when it sent -323 the message: "Highest praise is due a Marine Corsair who followed his target into our heavy close range fire in successfully pressing home his attack on an approaching Jill." In the 1990s, when the WILEY held its first reunion, Muse was made an honorary crew member.

Total for the day: Another 24 3/4 victories and 11 enemy aircraft damaged, which tied the record of 24 3/4 victories of 22 April. By each scoring four victories, Joe Dillard, John Ruhsam and Bob Wade became aces. Two Corsairs were hit by friendly AA fire and were repaired on base.

Concurrent with the kikusui, the Japanese Army on Okinawa launched a brutal counterattack on American troops. The Army actually caused fewer casualties than the kamikazes, which killed 472, wounded 568, and hit nine ships (eight were put out of action for the duration). About one in seven of the kamikazes were successful in their attacks, but no conventional aircraft were successful. (from S.E. Morison, VICTORY IN THE PACIFIC, p.391-2). To support their counteroffensive on shore, the JAAF had concentrated their attacks on carriers and gunline shipping (a hit was made on the BIRMINGHAM which had been shelling Japanese troops). The JNAF, however, seemed to have abandoned any hope of rescuing the island and was only intent on inflicting losses on shipping, regardless of its worth.

4 May: Corp. Karl Burns was wounded by shrapnel as an artillery shell landed in the squadron area in an evening attack. Burns was evacuated.

5 May: "We made a big improvement on the tent, which makes it much more comfortable. We built a floor for it, which looks good. Now everything inside won't get so dusty. The food is still good. Today for lunch we had fresh pork, carrots, potatoes, and biscuits, with canned fruit for dessert." Henry Brandon letter

5 May Close Air Support/Death of Major Arthur Turner

Mission: 1530-1837 Attack Japanese 32nd Infantry Regimental Headquarters and adjacent AA gun emplacements in southern Okinawa. Toward the end of April, Gen. "Vinegar Joe" Stillwell decided to renew the offensive on the Shuri Line. The 1st and 5th Marine Divisions relieved the exhausted 27th Division on the west flank, and the 77th relieved the 96th in the center. Refreshed, a new offensive began on 2 May, but the weather, terrain and fanatical Japanese resistance slowed the advance.

Corp. Roger Archambault remark: "Highway Route #1 ran north to south on the west coast of the island. Military ambulances crowded the road, bumper to bumper, night and day carrying the Marine and Army dead and wounded from the combat zone on the south to the evacuation beaches en route to the hospitals on Guam and Hawaii."

Major Art Turner led a combined flight from -323 (eight F4Us armed with two 500 lb. G.P. bombs and eight rockets) and -312 (eight F4Us armed with two napalm tanks and eight rockets). Upon reporting to station, Turner was cleared to attack, and he circled at

In a letter on 9 May, Henry Brandon writes: "I'm sure tired tonight as I have been strapped in one of these 'cuties' (F4U) for over 7 hours today and you just can't imagine how sore my sitting down place is." ***Courtesy of Henry Brandon.***

6,000 feet over the target area. Turner made section runs (two planes) with main gear down, its fairing acting as a dive brake, which was standard procedure. Broering: "Whenever you dropped your landing gear in a Corsair it would corkscrew and be difficult to handle. In the briefing the evening before we tried to talk him (Turner) out of it, but he wouldn't change." Turner, followed by his wingman, Warren Broering, deployed his main gear (dive brakes) and gear to slow his aircraft for his run on the target. Previously Japanese AA fire had been sparse or mostly non-existent, but Turner's aircraft was hit by AA fire, setting it aflame. 1Lt. Aquilla Blaydes reported seeing Turner bail out with his chute opening, but he drifted behind enemy lines and was captured. A post strike search failed to discover either Turner or his chute. There was much unsubstantiated scuttlebutt among the squadron that the Japanese had captured Turner, tied him to a tree, and used him for bayonet practice. Other rumors had it that his voice was transmitted over loud speakers directed toward our front lines while he was being tortured. Several days later Tokyo Rose announced that a Marine Major had been captured on Okinawa and returned to Japan. During a -323 reunion in Hawaii members found his headstone memorial (e.g. no body) in the famous Punch Bowl Military Cemetery on Oahu.

Axtell: "On Okinawa there wasn't much Jap AA fire, but there was a lot of small arms fire, and unfortunately, a lot of this was friendly fire! The small arms fire went up to 3,000 feet. Plus, there were artillery zones on each side, and you could fly right through it and not know it. There were a lot of our aircraft coming back with holes in them. It had to come from somewhere."

Despite the loss of Turner, the seven planes of -323 dropped their bombs and -312 dropped their napalm tanks, causing large fires. The entire flight, then joined up and initiated section rocket runs, firing eight in salvo.

6 May Close Air Support

Mission: 1530-1815 Attack a bridge and emplacements in northwest Naha, the largest town and capital of Okinawa. Marine divisions were making slow progress, being under the heavy and accurate artillery fire from enemy positions on the western face of the Shuri Heights. They captured the small town of Amike that overlooked Naha a half mile across a bay.

Major Dorroh led four F4Us armed with two 500 lb. G.P. bombs and eight rockets, and was instructed to circle west of Naha as no mission was available at that time. They circled for two hours waiting for an assignment. Dorroh was then told to join and follow seven TBMs who had been briefed on the target and knew exactly what to strike. Two runs were made, the first a glide bomb attack and the second a rocket attack. Damage assessment was difficult due to the smoke and haze over the target.

8 May John Ruhsam letter: "What a week this has been, going all the time. I tried to write before, but I never had a chance. Today I have flight duty, but it is raining like all sin outside. Of course, there is no flying under these conditions. It's colder than ever now, and is really miserable with all the mud and rain.

You probably already have heard what happened the other day from the newspapers. Bob and I ran into a turkey shoot (On 4 May, Ruhsam shot down four Vals and damaged three others, and Wade got four Japs while -323 shot down a record 24 1/2 Japs-ed.) I had a chance to shake the General's hand (Gen. F.F. Mulcahy ed.) afterward, and gave a long line of stuff to a bunch of correspondents, Norman Page and some guys from the Chicago Tribune. My score at present is six.

9 May: "I'm sure tired tonight, as I have been strapped in one of these 'cuties' (F4U) for over 7 hours today, and you can just imagine how sore my sitting down place is. I have a pad to sit on, but after so long even a cushion begins to feel like cement. You should have seen all the different positions I assumed in the cockpit." Henry Brandon letter

10 MAY COMBAT

Although the fifth kikusui of 3-4 May was successful, it marked the turning point for American troops on Okinawa. They had withstood the Japanese counterattack and were now making gains in fighting on the difficult south end of the island. Also, the war in Europe had ended two days before and spirits were high. The Japanese launched their sixth kikusui attack on the evening of the 10th.

At 1730 1Lt. Francis Terrill led a two plane section on a picket ship patrol 50 miles west of Zamba Misaki. After about an hour and a half of patrolling, Terrill saw an Army Hamp (?) carrying a torpedo at 3,000 feet at a position about one mile starboard of the picket. It was low on the water, and about to make run on the destroyer. Terrill nosed over, followed by his wingman, 1Lt. Glen Thacker, and made a stern run coming in from slightly above at 5 o'clock. He opened fire at 1,000 feet and got hits on the wing roots and engine. The doomed Hamp wildly dropped its torpedo and then pulled straight up in flames, and Terrill continued to follow, still shooting and closing fast. He needed a few more bursts to finally explode it.

Al Wells: "Bob Muse found there was scuttlebutt going around that some visiting general had written Washington about the harrowing conditions on Okinawa. The general stated that the pilots were flying day and night and were under constant bombing and strafing attacks and needed some R&R. Muse encouraged everyone to do their duty and make the general look good, and maybe even crash an airplane. Of course, everyone laughed. That day we taxied out along the semi-circular, half-moon taxiway. The Corsair had that big nose sticking out in front, so normally we had to S-turn to see during taxi. But that day I decided that S-turns wouldn't be necessary, because it was a curved runway and I could see. But somehow I didn't see, and just happened to look to the right and there was a guy on a tractor, and I'm about to hit him. I jammed on the brakes, the plane noses in, and I'm hanging by my shoulder straps. A jeep comes roaring up, and Muse jumps on the wing yelling, 'Nice job, Little Bub!' I think to this day he thinks I did this on purpose to get us some R&R."

10 May Close Air Support

Mission; 1530-1745 Attack Japanese troops dug in on a ridge in the Yonabaru area. The Marine troops continued their assault on the tough Japanese defensive complex, anchored on ridges and commanding ravines and draws up, which the Marines had to fight to dislodge to assault the Japanese above. On 7 May, Germany had surrendered, and now Japan fought alone but with more resolve and desperation.

Major Axtell led eight -323 and four -312 F4Us loaded with two 500 lb. bombs and eight rockets. Axtell circled the target area while the troops there marked the well-concealed Japanese troops with white phosphorous shells. However, too many phosphorous shells were fired in the same area and caused confusion in the air. Despite the assurances that naval gunfire in the area would cease during the air attack it continued, even though there was a naval gunfire spotting plane in the area throughout the attack. Three runs were made, one dive bombing, one glide bombing, and a final rocket run. Around the clock strafing runs on the target followed. Results

Intelligence had advised the squadron that a FM-2 had been captured by the Japanese and was flying recon unmolested over the island. The rogue Wildcat was .ID'd by an inverted 'T' on its tail. Ed Murray made a pass on the pictured FM-2 only to find out it was genuine US Navy issue when it landed at Kadena. Needless to say the -323 pilots involved did not seek out the PO'd Navy pilots. ***Courtesy of Norman Miller.***

of the attack could not be observed due to smoke and haze in the area.

OOPS!

Intelligence alerted the squadron that the Japs were flying a captured FM-2, an updated version of the F4F Wildcat, for recon and spotting purposes. Henry Brandon was flying wing to the division leader when he saw a lone aircraft about 15 miles away. He called out the aircraft to the rest of the unit, but no one could see it. Brandon closed and identified it as a FM-2. The intelligence bulletin had advised that there was an inverted "T" on the rudder. As Brandon slid over toward the bogie to ID the inverted T, he hesitated as he looked into the cockpit and saw that it was pretty well filled with pilot. That puzzled him, as most Japs were pretty small. He saw the inverted "T" when he looked over. Brandon called in his ID. Ed Murray, who was following just behind, came in firing all his guns, but missed. The FM-2 dropped his gear and appeared to be trying to get in to land behind Jap lines just beyond Kadena. Brandon came up on the "Jap's" tail, ready to fire from above and behind. At the same time a radio call came in from Bob Lejonstein, the fourth member of the division, reporting that there were more FM-2s with the same markings that were flying just below. The four U.S. Navy FM-2s landed at Kadena, but Brandon made every effort to avoid their pilots when he landed.

10 May: The squadron received 9 new planes.

11 MAY COMBAT

After the tentative attack the evening before, 6 Kikusui launched 150 aircraft (70 JNAF and 80 JAAF). Although only four ships were hit and none sunk, 10 May was to be the worst day for Navy men. At just after 1000, a Zeke and then a Judy hit the carrier BUNKER HILL, killing 396 and wounding 264 for the largest single loss in a single attack. Combined with 65 dead and 105 casualties wreaked on Picket Radar Station 15, this was the highest daily number of kikusui-inflicted casualties of Operation Iceberg.

Combat 1

1Lt. Charles Martin and his wingman, 2Lt. Everett Yager, led a division assigned to CAP from Kadena at 0730. After reporting to the Fighter Director, Martin and Yager were vectored 15 miles on a heading of 340 degrees from Izena Shima. At 0945, Martin heard over his radio that bogies had been sighted below and immediately descended through the haze, followed by Yager. Martin broke through the haze at 1,000 feet and spotted a Tojo below at 50 feet about to make a bombing run on a destroyer. Martin made a run from above at 4 o'clock, opening fire at 900 feet. His tracers hit the cockpit area, and it began to smoke badly. The Tojo jettisoned its bomb, hit the water on its belly, and bounced off back into the air. Martin salvoed a second burst. Two of his guns jammed, but the other four were enough to flame the Jap and crash it into the sea.

Combat 2

1Lt. Ed Keeley and his wingman, 2Lt. Larry Crawley, were the second section of the Martin/Yager division that had left Kadena at 0730. They were vectored on a heading of 350 degrees from Izena Shima by the Fighter Director to investigate bogies reported in that sector. At 0830, at 3,000 feet and about 15 miles from Izena Shima, Keeley observed a Tojo flying north at 3,200 feet. He made a run from below at 2 o'clock, opening fire at 900 feet. The Tojo tried to evade with a sharp right turn, but Keeley had no problem turning with him. He fired again and got hits to the cockpit. The Jap smoked badly and split-essed into the sea.

1lt. Ed Keeley and his wingman, 2Lt. Larry Crawley, had a day to remember, being credited with helping to save the beleaguered destroyer picket ship, HUGH W. HADLEY, from a concentrated kamikaze attack. ***Courtesy of Bill Drake.***

2Lt. Larry Crawley shot down a Dinah and three Nates. Crawley recollected: "We didn't have time to think, they just kept coming and we just reacted." ***Courtesy of Henry Brandon.***

1Lt. Ed Keeley shot down a Tojo and then three Nates. Both Keeley and Larry Crawley were cited by the destroyer HADLEY fighter director for their "flying skill and cool courage...in driving the planes away from the ship." *Courtesy of Jody O'Keefe.*

Keeley recovered, pulled up, and he and Crawley started off on a new 340 degree vector. Soon, reaching 14,000 feet, they sighted seven Nates, flying in two divisions low over the water toward our shipping. Keeley peeled off inside Crawley and hit one Nate on his first pass from above at 12 o'clock, opening fire at 900 feet. The Nate, hit in the engine and cockpit, smoked and crashed into the sea. After the kill, Keeley pulled up and saw a Nate on his tail. He easily pulled up and away from the ancient, fixed-gear Nate and came around out of the sun at 8 o'clock in a classic maneuver. He opened fire at 900 feet and closed fast, getting hits around the wing roots. The fragile Nate caught fire and crashed. Keeley again swung around in recovery and saw a third Nate, low over the water and making a run on a besieged destroyer. He closed from slightly above at 6 o'clock and fired four or five long bursts along the fuselage and cockpit. The Nate, entirely in flames, continued to bear down on the destroyer, and finally remnants crashed into the ship.

Crawley made his kills shortly after he had joined up again with Keeley. He first saw a Dinah that was below, just off the water and proceeding south accompanied by a Nate. Crawley's first pass on the twin-engined Jap bomber came from above at 8 o'clock, opening fire at 900 feet. He closed quickly and saw his tracers hitting the engine. The bomber caught fire and crashed into the ocean.

Keeley and Crawley were vectored 330 degrees to a point 10 miles off Izena Shima. Crawley intercepted two Nates. The first was destroyed from above at 5 o'clock with hits in its engine. Crawley climbed 500 feet and saw the second at wave top. He peeled off, came in from above at 5 o'clock, and opened fire at 900 feet. His tracers hit the Nate's wing roots, and it flamed and crashed, ending a successful day's combat for the pair.

Crawley's reminiscence on the action: "We didn't have time to think, they just kept coming and we just reacted." This modest appraisal and the description from Aircraft Action report #34, which was done after the battle, does not do justice to the exploits of Keeley and Crawley. It was later discovered that the destroyer in this encounter was the HUGH W. HADLEY (DD-774). Because of the high losses to the picket destroyers, she was taken off outer patrol duty only the afternoon before and transferred to picket ship duty at station 15. Here she was joined by the EVANS (DD-552) and four

After the Marine pilots left the HUGH W. HADLEY (DD-774) she was again overwhelmed by a simultaneous attack by ten kamikazes. Her AA gunners shot down all ten but three crashed the destroyer which was saved by heroic effort by her crew. *Courtesy of the USN.*

Keeley (L) and Crawley (R) are joined for a celebration dinner by 1Lt. Charles Martin who shot down a Tojo later on the same mission. ***Courtesy of Jody O'Keefe.***

smaller AA ships. Early that morning she began to pick up bogies that were part of the sixth kikusui massed kamikaze attack, comprised of 150 aircraft. For nearly two hours the HADLEY and EVANS came under attack, maneuvering at high speed, AA shooting at the attackers and directing CAP. The EVANS took several serious hits and went dead in the water. It was during this time that Keeley and Crawley came on the scene. Lt. J.T. Stevenson, the Fighter Director of the HADLEY, writes of their attack in BATTLE EXPERIENCE No. 24 (p.7-8), "Both Ruby 15 (the call sign for Kadena Marine air squadrons, Keeley was Ruby 15-3 and Crawley was Ruby 15-2 -editor) planes began picking off the stragglers at the beginning of the action, then opposed raid 4, estimated at 20-30. When enemy planes closed, these two planes came in with them. One very outstanding feat by one of these planes was that, though out of ammunition (Keeley ed.), he twice forced a suicide plane out of his dive on the ship, and the third time forced him into such poor position that the plane crashed through the rigging but missed the ship, going into the water close aboard. This was done while all guns on the ship were firing at the enemy plane. The highest award for flying skill and cool courage is not too much for this pilot. His wingman stayed at masthead height in the flak and assisted in driving the planes away from the ship." (Note: Robert Sherrod in his

On 12 May, John Ruhsam and Bob Wade (above) flew a picket patrol and shared a Dinah victory. Wade flew as Ruhsam's wingman and were very close friends and often split air victories when, in fact, one or the other had actually downed the enemy. ***Courtesy of Norman Miller.***

Even aces have to do laundry. John Ruhsam does his laundry in a portable washer/ringer. The multi-purpose steel helmet can be seen on a tripod in the foreground. ***Courtesy of John Ruhsam.***

HISTORY OF MARINE CORPS AVIATION, p.394, gives Keeley and Crawley credit for this action.)

After the Marines left, the HADLEY continued alone, but finally at 0920 was overwhelmed by a simultaneous attack by ten kamikazes. The AA gunners shot down all ten, but three, including one Baka, hit the destroyer, killing 28 and wounding 67. The ship was abandoned, but the damage control parties remained aboard. Through heroic and determined effort the ship remained afloat and arrived at Ie Shima. By the time the ship reached the U.S., the war was over, and it was sold for scrap.

11 May: "It sure is good news about the European war, and I suppose that they are having a big celebration back in the states. The war on this side isn't over yet, and I believe it is going to take a while yet to get it finished." Henry Brandon

12 MAY COMBAT

The last CAP of the day took off at 1730, a four plane division under Capt. Joe McPhail. John Ruhsam and his wingman, Robert Wade, of the second section, flew patrol for two hours and were at 8,000 feet, 40 miles southwest of Kadena. The two spotted a single Dinah flying towards them at about 5,000 feet. The Dinah had been flying east, straight and level toward a destroyer. Ruhsam tallyhoed and chased the Jap, followed by Wade. The Dinah nosed over and began jinking as it started its run on the DD. Ruhsam opened fire at 900 feet from slightly above and fired bursts from 3 to 6 o'clock onto his tail. His speed caused him to overrun, and the Jap rolled over and started down. As Ruhsam moved by he noticed his .50 hits in the Dinah's fuselage. Wade then fired a few short bursts from 600 feet at 5 o'clock, hitting the Dinah in the cockpit, causing it to smoke and crash and explode into the sea, narrowly missing a destroyer. The two shared the victory and returned to base in the dark at 2000. Ruhsam log book: 'Night landing again. Friendly AA raised Hell on the way home. Really glad to see home again."

12 May Close Air Support

Mission: 1630-1845 targets of opportunity, consisting of a landing craft and a bridge. On the 11th Gen. Simon Buckner ordered an all out offensive, with the Tenth Army taking control of the entire operation. Despite fresh troops and a four division offensive, the American attack quickly deteriorated and was subverted into a succession of pitched, hand to hand battles.

Major Axtell led a division equipped with two 500 lb. G.P. bombs and eight rockets, and they were instructed to orbit until a target could be assigned. After an hour they were assigned to patrol the southern end of Okinawa below a line running east to west from Yonabaru to Naha and were told to report any worthwhile targets. Everything below seemed to be dug in and the area destroyed beyond recognition. After carefully searching the area, all that was seen was a truck, a bridge and small landing craft tied to a quay off Itoman. Given permission to attack the bridge and landing craft, two rocket runs, two glide bomb runs and two strafing runs were made with probable serious damage.

Axtell: "I flew hundreds of hours, many on instrument conditions, on CAP or over Radar Picket Ships holding at altitude awaiting an assignment to intercept. The opportunity to engage the enemy in combat was a crap roll—it happened to me only three times."

12 May Rescue Escort

Four F4Us led by Capt. Charles Moore and his wingman, 1Lt. Henry Brandon, left Kadena at 0445 to fly escort for a PBM, Martin Mariner, in search of survivors of a B-29 that had ditched north of Okinawa. The B-29 had been part of a 102 bomber raid on the Kawashini Aircraft Company in Kobe that had met both AA fire and interceptors. After 3 1/2 hours, three life rafts were sighted. Hank Brandon: "When we reached the survivor's rafts an American submarine rescue picket had surfaced nearby. But when it saw our aircraft it immediately crash dived, not taking a chance we were Japanese. The PBM landed on the water and picked up all survivors."

13 May Close Air Support

Mission: 1630-1855 Strike radio towers and Shuri Castle in northern Shuri Town.

1Lt. Vernon Ball led four Corsairs armed with two 500 lb. bombs and eight rockets, reported in to the CASU and were instructed to proceed to Yonabaru to contact a TBF which would spot the target area. The TBF called in the target by grid coordinates and made two solo runs on the target. His first run was a dummy run, and on the second he dropped a marker bomb.

On 13 May, during a close air support mission on Shuri Castle, 1Lt. Ed Murray's F4U disintegrated in mid-air. Speculation was that Murray's 500 lb. bomb was hit by a Jap AA or a friendly 155mm howitzer shell that was being fired into the area by ground troops. *Courtesy of Henry Brandon.*

(L to R) Bill Drake, Bob Woods, Hots Terrill, and Eddie Murray in happier times. The squadron was shaken by the loss of the popular Murray. ***Courtesy of Jody O'Keefe.***

Ball initiated two glide bomb runs, followed by the division. One bomb was dropped on each run. The second bombing run was about to be initiated by 1Lt. Ed Murray and Henry Brandon, who continues the description of the mission: "We were to make individual runs on the castle itself, and we had broken off and Jack went in to drop his first bomb, and then I went in and dropped my bomb. I tailed in behind Jack, and Ed then went in to drop his bomb. He radioed that he was a little inside me, and asked me to pull out a little so that he could get an interval to drop his 500 lb. bomb. As he approached the target, about 1,000 yards in front of me, his aircraft just disintegrated into powder. I've never seen an aircraft disintegrate like that. We didn't know what had happened, and we reported to debrief that it was probably AA. Strangely, after the war while I was working at Vanderbilt University in Nashville, I came across a 'Long Tom' 155 mm gun crew member. We reminisced about our time on Okinawa and he stated that he remembered that on the 13th his crew had been firing on the target about the same time as our mission. They had received word to cease fire, but their howitzer had a round chambered and it was fired. They saw a flash that was probably the 500 pound bomb on Ed's plane being hit by the Howitzer round. Ed was the father of a son born while we were overseas, which he never saw."

Following Murray's accident, CASU instructed Ball to jettison all rockets on targets of opportunity south of the strategic bomb line, and the town of Kuwanga was hit.

13 May: "The last 3 or 4 days have been hard ones. I don't think I have ever been so tired in my life as I was last night after flying 9 hours. And the couple of days before that were just as bad. I have gotten a little rest today, so it hasn't been terribly bad. I think I have a "hop" later in the PM, which will be my only one for the day." Henry Brandon letter

14 May Major Richard Day, CO of VMF-312 also stationed at Kadena, was killed by AA fire. He was one of 23 Marine squadron COs to be killed in WW-2.

17 May The squadron received two new planes.

1Lt. Al Wells, hauling a piece of scrounged lumber for his tent floor, scored his first victories since getting the squadron's initial victory. On 15 May, he downed two Jills on a picket ship CAP to run his total to three. On the mission, wells was reluctant to fire on the bogie as he did not have firm ID until "big red oranges" came up at him from a Jap rear gunner. ***Courtesy of Henry Brandon.***

2Lt. Norman Miller, Well's wingman, got his only victory when he shot down "an airplane with a big red ball on its side." The Jap flew right in front of him, he dropped his flaps to slow down and got his shot. The Jill's rear gunner hit Miller's cowl flap but he was able to return to base without incident. ***Courtesy of Norman Miller.***

18 May Close Air Support

Mission: 1200-1330 Destroy barracks in Tomui Town. After the coordinated attack on the 12th, the struggle on land had again disintegrated into a series of bitterly contested battles for the high ground. The Marines took Sugar Loaf Hill, then Horseshoe Hill, then Crescent Hill, while the Army went from Dakeshi ridge to Wana Ridge, and then to Conical Hill. The Americans paid dearly for every foot of ground won, and then paid again to hold these tenuous positions that were very vulnerable to ruthless Japanese counter attacks.

Major Jeff Dorroh led two divisions loaded with two napalm tanks and eight rockets. When Dorroh went down to check the target designation he found that ASCU had done its job. The major led the rocket run and then climbed to altitude to effect the napalm attack. Large fires were seen, and the barracks and surrounding installations were demolished.

15 MAY COMBAT

Two divisions of eight F4Us, the last CAP of the day, took off at 1720 under 1Lt. Charles Martin. The second division was vectored to patrol south of Kume Shima, a large island 60 miles west of Kadena. After two hours of patrolling, the second section under 2Lt. Al Wells was vectored to intercept three Navy Jill attack bombers carrying bombs, or a torpedo. They were within ten miles of friendly shipping.

Wells describes his part in the combat: "We had been flying CAP over some picket ships and were expecting to be relieved. It was dusk, but we were ordered to stay on as intelligence had it that some Japs were coming down from Formosa. I was leading the second section. I saw a shadow come under us from the west. We had all this training in combat tactics; we flew in four plane divisions divided in two plane sections with two section leaders and their protecting wingmen. But when someone saw some Japs, it was every man for himself. Everyone took off like a bat-out-of-hell to shoot down a Jap. So I immediately dropped to the water so I could silhouette the plane against the sky. I saw him, but I was going much faster. As I came up on him I realized that I was going to over run him. I didn't want to shoot because I didn't have any firm ID on him in the dark. Sometimes we had TBFs out there, flying alone on patrol. I put the gear down and lowered the flaps to decrease speed. I got behind him but still didn't want to shoot, but then he fired at me. It looked like he was throwing oranges at me. I was in close and fired at 300 feet at the Jap, which was flying only about 20 feet off the water. It burned briefly and went right in. As he went in, I turned around and came back and silhouetted another Jap against the sky. I made a slight deflection run at 600 feet, astern level, as he shot back at me. I put him in the water—the hits, flames and crash into the ocean occurred almost simultaneously. I always thought they were Judys, but the official record states they were Jills." (The Jill was widely used late in the war against Navy shipping, both in kamikaze and conventional attacks. It first appeared in the Marinas Campaign as a replacement for the Kate dive bomber. It would have been considerably more effective if it were flown by more experienced crews, which were in limited supply.)

2Lt. Norman Miller, the wingman, destroyed his Jill at the same time. Miller: "We were headed home from picket patrol at dusk. We were flying with our wing lights on, as we felt the air was secured from Jap fighters. I was flying at about 500 feet, and suddenly, I saw this airplane with the red ball on the side fly right across my path. I immediately dropped my flaps to slow down and I got on his tail. I was about 200 feet behind, and I started firing, booting my rudders, when he released a torpedo. The tail gunner was shooting back at me. He hit me, and my cowl flaps popped open, which was no big thing. I fired, and the Jap began to smoke and did a slow descending curve into the ocean. It then burst into flame and crashed into the ocean."

16 May Death of Leon Reynolds

Engineering Officer, Capt. Fred Ritter: "Keith Fountain had brought the aircraft back from a mission and reported that the oil pressure was vacillating. Usually engines were changed every 400 hours,

16 May. On the previous day Keith Fountain's aircraft had given him problems and was overdue for an overhaul. Maintenance Officer, Fred Ritter, wanted to tow the aircraft the five miles to Yonton but 2Lt. Leon Reynolds (above) volunteered to fly it over. On the way, the engine failed and Reynolds, not having much altitude on the short hop, was forced to crash land and was killed. ***Courtesy of Jody O'Keefe.***

Yonton airfield viewed from Kadena. The two airfields were only five miles apart. ***Courtesy of Norman Miller.***

but this one had gone way beyond that. I suggested that we tow it over to Yontan, but Reynolds wanted to fly it the three miles. I guess the engine must have froze, and he went down." Reynolds made a gear up landing and was reported to be standing near the downed aircraft, but was dead when we reached him."

"When a squadron member was lost I wrote letters to the family. It was a difficult and personal moment. I emphasized the positive. I cited the contributions he had made for the benefit of the squadron. I told of the love and affection we had for him, and how much we would miss him." George Axtell

16 May TBM Accident Robert Carleton diary: "About 1500 this afternoon, I saw a terrible accident. A TBM (Grumman Avenger 3-man bomber) was going over the field about 100 feet off the deck after taking a wave off. As it got near the tower the tail gunner either jumped or fell out of the plane. He landed about 50 feet from me and bounced and rolled about 50 feet."

17 MAY COMBAT

Combat 1

A two plane section led by 1Lt. James Feliton and backed up by his wingman, 2Lt. Stuart Alley, left Kadena at 1445 on a picket CAP. They circled the picket area off Kume Shima for four hours before being vectored to an enemy plane by the Fighter Director.

Feliton spotted the bogie, identified as a Val, flying below at 500 feet. He made the first pass, followed by Alley from 9 o'clock

S/Sgt. Robert Carleton kept a daily diary which gave the enlisted man's view of the war. ***Courtesy of Norman Miller.***

2Lt. Stuart Alley, who joined the squadron at Okinawa, scored his first victory, a Val, on the 17th. ***Courtesy of Norman Miller.***

2Lt. Keith Fountain got his only claim of the war when he shared a Val with Francis Terrill. ***Courtesy of Bill Drake.***

1Lt. Charles Allen led the four plane division consisting of Lts. Strickland, Feliton, and Blackwell to seven victories. Allen contributed two Tojos to the aggregate. Allen is seen here with the squadron Intelligence Officer, Tilly Ferdenzi. ***Courtesy of Norman Miller.***

and above, and fired at 600 feet, but had too much speed and overran. The panicked Val went into a dive, taking violent evasive action to the right and left. The Marine duo recovered from the first pass and pulled up and attacked again from above. During this second run Alley, coming in from 1,000 feet, passed Feliton, moved out in front and opened fire from above at 900 feet. The Jill, flying at 100 feet, was hit by Alley's tracers in the cockpit and crashed in flame.

Combat 2

On the last mission of the day, 1Lt. Francis Terrill led four Corsairs on a CAP in the vicinity of Tonaki Shima, a small island lying between Kerama Retto and Aguni Shima, a gateway to the American anchorage. The division patrolled for four hours before it was vectored off Tonaki Shima to investigate a bogie. While orbiting at 3,500 feet, Terrill sighted a Val heading east at 2,000 feet. Terrill quickly peeled off, followed by the rest of the eager division. The entire division took a few shots at the Val, as they all overshot in their excitement. The Val was left smoking slightly, and Lts. Terrill and Keith Fountain raced to make a quick recovery, regained the altitude advantage and then made the second pass, abreast, from above at 6 o'clock. The besieged Val dropped to wave top level making violent turns to the right and left. The Marines opened fire at 900 feet and hit the Val, which started to catch fire as it crashed into the sea for a shared victory.

19 May Close Air Support

Mission: 0625-0815 Destroy Naha prison and surrounding compound.

Major Axtell led 11 aircraft armed with two 500 lb. A.P. bombs and eight rockets. The target was easily identified, and the first run was a rocket attack with 53 of 77 (of 88 carried) hitting the target area. As the flight recovered and joined up the weather had closed in to solid overcast with a 1,200 foot base. Because of the weather only nine of the 22 bombs carried were released, and only five of these hit the target. The mission was a failure, causing only slight damage.

Air base and road development had priority over all other base development. When the monsoon rains of late May bogged down the Tenth Army's advance, Gen. Simon Buckner suspended air base

Two victors on the 25th are seen here. Front of: (L to R) Francis Terrill, Glenn Thacker, and driver, George Graham. Rear of jeep: (L to R) John Strickland, Stuart Alley, and Harold Edelson. Strickland got a Zeke and Tojo and Alley added a Tojo. ***Courtesy of Norman Miller.***

1Lt. Jim Feliton was credited with two Tojos.. He had previously served at Guadalcanal and scored a victory over a Zero on 19 October 1942. ***Courtesy of Norman Miller.***

construction, and all available engineers were assigned to work on the supply roads. When good weather returned in June air base development accelerated, with Kadena, Yontan and Ie Shima bases being completed, and new bases built on Ie Shima and on the eastern side of Okinawa.

24 May: "At the present time I'm on standby in my plane on the runway. I have brought my pen and some paper along so I can write to you. Planes whiz by me one after another and make lots of noise, but otherwise this is really a good place to write a letter. I have the plotting board pulled out, and it makes a perfect place to write. Much better than my desk up at the tent." Henry Brandon letter

25 MAY COMBAT

The fast carriers of Task Force 58 had hit Kanoya on Kyushu, the Headquarters for the Fifth Naval Air Fleet kamikaze base on 23 and 24 May. They destroyed 84 aircraft that were slated for the seventh Japanese kikusui attack. Only 65 Japanese Navy aircraft were available because of the U.S. fighter sweeps, but the Japanese Army was able to marshal about a 100. Several kamikazes made a series of attacks close to midnight, but the main attack was slated for the next day. Fortunately for the Japanese, rain and low cloud shrouded the attack that was delivered between 0835 and 0905.

The Kawasaki Ki-44 Tojo was a single seat front-line Japanese Army fighter from its introduction in mid-1942. On 25 May the JAAF sent up a group of Tojos as part of 100 aircraft of the seventh kikusui. The squadron claimed seven and damaged three. ***Courtesy of James Lansdale.***

2Lt. Tom Blackwell shot down a Tojo, damaged another and then damaged a Tony in the battle. *Courtesy of Bob Woods*.

Charles Spangler fully loaded for combat damaged a Tony. *Courtesy of Norman Miller.*

In the evening of 24/25 May, as part of kikusui #7, the Japanese launched a remarkable kamikaze attack on Yonton Airfield. Nine Sally Ki-21 bombers carrying paratroopers followed a conventional air attack on Yonton. Only one Sally survived American CAP and AA. It was able to crash land and its paratroopers leapt from the bomber's nose to attack the field. In this photo the crashed Sally is shown with a pile of window anti-radar chaff laying in front of the nose which has been removed by the departing Japanese paratroopers. *Courtesy of the US Army*.

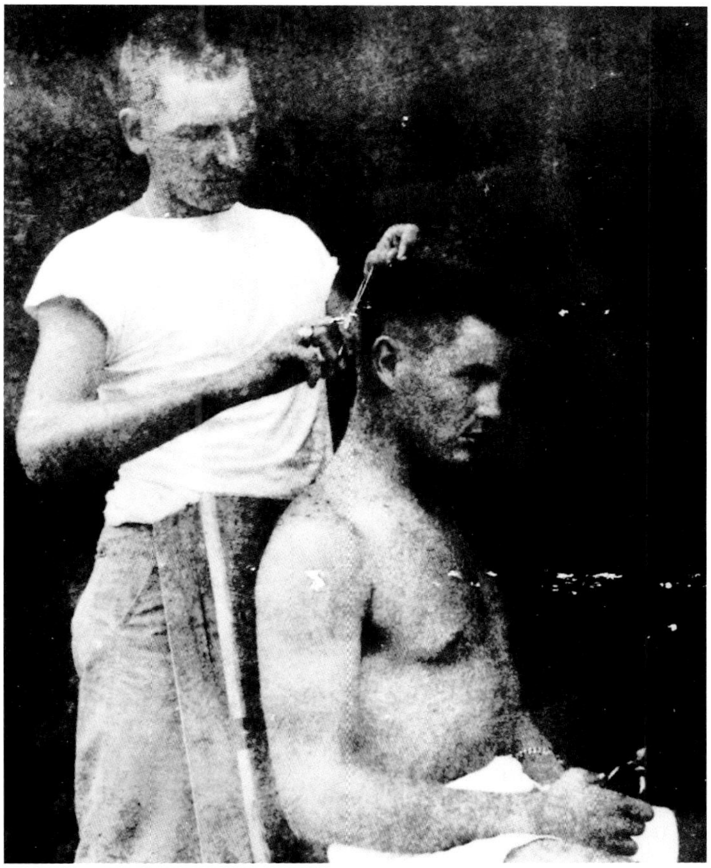

1Lt. John Strickland destroyed a Zeke and Tojo. He is seen here cutting Bill Hood's hair. ***Courtesy of Del Davis.***

Combat 1

A division of Death Rattler Corsairs led by 1Lt. Charles Allen and comprised of his wingman, 1Lt. John Strickland, and second section leader, 1Lt. James Feliton, and his wingman, 2Lt. Thomas Blackwell, were the first mission of the day, leaving at 0500. After patrolling 3 1/2 hours off Iheya Shima, Strickland spotted a mixed bag of nine bogies (six Tojos, one Tony and two Zekes) flying south at 2,000 feet in sections under the 4,000 foot cumulus overcast. The Corsairs were 10 miles northeast of the island at 3,500 feet. Strickland peeled off and closed fast from above on a Zeke at 7 o'clock, opening fire at 1,200 feet. He pulled over to the 6 o'clock position and fired his next burst, hitting the Zeke in the fuselage. Pieces were seen flying off the Jap's canopy, and it made a tight right turn, flipped over on its back, and crashed into the sea.

Lt. Allen made a run on a Tojo from above at 6 o'clock. He opened fire at 900 feet, and his tracers hit along the fuselage and into the canopy. The Tojo was seen to smoke and crash into the sea. On his recovery, Allen sighted a second Tojo directly ahead flying south at 1,500 feet. He closed at 6 o'clock, level, opening fire at 900 feet and watched his tracers converge on the cockpit. The Tojo made a violent snap roll and joined its predecessor.

Meanwhile, Blackwell engaged two Tojos and the Tony. His first run was on a Tojo from above, at 6 o'clock. He fired a short burst at 1,000 feet and got fuselage hits. Upon being hit the Tojo evaded by pulling up sharply, but the Corsair had no problem following. Blackwell got a long burst from 600 feet and the Jap exploded. In flying through the debris Blackwell sustained minor damage to his rudders and elevator.

Lt. Feliton also destroyed two Tojos. His first, flying at 2,000 feet, was destroyed from above at 6 o'clock, opening fire at 900 feet and causing fuselage hits and flames and a crash into the sea. On recovery, Feliton went after the second Tojo dead ahead at 2,000 feet. He closed at 6 o'clock level and opened fire at 900 feet, knocking the Tojo's bomb from its pylon. His second burst scored multiple hits on the fuselage, and the Jap rolled over on its back and smashed into the sea.

The flight joined up and chased the remaining bogies toward the southwest. Strickland caught up to a lagging Tojo and shot it down as he closed fast from the 6 o'clock position level and fired from 500 feet. The Tojo evaded with a sharp right diving turn and was able to get another burst before he overshot. The flight saw it flip over and hit the ocean.

Combat 2

The second mission of the day also took off at 0500. Capt. Bill Van Buskirk led the division to CAP 40 northwest of Ie Shima. After circling in heavy overcast for 3 1/2 hours, 2Lt. Stuart Alley at 500 feet sighted a single Tojo approaching above at 4,000 feet. It took Alley an instant to realize that the Jap was making a run on him from above at 11 o'clock. Alley pulled up his nose and fired at the closing Tojo. The two opponents fired short bursts at each other. Alley noticed pieces flying off the Tojo's fuselage and the engine smoking slightly. Both adversaries overshot each other and scrambled to gain the altitude advantage. The Corsair gave its pilot this superiority, and Alley initiated his second pass from above at 12 o'clock. Alley got a few hits on the engine and again overran the Jap. He again recovered quickly and got the altitude advantage. A third pass was then made from slightly above at 6 o'clock, closing fast and firing at 1,000 feet. The Tojo, smoking heavily, jinked violently, dove for the water, crashed and exploded.

Lt. Spangler then went after two Tojos flying above at 4,500 feet. He fired a long burst at one of them from 900 feet at 7 o'clock, and it went into a sharp left turn and then turned to the right. Spangler

A Japanese paratrooper lies dead near the C-46 transport he helped destroy. ***Courtesy of the US Army.***

A 70,000 gallon fuel dump was set on fire at Yonton during the Giretsu attack and was seen from Kadena. Nine aircraft were destroyed, two Americans killed and 18 wounded. The raid put VMF-323 and the entire island on edge, and there were many sleepless nights. *Courtesy of the USMC via Steve Stuczynski.*

Post-attack inspection of the Sally bomber at Yonton. *Courtesy of Henry Brandon.*

then opened fire a second time after closing at 6 o'clock low. The badly smoking Tojo disappeared into a cloud for a damaged credit.

24/25 May Giretsu Suicide Attack on Yontan

As part of Kikusui #7, on the night of 24/25 May, the Japanese launched a remarkable kamikaze attack on Yontan airfield. Nine Mitsubishi Sally Ki-21 bombers of the 3 Dokuritsu Hikotai, carrying paratroopers from the Giretsu Kutei Tai regiment, followed six formations of conventional bombers to Okinawa that had attacked Yontan, Kadena, and Ie Shima airfields. Four of these Sallys were destroyed by U.S. CAP, and four more were shot down by heavy AA fire as they descended toward Yontan. At 2230, the remaining

In his letter of 26 May, Henry Brandon writes, "It's been raining steadily and the rising water is threatening to run us all out of our little tent....the mud really gets on your nerves." *Courtesy of John Ruhsam.*

Toward the end of May there was another period of heavy rains. The ordnance tent floor went under water. *Courtesy of Jody O'Keefe.*

Sally crash-landed, skidding along the runway to a stop. Ten Japanese paratroopers armed with submachine guns leaped from the bomber's nose and hatches and attacked parked planes, fuel and ammunition dumps with explosive charges and phosphorous grenades. Two Americans were killed and 18 wounded before the raiders were subdued. The raid destroyed nine aircraft, damaged 26 more and set 70,000 gallons of gasoline aflame.

Enlisted man James Barrett describes the incident: "From Kadena we could see the flames leaping up to the skies on Yontan, only four miles away. There was a -323 component to the defense that was organized that night. Major Axtell assembled us and told us that we had to prepare for a similar Japanese attack on Kadena. We were sent out to the air strip with loaded rifles and instructed to shoot at any plane that would attempt to land. We were lined up along the east side of the airstrip, ready for anything. During the night, through the pitch darkness, we could hear the clank, clank of tanks moving at a little distance from us. The night wore on and nothing happened at Kadena. But as dawn began to break we found that we were staring at a long row of tanks with their cannons pointed directly at us. Someone hastened over to tell them we were on their side, and we got a sort of apology from the officer who was supposed to secure us after the tanks were in place. We were really lucky that no enemy planes landed at Kadena that night."

Warren Broering: "The intelligence for the Jap parachute drop was very good, and we were put on alert. I was in the tent with Del Davis, Bob Wood and Charlie Martin, and we were ready for anything. We each were on watch for about two hours so the others could sleep. No one was supposed to be outside except those on guard duty. Del Davis and I had our cots facing the door flap so we could see out. Also, it was pitched on a wheat field so that the stubble would crackle if someone stepped on it and we could hear them. I was on watch, and I heard noise outside, so I challenged the intruder for the password. Before he even had a chance to return the password, Del woke up and fired away with his .45 at point blank range. The guy went down screaming, but Davis had somehow missed. It was lucky he was such a bad shot." The intruder was Jesse James, an enlisted "man," who had lied about his age to get into the Marines. The 16 year old James was the unit's misfit/mascot/psycho and was always in trouble with Axtell.

26 May: "It has been raining steadily, and the rising water is threatening to run us all out of our little tent, but maybe it will stop tonight. I hope. This mud really gets on your nerves. It gets messy around here . Every time we come in the tent we take our shoes off to avoid messing up our floor. Aren't we particular old ladies?" Henry Brandon letter

"Our engineers tended to build in low areas on the island and ignored the rice paddies and drainage systems which the Okinawans had engineered for centuries. During a particularly rainy period our ordnance area was flooded so that only the top of our truck and tent was above the water." James Barrett

28 MAY COMBAT

After losing over 200 planes during the seventh kikusui attack the eighth massed kikusui attack was quickly organized for the 27th. The weather was even worse than on the previous attack on the 25th and had interfered with U.S. land-based operations on the 27th. No sorties were flown by -323, and flights by other units which did get aloft were often recalled or couldn't contact the kamikaze formations. The Japanese attacks were relatively successful, getting hits on nine ships and sinking or putting eight out of action for the remainder of the war. Only 47 of 110 aircraft (a relative figure compared to previous attacks) which took part were lost, so the attack was continued the next day.

Combat 1

At 0500, 1Lt. Del Davis, with his wingman, 2Lt. Robert Woods, led his division of 1Lt. Jack Broering and his wingman through the dawn overcast to a patrol area east of Zampa Misaki (this location is off the east coast of Okinawa). After 2 1/2 hours on CAP the Fighter Director vectored them to a point 40 miles east of Zampa Misaki to check out a bogie report in the area. Broering: "The controller called out a bogey, and it remained in the same relative position, so it was apparent that it was shadowing us in the cloud layer above. We broke up; my section going above the clouds and the other below. The bogie must have thought the whole flight was coming up, so he went down." Davis: "I picked up a visual contact

1Lt. Del Davis (R) and his wingman, 2Lt. Bob Woods, shared a victory over a Tojo. Davis got so low in his pursuit of the Jap that his prop kicked up sea water. ***Courtesy of Norman Miller.***

1Lt. Harold Edelson joined with 1Lt. John Strickland after they became separated from their flight and shared a Sally bomber victory. ***Courtesy of Henry Brandon.***

on a single fighter at about one mile in the 12 o'clock position. The bogie sighted us and entered the overcast below. I instructed the second division to remain above the overcast in the event the fighter decided to climb back on top. Woods and I descended on a westerly course and broke out between two small islands at about 300 feet. I did a 180 turn to the east and immediately picked up the target, a A-6M Zero (ed. note: the ACA report states a Tojo) at about 800 feet dead ahead, headed for the Picket Ships." Davis, followed by Woods, initiated a run from above at 6 o'clock, and both pilots opened fire. Their fire converged on the cockpit, and the Jap jettisoned two small bombs and dove for the water. They followed him down, getting a few more hits, resulting in smoke and an explosion to share the victory. Davis, "I was surprised that during this encounter I had gotten so low on the water that my propeller was picking up sea water.

Combat 2

The second division of Corsairs led by 1Lt. John Strickland also took off at 0500 to fly CAP over Ie Shima. After several hours they saw an Army twin-engine Sally bomber flying 1,000 feet above at 3,000 feet. Strickland led the division through the overcast to press home the attack. 2Lt. Jim Carey, flying on Strickland's wing, opened fire first from 1,200 feet but made no hits. The alerted Sally pulled up into a cloud, but Strickland caught glimpses of it making violent course changes in the thin cloud.

Strickland and 1Lt. Harold Edelson became separated from the rest of the division while in the clouds and joined up. Upon breaking through the clouds they found themselves slightly above and astern of a Sally. The Sally's tail gunner opened fire as it began its bombing run on the shipping off Ie Shima. The Marines opened fire simultaneously and silenced the tail gunner. The Sally, intent on its attack, blandly jinked and continued into a steeper dive with Strickland and Edelson closing fast. They hit the silver bomber in the fuselage and port engine, which began to smoke badly as it broke through the overcast over friendly shipping. Both friend and foe came under AA fire. Nonetheless, both continued their attack and followed the Sally down until they saw it crash and explode. Upon his return to base Strickland found that his right wing was damaged by AA fire, which was repaired on base.

28 May: "This rain situation is really getting critical. We haven't had any sunshine now for over a week, and everything around here is filled with water. There is absolutely nothing for us here except work, sleep, and eat, and that old routine is really getting tiresome. But I know that we are having a much easier time than the others here on the island." Henry Brandon letter

29 May: "Nothing except rain for days now. The mud is deep as usual, so we slip and slide around. I haven't flown much in the past week, just the way the schedule and weather work out. Time is beginning to become heavy on our hands now. We do nothing but work and wait, with no outside activities of any sort. If we had a chance to go swimming or something it might break the monotony. It looks like I won't get much of a rest leave, either. We are overdue now because someone is fouling up along the line. Just a second ago a couple of goats found my socks, and I had to shoo them away. They have been getting pesky of late and try to get into our tent." John Ruhsam

Charlie Allen and Bob Wade are visited by two of the many pesky goats that roamed the airfield. Nothing was safe from their pillaging. ***Courtesy of John Ruhsam.***

29 May Close Air Support

Mission: 0940-1120 Strike targets of opportunity in south Naha. After the capture of high ground on the eastern flank some gains were made in the middle of the month. But then the infantry advance again became desperately slow. The Shuri Line was showing some cracks.

Major Jeff Dorroh was acting as an Air Coordinator for a 24 plane close air strike to south Okinawa. He was to observe the weather over the target and found it to be solid overcast to 500 feet, and called to cancel the strike. Meanwhile, Capt. Bill Van Buskirk, the strike leader, had already taken off and soon joined up with Dorroh over the Naha area. Dorroh and Van Buskirk were armed with a napalm tank and 500 lb. bomb each and eight rockets. CASU assigned them a target consisting of two ridges lying about 1,500 yards south of Naha airfield. Upon verifying the target the two saw numerous caves containing troops and light and medium gun emplacements. The napalm tanks were released first to burn off any camouflage. Then the two 500 pounders were dropped, followed by sixteen rockets, eight of these by the Air Coordinator's (Dorroh) smoke rockets. Both sides of the ridges were hit, and several direct hits were made on the caves. Results were judged to be excellent.

30 May: "For the first time in days the sun has shown, not for long, but long enough to let us know it is up there somewhere. Last night we had two inches of water all over the floor of our tent. So this morning the sides are all tied up, and all my things are being aired or dried out as much as possible before the next deluge.

Every night we start having a movie, and nearly every night it is never finished. Last night, for instance, all went fine until it was half over and the clouds burst above us. The night before an air raid stopped it, and the night before that it was the rain again. Four nights ago we actually got through an entire movie only because they showed it through the rain. Unfortunately, we had seen that one before. Last night was a big night, as I got word that I am a 1st. Lieutenant. It isn't completely official until they write up the papers and sign them. But I am as far as the pay voucher is concerned. It was a long grind of 20 months, but finally they got down to my number. We have heard those peace rumors out here, too, and it seems so far away. People don't know how determined the Japanese fight. I may be wrong, I hope so, but I don't think they will give up for one long, long time. We're just going to have to go in and drag them out of every hole. They just don't live, think, or exist in the same way we do." John Ruhsam letter

31 May Close Air Support

Mission: 1430-1700 Attack enemy dugouts and entrenchments along a ridge 2,000 yards south of Naha Airfield. Pilots were briefed on a

2Lt. Bill Drake, playing G.I. Joe and brandishing a Japanese samurai sword which was probably the most valued of Japanese souvenirs. ***Courtesy of Henry Brandon.***

Tilly Ferdenzi ceremoniously beheads Bob Muse with his newly acquired samurai sword. ***Courtesy of Norman Miller.***

Displaying a captured Japanese flag are: Front Row: (L to R) Del Davis, Harold Edelson (behind flag), Larry Crawley, and Bill Drake (looking down). Middle Row: (L to R) Bob Wade, Mindy Muse, Al Wells, Bob Wood (cap), and Ed Keeley. Back Row: (L to R) Razor Blaydes, Tilly Ferdenzi, Harold Tonnessen (playing the accordion). *Courtesy of Jody O'Keefe.*

A -323 F4U carrying a 160 gallon paper napalm tank. This photo was probably taken later in the campaign as the fighter shows wear and tear on the paint job. ***Courtesy of Norman Miller.***

prearranged target. Because of poor visibility—9/10ths cumulus and 200 foot ceiling—over this target, another target was assigned.

Major Jeff Dorroh, acting as Air Coordinator, was loaded with two 500 lb. bombs, tail fused for 8-11 second delay and eight FS (smoke) rockets. Capt. Felix Cecot led the strike force of ten F4Us armed with two napalm tanks and eight rockets. After a dummy run, Dorroh pushed over at only 150 feet and 5 degrees due to the weather and dropped his bombs. Cecot's flight pushed over at 100 feet and 10 degrees and dropped 17 napalm tanks at 50 feet. The rest were not dropped, as the pilots were not on target and were in close proximity to our troops. On the third run 59 of 80 rockets were launched along a 300 yd. slant from a 100 foot push over at 10 degrees, all hitting the target area. The remaining rockets were not fired because pilots were not sure of target designation. Results were not observed.

MONTHLY SUMMARY

MAY
Personnel: 291
Officers: Marine: 61 — Enlisted: Marine: 223
Navy: 1 — Navy: 6
Personnel lost: 2Lt. Leon Reynolds
Maj. Arthur Turner
1Lt. Edward Murray

Aircraft
on hand: 23 FG-1Ds — 10 F4U-1D
Aircraft lost: 6 F4U-1Ds

Missions: 208/31 flying days
Combat Air Patrol: 123
Picket Ship Patrol: 67
Close Air Support: 16
Miscellaneous: 2
2822 hrs./1006 indiv. Flights/1002 combat missions
Encounters: AA: 4 Enemy A/C: 14
Enemy A/C destroyed: 52 3/4
probable: 0
damaged: 14

CHAPTER 26
June
Closing Down

1 June Close Air Support
Mission: 0930-1200 Attack buildings, barges, underground emplacements in Kyamu. Two months into the campaign the loss in life and equipment was incomprehensible. In the bitterly contested south, American infantry forces had advanced just 400 feet per day from 8 April until the end of May. Here the Japanese had lost 64,000 men. More inconceivable were the 200 Japanese prisoners taken only because they were either badly wounded or unconscious. American casualties (killed, wounded, and missing) amounted to over 26,000, but while American killed amounted to only a tenth of the total Japanese killed, this was an unacceptable figure. Onshore equipment losses were obscured by the devastation to offshore shipping. The Shuri Line had all but crumbled, and the Japanese withdrew. However, the weather and American indecision and inaction allowed them to set up defensive positions further south. Here they continued their dogged defense; delay, inflict maximal damage, retreat, and die.

Capt. Felix Cecot led a division armed with two napalm tanks and eight rockets. After reaching station, the flight was instructed to pick a target of opportunity below the strategic bomb line. Kyamu Town on the southeastern tip of Okinawa was chosen. The napalm was dropped first followed by the rockets. The mission produced mediocre results, with a few fires started and few, if any, buildings and barges destroyed. After the attack the flight continued on a two hour CAP before returning to base.

2 June Close Air Support
Mission: 1055-1215 Attack gun emplacements and caves south of Yuza Town. Using recon photos, the target had been well briefed on the ground prior to take off. Once over the target the pilots had no problems identifying the target and were further aided by an Air Coordinator, who verified the target with smoke rockets. Major Axtell led three napalm and rocket equipped divisions over the target. Due to the efficient briefing and air coordination, this mission was considered one of the better close air support missions flown thus far. Enemy emplacements and caves were accurately hit by rockets, and napalm started large and serious fires.

2 June 13 replacement pilots join squadron

3 June Combat
With the eighth kikusui on 27-28 May, the Japanese had depleted their stock of aircraft, so much so that on the 30th, no Japanese aircraft appeared over Okinawa, for the first time in 66 days. The ninth kikusui that commenced was a small one spread over five days, and only 50 aircraft took part. It was apparent that by the end of May that Japanese air attacks were declining in number and potency. Despite the significant destruction to American shipping caused by the kamikazes, the Japanese no longer had the aircraft in reserve to absorb the staggering losses suffered in the TEN-GO operations. Japanese military leaders now recognized that they were powerless to drive away the huge Allied task force lying off Okinawa without committing every remaining aircraft in inventory. The Japanese had decided that the final battle would take place on the Japanese homeland and were intent on conserving their aircraft reserve.

1Lt. Al Wells scored two hard-won victories against the last of the experienced, skilled Japanese pilots flying Zeke (Zero) fighters to become an ace. Upon first seeing the bogies, Wells identified them as Japs as he tally-hoed, "they're too beautiful to be ours". ***Courtesy of Bob Woods.***

2Lt. Bill Drake became an ace when he shot down four Zekes. In the swirling aerial battle, named the "Big Hairy Dogfight," Drake ran out of ammo and his fuel gauge malfunctioned when he was bounced by a formation of fighters. Fortunately they were P-47s which escorted him back to base. *Courtesy of Henry Brandon*.

2Lt. Jerry Conners contributed to Zekes to the squadron's nine victories. He almost contributed another unwanted victory to the total when he just missed Al Wells in the chaotic battle. *Courtesy of Bill Drake*.

Combat 1 "The Big Hairy Dogfight"

At 1000 on 3 June, a four plane division took off from Kadena. The division was led by 1Lt. Cy Dolezel (Ruby 1) and his wingman, 2Lt. Bill Drake (Ruby 2), while the second section was led by 1Lt. Al Wells (Ruby 3) and his wingman, 2Lt. Jerry Conners (Ruby 4). They had been flying CAP over the invasion beaches of Iheya Shima for about an hour when they were asked to join up with another division of Corsairs out of Ie Shima. The two divisions were at 13,000 feet, 20 miles west of Iheya Shima, and were given a vector to 20,000 feet on a course of 090 degrees. The Ie Shima division remained at 13,000 feet while Dolezel was ordered to take his division to 20,000 feet. They broke through the overcast at 15,000 feet, and at 16,000 feet the division was confronted by a large formation of 24 aircraft. They were immediately identified as Japanese Zeke fighters, which were apparently on a fighter sweep to oppose our landings on Iheya Shima. "They're too pretty to be ours," thought Wells. There was an old adage among Navy and Marine flyers: "If it's beautiful, it's a Jap." Japanese aircraft were generally clean, no lumps or bumps, smooth, faired lines with sleek, rounded noses and slim fuselages. These weren't old, lumbering Val, Nate or Jill suiciders flown by inexperienced pilots, but a sky full of Zekes (Zero Navy A6M) looking for a fight. The Japs had a speed and 2,000 foot altitude advantage over the Marines who were still climbing out of the clouds. It was too late to dive back into the safety of the clouds, so the Corsairs kept on climbing. The Japs dropped their belly tanks and dove to attack, while the Marines employed the SOP of trying to turn on the Japs' tails. The Japs unbelievably missed on their first pass, and the battle continued down to the deck and turned into, as Dolezel describes it: "One big, hairy dogfight." U.S. fighter doctrine was not to dogfight the more maneuverable Jap fighter, but to employ a two plane, leader and wingman, scissors attack tactic. Now each of the -323 pilots was on his own, with no other option but to engage the swirling Japs and try to join up with another Corsair.

Dolezel turned with the two Zekes that attacked him and followed them into the clouds. The three fighters came out of the clouds

1Lt. Cy Dolezel is pointing to a 20mm cannon hole put there by a Zeke after he had shot down another Zeke. The shell went through the fuselage and exploded against the armor plate behind his head, knocking him silly for a few seconds. ***Courtesy of Bill Drake.***

1Lt. Charles Spangler led a three plane flight of 2Lts. Dewey Durnford and Stuart Alley on a CAP and splashed a Val. ***Courtesy of Norman Miller.***

2,000 feet below. One Jap had drifted to Dolezel's left in a diving spiral. Dolezel followed him as he came out of the spiral and leveled out and began a roll. A quick spurt from the Corsair's .50 calibers hit him as he turned on his back and flamed him. Dolezel dove through cloud to about 10,000 feet looking for Drake. Unable to find him, Dolezel climbed back to 16,000. As he broke out of the clouds, he again encountered the Zekes, six of them. Dolezel made the mistake of trying to turn and dive back into the clouds. As soon as he came out of his turn Dolezel says, "It felt like I was hit in the back of the head with a baseball bat." He went into his dive into the clouds with his head ringing and came out at about 12,000 feet. He circled around trying to compose himself and figure out what happened. A 20 mm Jap cannon shell had exploded against the armor plate behind his head. It hadn't penetrated, but the concussion knocked him silly for a while. Fortunately, he saw Jerry Conners and left for Kadena.

The Mitsubishi A6M Zeke was the ubiquitous Zero. The Zekes which appeared over Okinawa were usually early models flown by experienced pilots to led the barely trained kamikaze pilots to the island or as decoys used to draw off the US CAPs and allow the kamikazes to attack against lesser opposition. On 3 June, nine were shot down by the Death Rattlers. ***Courtesy of James Lansdale.***

2Lt. Stuart Alley shot down three Vals to become an ace with his fifth victory. ***Courtesy of the USMC via Steve Stuczynski.***

2Lt. Dewey Durnford shot down a Val and then a Nate to become the twelfth and last Death Rattler ace of the war. On 17 May 1953, while flying a F-86 for the 5th FIW over Korea, Durnford (shown in Korea) shot down a MIG-15. ***Author's collection.***

At the start of the dogfight, Jerry Conners broke out a little behind Dolezel, Drake and Wells. He continued in a steep climb to the left trying to get on the Jap's tails. Three Zekes made a section run on Conners, but in their haste led him too much and their tracers whizzed past his prop. Conners lost his composure. Instead of turning into his attackers, he urgently shouted for help in his mike and looked for Wells, his section leader. As he closed behind Wells he was set upon by two Zekes from one o'clock, one high and one level. Conners was behind and slightly below Wells. The Zeke on level went after Wells' tail, leaving the higher Zeke to get Conners. As the Zeke went after Wells, the Marine pilot made a steep right turn in front of Conners, who squeezed off a quick, accurate burst from 600 feet. Conner's .50s blasted the Jap out of his turn and caused it to dive into flames. Conners says, "I almost scored double, as my bullets just missed Al's wing up ahead." What happened to the second high Zeke is a mystery, as Conners didn't see him. He either didn't fire or fired and missed. As Conners joined Wells, the section leader spotted a Jap and firewalled it, leaving Conners alone again. Again the solitary pilot was attacked by two Zekes, one dead on and the other from about two o'clock. The Zeke on the head-on collision course and Conners started firing simultaneously at about 700 feet in a game of chicken. The Jap suddenly pushed his nose down to escape under the Corsair. Conners also pushed his nose down, which put the Zeke into his field of fire, tearing into the cockpit, setting the Jap on fire. Conners spotted Wells again, but was unable to join up as Wells was in a whirling, vertical dogfight. Conners followed the fight, watching as the Zeke was unable to pull out of his dive and plunged into the sea. Conners caught a glimpse of Wells as he climbed into a cloud and took off after him. As Conners pulled out of the cloud he saw a Corsair off to his right and thought Wells had crossed over in front of him in the cloud. Looking over Conners saw that it was Dolezel with a large hole in his canopy and his radio antenna draped around his stabilizer. The two pilots headed home.

Bill Drake had lost Dolezel in the first encounter and was searching to rejoin him when two Japs cut across his nose to the right. Drake followed one section of Zekes to 17,000 and fired on the tail end Charlie, but his tracers were crossing behind the target. Drake swung his nose slightly below to a 5 o'clock position and walked a long burst of bullets up the fuselage into the cockpit that burst into flame. The Jap exploded, throwing chunks of airplane towards Drake. He chased the second Zeke and made a 3 o'clock run, hitting it in the cockpit, which also flamed violently. While trying to relocate Dolezel, he saw three Zekes flying to the west below him. The one on the left flew on unaware, and Drake closed on it at 4 o'clock. His bullets once again hit the cockpit and the Zeke burst into flame. He went after the other two Zekes, but overshot. Wanting company, Drake looked around for any Corsair, but when he looked into his rear view mirror he saw, to his dismay two Zekes on his tail, sandwiched, one on each side. He jammed the nose down, firewalled the throttle, and hit the water injection. Screaming down some 7,000 feet at 500 mph he pulled away from the Japs, who broke off at 7,000 feet and pulled up. With all that speed built up, Drake decided to take off after the Japs. The Corsair easily could out climb the Zeke, and Drake soon had the inside Jap

1Lt. Bob Wade shared a Val victory with John Ruhsam. The half victories for each gave seven apiece to tie them with Jerry O'Keefe with seven for the most in the squadron. Wade (shown in Korea) flew with the 51st FIW in Korea and shot down a MIG-15. ***Author's collection.***

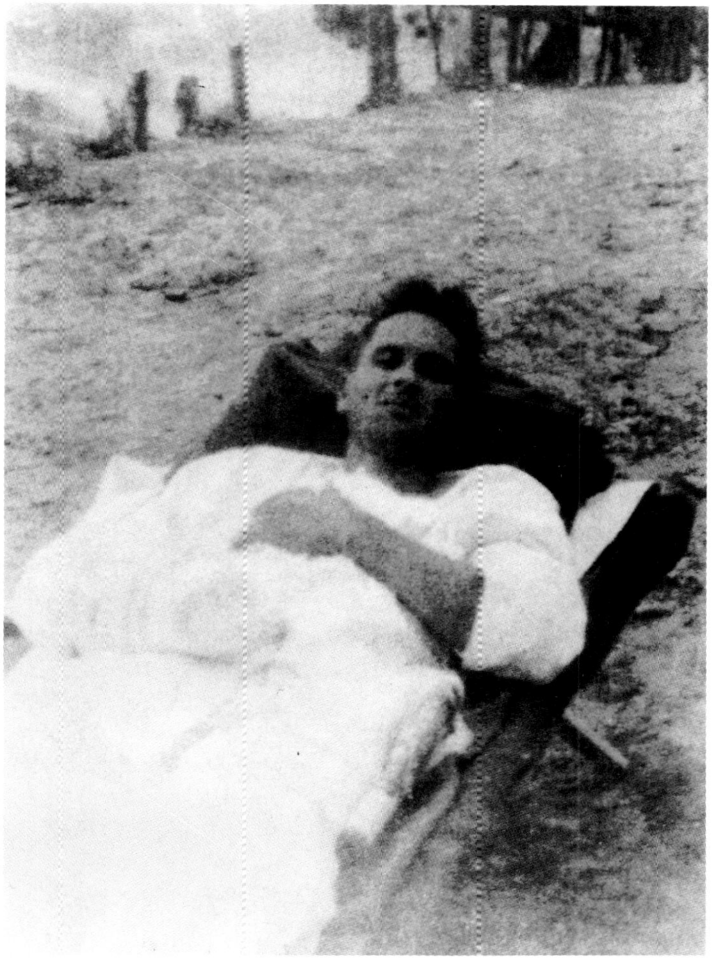

Sgt. Earl Barr ready to evacuate after burning himself while washing clothes with gasoline. ***Courtesy of Harley Brock.***

in his sights and shot about 200 rounds into it. The bullets hit the cockpit, and again the plane burst into flame (due to the unprotected fuel tank in front of the pilot, it was disclosed at debrief later). The Jap wingman made a sharp left turn to escape, but Drake kicked left rudder and squeezed off about 100 rounds before he ran out of ammo. He came up on the Jap's left and could see some smoke trailing out of his wing root. It appeared that the Jap would make it home, and Drake briefly considered ramming, but discretion was the better part of valor, and he turned home with four victories and a damaged. When he checked his instrument panel he found his compass spinning wildly, and his fuel and engine temperature gauges out. Drake realized that he had no idea which direction Kadena would be and requested help over the radio. He reached Conners and Dolezel, who were unable to help. Drake crossed a small island and dropped down to 1,000 feet to try to get his bearings. As he looked into the distance he saw another Zeke at about 5,000 feet. Out of ammo, this was not the best tactical position to be in. Instinctively ducking down into his seat so as not to be seen, Drake tried to sneak away. As he looked back he saw the Jap turn away, maybe also out of ammo or low on fuel. Drake climbed, looking around, and he saw a formation of fighters barreling in a dive towards him and he thought he was dead man. Drake saw that the fighters were mid-wing, not low-wing Zekes, and identified them as Air Force P-47s. He put his Corsair in position for the P-47s to see its gullwings and they broke off the attack. Drake was escorted home by the Army with four victories and a probable.

On the first attack, Al Wells concentrated on getting out of the way while taking quick shots at the swarming Japs. He had to jink around to keep the Japs off his tail, but he couldn't get any decent shots and was wasting ammo. Suddenly, one flew across his nose and he turned with it, firing and getting hits, starting it smoking. Wells had turned so tightly that he stalled out and went down with him through a layer of clouds. Wells recovered from the stall in the cloud layer, and when he broke through he saw the damaged Jap below him. Wells fired again, hitting the cockpit, setting the plane aflame. Wells found himself below the lowest cloud layer at about 8,000 feet and began to climb to rejoin the battle. As he began a climbing turn he saw a Zeke just below and about 500 yards away.

Wells continued his turn after the Jap, who saw him and went into a steep dive toward the deck. Wells firewalled the throttle, put it in low blower, hit the water injection, and took off after the Jap. Wells caught up and was fixing the easy victim in his sights when the easy victim "zoomed straight up, and did this damn gook thing, like he was on a string." Wells yanked back on the stick, but there was no way that the Corsair could turn with the Zeke. Before Wells knew what was happening, the Jap was rocketing down from 1,500 feet above, head on, in a 60 degree dive, on his back, his guns firing at him. Wells was also climbing at 60 degrees and firing. "At first I thought he was going to ram me." The two fighters closed on each other, firing and missing, the Jap's bullets passing overhead and Well's passing under the Jap, which happened to be over, as the Jap was inverted. Wells finished his climb and turned after the Jap, who was again below and departing. Wells goosed the Corsair again and caught the Jap, who again went "into the same damn zoom, up, over and down on me. This happened not twice, but several times! I kept blacking out during every one of those steep pull ups." Finally, Wells decided that his luck was running out and he needed to try something different. He decided to nose up a little in the climb to get a better shot at the Jap. But that also meant there was a greater chance of the two planes colliding, especially if the Jap decided to nose down just a little! "We went into the same old dance-chase, climb, loop and dive. I went up on his tail and he again flipped on his back about 1,500 feet above me and then dove on me. My tracers were again sliding under him. so I quickly pulled the nose up, and I thought I saw some hits go in. I quickly pushed the nose back down, and the Jap roared over on his back, just missing me. He came so close that I could see the flames just starting in his cockpit. He stayed on his back all the way to the drink. He hit the water with just a splash—there was no explosion. He was a really good pilot, and gave me the greatest scare of my life. It was the only time in my life that my mouth was like cotton and I couldn't swallow." Wells saw oil slicks on the water where planes had gone in and

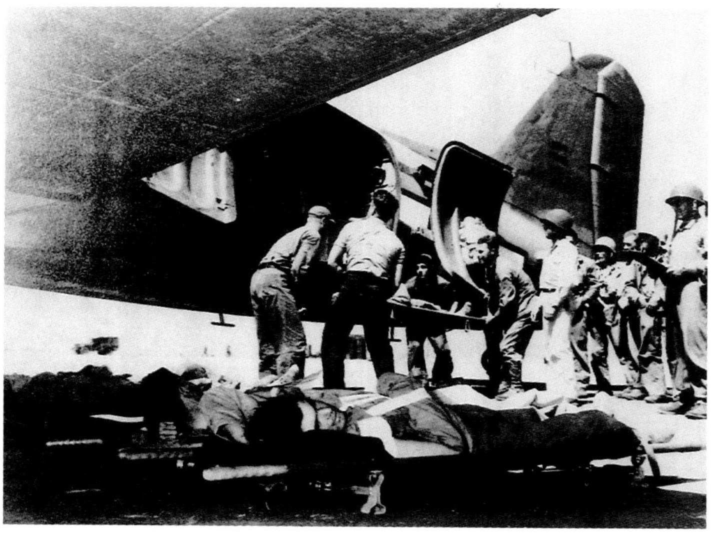

During the Okinawa campaign the use of air evacuation came into wide use. About 40% or more of the more than 15,000 casualties were evacuated by air to hospitals in the Marianas and, if necessary, to Hawaii or the Mainland. ***Courtesy of the USMC via Steve Stuczynski.***

This is a strike photo of the 8 June close air support mission on a Jap-held ridge on the southern outskirts of Tomui Town to work with troops advancing toward the town. ***Courtesy of the USMC via George Axtell.***

figured that the odds of one of the division being one of those slicks were pretty high. His radio was out and he headed home. On the way he looked up and saw four Corsairs streaking down on him. Wells couldn't call them because of his radio being out and just had to hope they would recognize him before they shot him down. They broke off, and Wells recognized it was Joe Dillard's division rushing to the fight that was over. Wells followed them and searched for an hour with them before they all went back to Kadena.

Combat 2

At 1015, a three plane flight led by 1Lt. Charles Spangler, and including 2Lt. Dewey Durnford and 2Lt. Stuart Alley, took up CAP 40 miles off the Okinawa beachhead (Zampa Misaki). While flying at an altitude of 700 feet, Spangler sighted a Val on an opposing course at an altitude of 500 feet. He swung his division around on the Val's course and made a pass from above at 6 o'clock. The Val jettisoned its bomb and dove to the deck to escape. Spangler overshot on his pass, and Alley followed him in from above and opened fire at 900 feet at 6 o'clock, hitting the cockpit. The doomed Val dove and crashed into the sea.

The trios, on another vector, were directed to five more Vals and a Nate heading toward nearby shipping. From 1,000 feet Spangler led his division in from above at 4 to 7 o'clock. Spangler, closing fast, hit a Val from 900 feet and saw it splash as he made a wing over on recovery.

Alley then opened fire on a Val from above at 6 o'clock from 1,000 feet, tattooing its fuselage and finally exploding it. A second Val flew dead ahead of Alley and was also dispatched from 6 o'clock and 1,000 feet.

Meanwhile, Durnford closed from above and 5 o'clock on a Val in a diving turn and opened fire at 700 feet. The Val flamed brightly and crashed into the sea. On recovery Durnford saw the Nate at 2,000 feet, closed from 5 o'clock below, and fired a long burst from 900 feet. The Nate split-essed and went into a climbing turn. Durnford followed and hit him at 8 o'clock low. The Nate went into a tight turn, spun, and crashed into the sea.

Combat 3

A division led by Capt. Joe McPhail left on CAP at 1230, headed for Iheya Shima. After 4 1/2 hours of boring non-eventful flying, Ruhsam log book: "The division was flying late afternoon CAP. Splashes all around, but no vectors for us. Wade spotted a bogey in his rear vision mirror (flying on an opposite course), and we whirled around and gave chase. The plane was about 2,000 feet above and five miles away. He pushed over in a dive to gain speed, so we poured on the coal. Coming up from behind we could see the fixed landing gear. We tallyhoed and barreled in. Caught him at about 1,500 feet, and both Wade and I started firing. He (the Val) turned to my side, and I had another beautiful shot. He began to burn and rolled over. I over ran and got caught below. Jammed the stick forward and went about 2 feet away, and could see both the pilot and gunner. The rear gunner was fighting to get out of the plane, but it went straight in and blew up on the water. Wade and I split."

Score for the day against front-line, experienced Japanese fighter pilots: Death Rattlers downed 9 Japs, while the Japs dented one F4U seat armor plate. Claims for -323: Drake: 4 Zekes (1 Zeke probable); Wells: 2 Zekes; Conners: 2 Zekes: and Dolezel: 1 Zeke. Drake and Wells became aces, each scoring their fifth victories.

P-47s of the USAAF's 507th FG had previously flown from Ie Shima and raided Kyushu on the southern tip of the Japanese Homeland. Major Axtell lobbied for permission to lead a Marine F4U strike against Kyushu to prove the Corsair had enough range to do so. Shortly after noon on the 10th, Axtell led 24 F4Us to attack airfields there. Strafing runs resulted in the destruction of 13 enemy aircraft on the ground. ***Courtesy of George Axtell.***

3 June: "Well, I guess our writing days will soon be over. You can catch the next train for the West Coast. My orders are in, and I probably will get them soon, but there may be some delay in transportation. I may have to wait for a plane for a couple of days or a couple of weeks. I expect to be home within a month anyway. My flying days here are over. My last hop was on May 31, so you don't have to worry about your 'old man' now." Henry Brandon letter

5 June Earl Barr Accident. Sgt. Earl Barr burned hand and leg while washing clothes with 100 octane gasoline.

5 June: "I feel a little funny, the war being over for me and I am returning home, just where I want to stay the rest of my life. But, I sure am going to be glad to get away from the mud and dirt and get back to living like a civilized being with my little wife." Henry Brandon letter

7 June: 2 replacement pilots join squadron

13 pilots transferred on completion of their tour of duty

8 June Close Air Support

Mission: 0730-0930 Close Air Support on a Jap-held ridge on the southern outskirts of Tomui Town to work with troops advancing towards the town.

Major Axtell acted as Air Coordinator for eight VMF-322 Corsairs. Ground troops fired two white phosphorous shells on each end of the ridge to mark the extremities of the target. Axtell then further pinpointed the target by accurately dropping two 500 lb. G.P. bombs on the ridge crest. -322 came in on their napalm and rocket runs and caused heavy damage. It was determined that well-briefed and coordinated pilots aided by accurately marked targets achieved successful results.

George Axtell: "As the air coordinator I was assigned to mark the target area. The ground coordinator would radio me the o'clock position from observing my direction of flight. I would either fly a trial run or fire smoke marker rockets. The ground coordinator would give me the results and corrections for what I hoped would be the final run. The squadron would then roll on in and drop its ordnance. My wingman and I would climb to the tail-end Charlie position and drop our ordnance."

8 June: "I guess this is the most excited that I have ever been. I didn't sleep but about an hour last night. I haven't had much time, for I am getting on a plane in about an hour and will be on my way home to you. I hope to be there within a week or so. Give everyone at home my regards. I know I'm about the happiest man in the world to be coming home to my wonderful wife." Henry Brandon letter

10 JUNE COMBAT

After the success of the Navy's fast carrier attacks on southern Japan, Major Axtell had been anxious to mount the first Marine land-based fighter attack on the airbases on Kyushu. U.S. Army P-47 Thunderbolts of the 507th Fighter Group based on Ie Shima had made the first AAF sweep of the Japanese homelands on 24 May. Headquarters felt that the Corsair didn't have sufficient range for the mission, but after much planning and politicking Axtell got his wish. Axtell: "There was interservice competition, and I wanted to fly a mission to Japan, especially after the Army with special long-range P-47s flew there. I was told that our F4Us didn't have enough range, but we knew we could lean out and get there and back. Early in the morning I got a call to go up to the operations center and see (M.Gen. Fred F.) Mulcahy. He said that I had been bitching long and loud and now I could go. I asked when, and he said now. That gave us only a couple of hours to get ready, but we knew what we were doing." Targets were to include enemy aircraft encountered in the air, parked on the ground and the installations at Kitahara, Kokubu and Kanoya airfields.

The combined fighter sweep was to include 24 F4Us of VMF-323 (including four to act as an escort for a rescue PBY Dumbo) and four F4Us of VMF-312. Since many replacement pilots had arrived and it was near the end of the tour for many pilots, Axtell asked for volunteers. Of course, almost every veteran volunteered. Del Davis recalls, "Several of us were relieved for Stateside duty and directed to turn in our flight gear. I went to the supply tent and was given a receipt for my gear and told to toss it into a fire, but I couldn't do this. The next day Major Axtell called us together and asked for volunteers." The pilots were given a quick briefing by intelligence on the Kyushu airfields, and Axtell and his staff had previously worked out a flight and attack plan.

On taking off at 1215, Major Axtell, the flight leader, and his flight made one circle of the field and started out on course. Del Davis: "I was in the back of the pack for launch. I looked over to my left and saw my wingman (Bob Woods) waving his arms and pointing to his watch. Not knowing what the hell he meant, I gave him a thumbs up. To my dismay, he shut down his engine and ran to the billeting area. He quickly returned, waving his Bible, which he never flew without." All guns were tested over the water, and the flight then joined up in a column of divisions, climbing at an IAS of 145 knots at 1700 rpm with 32 inches of manifold pressure to an altitude of 9,000 feet. The flight then climbed to 15,000 feet and leveled off, changing formation from a column of divisions to a line of divisions and DR'd (dead reckoning) towards Japan. Within 50-75 miles of Kyushu the flight changed settings to 2000 rpm and an IAS of 150 knots and climbed to 20,000 feet. Power was then reduced to 1700, rpm and the flight cruised over the southern tip of Kyushu, waiting for Japanese interceptors.

On the Kyushu mission 1Lt. Joe Dillard downed a Judy over Kitahara Airfield for his 6 1/3 victory and to score the last of the Death Rattler's 124 1/2 victories. *Courtesy of the USMC.*

At 1400, when Jap opposition didn't materialize, Axtell ordered the divisions to form up in their pre-assigned positions for the attack. To provide air cover for designated attack aircraft, eight aircraft were stacked at 15,000 feet, eight at 18,000 feet, and eight at 20,000 feet, including Axtell. Al Wells continues the account: "Everyone was excited. Looking down, one of the pilots called out three or four aircraft taking off (from Kitahara airfield). He announced, 'Hey, they're taking off down there.' The whole squadron was eager to shoot down one last Jap. The eight lowest Corsairs were supposed to break first, but were joined by the middle eight. The eight with Axtell didn't dare move. George was up there yelling in the radio, 'Join up, join up.'"

On the flight's first run one Judy was shot down by 1Lt. Joe Dillard as it was in the traffic pattern preparing to land (they weren't taking off as first reported) at Kitahara. Dillard made one pass from 6 o'clock above and hit it in the cockpit, and it crashed into the ground in flames. This was the 124 1/2 and last Death Rattler aerial victory of the war. This was the first of four simultaneous low on deck, high speed strafing runs made from NE-SW and SE-NW. Del Davis: "We rolled into Kitahara under AA fire. My first firing pass was down the runway to the east. A fighter was taxiing for takeoff, and when I fired the pilot jumped from his plane and took off towards the side of the runway while his aircraft was consumed by flames." In addition to Dillard's Judy, it was estimated that a Tojo, two Tonys, eight other unidentified aircraft and four probables were destroyed in the strafing attack.

Kokubu was the next target. Again there were four simultaneous strafing runs being made from NE-SW. Damage was estimated to be one Tony destroyed on the ground and four unidentified damaged. Kanoya was next, and using the same strafing tactics NE-SW and SE-NW, two unidentified bombers were destroyed on the ground and three probably destroyed.

On the way into Okinawa the flights were running low on fuel, and Axtell radioed and alerted all Okinawa airfields that his Corsairs could be landing anywhere. The mission returned at 1730.

Anti-aircraft fire was of moderate intensity and relatively inaccurate. Two Corsairs sustained medium damage from light and medium AA over Kanoya that was repaired back at base. However, one suffered holes in the left wing and wing root and was considered damaged beyond repair. Walter Bestwick: "I sustained an anti-aircraft hit to my propeller and my right wing while over Kyushu.

With the damaged propeller my engine ran rough, and it took a little of nursing to get home safely."

The after action report on the five hour mission assessed the damage, "as slight to serious. Large fires were observed due to the burning aircraft on the ground. Barracks, anti-aircraft gun positions and hangars were well strafed." VMF-323 expended 15,600 rounds of 50 caliber (VMF-312, 3,200 rounds). A total of 14 aircraft were destroyed, seven probably destroyed, and four damaged. The report went on to state, "All pilots participating in this sweep feel that land based fighter sweeps from this area (Okinawa) could be fruitfully executed. However, since this was the first sweep attempted, it is believed that all pilots are now cognizant of the many phases of carrying out a sweep of this kind, which prior to yesterday, were unknown."

13 June Close Air Support

Mission: 1430-1645 Attack Jap command post along a ridge 500 yards southwest of Mabuni Town. On this day 16 pilots joined the squadron as replacements.

Utilizing the successful pre-mission briefing and Air Coordinator procedure, this close mission produced effective results. Major Axtell again acted as Air Coordinator, marking the target with two 500 lb. G.P. bombs with 8-11 second delay fuses. Capt. W. Hammer, leading 24 F4Us loaded with two napalm tanks and eight rockets, hit the ridge. Two 12 plane flights attacked the target in column, first dropping 44 napalm tanks and then firing 158 rockets.

13 June CAP

Twelve aircraft left at 0500 on a CAP led by Capt. C. Z. Walker. John Ruhsam: "Today while flying I spotted a couple of small boats away out from one of the numerous islands. I thought that I might have something for sure, so we went down for a look. We looked them over good, but they looked too much like civilians to shoot at. I bet we scared the daylights out of them, as they stood up in their little canoes and waved their shirts at us not to shoot."

13-15 June Replacement and Transfer Pilots: On the 13th of June, 16 replacement pilots joined the squadron. On the completion of their tour of duty on the 14th, 17 pilots were transferred, and the next day nine more were transferred.

13 June: "Well, VMF-323 just isn't the same squadron any more. I don't know half the men who represent our numbers out here now. What a swell gang we did have; I don't suppose they will ever find a group of men who will get along together as well as we did or accomplish as much." John Ruhsam letter

Del Davis: "In the middle of June they put us on a battle wounded Curtiss Commando (R5C) from Okinawa. It was a hairy trip, as we were island hopping across the South Pacific, making a few exciting landings and running into some really bad weather. From Hawaii we were put on a Pan Am Flying Clipper sea plane. My space was a night pallet in the hull of a pontoon. During the day the bar was open, and it was very enjoyable. The 2,200 mile flight took about 23 hours to San Francisco."

Bill Drake and four others were fortunate to fly on the Pan American Clipper and got back to the States in less than a week. Jack Broering was not so lucky. He was flown to Guam but was bumped, and spent three or four days there. He then hitched a ride and flew to Johnson Island, a refueling stop that lies about 1,000 miles west of Hawaii. Here a new list of passengers to Hawaii was posted, which included a newly arrived USO group, which didn't make the bumped military passengers happy. Fortunately, Broering's name was on the list, and he was off to Hawaii. He spent a few days there trying to connect to the States.

John Ruhsam, Joe McPhail, Norm Miller, Glen Thacker, and Warren Bestwick were among those who were transferred to the Palau Islands. They began flying strike missions beginning on 26 June and stretching into August, mostly in the Babelthop area. McPhail: "We bombed islands that had been by-passed. Probably to keep the Japs from growing sweet potatoes!"

"When Glen Thacker left Palau on a troopship he got so seasick that he had to get off on the Marshall Islands. We tried to talk him out of leaving the ship because there were so many men waiting to get back to the States, but he was so miserable he just had to leave. It took Thacker nearly three months to finally reach home." John Ruhsam

15 June Close Air Support

Mission: 1330-1500 Give close air support to elements of the 27th division by attacking an enemy strong point along a ridge west of Kushi-Take in north central Okinawa. Eight F4Us led by Capt. W. Hammer circled over the target area, while the troops on the ground marked it with W.P. (white phosphorous) shells. Three runs were made, the first a napalm run releasing 44 tanks, and two rocket attacks launching four per plane on each run, totaling 58 rockets. The mission was culminated by strafing runs.

During this mission USMC and *LIFE* magazine photographer, 1Lt. David Douglas Duncan, strapped himself into a modified auxiliary fuel tank with a Plexiglas nose. The tank was attached under the port wing of a USAAF, 28th PRS Lockheed F-5E Lightning, which was the photo-recon version of the P-38. For the most dramatic photographic effect, Duncan had requested that the F-5 pilot

Two -323 divisions take part in a 15 June close air support mission over Kushi-Take, a fortified ridge in north central Okinawa (the ridge is located on the peak in the upper right of the photo). The mission was photographed by USMC and LIFE magazine photographer, 1Lt. David Douglas Duncan. ***Courtesy of the USMC.***

Duncan crawled into a specially-designed belly tank mounted under the wing of a 28th PRS F-5E, photo-recon version of the P-38. ***Courtesy of the USMC via Steve Stuczynski.***

Duncan is seen here cleaning the Plexiglas nose of the belly tank. Duncan took 35mm stills and movie film of the mission. ***Courtesy of the USMC via Steve Stuczynski.***

place him 40 to 50 feet behind the F4U when it fired its rockets. However, when the Corsair salvoed its rockets, the turbulence was so great that the F-5 was blown on its right wing and then headed down. It was momentarily knocked out of control, and nearly crashed into the target ridge before recovering.

A message received from the ground troops after the attack stated that it had been well executed, and the attacking aircraft were on target with their rockets and started large fires along the ridge crest.

16 June AN ERA ENDS

16 replacement pilots joined the squadron. Major Martin E.W. Oelrich relieved Major George Axtell. The new CO, Major Oelrich, was an uncompromising officer who demanded rather than earned respect, and consequently the squadron's morale deteriorated. Oelrich's goal was to have VMF-323 be assigned as part of the

A view VMF-323 returning from the support/PR mission taken from a 2nd MAW TBF Avenger. ***Courtesy of Norman Miller.***

The Corsair fired a salvo of eight rockets, and the F-5 was following so closely in order to give Duncan a close up that the rocket blast almost caused it to crash. ***Courtesy of the USMC via Steve Stuczynski.***

On his day of departure from Okinawa, Major Axtell is surrounded by his ground officers, (L to R) Tilly Ferdenzi, Ed Lynn, Sol Mayer, Paul Rix, (Axtell), Al Taylor, Capt. Sinkwood, Doc Tom Dussman, and George Graham. Sinkwood was the new adjunctant. Graham and Lynn left with Axtell. ***Courtesy of Jody O'Keefe.***

On the behalf of the ground officers, Ed Lynn presents Major Axtell a Japanese samurai sword before he left the island. ***Courtesy of Jody O'Keefe.***

Occupation Forces of Japan. He wanted to shape up a proud outfit with an outstanding record that needed no shaping up. Axtell's one big family was no more. While most of the pilots had transferred out by mid-June, most of the enlisted personnel stayed on. Things got so bad that one night the sign in Mayer's mess was changed from "Where the Aces Meet to Eat" to "Where the Aces Met To Eat." One incident in which a pilot error or a fuel selector valve caused the loss of an aircraft led to the court marshal of a PC who fueled the plane. This incident galvanized a rift between officers and enlisted men.

Sol Mayer: "In the Marines there was a division between the officers and enlisted men, and even between the officers themselves. There was a division between those who didn't fly, the "ground crunchers," and those who did. But in our squadron there wasn't any division between any of us, we were like one big family. But this wasn't so after Major Oelrich took over."

Harold Hohl: "When Major Oelrich took over, he flew as my wingman while I took him out on the various types of missions we flew—CAP, picket ship patrols, and so forth. He was entirely different from Major Axtell, and we didn't see eye to eye on a lot of things. He was critical of all of us, and caused more problems than he was able to solve. I was in morning mess wearing what I had always wore, but he wanted us in clean, pressed khakis so, I had words with him about this and after this words continued."

PC Donald Hitchings: "We (VMF-323) had more than the Marine Corps Spirit, we were a family. With Axtell, we had so much going on in the air, everything was loose. Everybody knew their jobs and did them. There wasn't time for anything else. By July the war was winding down and there wasn't much to do in the air, or with the free time on the ground. These factors, and when Major

Major Martin Oelrich (L) replaced Axtell as CO in mid-June and quickly became unpopular with his by-the-book brand of leadership. ***Courtesy of Jody O'Keefe.***

2Lt. Jim Carey joined the squadron on Okinawa with several of the other pilots and they stayed on and flew out of Awase Airfield under Major Oelrich. ***Courtesy of Norman Miller.***

Axtell and his pilots left, led to a general let down that didn't help Major Oelrich's popularity. The spirit just wasn't there anymore after they left."

17 June Close Air Support
Mission: 1330-1500 Attack enemy artillery and mortar emplacements along the ridge east of Nagagusuku Town. 17 June marked the end of organized resistance on Okinawa. The Japanese were losing 4,000 men per day, as they had been relentlessly hit by naval gunfire, artillery and aerial close air support. This combined with the determined infantry assault caused the Japanese to crack and then crumble. They broke up into small groups and continued to fight guerrilla style. For the first time in the war Japanese prisoners were taken, with 997 taken on 27 June, the most for any single day in the war. However, many thousands committed suicide, including Gen. Mitsuru Ushijima, Gen. Isamu Cho, and their staff. Capt. W. Hammer led eight -323 F4Us and four -322 F4Us on four runs in column. On the first run 17 bombs were dropped (-323 carried two 500 lb. and -322 carried one 1,000 lb.). The second and third runs were rocket runs firing 69 rockets, and the final run was a strafing attack. The well briefed attack was a success, as there was no problem in target ID and ground-to-air communications were excellent.

17 June Strike Mission
Mission: 1330-1700. Two divisions led by 2Lt. William Baker hit installations on Amani O Shima. Baker was listed as MIA and later KIA.

18 June Close Air Support
Mission: 0645-800 Attack enemy strong point holding up the advance of our troops along a ridge running southeast from Kiyami Town. Capt. W.L. McCleary led two divisions armed with two napalm tanks and eight rockets. A rocket run was made first, eight rockets fired in salvo, and this was followed by the dropping of 16 napalm tanks. The napalm was noted as particularly effective against enemy troop positions.

18 June Close Air Support
Mission: 1530-1700 Again attack the enemy strong point along a ridge running southeast from Kiyami Town. Eight F4Us led by Capt. Ford Coffman were joined by eight -322 F4Us, all armed with one 1,000 lb. bomb and eight rockets. Two runs were made. The 1,000 pounders were released first, but two failed to release properly and had to be jettisoned into the sea. The rockets were fired on the second run, eight in salvo. All bombs and rockets were observed to hit the target, but actual damage was difficult to assess because of the smoke over the target. Also, there was confusion at the target because the two squadrons arrived at the target together and should have been staggered.

On 18 June, well-known war correspondent, Ernie Pyle, was hit in the head and killed when his jeep was ambushed by a machine gun on Ie Shima Island, which lies just off the Motobu Peninsula. ***Courtesy of the US Army.***

18 June Death of Ernie Pyle

On 18 June, Ernie Pyle, America's most eminent war correspondent, was riding in a jeep through captured territory on Ie Shima, an island off the Mobutu Peninsula. A Japanese machine gun opened fire, and the jeep's occupants took cover in a ditch, where Pyle was hit in the temple by a bullet. A makeshift sign was erected at the site: "At this spot the 77th Infantry Division lost a Buddy, Ernie Pyle."

18 June Death of Gen. Buckner

On 18 June, from atop a ridge, Gen. Simon Bolivar Buckner, the commander of the 10th Army, and his entourage were watching the newly arrived 8th Marines moving through a valley below. With all the activity, Japanese gunners on the opposite ridge recognized that something was going on and shelled the area. Shells hit a nearby coral outcrop, and a piece of coral struck Buckner in the chest, killing him. Buckner was the highest ranking American officer to be killed in action in WW-2. Gen. Roy Geiger took command and became the only Marine and aviator from any service to command a field army, albeit for only for five days when he was relieved by Gen. Joseph Stillwell. But the land battle was over by then.

A Catholic mass is celebrating on 26 June in Thanksgiving for the securing of the southern end of the island by Chaplain E.B. Kelly. Religious services were mostly held outdoors. ***Courtesy of the USMC via Steve Stuczynski.***

On 18 June, Gen. Simon Bolivar Buckner (L), commander of the 10th Army was struck in the chest and killed by a coral fragment dislodged by an artillery shell. He was the highest-ranking US officer killed in WW-2. USMC Gen. Roy Geiger (R) took Buckner's post and became the only aviator of any service to command a US field army. ***Courtesy of the USMC.***

John James was an enlisted man who joined the squadron at Cherry Point. James, obviously nicknamed "Jesse," joined at underage 16 and was constantly in trouble from day 1. He finally was wounded on an illicit souvenir hunt and sent home. ***Courtesy of Francis Maggliocco.***

Jim Barrett (2L) and Roy Cassell (far R) enter Naha on a souvenir hunting expedition. ***Courtesy of James Barrett.***

19 June Close Air Support
Mission: 0730-1120 CAP. Four plane CAP led by Capt. Ford Coffman also strafed a possible radar installation at the edge of a cliff on Sotsuko Zaki on the southwestern tip of Amami O Shima with unobserved results.

23 June Dumbo Escort
Mission: 1330-1740 To fly cover. Twelve F4Us led by Capt. W. Hammer, plus four F4Us to fly as Dumbo escort, were to fly escort for 18 VTB and 24 VFB on a mission to attack Ishigaki Shima on Sakishima Gunto. No Japanese were encountered, and rockets were fired on airfield installations. 1Lt. Gustave Broberg made a water landing off Ie Shima and was safely picked up by a destroyer.

25 June Two pilots were transferred on completion of their tour of duty.

26 June Strike Mission
Mission: 0915-1415 CAP and targets of opportunity on Okinoerabu Shima. Capt. F. Rotter led eight F4Us to hit targets of opportunity in the vicinity of China Town. A total of 64 rockets and 3,600 rounds of ammunition were expended on buildings northwest of town. Damage was judged to be slight.

28 June Combined Strike Mission
Mission: 0630-0915 Combined strike. Maj. Oelrich led 16 aircraft on a combined strike mission with VMF-312 and-322 to hit aircraft facilities, runways, and installations at Kikai Shima. Medium fires were started along the taxiways and nearby revetments.

29 June: One of the major pastimes was collecting Japanese souvenirs as James Barrett relates: "After the island was supposedly secured, some of us went down to the front lines without permission to look around and collect souvenirs. There were Japanese soldier and civilian bodies everywhere, and we saw wounded women and children, many with maggots in their wounds. There were Japanese rifles lying everywhere, so we started looking for small souvenirs in caves abandoned by the Japanese. We found a cave with a double entrance separated by a small pillar. None of us were willing to go in except (T./Sgt. Edwin) 'Tiny' Mascal, nicknamed for obvious reasons, who volunteered to crawl in on his hands and knees. He found a pistol, and as he grabbed for the pistol he looked up into the face of a Japanese soldier. We heard some kind of frightened yelp, and he backed out as fast as he could. Just as he exited, a grenade came rattling out behind him. We dodged away, and he ducked around the other side of the pillar, but still got some shrapnel into his back. Two Japanese soldiers ran out of the cave, but we let them go especially when one of the men, with a rifle forgot to take off the safety. When we got back to Kadena we had to doctor Mascal ourselves, as he couldn't report his injury because we weren't supposed to be at the front. To add insult to injury, word got around that Tiny had a Japanese pistol, and during the night his tent and sea bag were slit open and the pistol stolen."

Souvenir hunting could be dangerous. Joseph "Jesse" James went down to the front lines without permission to play infantryman and look for souvenirs. He got caught in an American mortar barrage and was wounded and evacuated.

Ed Coogan (L) and Rocco DeMilia search through the demolished town of Naha for souvenirs. ***Courtesy of Rocco DeMilia.***

Monthly Summary

JUNE

Personnel: 295
Officers: 62 Enlisted: 223
Personnel lost: 1Lt. William Baker

Aircraft		
on hand:	7 F4U-1Ds	25 FG-1Ds
Aircraft lost:	3 FG-1Ds	1 F4U-1D

Missions:	Original pilots: 68	Replacement Pilots: 130
	Combat Air Patrol: 46	Combat Air Patrol: 96
	Picket Ship Patrol: 16	Picket Ship Patrol: 14
	Close Air Support: 5	Close Air Support: 14
	Miscellaneous: 1	Miscellaneous: 6

3745 hrs./1248 indiv. Flights/1242 combat missions
Encounters: AA: 9 Enemy A/C: 4
Enemy Aircraft destroyed: 17
probable: 1
damaged: 0

End of tour and replacement pilots:
2 June: 13 pilots join
7 June: 2 pilots join
13 pilots end tour
13 June: 16 pilots join
14 June: 17 pilots end tour
15 June: 9 pilots end tour
15 June: 16 pilots join

Partial Roster of New Officers and Pilots

Commanding Officer: Maj. Martin E.W. Oelrich

Majors:
O.H. Brueggeman E.J. Nelson

Captains:
F.G. Coffman W.L. McCleary
M. Dietrich F.F. Rotter
W. Hammer J.T. Steen
G.E. McClane C.Z. Walker

1Lts.:
J.T. Bonner J.J. McBride
G.T. Broberg W.C. McCallister
E.G. Dick R.C. McKean
B.H. Duncan O.C. Nance
K.- Flynn J.M. O'Kelley
A.S. Johnson W.K. Paramenter
A.C. Livermore L.R. Tillery

2Lts.:
R.M. Allensworth R.L. Hammerley
W.O. Baker J.L. Scott
C.A. Broudy B.B. Sessions
N.E. Brown H.B. Thayer
A.E. Dichak D.S. Thomas
C.L. Floyd D.R. Tuff
W.D. Gist C.A. Willis

2Lts. who joined in April and stayed on:
Jim Carey Jerry Conners Harold Hohl

Compiled by Bill Wolf

CHAPTER 27
Anticlimax
July, August, September

After the cessation of hostilities on Okinawa on 2 July the squadron's operations became ho-hum at best, as described by the monthly summary: "All Combat air patrols proved to be negative, no enemy aerial contacts having been made during this month. However, during this period, escort and strike missions ranged from Kyushu to the southern most tip of Sakashima Gunto. Special combat air patrols ranged as far west as the China coast. These were flown as cover for elements of our fleet operating in this area."

1 July Escort
Mission: 1545-1015 Escort bombers on strike mission. Three divisions led by Capt. L.W. McCleary left Kadena to escort 24 B-25s on strike mission to destroy enemy aircraft, aircraft installations, and dispersal areas on Chiran Airfield, Kyushu. This flight flew medium cover over the bombers and encountered no intercepting enemy aircraft.

1 July Combat Air Patrol
Mission: 1115-1710 over southern Kyushu. A division led by Capt. J.T. Steen flew CAP over Chiran, Kagoshima, and Kanoya Airfields on southern Kyushu. The patrol was flown over this area for two hours at 18,000 feet, and no intercepting aircraft were encountered.

4 July Combat Air Patrol
Mission: 1000-1300. Eight fighters led by Major O.H. Brueggeman went out on CAP. The Fighter Director controlling the mission directed Bruggeman's division to strafe gun emplacements near Yami Town on Okinoerabu Shima. Several small fires were started as "the gun emplacements were well strafed."

On a 1730-2035 CAP, division leader 1Lt. Gustave Broberg overshot the field on landing and suffered a compound fracture of his right arm. His aircraft was damaged beyond repair.

5 July: Shortly after the island was secured, the Marines turned over a large ammunition dump to the Army. The next day it went up in a spectacular explosion, a day late for the 4th of July.

7 July Strike Mission
Mission: 1350-1730. Twelve fighters loaded with bombs and rockets, led by Major O.H. Brueggeman, flew to Amani O Shima to hit a radar installation there. Due to bad weather over the target, -323 attacked targets of opportunity on Tokuna Shima and Okinoerabu Shima. The damage to the revetments, buildings, and AA gun emplacements was judged "slight to unobserved."

8 July Rocket Test Firing Mission
Mission: 1000-1125. Capt. L.W. McCleary and his wingman fired a total of 15 rockets on targets of opportunity on Okinoerabu Shima, consisting of dugouts on the northwestern coast and a building on the eastern coast. The two also expended 2,400 rounds of .50 caliber with "slight to unobserved damage."

9 July**:** Sol Mayer: "A short time after Major Axtell left the mess building burned down one morning. It was nothing but canvas over a wooden frame, so it burned down to the ground. One of the stoves exploded, and one of the guys got burned trying to put out the fire. Major Oelrich decided to divide the men into three groups to eat elsewhere. But I had the next meal ready before he could even make up the list. I served steak and real mashed potatoes and chocolate cake for dessert."

10 July Strike Mission
Mission: 1015-1430 Escort for medium bomber strike mission. Capt. L.W. McCleary led 16 F4Us from Kadena at 1015 to escort AAF B-25s also based at Kadena on a strike mission to Chiran Airfield, Kyushu. The flight failed to make contact at the rendezvous point with the other escorting aircraft or the bombers after vainly orbiting the rendezvous point for an hour. McCleary then led his 16 fighters to strafe airfield facilities at Wan Airfield, Kikai Shima. One pass was made, and "it was believed that five medium AA emplacements were knocked out." A 100 foot landing barge in Minato Wan was also strafed, but definite damage assessment was not ascertained.

The squadron suffered their largest losses of the war. Three aircraft were hit by anti-aircraft fire. One pilot, 1Lt. Walter Paramenter, was listed as MIA, one made a successful ditching 1 1/2 miles south of Kaiki, and one made a successful wheels up landing at Kadena, writing off the aircraft.

11 July Strike Mission
Mission: 0555-0900 Strike mission to Kyushu. Twenty F4Us led by Major Martin Oelrich took off from Awase at 0555 on a strike mission to hit airfield facilities and installations at Kokubu Airfield on Kyushu. Because of the solid overcast over Kokubu, this flight dropped their bombs on buildings, warehouses, and a factory in Miyazaki Town, north of Miyazaki Airfield. Japanese AA was moderate, and "a direct bombing hit was observed on what looked to be a medium sized factory building east of town."

Harold Hohl: "These young Majors had no combat experience, and on a hop up to Kyushu on July 11th, we were led into a big

Opposite:* S/Sgt. Frank Maggliocco and Corp. Alfred Cerniello pose on a drop tank on Awase Airfield. The squadron moved to Awase on 15 July without curtailment of operations. The base had better "campsite and line" facilities than Kadena. *Courtesy of Frank Maggliocco.

thunderhead and there were problems. I went into a graveyard spiral and was lucky enough to pull up just as the prop wash churned water off of Kakashima Bay. I was totally disoriented when I pulled up, and I almost went into the trees of the volcano. When I returned to base I was so shook up that I grounded myself for several days."

12 July Escort Missions

Two escort missions were logged. The first, 0625-1050, had 12 aircraft led by Capt. L.W. McCleary escorting 60 Kadena-based AAF B-25s on a strike mission to Kanoya Airfield without combat. The second, 1600-1930, acted as Dumbo escort as part of a strike hitting the airfields at Miyako on Sakashima Gunto.

15 July: The base of operations was changed from Kadena to Awase. The change necessitated no curtailment of operations, as a major 24 aircraft escort mission was launched to Kyushu, along with two CAPs. The War Diaries state: "Here at Awase our campsite and line facilities are more than adequate. Living and working conditions are better than they were at Kadena, and all hands are pleased with the new setup.

"Active steps are being taken to ensure recreational activities for all, and messing conditions, although a bit crowded in spots now, are being remedied as rapidly as existing conditions will allow."

"Awase airfield accommodations were better than Kadena, as the tents were canvas stretched over wood framework with wooden deck floors. During the big battles of April, May, and June, church attendance reached overflow capacity. Mass was held in a tent with its sides rolled up. The alter was a plank laid across two 55 gallon drums. The Priest stood in the mud with his pants cuffs pulled up.

At Awase there was a large Quonset hut chapel that, since the danger was over, was no longer well attended, much to the chaplain's chagrin." James Barrett

17 July Strike Mission

At 0520 Capt. L.W. McCleary led 16 aircraft on a strafing and bombing mission to Miyara Airfield on Ishigaki Shima.

19-20 July: The island was issued a typhoon warning. The planes were tied down for an expected typhoon. James Barrett: "We stayed up all night. Each man had a hammer, a handful of nails, and extra boards to reinforce the tent framework, but we only got heavy rains and gusty winds the next day. Little damage was done, as the island only received a glancing blow."

"J.T. Kennedy (Sgt. James) was our moonshine expert. He went up to the mess tent where the food stores were located with his sleeves rolled up so the guard couldn't see his down stripes (i.e. lesser sergeant's rank). He would regale the young guard with tales of his invented exploits as a grizzled veteran of Guadalcanal and the old days in the Corps. While the guard was being occupied, we would go under the back of the tent and take cases of apricots and other canned fruit that would ferment. Kennedy had a 12-15 gallon crock and added the fruit and yeast and sugar, and after some nurturing we would have a fermented beverage. It's fortunate that no one ever inspected under our beds, or we would have been in big trouble." James Barrett

24 July Escort

On a two division Dumbo escort at 0920 in conjunction with a B-24 photo mission over Kyushu. On the return to Awase, 2Lt. H.L. Hammerly was forced to ditch and, ironically, was picked up uninjured by a Dumbo PBY.

29 July Escort

Major Oelrich took off at 0900 with 12 F4Us to escort a F6F photo mission to Kyushu. Six planes of this mission strafed targets of opportunity along the southeastern coast of Kyushu. Barges, small boats, dock facilities, radar stations, and repair facilities were "well strafed."

Monthly Summary

JULY
Personnel: 307
Officers: 69 Enlisted: 238
Personnel lost: 1 1Lt. Walter Permenter

Aircraft on hand:	7 F4U-1Ds	21 FG-1Ds
Aircraft lost:	6 FG-1Ds	1 F4U-1D

Missions: 136/30 flying days (1 bad weather day)
Combat Air Patrol: 116
Picket Ship Patrol: 7
Close Air Support: 4
Escort: 9

2771 hrs./924 indiv. Missions/914 combat missions
Encounters: AA: 4 Enemy A/C: 0

AUGUST: The War Winds Down to a Stop

The war was winding down in August, as the War Diaries divulge: "During this month no enemy aerial opposition was encountered and....flight activity has been of a routine nature and of negative results. To compensate for this curtailment of flight activity, active steps have been taken by the Commanding Officer to ensure proper use of leisure time by all hands. Daily swimming trucks to the beach have met with the approval of all squadron personnel, and the proposed program of organized competitive athletics by our recreation officer will prove to keep all hands actively engaged in some pastime during this period of relative inactivity." The relative inactivity began early in the month when bad weather grounded all flights from 1-4 August.

8 August Strike Mission

Mission: 1300-1745 to southern Kyushu. Seven aircraft led by Capt. C.Z. Walker left Awase on a strike mission to attack Chiran Airfield, Aoto Town, Goryo town, and radio installations at Shimami on Tanega island. Rockets and strafing "started small to medium fires at most of the targets hit. Anti-aircraft fire encountered was meager and inaccurate."

8-9 August: "After the first bomb (A-bomb on Hiroshima on 6 August) went off, word went out that Japan had surrendered. To celebrate every weapon, on the island and off shore, was fired. You could practically read a newspaper by the light from the tracers in the sky. The guy next to me, J.T. Kennedy (Sgt. James), got hit in the back with a spent .45 bullet, which penetrated just under his skin. It was removed by P/M 3c, Stan Goff, the corpsmen on base and caused minor damage.

We had a radio in our tent, and Grady (M/Sgt. Edmund) came out and told us that he heard that we had some kind of new kind of explosives called "atoms or something." From my three years of college science I realized that the atom had been split. Later the radio reports had difficulty in explaining the nature of the atomic bomb to the public." James Barrett

11 August Combat Air Patrol

While on a 1000-1320 CAP led by 1 Lt. J.T. Bonner, the Fighter Director directed the flight to strafe two unidentified aircraft on Tokuno Airfield on Tukuno Shima. One strafing run was made through medium AA fire with unobserved results.

13 August Combat Air Patrol

The last interesting mission of the war took place when Capt. M. Dietrich was requested by the Fighter Director to leave CAP and lead his division to strafe Wan Airfield, Kaiki Shima. A Betty bomber was left burning at the southern end of the field.

14-15 August: The atomic bombings of Hiroshima on the 6th and Nagasaki on the 9th caused Emperor Hirohito to finally intervene and accept the provisions of the Potsdam Declaration on the 14th. On the 15th, the Japanese heard their Emperor's voice for the first time, as the Emperor addressed his "Good and Loyal Subjects," explaining his decision "to effect a settlement of the present situation." It was not until 2 September, on an ordinary mess table covered by a green cloth on the Battleship MISSOURI's verandah deck, that two sets of surrender documents, one in Japanese and the other in English, were ready to sign. At shortly after 0900, Japanese Foreign Minister Mamoru Shigemitsu affixed his signature to the documents, ending the Pacific war after 1,364 days of bloody battle.

Even though the Emperor had signed the surrender document, there were fears by both Nimitz and MacArthur that Japanese soldiers, sailors, and pilots would be coerced by die hard officers to oppose the occupation, though the Emperor's wishes were observed and no incidents transpired. VMF-323 continued to fly CAP missions, 64 for the remainder of August, and as the War Diaries for September describe: "During the period covered in this report this squadron's flight activities consisted mainly of combat air patrols and observation flights to Kuchino Shimo and Tukara Gunto. During the month no enemy aerial opposition was encountered. Due to the cessation of hostilities, flight activities have been curtailed, and the Commanding Officer has taken steps to ensure proper use of leisure time by all hands. The swimming truck has continued to

Roger Archambault joined the squadron in North Carolina and served after the first group of pilots went home. "After the atomic bomb fell everyone got going home fever." He left on 5 October on the carrier, SHANGRI-LA and arrived in California on 21 October. After a 30 day furlough he was discharged on 5 December. ***Courtesy of Jody O'Keefe.***

make its trip to the beach, and areas for basketball and baseball have been made available for competitive athletics."

MONTHLY SUMMARY

AUGUST
Personnel: 291
Officers: 55 Enlisted: 236
Personnel lost: 0

Aircraft on hand: 6 F4U-1Ds 18 FG-1Ds
Aircraft lost: 1 F4U-1D

Missions:	Through 15 August: 43	After 15 August: 64
	Combat Air Patrol: 34	Combat Air Patrol: 64
	Picket Ship Patrol: 4	Picket Ship Patrol: 0
	Close Air Support: 2	Close Air Support: 0
	Escort/Misc: 3	Escort/Misc.: 0

2091 hrs./763 indiv.flights/752 combat missions
Encounters: AA: 4 Enemy A/C: 0

SEPTEMBER: The War's Over, So Why Don't We Go Home?
6 September: 2Lt. Howard Thayer suffered a stoppage in his oil system, or lack of oil, and crashed on a CAP off Tokuno Shima. He was rescued, uninjured.

13 September: Veteran, 2Lt. Jerry Conners, sustained hydraulic and CO_2 failure and crashed, uninjured, ten miles east of Awase.

16-17 September: The squadron was getting ready to go to Japan when the second typhoon warning was issued. All the shipping and aircraft mostly left the area or were again secured. The men spent the night in the mess hall. Top winds were recorded at 120 mph with very heavy rain. After the storm there was a shortage of food, and the men were served beans and rice for every meal for a number of days.

23 September: 2Lt. Charles Willis damaged a wing tip while taxiing. Willis was unhurt, and the wing tip was replaced.

25 September: VMF-323 CO, Major Martin Oelrich, was detached to HdqSq-33, MAG-33, and Major O.H. Brueggeman assumed the duties of Commanding Officer.

26 September: Eleven officers and 71 enlisted men joined the squadron from VMF-312, MAG-33.

27 September: Seventy-eight enlisted men were transferred to MWSS-2 for assignment to the U.S.

29 September: Major O.H. Bruggeman was detached to Pers.Grp.,MCAD, Miramar, San Diego, and was replaced as CO by Captain Dietrich.

GOING HOME
Thus ended the World War II chronicle of the Death Rattlers, and the remaining men were looking forward to going home. Carriers were ideally suited for transporting large number of troops home because of their huge hangar areas. The first priority was the Recovery of Allied Military Personnel (RAMP) who were POWs of the Japanese. "Magic Carpet" was the operation to transport troops back to the States. Because the atomic bomb unexpectantly shortened the war the military was unprepared for this task. On 9 September 1945, R.Adm. H.S. Kendall was assigned command of TG 16.12 and Magic Carpet. Although things got off to a slow start with only 8,241 of 259,856 men being transported in September, October was better, with 370,596 of 695,486 transported. Between October 1945 and May 1946 over 1,308,000 persons were transported. Eight large Essex class carriers were pressed into service to transport troops home. Carrier crew compliments were reduced, and extra galley facilities and three to five tier bunks were installed on the hangar decks to accommodate the returning troops.

Roger Archambault was an AAM (Aviation Machinists Mate) with the Squadron from its inception at Cherry Point in July 1943. "After the A-bomb was dropped we became more relaxed, and 'going home fever' crept in the area. Finally, we were relieved and replaced by new men and transferred to a transit center to wait for transportation stateside. They selected men to leave by the point system. Points were given for days overseas, time in service, decorations, etc. I had 50 points and got a ride on the SHANGRI-LA (CV-38 ed.) on 5 October. We slept on the hangar deck with two small blankets, but it didn't matter because we were going home. We arrived at San Pedro, California, on October 21st, after sailing near Alaska to avoid a typhoon. We were taken to Camp Miramar and granted a 30-day furlough. I headed home to Springfield, Massachusetts, and afterwards reported to Cherry Point for discharge on 17 December 1945.

James Barrett: "I went home on the SHANGLI-LA. I volunteered for laundry duty, which turned out to be good luck. I got to eat in the regular crew's mess and didn't have to wait. Most important, I got my own bunk below decks and didn't have to sleep on the cold hangar deck."

Most of the squadron returned to civilian life, and some remained in the military. But for all, World War II was the best of times and the worst of times. It shaped the course of world history and the course of personal history.

Because the dropping of the atomic bombs unexpectantly shortened the war, "Operation Magic Carpet" was initiated to transport the troops home. The SHANGRI-LA (CV-23) was one of eight ESSEX Class carriers which had to be equipped with extra galleys and cold, draughty five tier bunks on the hanger decks. *Courtesy of the US Navy.*

CHAPTER 28

Victory

The Cost and Worth

By the 21st of June major Japanese resistance had ceased, and the mopping up operations were finished by the end of the month. On 2 July the campaign was officially declared ended.

The Americans expended 7.5 million (37 mm to 8 inch) howitzer rounds, 60,000 (5 to 6 inch) naval gun shells, 392,000 hand grenades, 20,360 rockets, and slightly less than 30 million machine, rifle, and pistol rounds in the battle.

The final loss in American casualties was the highest sustained in any operation against the Japanese. Battle casualties were 49,151, of which 12,520 were killed or missing and 36,631 wounded. Army losses were 4,675 killed and missing, and 18,099 wounded; Marine losses (including TAF) were 2,938 killed and missing, and 13,708 wounded; Navy losses were 4,907 killed and missing, and 4,824 wounded. Army nonbattle casualties numbered 15,613, and Marine 10,598. There were 36 ships sunk and 368 damaged. Between 1 April and 1 July, 763 aircraft were lost. The Americans demonstrated that they were able to defeat the Japanese no matter how determined their resistance. The victory provided a staging base for the large number of troops and a fleet anchorage for the invasion of Japan, along with airfields close to Japan. The costly victory was a sobering harbinger of the cost of the future invasion of the Homelands.

The Japanese were capably led and fought a determined battle on difficult terrain, which they had heavily and cleverly fortified to inflict maximal losses to the enemy. The Japanese lost an estimated 110,000 dead and 7,400 wounded and/or taken prisoner. They lost 7,800 aircraft, 16 ships sunk, and four damaged. In the end they gave up 640 square miles of land that was only 350 miles from Kyushu, the southern tip of the Japanese mainland. The loss of Okinawa provided a staging area for the invasion of the Japanese Homeland, OPERATION CORONET, scheduled for the spring of 1946. Okinawa provided excellent fleet anchorages, and aircraft flying from its improved airfields were able to attack Japan directly with minimal opposition.

During the six week campaign the Okinawan civilian population suffered immeasurably. Nowhere in the Pacific had a noncombatant population endured such intense devastation. As the battle moved southward civilians were forced to hide in caves, and more died in the south than the total number of soldiers on both sides! It is estimated that over 150,000 Okinawans, a third of the total population, lost their lives, two thirds of these during the last ten days of June. There were thousands of corpses scattered on the southern end of the island, and no Okinawan family escaped the ravages of the battle. The island and its people had suffered total cultural and material devastation that remains virtually unknown and unrecorded.

The battle for Okinawa was the final great battle of World War II. As the preparations for the invasion of Kyushu were being made in August 1945, the dropping of the atomic bombs on Hiroshima and Nagasaki forced an early Japanese surrender and ultimately saved thousands of Japanese and American lives.

Japanese propaganda had convinced the Okinawans that the American invaders were barbarians and the population fled south in front of the advancing Americans. ***Courtesy of John Ruhsam.***

Nowhere in the Pacific did a civilian population endure such intense devastation as did the Okinawans. A third of its population, 150,000, lost their lives, and the island suffered total material and cultural devastation. ***Courtesy of John Ruhsam.***

CHAPTER 29
Death Rattler Legacy

By 13 July, TAF claimed 625 Japanese aircraft destroyed and 29 probables with MAG-33 pilots destroying 214 and VMF-323 124 1/2 of those. TAF flew 118,982 hours and 38,192 sorties, expending 4,102,559 rounds of .50 cal. ammunition, and 445,748 of 20 mm. Some 4,161 tons of bombs, almost a million pounds of napalm, and 15,691 rockets were released.

The Death Rattlers validated themselves as one of the Marine's premier squadrons, establishing many new records.

The 24 3/4 Japanese aircraft destroyed by seven pilots on 28 April was the highest recorded score for a single Marine squadron in a single action. One week later, on 4 May, the squadron again shot down 24 3/4 aircraft in the morning's combat by 16 pilots. The 91 1/2 enemy aircraft shot in a month's period was a new high, surpassing the previous record of 85 1/2. VMF-323 topped the previous six week record of 104 1/2 by one.

The 124 1/2 victories were the highest in the Okinawa Campaign, Navy and **Marine squadron** totals:

VMF-323 124 1/2 F4U Okinawa (Kadena)
VF-83 122 F6F ESSEX
VF-9 93 1/4 F6F YORKTOWN
VF-17 89 F6F HORNET
VF-30 77 F6F BELLEAU WOOD
VBF-17 76 F6F HORNET
VMF-311 71 F4U Okinawa (Yontan)
VBF-83 60 F6F ESSEX
VF-82 60 F6F BENNINGTON
VMF-312 59 1/2 F4U Okinawa (Kadena)
VF-47 56 1/2 F6F BATAAN
VMF-224 54 F4U Okinawa (Yontan)

and were the seventh highest victory total scored by a Marine Squadron in World War II.

VMF-121 208
VMF-221 185
VMF-112 140
VMF-215 137
VMF-212 132 1/2
VMF-223 132 1/2
VMF-214 127
VMF-323 124 1/2

Of the 124 1/2 victories, VMF-323 shot down :
80 1/4 Japanese Navy Aircraft
44 1/4 Japanese Army Aircraft
including:

Val: 51 3/4 (JNAF)	Tony 5 (JAAF)	Judy: 2 (JNAF)
Zeke: 16 (JNAF)	Jill: 4 (JNAF)	Lily: 1 (JAAF)
Nate: 16 (JAAF)	Hamp: 2 1/2 (JNAF)	Ida: 1 (JAAF)
Tojo: 11 (JAAF)	Kate: 2 (JNAF)	Sally: 1 (JAAF)
Dinah: 8 1/4 (JAAF)	Betty: 2 (JNAF)	Helen: 1 (JAAF)

VMF-323 was awarded:

The Presidential Unit Citation (Navy) Streamer with one Silver Star for its action over Okinawa 4 April-14 July 1945.

Asiatic-Pacific Campaign Streamer with two Bronze Stars.
Okinawa Gunto 2 April-14 July 1945
3rd fleet Operations Against Japan 15 July-15 August
World War II Victory Streamer 1 August-31 December 1946

When Majors Axtell, Dorroh, and 1Lt. O'Keefe became aces in one action, it marked the first time that three Marine pilots went from no victories to five or more in one action. Only ten Marine pilots became "aces-in-a-day" during WWII. (Capt. Herbert Valentine of VMF-312 shot down 5 1/2 Japanese on 5 May over Okinawa after he had scored a half victory on 16 April.)

Major Dorroh's six victories in one action was the highest individual score since 7 April 1943, when Capt. James Swett of VMF-221 shot down a Marine record seven Jills over Bougainville.

The 12 VMF-323 aces were second to the 14 VMF-121 aces (11 F4F aces in the first tour and 3 F4U aces in the second tour), but -323 had the most aces in one tour.

The 12 VMF-323 aces were:

7 O'Keefe, Jeremiah	6 Axtell, George
7 Ruhsam, John	6 Dorroh, Jefferson
7 Wade, Robert *	5.5 Hood, William
6.33 Dillard, Joseph	5 Alley, Stuart
6.33 Durnford, Dewey	+5 Drake, Charles
6.08 Terrill, Francis	5 Wells, Albert

* scored 1 victory Mig-15 Korea (51 FIW)
\+ scored 0.5 victory MiG-15 Korea (4FIW)

Top Okinawa aces were (all USN/F6F):
12.5 Valencia, E.A. Lt. VF-9
10 French, J.B. Lt(jg) VF-9
9 Mitchell, H.E. Lt(jg) VF-9
8 Johnston, J.M. Lt(jg) VBF-17
7.5 Foster, C.C. Ens. VF-30

(Note: VF-9 (YORKTOWN), known as Valencia's Flying Circus, scored 93 1/2 victories over Okinawa, including 30 3/4 on 4 May and 24 on 11 May. It had 14 aces on this, its third tour. Lt. Eugene Valencia's division of four aces scored 43 1/2 victories and boasted three double aces (see table above). VF-83 (ESSEX) scored 122 victories, including 56 on 6 April and 24 on 4 May. It had 12 aces.)

CHAPTER 30
Death Rattler Aces

WADE, Robert (Bob) 1Lt. (s/n 030908) 7 Victories
DOB: 31 October, 1923, Jenkintown, PA
Died: 10 November, 1991, Santa Ana, CA
Biography:

Wade gained his first exposure to flying in the early 1930s. During high school at Elkins Park, PA, he worked at the airport during the summer to pay for flying lessons. Upon graduation he entered the Naval Aviation Cadet Program. He was commissioned a 2Lt. in the Marine Corps on 23 October 1943.

He originally trained on Dauntless SBD dive bombers, but switched to the Corsair and joined VMF-323 in January 1944, with 645.5 hours of training. Wade destroyed eight Japanese aircraft and damaged three others during his tour (15 combat missions), and received the Navy Cross, the DFC, and three strike/flight Air Medals. After being relieved, he transferred to VMF-122 on Peleliu until the end of the war. He was released to inactive duty in January 1946.

He returned to active duty in October 1946, and saw an additional 40 combat missions in Korea with VMF-311 from July to November 1952. He received two additional strike/flight Air Medals during this tour. Subsequently, he was assigned to exchange duty with the Air Force, flying F-86 Sabres with the 16th Fighter-Interceptor Squadron, 51st Fighter-Interceptor Wing from December to March 1953, in 20 combat missions. On 20 January, Captain Wade shot down a MiG-15. In his Air Force tour he received an Air Force DFC and two strike/flight Air Medals.

After a medical retirement in 1964 as a Lt. Colonel, Wade joined McDonnell-Douglas Astronautics.

Date	Time	Enemy	a/c Location
1945			
4-15	1900	2 Tony	25 mi. NW of Ie Shima
5-4	0830	2 Val	25 mi. NW of Ie Shima
	0830	2 Nate	"
	0830	3 Nates dam.	"
5-12	1930	0.5 Dinah	40 mi. SW Kadena AF
6-3	1700	0.5 Val	10 mi. W of Ie Shima
1953			
1-20	1505	Mig-15	near Yousu-dong

TOTAL: 8/0/3

Ten of the Twelve Death Rattler aces (L to R) Maj. George Axtell (6 victories), Maj. Jeff Dorroh (6), 2Lt. Stuart Alley (5), 1Lt. Al Wells (5), 1Lt. Francis Terrill (6 1/6), 2Lt. Bill Drake (5), 1Lt. Joe Dillard (6 1/3), 1Lt. Jerry O'Keefe (7), 2Lt. Dewey Durnford (6 1/3), 1Lt. Bill Hood (5 1/2). Missing are John Ruhsam (7) and Bob Wade (7). ***Author's collection/USMC.***

BOB WADE *Courtesy of Jody O'Keefe.*

JOHN RUHSAM *Author's collection.*

RUHSAM, JOHN W. 1Lt. (s/n 030883) 7 Victories
DOB: 7 September, 1922, Albert Lea, MN

Biography: Ruhsam enlisted in the Naval Flight Training Program while a student at Iowa State College. He received his wings and commission as 2Lt. in the Marine Corps on 1 October 1943. Ruhsam was assigned to the 2 Marine Air Wing and was assigned to VMF-323 in early 1945 at Espiritu Santo.

He flew 20 combat missions and received a Navy Cross, two Air medals, a strike/flight DFC, and three strike/flight Air Medals. Ruhsam was a career Marine aviator and received a Letter of Commendation, with Ribbon and Combat "V," for the period 17 April to 24 September, 1952. He retired from the Marine Corps in 1969 as a Colonel.

Date 1945	Time	Enemy	a/c Location
4-12	1430	Zeke	Motobu Peninsula
4-15	1900	Tony	Kawata Wan
5-4	0830	4 Vals	25 mi. NW of Ie Shima
	0830	3 Val dam.	"
5-12	1930	0.5	Dinah 40 mi. SW of Kadena AF
6-3	1700	0.5	Val 10 mi. W. Of Iheya Shima

TOTAL: 7/0/3

O'KEEFE, Jeremiah J. 1Lt. (s/n 025432) 7 Victories
DOB: 12 July, 1923, Ocean Springs, MS

Biography: Born in Ocean Springs, MS, the young O'Keefe's family moved to Biloxi, where he went to Sacred Heart Academy where he co-captained the football team in 1941. Following graduation from Soule Business College in New Orleans, he entered Navy flight training. He received a 2Lt. Marine Corps Reserve commission on 16 June 1943 at the age of 19. On his VMF-323 tour he received a Navy Cross, a DFC, and two strike/flight Air Medals before returning to the U.S. in late June 1945.

He graduated from Loyola University in 1948. He returned to his home in Biloxi, went into the funeral home business, and started his own insurance company. He served in the Mississippi legislature for one term from 1960 to 1964. He was elected to two terms as mayor of Biloxi from 1973 to 1981. He was awarded many outstanding citizen awards for his work for Biloxi. In 1995, O'Keefe was awarded $500 million in a breech of contract suit against a major company in the funeral business. He has established the O'Keefe Charitable Foundation. He and his wife had 13 children, and 38 grandchildren and counting.

Date 1945	Time	Enemy a/c	Location
4-22	1830	5 Val	50 mi. N. Of Aguni Shima
4-28	1830	2 Nate	70 mi. NW of Zampa Misaki

TOTAL: 7/0/0

DURNFORD Jr., Dewey F. 2Lt. (s/n 032195) 6.33 Victories
DOB: 23 October, 1922, Milwaukee, WI

Biography: After attending Ohio State University, Durnford graduated from the Navy's flight training school, joined the Marine Corps, and was commissioned a 2Lt. at Pensacola on 16 November 1943. He arrived at Okinawa with 489 hours of flying time, and while there earned three DFCs and three strike/flight Air Medals.

Durnford remained in the service after the war and returned to combat during the Korean War. He flew 75 combat missions in a tour with the Marines, and then flew F-86Fs with the 335th FIS of the 4th FIW on an exchange tour with the USAF. He shared the destruction of a Mig-15 on 17 May 1953. In Korea he received an Air Medal, four strike/flight Air Medals, and an Air Force DFC and two Air force Air Medals. He later served a year in Vietnam and retired from the Marines as a Colonel on 1 March 1971.

Date	Time	Enemy a/c	Location
1945			
4-12	1515	.33 Betty	71 mi. NW of Ie Shima
4-16	0930	Lily	30 mi. N of Ie Shima
	0930	Helen (Betty?)	30 mi. W of Yontan
4-28	1830	2 Nate	70 mi. NW of Zampa Misaki
6-3	1330	Val	40 mi. E of Zampa Misaki
	1330	Nate	"
1953			
5-17	1540	.5 MiG-15	near Sinuiji

Total 6.88/0/0

DILLARD, Joseph V. 1Lt. (s/n 023880) 6.33 Victories
DOB: 14 February, 1923, Kenton, OK
Died: September, 1983, Alameda, CA

Biography: Dillard was born on 14 February and appropriately named Joseph Valentine. He was commissioned a 2Lt. in the Marine Corps on 16 May 1943 and promoted to 1Lt. on 30 November 1943. On 10 June 1945 he claimed the last Death Rattler victory of World War II when he shot down a Judy over Kyushu. Dillard received a DFC and an Air Medal, along with three strike/flight Air Medals.

JERRY O'KEEFE ***Courtesy of Henry Brandon.***

Date	Time	Enemy a/c	Location
1945			
4-15	1830	.33 Val	65 mi. SE N tip of Okinawa
4-28	1845	Kate	50 mi. NW of Ie Shima
5-4	0830	.5 Val	20 mi. N of Aguni Shima
	0830	.5 Dinah	"
	0830	2 Dinah	"
	0830	Val	"
6-10	1415	Judy	Over Kitahara AF, Kyushu

TOTAL 6.33/0/0

TERRILL, Francis A. 1Lt. (s/n 023349) 6.083 Victories
DOB: 14 July, 1920, Manhattan, MT
Died: 12 January 1946

Biography: Following his completion of the Naval aviation cadet program at Corpus Christi, TX, he was commissioned as a 2Lt. in the Marine Corps Reserve on 3 July 1943. He was promoted to 1Lt. on 31 May 1944. He received two DFCs, an Air Medal, and a strike/flight Air Medal.

Returning to the U.S., Terrill was killed in a ground aircraft collision on 12 January 1946, near Shreveport, LA, while serving with VRF-3.

Date	Time	Enemy a/c	Location
1945			
4-15	1830	.33 Val	65 mi. SE N tip of Okinawa
4-28	1640	2 Val	50 mi. NW of Izena Shima
5-4	0830	Dinah	30 mi. N of Aguni Shima
	0830	.25 Dinah	"
	0830	Val	"
	0830	2 Dinah dam.	"
	0830	2 Val dam.	"
5-10	1925	Hamp	50 mi. W of Zampa Misaki
5-17	1910	.5 Val	2 mi. S of Tonaki Shima

TOTAL 6.0833/0/4

DEWEY DURNFORD ***Author's collection.***

JOE DILLARD *Courtesy of Henry Brandon.*

FRANCIS TERRILL *Courtesy of Norman Miller.*

DORROH, Jefferson D. Major (s/n 09314) 6 Victories
DOB: 14 March, 1921, Corona, CA

Biography: Dorroh moved to Eugene, Oregon, and attended the University of Oregon. While there he enrolled in the Navy's V-5 program in September 1941. In June 1941 he entered the advanced Civilian Pilot Training program and finished the course at Albany, Oregon, on 8 July 1941. The next day he traveled to Seattle, and on 9 July he enlisted in the Navy's pilot training program as a cadet. He graduated at NAS Miami and was commissioned as 2Lt. in the USMCR on 12 March 1942. After a brief time as a flight instructor at various Naval Air Stations, he was promoted to captain on 31 May 1943, and joined VMF-323 in September 1943 at Cherry Point NAS. He was promoted to Major on 25 September 1944.

Dorroh was the XO on Okinawa, and in 29 missions saw combat only once, but made the most of it. He scored six victories on 22 April, the second highest USMC total in one day. For this action he was awarded the Navy Cross. He also was awarded a strike/flight DFC and three strike/flight Air Medals. He was released from active duty on 1 November 1945. Dorroh subsequently obtained a law degree and became an Oregon Senior Judge.

Date	Time	Enemy a/c	Location
1945			
4-22	1830	6 Val	50 mi. N of Aguni Shima
	1830	2 Val prob.	"
TOTAL 6/2/0			

AXTELL, George C. Major (s/n 06857) 6 Victories
DOB: 20 November, 1920, Ambridge, PA

Biography: After graduating from high school in 1938, Axtell attended the University of Alabama. He entered the USMC in July 1940 as a Marine Aviation Cadet. He was commissioned as a 2Lt. and designated a Naval Aviator on 12 May 1941. Following flight school, he was sent to the U.S. Navy's postgraduate school to study meteorological engineering, from which he graduated in March 1943.

Promoted to major on 15 May, 1943, he was assigned to command the newly formed VMF-323 squadron at Cherry Point, NC, as the youngest Marine Squadron CO. He led the Death Rattlers on a highly successful tour over Okinawa and became an ace-in-a-day on 22 April 1945. He received a Navy Cross, an Air Medal, and four strike/flight Air Medals.

JEFF DORROH ***Author's collection.***

BILL HOOD ***Courtesy of Jody O'Keefe.***

Axtell remained in the USMC. His next assignment was CO of Marine Carrier Air Group (MCVG)-16, and then as CO of VMF-452 until January 1947. During the Korean War Lt.Col. Axtell flew combat with the 1MAW and later served as CO of Marine Aircraft Attack Squadron-312 from 12 July to 4 October 1952, aboard the SICILY, receiving a Gold star in lieu of a second DFC, as well as two strike/flight Air Medals in 41 combat missions. His career took him to various command and staff assignments in the U.S., Japan, and the Pacific. He became a Colonel in July 1959 when he was CO of MAG-12. He graduated from the National War College in June 1964. In Vietnam Axtell received the Legion of Merit and a Gold Star in lieu of a second LM. He returned to the U.S., was promoted to Brig. Gen., and became Assistant Chief of Staff of Staff G-4, receiving a third LM. He was promoted to Maj.Gen. and became CO of 2MAW, and then became a Lt.Gen. and was CO of FMF Atlantic. Axtell retired on 1 September 1974, receiving a DSM. Axtell holds BA and MA degrees from George Washington University.

Date	Time	Enemy a/c	Location
1945			
4-22	1830	5 Val	50 mi. N of Aguni Shima
	1830	3 Val dam.	"
4-28	1830	Nate	70 mi. NW of Zampa Misaki

TOTAL 6/0/3

GEORGE AXTELL ***Author's collection.***

STU ALLEY ***Courtesy of the USMC via Steve Stuczynski.***

HOOD Jr., William L. 1Lt. (s/n 027514) 5.5 Victories

DOB: 7 May, 1924, Kalamazoo, MI

Died: KIFA 4 August 1946

Biography: After completing the Navy pilot training program he was commissioned a 2Lt. in the USMC on 16 July 1943. Hood was one of the core pilots from the squadron's formation at Cherry Point. On 30 June 1944 he was made a 1Lt. He flew 39 combat missions with -323 and received two DFCs and two strike/flight Air Medals. Hood was killed in a private light plane accident while on leave at Benton Harbor, MI, on 4 August 1946.

Date 1945	Time	Enemy a/c	Location
4-27	1830	2 Nate	50 mi. N of Aguni Shima
	1830	0.5 Val	"
	1830	0.5 Val	"
	1830	0.5 Val	"
	1830	2 Val dam.	"
4-28	1640	2 Val	50 mi. NW of Izena Shima

TOTAL 5.5/0/2

BILL DRAKE ***Courtesy of Bill Drake.***

ALLEY, Stuart C. 2Lt. (s/n 031495) 5 Victories

DOB: 14 May, 1924, Dayton, Ohio

Died: 21 January 1960 Grand Prairie, TX

Biography: Alley joined the Marine Corps in 1942, and applied for Naval flight training following graduation on 16 October 1943. He received a DFC and three Air Medals.

Date 1945	Time	Enemy a/c	Location
5-17	1900	Val	Kume Shima
5-25	0900	Tojo	40 mi. NW of Ie Shima
6-3	1330	3 Val	40 mi E of Zamba Misaki

TOTAL 5/0/0

DRAKE, Charles W.(Bill) (s/n 031331) 5 Victories

DOB: 14 April, 1923, Maplewood, NJ

Biography: Bill Drake attended Dartmouth University (NH) prior to joining the Marine Corps in the summer of 1942. He entered the Navy V-5 program and completed his primary training at Squantum, MA. He graduated at Pensacola on November 1943, and was commissioned a 2Lt. in the Marine Corps, after which he took operational training at Opa Locka, FL. During his 31 combat missions he was awarded a Navy Cross, an Air Medal, and a DFC. He separated form the service in January 1946. He graduated from Dartmouth, and upon returning to New Jersey, entered the warehousing and transportation business before going into publishing.

Date 1945	Time	Enemy a/c	Location
5-4	0830	Val	20 mi. N of Aguni Shima
6-3	1245	4 Zeke	20 mi. W of Iheya Shima
	1245	Zeke prob.	"

TOTAL 5/1/0

AL WELLS ***Courtesy of Norman Miller.***

WELLS, Albert P. 1Lt. (s/n 026538) 5 Victories

DOB: 10 April, 1922, New York City, NY

Biography: After completing Navy flight training he was commissioned as a 2Lt. in the USMC on 1 July 1943. Wells took bomber training at Opa Locka, FL, and transferred to fighters. He trained at El Toro and joined VMF-323 at El Centro in January 1944. He became a 1Lt. On 21 December 1944 Wells received two DFCs, an Air Medal, and a strike/flight Air Medal. Wells scored the squadron's first victory, destroying a Tony on 12 April. After the war Wells remained in aviation for 40 years, both in the cargo and passenger airline business, including a stint as the CEO of Hawaiian Air.

Date	Time	Enemy a/c	Location
1945			
4-12	0535	Tony	Nakagusuku Wan
5-15	1930	2 Jills	20 mi. S of Kume Shima
6-3	1245	2 Zeke	20 mi. W of Iheya Shima

TOTAL 5/0/0

The "General," and wife, Shirley. Except for close friends in the unit, many VMF-323 members still refer to Axtell as General or Major.

Death Rattler group photo with Gulf of Mexico "kills" during an annual fishing trip sponsored by Jerry O'Keefe (author on right).

Jerry O'Keefe, 53 years later. A successful businessman and politician (mayor of Biloxi, MS, and a state senator for MS).

Friends in war and friends in peace. Al Wells (L) and Hank Brandon (R) continue their 55 year friendly rivalry by comparing the size of their cathes.

VMF-323 CLAIMS

12 April-10 June 1945

Date	Time	Claim	Pilot	Location
4/12	0530	Tony	1Lt.Al Wells	Nakagasuku Wan
	1430	Zeke	2Lt.Warren Bestwick	Motobu Peninsula
	1430	Zeke	2Lt.Warren Bestwick	Motobu Peninsula
	1430	Zeke	CaptJoe McPhail	Motobu Peninsula
	1430	Zeke	1Lt.John Ruhsam	Motobu Peninsula
	1430	Zeke prob.	1Lt.Glenn Thacker	Motobu Peninsula
	1515	Betty(.33)	1Lt.Del Davis	71m NW Ie Shima
		(.33)	2Lt.Dewey Durnford	"
		(.33)	1Lt.Chas. Spangler	"
	1530	Jack prob.	Capt.Felix Cecot	Above Ie Shima
4/15	1830	Val (.33)	1Lt.Joe Dillard	65m SE northern
		(.33)	1Lt.Francis Terrill	tip of Okinawa
		(.33)	1Lt.Harold Tonnessen	"
	1830	Zeke (.5)	1Lt.Chas. Allen	N tip of Okinawa
		(.5)	1Lt.John Strickland	"
	1830	Tony	1Lt.Fred Zehring	Off NW Okinawa
	1900	Tony prob.	2Lt.Warren Bestwick	Over Kawata Wan
	1900	Tony	1Lt.John Ruhsam	Kawata Wan
	1900	2 Tony	1Lt.Bob Wade	Kawata Wan
4/16	0900	Hamp	1Lt.Ed Abner	60m N Ie Shima
	0900	Hamp (.5)	1Lt.Ed Abner	60m N Ie Shima
	0930	Lily	2Lt.Dewey Durnford	30m N Ie Shima
	0930	Betty	2Lt.Dewey Durnford	30m W Yontan
	1000	Kate (.25)	2Lt.Larry Crawley	4m W Zampa
		(.25)	1Lt.Ed Keeley	Mikaki
		(.25)	1Lt.Chas. Martin	"
		(.25)	2Lt.Everett Yager	"
4/22	1830	2 Val	1Lt.Ed Abner	50m N Aguni Shima
	1830	Val dam.	1Lt.Ed Abner	"
	1830	Val	1Lt.Chas. Allen	"
	1830	Val prob.	1Lt.Chas. Allen	"
	1830	5 Val	Maj.George Axtell	"
	1830	3 Val dam.	Maj.George Axtell	"
	1830	6 Val	Maj.Jeff Dorroh	"
	1830	2 Val prob.	Maj.Jeff Dorroh	"
	1830	2 Nate	1Lt.Bill Hood	"
	1830	Val (.5)	1Lt.Bill Hood	"
	1830	Val (.5)	1Lt.Bill Hood	"
	1830	Val (.5)	1Lt.Bill Hood	"
	1830	2 Val dam.	1Lt.Bill Hood	"
	1830	5 Val	1Lt.Jerry O'Keefe	"
	1830	2 Val	1Lt.Norm Theriault	"
	1830	Val (.25)	1Lt.Norm Theriault	"
4/28	1640	2 Val	1Lt.Vern	Ball 50m NW Izena Shima
	1640	2 Val	1Lt.Bill Hood	"
	1640	Val	1Lt.Ed Murray	"
	1640	Val (.5)	1Lt.Ed Murray	"
	1640	Ida	1Lt.Ed Murray	"
	1640	2 Val	1Lt.Francis Terrill	"
	1830	Nate	Maj.George Axtell	70m NW Zampa Misaki
	1830	2 Nate	2Lt.Dewey Durnford	"
	1830	2 Nate	1Lt.Jerry O'Keefe	"
	1845	Kate	1Lt.Joe Dillard	50m NW Ie Shima
5/03	1900	Judy	2Lt.Tom Blackwell	15m SW Aguni Shima
5/04	0830	Tojo	2Lt.Jim Bierbower	25m N Ie Shima
	0830	Val (.5)	1Lt.Aqulla Blaydes	20m N Aguni Shima
	0830	Val (.5)	1Lt.Joe Dillard	"
	0830	Dinah (.5)	1Lt.Aqulla Blaydes	"
	0830	Dinah (.5)	1Lt.Joe Dillard	"
	0830	2 Dinah	1Lt.Joe Dillard	"
	0830	Val	1Lt.Joe Dillard	"
	0830	Val	1Lt.Cy Dolezel	"
	0830	Dinah (.5)	1Lt.Cy Dolezel	"
	0830	Dinah (.5)	Capt.Bill Van Buskirk	"
	0830	Val	2Lt.Bill Drake	"
	0830	Val (.5)	2Lt.Harold Hohl	"
	0830	Nate	Capt.Joe McPhail	Near Ie Shima
	0830	Jill	1Lt.Bob Muse	20m W Ie Shima
	0830	4 Val	1Lt.John Ruhsam	25m NW Aguni
	0830	3 Val dam.	1Lt.John Ruhsam	Shima
	0830	Dinah	1Lt.Francis Terrill	30m N. Aguni
	0830	Dinah(.25)	1Lt.Francis Terrill	Shima
	0830	Val	1Lt.Francis Terrill	"
	0830	2 Dinah dam.	1Lt.Francis Terrill	"
	0830	2 Val dam.	1Lt.Francis Terrill	"
	0830	Helen	1Lt.Glenn Thacker	"
	0830	Dinah	1Lt.Glenn Thacker	"
	0830	Val dam.	1Lt.Glenn Thacker	"
	0830	Val	Capt.Bill Van Buskirk	20m N Aguni Shima
	0830	2 Val	1Lt.Bob Wade	25m NW Ie Shima
	0830	2 Nate	1Lt.Bob Wade	"
	0830	3 Nate dam.	1Lt.Bob Wade	"
5/10	1925	Hamp	1Lt.Francis Terrill	50m W Zampa Misaki
5/11	0830	Dinah	2Lt.Larry Crawley	30m NW Izena Shima
	0830	Nate	2Lt.Larry Crawley "	
	0830	Tojo	1Lt.Ed Keeley	"
	0830	3 Nate	1Lt.Ed Keeley	"
	0830	2 Nate	1Lt.Larry Crawley	10m NW Izena Shima
	0830	Tojo	1Lt.Chas. Martin	10m NE Izena Shima
5/12	1930	Dinah (.5)	1Lt.John Ruhsam	40m SW Kadena AF
	1930	Dinah (.5)	1Lt.Bob Wade	"
5/15	1930	Jill	2Lt.Norm Miller	20m S Kume Shima
	1930	2 Jill	1Lt.Al Wells	"
5/17	1900	Val	2Lt.Stuart Alley	Kume Shima
	1910	Val (.5)	2Lt.Keith Fountain	2m S Tonaki Shima
	1910	Val (.5)	1Lt.Francis Terrill	"
5/25	0845	Zeke	1Lt.John Strikeland	10m NE Iheya Shima
	0850	Tojo	2Lt.Tom Blaclwell	"
	0850	2 Tojo	1Lt.Chas. Allen	"
	0850	2 Tojo	1Lt.Jim Feliton	"
	0850	Tojo dam.	2Lt.Tom Blackwell	"
	0850	Tojo	1Lt.John Strickland	"
	0850	Tojo dam.	2Lt.Tom Blackwell	"
	0900	Tojo	2Lt.Stuart Alley	40m NW Ie Shima
	0900	Tojo dam.	1Lt.Chas. Spangler	"
5/28	0740	Tojo (.5)	1Lt.Del Davis	40m E Zampa Misaki
	0740	Tojo (.5)	2Lt.Bob Woods	"
	0820	Sally (.5)	1Lt.Harold Edelson	Over Ie Shima
	0820	Sally (.5)	1Lt.John Srtickland	"
6/03	1245	2 Zeke	2Lt.Jerry Conners	20m W Iheya Shima
	1245	Zeke	1Lt.Cy Dolezel	"
	1245	4 Zeke	2Lt.Bill Drake	"
	1245	Zeke prob.	2Lt.Bill Drake	"
	1245	2 Zeke	1Lt.Al Wells	"
	1330	3 Val	2Lt.Stuart Alley	40m E Zamba Misaki
	1330	Val	2Lt.Dewey Durnford	"
	1330	Nate	2Lt.Dewey Durnford	"
	1330	Val	1Lt.Chas. Spangler	"
	1700	Val (.5)	1Lt.John Ruhsam	10m W Iheya Shima
	1700	Val (.5)	1Lt.Bob Wade	"
6/10	1415	Judy	1Lt.Joe Dillard	Over S Kyushu

TOTALS: 124.5 Victories/ 7 Probables/ 20 Damaged

CHAPTER 31
Enlisted Men

VMF-323 Enlisted Bureaucracy on Okinawa
Sgt/Major Raymond Beckner
M/Sgt. Lloyd Bowman Leading Chief
M/Sgt. Archie Lebow Line Chief
M/Sgt. John Culleton Engineering Chief
M/Sgt. George Morrison Armaments Chief
M/Sgt. Edmund Grady Armorer
M/Sgt. Robert Brown Armorer
M/Sgt. William Elliott Hydraulic Mechanics
M/Sgt. Richard Misch Propeller Mechanics
M/Sgt. Stanley Parrish Metalsmiths
M/Sgt. Thomas McLaughlin Fabric Workers
M/Sgt. Elwood Hand Aviation Supply
M/Sgt. William Kuck Aviation Supply
M/Sgt. Eugene Yongeman Radar Chief
M/Sgt. Henry Garrard Radar Mechanics
M/Sgt. Jerry Blake Motor Transport
M/Sgt. Lowell Frye Dispatcher
M/Sgt. Lonnie Herdon Mess Sargeant

Plane Captains: (L to R) Top Row: T/Sgts. James Buckley, Paul Pentheny, Don Hitchings, and Stan Woszcyna. Bottom Row: T/Sgt. Paul Finney, S/Sgt. Frank Maggliocco, M/Sgt. Lloyd Bowman. Courtesy of *Don Hitchings*.

S/Sgts. Albert Magley (L) and Harley Brock shoot the bull outside their tents at Pendleton. *Courtesy of Harley Brock*.

(L to R) S/Sgt. Frank Maggliocco, Sgt. James Kennedy, Corp. Joe Bassani, and M/Sgt. Robert Brown. *Courtesy of Bill Drake*.

Jerry Bennett (Plane Captain). *Courtesy of Norman Miller.*

T/Sgt.Paul Pentheny exiting the cockpit of a well-worn Corsair. *Courtesy of John Ruhsam.*

Nordia Mikelson (Plane Captain). *Courtesy of Norman Miller.*

Norm Caron (Plane Captain). *Courtesy of Norman Miller.*

Don Hitchings (Plane Captain). *Courtesy of Norman Miller.*

Harry Gracy (Plane Captain). ***Courtesy of Norman Miller.***

John Cox (Mechanic). ***Courtesy of Norman Miller.***

Earl Barr (Plane Captain). ***Courtesy of Norman Miller.***

Hotel California. At Kadena the hydraulics section named their tent after the Clark Hotel, a Los Angeles enlisted men's hangout. On the left is James Martin and on the right is Bill Elliott. ***Courtesy of Harley Brock.***

Legend for Comprehensive Enlisted Man Roster VMF-323

Rank Code

A- Master Sargeant
B- Technical Sargeant
C- Staff Sargeant
D- Sargeant P- Pharmacist (Navy)
E- Corporal
F- Private First Class
G- Private

X- on squadron roster as of date

Compiled by Harley Brock

Comprehensive VMF-323 Enlisted Roster 1943-45

RANK	LAST	FIRST	Aug43	Jan44	Apr45	JOB#	JOB TITLE
A	BECKNER	Raymond C.			X	584	Sgt Maj
A	BLAKE	Jerry M.		X	X	213	Motor Trans
A	BOWMAN	Lloyd	X	X	X	752	Leading Chief
A	BROWN	Robert E.	X	X	X	911	Armorer
A	CULLETON	John F.	X	X	X	752	Eng. Chief
A	DUDLEY	George L.	X	X	X	747	AMM
A	ELLIOTT	William W.	X	X	X	528	Hydraul. Mech.
A	FRYE	Lowell E.			X	410	Dispatcher
A	GARRARD	Henry O.	X	X	X	754	Rad Mech
A	GRADY	Edmund J.	X	X	X	911	Armorer
A	HAND	Elwood	X	X	X	826	Avn Supply Clk
A	HERNDON	Lonnie B.		X	X	824	Mess SGT
A	KUCK	William G.			X	826	Avn Supply Clk
A	LEBOW	Archie G.	X				Line Chief
A	MC LAUGHIN	Thomas M.		X	X	548	Fabric Worker
A	MISCH	Richard A.	X	X	X	687	Prop Mech
A	MORRISON	George E.	X	X	X	911	Armament Chief
A	PARRISH	Stanley R.		X	X	555	Metalsmith
A	STEWART	Frank H.	X	X	X	747	AMM
A	WILLIAMS	James D.	X	X	X	747	AMM
A	YONGEBERG	Eugene			X	542	Rad Chief
B	AMUNDSON	Ernest O.	X	X	X	747	AMM
B	BARNETT	James F.	X	X	X	911	Armorer
B	BEYERKOLER	Richard W.		X	X		Radar
B	BOROZAN	Steve		X	X	956	Carburator
B	BROWER	George C Jr.		X	X	911	Armorer
B	BUCKLEY	James A.	X	X	X	747	AMM
B	CARON	Norman P.	X	X	X	747	AMM
B	COCHRAN	Jack M.			X	501	Clk SGT Maj OFF.
B	CROSS	Robert C.			X	824	Mess SGT
B	DAUGHTON	John P.	X	X	X	—	Trans Mech
B	DE MILIA	Rocco A.	X	X	X	911	Armorer
B	FECKANCZ	Sam		X	X	747	AMM
B	FINNEY	Paul C.	X	X	X	747	AMM
B	HILBLACK	Dennis L.			X	754	Radar Operator
B	HIMMELBERGER	Arthur I.	X	X	X	747	Line Chief
B	HITCHINGS	Donald A.	X	X	X	747	AMM
B	KALUPONOV	Andrew	X	X	X	754	Rad Mech
B	LEE	Melvin		X	X	244	Truck Dr.
B	MARTIN	James H.		X	X	528	Hydraul Mech.
B	MASCAL	Edwin F.	X	X	X	747	AMM
B	MICHA	Charles H.		X	X	501	Clk SGT Maj OFF.
B	NIBLACK	Dennis L.	X	X	X	754	Rad. Operator
B	PENTHANY	Harold O. Jr.	X	X	X	747	AMM
B	PRESTON	George D.		X	X	954	Radar Tech.
B	SALSER	Floyd	X				Asst Line Chief
B	SLOAN	Albert			X	911	Armorer
B	VAIRA	John D.	X	X	X	911	Armorer
B	WARREN	Milton C.			X	911	Armorer
B	WOSZCYNA	Stanley J.	X	X	X	747	AMM
C	ALENGI	Joe N.	X	X	X	911	Armorer
C	BAKER	Edward J.			X	244	Truck Dr.
C	BARND	William H. Jr.		X	X	747	AMM
C	BENNETT	Jerome		X	X	750	Plane Capt.
C	BOYCE	Joseph	X	X	X	911	Armorer
C	BRENNEN	Donald P.		X	X	686	Instrument Mech
C	BROCK	Harley W.	X	X	X	747	Plane Capt.
C	BRUNO	John O.	X	X	X	911	Armorer
C	BRUNO	Joseph J.	X	X	X	911	Armorer
C	CARVER	Donald E.	X	X	X	747	AMM
C	CHAPMAN	Odie F.			X	114	Charge of Const.
C	CHESSMAN	Charles M.	X	X	X	747	AMM
C	CLEVENGER	Clarence L.	X	X	X	747	AMM

C	COOGAN	Edward J.		X	X	911	Armorer
C	CULVER	Leonard O.	X	X	X	747	AMM
C	DENNIS	Thomas A.			X	754	Rad Mech
C	DI PAOLA	Arthur P		X	X	245	Truck Dr.
C	DOWNS	Fred W.			X	275	Class. Clk.
C	FLEGEL	Wayne L.	X	X	X	747	AMM
C	GAWRON	Edward M.	X	X	X	826	Avn Supply Clk
C	GOODWIN	Dibble G.	X	X			Acting Sgt. Major
C	GRACEY	Harry A.	X	X	X	747	AMM
C	GUSTIN	M-N orton J.	X	X	X	911	Armorer
C	HEWITT	Charles B. Jr.		X	X	685	AVN Elect
C	HILL	Richard D.	X		X	641	Field Tele
C	HOLLAND	Vincent E.	X	X	X	747	AMM
C	HURLBURT	Elmer C.	X	X	X	56	Mail Clk.
C	KADASKY	Frank		X		750	Crew Chief
C	KARREN	Milton C.		X		911	Armorer
C	KROFFT	Robert M.	X	X	X	747	AMM
C	MAGLEY	Albert J.	X	X	X	501	Flt Clk
C	MAGLIOCCO	Francis J.	X	X	X	747	AMM
C	MIKELSON	Nordia	X	X	X	747	AMM
C	REGAN	John J.	X	X	X	776	Rad. Operator
C	SCHRESS	Joseph R.			X	60	Mess Clk
C	STEPHENS	David H.	X				Sq. Clk
C	STOVALL	Augone W.		X	X	687	Prop Mech.
C	UPHOUSE	Earl W.		X	X	754	Rad Mech
C	WALDEN	William T.	X	X	X	501	Eng. Clk.
C	WELFGOTT	Lawrance E.	X				
C	WILCZEK	Theodore R.	X	X		747	Mechanic
D	ANSEL	Eugene A.		X	X	60	Ck Sg Mess
D	BARR	Earl H.		X	X	747	AMM
D	BEYE	William P.	X	X	X	835	Material Clk.
D	BOENZI	Neal		X	X	747	AMM
D	BOKROS	Adrian N.			X	40	Auto Body Repair
D	BOSS	Ralph E.		X	X	911	Armorer
D	BOUCHARD	Roland R.	X	X	X	747	AMM
D	BOUCHILLION	Haward L.	X	X	X	747	AMM
D	BROWN	William R.T.	X	X		776	Radio
D	BUTCHER	William C.	X	X	X	911	Armorer
D	CARLTON	Robert W.		X	X	747	AMM
D	CLARK	Joe F.	X	X	X	685	Truck Dr.
D	COHEN	Samuel			X	776	RAD Op
D	COLUCCIO	Daniel F.			X	60	Ck Sg Mess
D	COMERFORD	John C.	X	X	X	555	Metalsmith
D	COX	John F. J r.		X	X	747	Mechanic
D	CRESCENTI	Turidio A.	X	X	X	911	Armorer
D	CUNNINGHAM	Harold B.	X	X	X	620	Para Rig
D	CUPCIELLA	Anthony			X	348	Auto Parts clk
D	DAIGLE	Rowland L.	X	X		747	Mechanic
D	DE ROCK	Lawrence A.		X	X	747	AMM
D	DI BENEDETTO	Michael A.		X	X	911	Armorer
D	DROLET	Maurice A.		X	X	50	Carpenter
D	ECERICH	Andrew G.		X	X	911	Armorer
D	EDWARDS	John H.	X	X		747	Mechanic
D	ELSON	Albert G.		X		911	Armorer
D	FITZGERALD	Gerald J.		X	X	501	Clk Sgt Maj
D	FOLCARELLI	Anthony P.	X	X	X	245	Truck Dr.
D	FRISCHKORN	Jay R.	X	X	X	956	Carb. Mech
D	GAIGAL	Joseph F.	X				Photographer
D	GASEK	Stanley R.	X	X	X	60	Cook
D	GATES	Dan H.	X	X	X	747	AMM
D	GRIFFFONI	Joseph	X	X	X	555	Metalsmith
D	GRIFFIN	Marley T.	X	X	X	747	Hydraul. Mech.
D	HERBERT	William			X	14	Trans Mech
D	HILL	Thomas Q.	X	X	X	747	AMM
D	HILL	Clyde K.	X	X	X	754	Radar Mech
D	HOPPER	Clyde L.	X	X	X	747	AMM

D	JOHNSON	Glenn A.		X	X	911	Armorer
D	JOHNSON	Harold D.		X	X		Rad. Operator
D	KADJA	Frank			X	245	Truck Dr.
D	KAELBER	Charles J.	X	X	X	747	AMM
D	KELLY	William M. Jr.	X				Mechanic
D	KENNEDY	James T.		X		911	Armorer
D	KENYON	Robert	X	X	X	620	Para Rig
D	KOZLOWSKI	Edward W.			X	60	Field Cock
D	KYNE	Gerald E.	X	X	X	911	Armorer
D	LANGSTON	Don N.Jr.	X	X	X	911	Armorer
D	LONDRAVILLE	Arthur W.	X	X	X	911	Armorer
D	MAHADY	Martin F.		X	X	911	Armorer
D	MAURER	Mark K.		X	X	911	Armorer
D	MICHAEL	Thomas J.			X	244	Truck Dr.
D	NEEB	Norman G.		X	X	245	Truck Dr.
D	NORTON	James L. Jr.	X				Material Clk.
D	OLSON	Roger J.	X	X	X	747	AMM
D	OSTENDORF	Otto W.		X	X	521	Gen Duty
D	OSTROSKI	Thaddeus T.	X	X	X	519	Aircraft Painter
D	QUILL	Ralph P.	X	X	X	245	Truck Dr.
D	RUSSELL	Gilbert P.		X	X	245	Truck Dr.
D	SAARI	Lynn E.		X	X	754	Rad. Operator
D	SHIPTON	Bart A.		X	X	245	Truck Dr.
D	ST CLAIR	Robert E.	X	X	X	566	Police SGT.
D	STEVENS	Edwin J. Jr.	X	X	X	747	AMM
D	TARRAVECHIA	Dick			X	754	Radar Operator
D	TIPPLER	Frank H.	X	X	X	555	Metalsmith
D	TIPTON	Alvin R.Jr.	X				
D	TOMSETT	Richard N.	X	X	X	754	Rad Mech
D	VAGNONI	Nicholas			X	60	Ck Sg Mess
D	VERSACI	Benedict J.		X	X	405	Clk Gen.
D	WENTZ	William R.		X		747	Mechanic
D	WILEY	Melvin N.	X			911	Armorer
D	WINGFIELD	Chester G.		X	X	911	Armorer
D	YANUSS	Quenton W.	X	X	X	747	AMM
E	ABRAMS	Sheldon E.	X				Radio Operator
E	ANDERSON	George			X	244	Truck Dr.
E	APPLEBAUM	Albert G.			X	521	Construction
E	ARCHAMBAULT	Roger L.		X	X	747	AMM
E	BASSANI	Joseph A.		X	X	747	AMM
E	BELANGER	Gerald H.		X	X	60	Ck Sg Mess
E	BICKFORD	John F.	X	X	X	747	AMM
E	BONNER	William U.		X	X	911	Armorer
E	BROOKS	Roger W. Jr.	X	X	X	747	Mechanic
E	BURGESS	John R.		X	X	747	AMM
E	BURNS	Karl H.	X	X	X	747	AMM
E	CALDWELL	Wilbur D.		X	X	911	Armorer
E	CAROTTA	Arthur F..		X	X	555	Metalsmith
E	CASSELL	Roy M.		X	X	911	Armorer
E	CERNIELLO	Alfred B.		X	X	747	AMM
E	CERTUSE	Aldo			X	244	Truck Dr.
E	COOK	Ernest W. Jr.	X	X	X	245	Truck Dr.
E	COOPER	Clifford H.	X	X		747	Mechanic
E	DESIBIA	Edward J.	X	X	X	245	Truck Dr.
E	DOKTER	Robert A.		X	X	747	AMM
E	DOWNES	Francis J.		X	X	747	AMM
E	DUBIN	Isadore		X	X	747	AMM
E	DWYER	John A.Jr.		X	X	747	AMM
E	FOX	Lester E.		X	X	641	Truck Op.
E	FUSE	Alfonco A.	X	X			Instrument Mech
E	GALLIER	Van M.		X	X	911	___
E	GILBERT	Herbart W.		X	X	641	Telephone OP.
E	GREGORCZY	AnthonyJ.		X	X	60	Cook
E	GREGORY	William J.		X	X	60	Cook
E	HARRISON	Chester L.		X	X	501	Clk SGT Maj OFF.
E	HEYNOLDS	Robert W.			X	747	AMM

E	HORTON	Thomas E.	X	X	X	911	Armorer
E	HUDSPETH	Charles C.Jr.	X	X	X	747	AMM
E	IKERD	William G.	X	X			Carb. Mech
E	J or KENNER	Edwin M.			X	911	Armorer
E	JACKSON	Eugene B.	X	X	X	747	AMM
E	JAMES	Joseph N.Jr.	X	X	X	911	Armorer
E	JAMES	Aaron A.Jr.		X	X	60	Cook
E	KENNEDY	John C.	X	X	X	747	AMM
E	LARSEN	Arnold L.			X	521	Truck Dr.
E	LOVERN	Ralph B.		X		521	Ground Defense
E	MASCLARETTE	Joseph R.		X	X	22	Barber
E	MASLAKOWSKI	Edward S.	X	X	X	55	Sq. Clk.
E	MC DONALD	Raymond E.			X	747	AMM
E	MCGREGOR	Harry A.		X	X	911	Armorer
E	McMASTER	Robert E.	X			747	Plane Capt.
E	MORRIS	John O. Jr	X	X	X	245	Construction
E	MUTTER	Howard E.	X	X	X	521	Flt Clk
E	NAYLOR	George C.			X	911	Armorer
E	NESPOLA	Frank A.	X	X	X	405	Clk
E	NICHOLS	Andrew J.			X	747	AMM
E	ORLANDELLA	Frank A.	X	X	X	114	Machinist
E	POWERS	Richard E.		X	X	911	Armorer
E	SCAROLA	Edward		X	X	911	Armorer
E	SHERWOOD	Leslie F.			X	245	Truck Dr.
E	SIEBER	Clyde B.		X	X	78	Electrician
E	SIEGEL	Julius M.	X	X	X	50	Carpenter
E	SILECHIA	Vito Jr.			X	940	Aerial Photo
E	STAFFORD	Dennis J.	X	X	X	747	AMM
E	STEVENS	James R.	X	X	X	747	AMM
E	STRANSKY	Paul			X	620	Para Rig
E	TILER	Maurice L.			X	911	Armorer
E	TOOMEY	Howard P.			X	50	Carpenter
E	WEIRICH	Robert A.		X	X	245	Truck Dr.
E	WILLIAMS	Reynolds W.			X	245	Truck Dr.
E	Y-ZIESSMER	John J.		X		60	Cook
E	YOZLOOSKI	Edward W.		X		60	Cook
F	ALESSANDRO	John J.		X		747	Mechanic
F	AUGUST	Micheal		X		911	Armorer
F	BALTHASAR	Victor H. Jr.		X		747	Mechanic
F	BOUC—BOC-N	Thomas A.	X	X		747	Mechanic
F	BOULDINCK	Walter W.	X	X		747	Mechanic
F	BRAULIEU	Charles R.		X		929	Truck Dr.
F	CALSPEGGIC	Frank		X		521	Ground Defense
F	CLARK	Thomas C.			X	911	Armorer
F	COMFREY	Christopher E.		X		704	Telephone OP.
F	COOKE	Thomas W. Jr.	X	X	X	521	Construction
F	COSELL	James S.		X		521	Ground Defense
F	COURAGE	Raymond W. Jr.	X				Electrician
F	COURTNEY	Howard H.		X	X	911	Armorer
F	COWING	Harry C. Jr.		X	X	704	Telephone OP.
F	DELL	Harold E.		X	X	747	AMM
F	DIONE	Eugene		X		6-5	Electrician
F	DUBE	Raymond L.		X	X	521	Ground Defense
F	EBERLE	Robert H.	X	X			Mechanic
F	FENTON	James P.	X	X	X		Mechanic
F	FERGUSON	James B.	X	X			Armorer
F	FREEMAN	Christian H.		X	X	521	Ground Defense
F	GERACI	John P.		X		704	Telephone OP.
F	GREYNOLDS	Robert W.	X	X		60	Mechanic
F	GULA	Daniel		X		704	Telephone OP.
F	HANSON	William B.	X			911S	Armorer
F	HARRIS	Robert D.	X	X		521	Ground Defense
F	HERKAN	Rudolph J.	X	X			Mechanic
F	HOFFMAN	Fred F.	X	X	X	704	Telephone OP.
F	HOPKINS	Harry N.	X	X	X	747	AMM

F	HORNSBY	Lucian	X				Armorer
F	HUMPHREY	Lester O.	X				Mechanic
F	JONES	Vincent B.	X				Armorer
F	KNOPF	George E.			X	245	Truck Dr
F	LACK	Walter F.	X	X	X	521	Construction
F	MC GARTLAND	John F.	X	X	X	521	Construction
F	MELSON	Kenneth E.	X	X			Mechanic
F	MIKSIC	Markus	X	X	X	521	Construction
F	NAVARRO	Robert A.			X	521	Construction
F	NEWHOUSE	Francis J. Jr.			X	521	Truck Dr
F	PALUMBIZIO	Alfred J.	X	X	X	747	AMM
F	QUESENBERRY	Genious E.		X	X	521	Construction
F	RHOUIS	Athol L.	X				Mechanic
F	RUBIN	Alexander		X		685	Electrician
F	SABATINO	Leonardo V.		X	X	521	Carpenter
F	SEXTON	Leland O.			X	911	Armorer
F	SHEGOGUE	Donald K.	X	X	X	747	AMM
F	SINGLETARY	Robert H.		X	X	911	Armorer
F	SLATER	George E.	X	X			Mechanic
F	SMITH	Harold R. Jr	X			245	Truck Dr
F	STEINLE	James N.			X	911	Armorer
F	STROUSKI	Alexander		X		521	Ground Defense
F	TAYLOR	Raymond B.	X	X		747	Mechanic
F	TOCCI	Frank R.			X	686	Instrument Mech
F	TOMLINSON	Fred J.		X	X	521	Ground Defense
F	WINDHAM	Louis E.	X				Carpenter
F	WITHROW	Richard W.		X	X	519	Aircraft Painter
F	ZARRA	John A.	X	X	X	521	Comm
G	BECKER	Marvin R.	X	X		521	Ground Defense
G	BERGERON	Omer J. Jr.	X	X		521	Ground Defense
G	CLARK	James M.	X	X		769	Storekeeper
G	CUBIC	George J.		X		747	Mechanic
G	DE STEFANO	Bart			X	521	Gen Duty
G	DECKER	Chase S.	X	X		521	Ground Defense
G	DIETRICH	Henry L. Jr.		X		704	Telephone OP.
G	EGGESTEIN	Orivilla R.			X	521	
G	FENTON	John F. Jr.	X				Mechanic
G	FORTE	Angale	X	X			Mechanic
G	FOX	Carl F.		X		521	Ground Defense
G	FREAR	Harold E.	X			929	Truck Dr.
G	HART	John E.	X	X			Mechanic
G	KANAD	Martin	X		X	245	Truck Op.
G	KELLI	Guiseppe	X				Mechanic
G	KNIGHT	Randal L.	X	X			Para.
G	KRIEN	Steve F.	X				Mechanic
G	KRISS	Steve F.	X	X		747	Mechanic
G	LEWISON	David J.			X	521	Gen Duty
G	MAIGRET	Roger M.	X				Mechanic
G	MILLETICH	Matteo		X		929	Truck Dr.
G	MUSIAK	Henry	X	X		929	Truck Dr.
G	POPE	James F.		X		521	Ground Defense
G	ROIANO	Thomas N.		X		521	Gen Duty
G	RYAN	Thomas J.		X		521	Ground Defense
G	SELIG	William H. Jr.	X	X		929	Truck Dr.
G	SIBILLIA	Peter A.		X		521	Ground Defense
G	SOLOMONS	William	X	X		521	Ground Defense
G	TIMBERA	Louis	X	X		50	Carpenter
G	TRIOLO	Charles S.	X	X		548	Fabric and paint
P	GOFF	Stanton M.		X	X	521N	Corpman
P	MYNATT	James P.			X	521N	Corpman
P	ROGERS	William H.		X	X	521N	Corpman
P	SADOWSKI	Edward		X	X	521N	Corpman
P	SHAW	Harry L.		X		521N	Corpman
P	SLAGLE	Robert E.		X	X	521N	Corpman
P	WHITTEN	Payson M.		X	X	521N	Corpman
P	WOODRUFF	Stanley F.		X	X	521N	Corpman
P	YEATS	Amos T.		X		521N	Corpman

CHAPTER 32
Rattler Epilogue

KOREA

In July 1950, VMF-323, again flying the Corsair (but the F4U-4B version), was ordered to Western Pacific due to the North Korean invasion of South Korea. On 6 August, the Death Rattlers, led by CO Major Arthur Lund, entered combat aboard the USS BADOENG STRAIT (CVE-116) when it flew close air support missions in the defense of Pusan. In September, it flew missions in support of the Inchon invasion, and in December it covered the withdrawal of the 1st Marine Division from encirclement by the Chinese Communists who had entered the war, and tried to stem their advance from the Yalu.

In early 1951, the squadron became land-based, moving to Bofu Airbase in Japan and then to K-1 near Pusan. During this interim they flew mainly armed recon flights. In June, the squadron was assigned to the USS SICILY (CVE-118) were it flew naval gunfire spotting, close air support, armed recon, and CAP in order to blockade the northwest Korean coast. In late September, the squadron again was land-based until they left Korea on 2 July 1953. During this time the squadron was redesignated VMF to VMA to reflect its attack role, and flew half AU-1s, which were F4Us designed for the attack role. The majority of its missions were close air support and air interdiction missions.

VIETNAM

On 1 December 1965, the Death Rattlers, now designated VMFA-323, arrived at Da Nang Airbase, Vietnam. The squadron was an attack unit flying the F-4B Phantoms and primarily flew CAPs and air-to-ground weapons delivery missions. In May 1967, VMFA-323 played a significant role in the defense of Khe Sahn. After a distinguished deployment in Vietnam, the Death Rattlers were relieved on 1 April 1969, having flown 17,000 combat sorties. The Command Chronology for March 1969 stated:

"When the Death Rattlers return to combat, they will have much to live up to if they are to match the record they have set during this combat tour."

Death Rattler Song:

Down in the islands, across the blue sea
Down in the islands, across the blue sea
Write me a letter, send it to hell
Send it in care of Major Axtell
We'll lick these Jap boys, we'll lick them well
'Cause we've got Major Axtell
Across the blue skies boys, we'll chase them to hell
Flying and shooting like Major Axtell
Out from the islands, o'er the blue sea
Comes that great squadron-323
All our airplanes, all of our mechs
All our pilots, physical wreaks
I'll get there some day, into Japan
Not just as a tourist but a flying wildman
Let's drink a toast, while on a spree
To the best outfit, VMF-323
Sung to the tune "Birmingham Jail," or "Down by the Valley."

Bibliography

Interviews (Taped telephone and personal)

Allen, Charles (Sherwood, AR)
Allen, Charles (via Dorothy Spangler)
Archambault, Roger (Belchertown, MA)
Axtell, George (Weaverville, NC)(+ letters & e-mail)
Axtell, George (via Dorothy Spangler)
Barrett, James (West Allis, WI) (+ e-mail)
Bassani, Joe (Deerfield Beach, FL)
Bestwick, Warren (Bellingham, WA) (+ e-mail)
Bestwick, Warren (via Dorothy Spangler)
Bierbower, Jim (Asheville, NC)
Blaydes, A.M. (Pensacola, FL)
Brandon, Henry (Ocala, FL)
Brandon, Henry (via Dorothy Spangler)
Broering, Jack (via Dorothy Spangler)
Brock, Harley (Riverside, CA)(– e-mail & letters)
Conners, Jerry (Palisades, CO)
Coogan, Ed (Ocala, FL)
Crawley, Larry (Portland, OR)
Crawley, Larry (via Dorothy Spangler)
Davis, Del (Vista, CA) (+ letters)
DeMilia, Rocky (Wethersfield, CT)
Dolezel, Cy (E.Jordon, MI)
Drake, Bill (Brookside, NJ) (+ letters)
Durnford, Dewey (Rockledge, FL)
Dussman, Dr. Thomas (via Dorothy Spangler)
Finney, Paul (Toone, TN)
Fountain, Keith (via Dorothy Spangler)
Hitchings, Don (Hopkinton, MA)
Hoel, Harold (Costa Mesa, CA) (+ letter)
Lee, Mel (Hoboken, NJ)
Magliocco, Frank (Willmantic, CT) (+ letters)
Mayer, Sol (New Orleans, LA)
Mayer, Sol (via Dorothy Spangler)
McPhail, Joe (Houston, TX) (+ Letter)
McPhail, Joe (via Dorothy Spangler)
Miller, Norman (Dumfries, VA)
Miller, Norman (via Dorothy Spangler)
Muse, Bob (Boston, MA)
O'Keefe, Jerry (Ocean Springs, MI)
Ritter, Fred (Rochester, NY)
Ruhsam, John (Sarasota, FL) (+ letters)
Ruhsam, John (via Dorothy Spangler)
Spangler. Charles (via Dorothy Spangler/7 tapes)
Thacker, Glenn (Lakeville, IN)
Theriault, Norm (N. Ft. Myers, FL)
Tonnessen, Harold (E. Sandwich, MA)
Tonnessen, Harold (via Dorothy Spangler)
Wells, Al (Miami, FL)
Wells, Al (via Dorothy Spangler)
Woods, Robert (Dalles, OR)

Diaries and Letters

Brandon, Henry (Collection of Letters)
Carleton, Robert (Diary via Dorothy Spangler)
Comstock, Byron (Letter via Dorothy Spangler)
Ruhsam, John (Log book via Dorothy Spangler)
Ruhsam, John (Letters to his parents)
Spangler, Dorothy (Letter about Charles Spangler)

Microfilm

An Evaluation of Air Operations: The Influence of Air Power on the Okinawa Operation. 11 October 1945.
Muster Roll of Officers and Enlisted Men of the Marine Corps VMF-323 1 August 1943 to 1 August 1945.
VMF-323 Aircraft Action Reports Nos.1-61.
War Diary: Marine Fighting Squadron 323 1 June 1944 to 31 October 1945.

Periodicals

Infield, Tom, "Last Stand Before Dropping of Atomic Bomb," *Philadelphia Inquirer*, 1 April 1995, p.1.
Larson, Eric, "Fight to the Death," *TIME,* 9 December 1996, p.62.
Martin, 1Lt. Harold, "A Very Bitter Fellow," *True, 1946, p.57.*
Neely, Frederick,"Wing Talk," *Colliers,* 18 August 1945, p.8.
US Marine Corps, "Historical Narration," news release, 26 August 1994.
Westell, Freeman, "Vought Corsair," *Wings,* June 1995, special issue.
Wolf, William, "Three Marine Aces in a Day," *American Fighter Aces Association Journal*, Summer 1990, p.6.
Wolf, William, "Fighter Aircraft Armament of World War II," unpublished article.
Wolf, William,"Suicide Samarai," *Wings*, February 1977, p.18.

Reunion

Reunion and fishing trip, 6-10 June 1998, hosted by Jerry O'Keefe, Destin, FL. Attending: George Axtell, Jerry O'Keefe, Al Wells, John

Ruhsam, Hank Brandon, Joe McPhail, Charlie Allen, Norm Theriault, Sol Mayer, Norm Miller, Harley Brock

Videos

American Sound & Video, "Remarkable F4U Corsair."
Video Scene, "Death Rattlers."
NVF, Warbird Check Outs, "Flying the F4U Corsair."
Wells, Joyce, "1982 Reunion Video," private production.

Books

Abrams, Richard. *F4U Corsair at War.* New York: Scribners, 1981.

Alexander, Joseph. *The Final Campaign.* Washington DC: Marine Corps Historical Center, 1996.

Appleman, Roy et.al. *War in the Pacific. Okinawa: The Last Battle.* Washington DC: US Army Historical Division, 1948.

Astor, Gerald. *Operation Iceberg.* New York: Donald Fine, 1995.

Baker, A.D. *Allied Landing Craft of World War Two.* London: Arms & Armour, 1985 (reprint of 1944 edition.)

Belote, James and Belote, William. *Typhoon of Steel.* New York: Harper & Row, 1970.

Brown, David. *Fighting Elites: Kamikaze.* New York: Gallery, 1990.

Charles, Roland. *Troopships of World War II.* Washington DC: Army Transportation Association, 1947.

Dean, Francis. *America's One Hundred Thousand.* Altglen, Pennsylvania: Schiffer, 1997.

DeChant, John. *Devilbirds.* Washington DC: Zenger, 1971.

Feifer, George. *Tennozan. New York: Ticknor & Fields, 1992.*

Foster, Simon. *Okinawa 1945: Final Assault on the Empire.* London: Arms and Armour, 1994.

Frank, Benis and Shaw, Henry. *History of US Marine Corps Operations in World War II, Victory and Occupation, vol. V.* Washington DC: USMC Historical Division, 1968.

Gow, Ian. *Okinawa 1945: Gateway to Japan.* Garden City, New York: Doubleday, 1985.

Guyton, Boone. *Whistling Death.* New York: Orion, 1980.

Inoguchi, Rikihei et.al. *Divine Wind.* Annapolis, Maryland: Naval Institute Press, 1958.

Isley, Jeter, and Crowl, Philip. *The US Marines and Amphibious War.* Princeton, New Jersey: Princeton University Press, 1951.

Lindbergh, Charles, *The Wartime Journals of Charles A. Lindbergh.* New York: Harcourt, Brace, Jovanovich, 1970.

Morrison, Samuel Elliott. *History of US Naval Operations in World War II, Victory in the Pacific, 1045, vol. XIV.* Boston: Little, Brown, 1961.

Nichols, Charles and Shaw, Henry. Okinawa: Victory in the Pacific. Tokyo, Japan: Charles Tuttle (reprint), 1966.

Olynyk, Frank. *USMC Credits for the Destruction of Enemy Aircraft in Air-to-Air Combat World War 2.* Ohio: Author, 1981.

O'Neill, Richard. *Suicide Squads.* London: Salamander, 1981.

O'Sheel, Patrick and Cook, Gene, *Semper Fidelis, U.S. Marines in the Pacific 1942-1945. New York, William Sloan, 1947.*

Pitzel, Gerald. *A History of Marine Fighter Attack Squadron 323. Washington DC: History and Museums Division, 1987.*

Sherrod, Robert, *History of Marine Corps Aviation in World War Two.* San Rafael, California: Presidio, 1980.

Spangler, Dorothy, D*eath Rattlers: Story of VMF-323 at Okinawa,* Unpublished manuscript, Los Angeles.

Styling, Mark. *Corsair Aces of World War 2.* Great Britain: Osprey, 1995.

Tillman, Barrett. *Corsair: The F4U in World War Two and Korea.* Annapolis, Maryland: US Naval Press, 1979.

US Army. *Airfield and Base Development, vol. VI. Washington DC:* Office of Chief Engineer, 1951.

US Navy. *Battle Experience No.24, Secret Information Bulletin,* "Radar Pickets and Methods of Combating Suicide Attacks Off Okinawa, March-May 1945." Washington DC: 1945.

US Navy. *Pilot's Notes for the F4U Corsair* (reprint). Milwaukee, Wisconsin: Aviation Publications, 1973.

US Navy Department. *Dictionary of American Fighting Ships, vol.I-VIII.* Washington DC: Naval History Division, 1959-81.

US Navy Department. *Building the Navy's Bases in World War II. Washington DC: Bureau of Yards and Docks, 1947.*

Warner, Denis and Warner, Peggy. *Sacred Warriors.* New York: Van Nordstrom, 1982.

Wolf, William. *Victory Roll: Flying the Aircraft of the Aces of World War II.* Unpublished manu- script, Ft. Lauderdale, Florida.

Index of Personnel and Photographs